The Balance of Power in World History

Also by Stuart J. Kaufman

MODERN HATREDS: The Symbolic Politics of Ethnic War

Also by Richard Little

THE ANARCHICAL SOCIETY IN A GLOBALIZED WORLD (*co-editor with John Williams*)
THE BALANCE OF POWER IN INTERNATIONAL RELATIONS
BELIEF SYSTEMS AND INTERNATIONAL RELATIONS (*co-editor with Steve Smith*)
GLOBAL PROBLEMS AND WORLD ORDER (*co-author with R.D. Mckinlay*)
INTERNATIONAL SYSTEMS IN WORLD HISTORY (*co-author with Barry Buzan*)
INTERVENTION: EXTERNAL INVOLVEMENT IN CIVIL WAR
ISSUES IN WORLD POLITICS (3rd edition) (*co-editor with Brian White and Michael Smith*)
THE LOGIC OF ANARCHY (*co-author with Barry Buzan and Charles A. Jones*)
PERSPECTIVES ON WORLD POLITICS (3rd edition) (*co-editor with Michael Smith*)

Also by William C. Wohlforth

COLD WAR ENDGAME (*editor*)
ELUSIVE BALANCE AND PERCEPTIONS IN THE COLD WAR
WITNESSES TO THE END OF THE COLD WAR (*editor*)
WORLD OUT OF BALANCE: International Relations Theory and the Challenge of American Primacy (*co-author with Stephen G. Brooks*)

The Balance of Power in World History

Edited by

Stuart J. Kaufman
Department of Political Science and International Relations
University of Delaware, USA

Richard Little
Department of Politics
University of Bristol, UK

and

William C. Wohlforth
Department of Government
Dartmouth College, USA

palgrave
macmillan

First published 2007 by
PALGRAVE MACMILLAN
Houndmills, Basingstoke, Hampshire RG21 6XS and
175 Fifth Avenue, New York, N.Y. 10010
Companies and representatives throughout the world

PALGRAVE MACMILLAN is the global academic imprint of the Palgrave Macmillan division of St. Martin's Press, LLC and of Palgrave Macmillan Ltd. Macmillan® is a registered trademark in the United States, United Kingdom and other countries. Palgrave is a registered trademark in the European Union and other countries.

ISBN 13: 978–0–230–50710–4   hardback
ISBN 10: 0–230–50710–7   hardback
ISBN 13: 978–0–230–50711–1   paperback
ISBN 10: 0–230–50711–5   paperback

This book is printed on paper suitable for recycling and made from fully managed and sustained forest sources. Logging, pulping and manufacturing processes are expected to conform to the environmental regulations of the country of origin.

A catalogue record for this book is available from the British Library.

Library of Congress Cataloging-in-Publication Data

The balance of power in world history / edited by Stuart J. Kaufman, Richard Little, William C. Wohlforth.
    p. cm.
    Papers presented at a workshop on Hierarchy and Balance in International Systems held at Dartmouth College, October 18–20, 2003.
    Includes bibliographical references and index.
    ISBN 0-230-50710-7 (alk. paper)
    1. Balance of power – History – Congresses. 2. International relations – History – Congresses. I. Kaufman, Stuart J. II. Little, Richard, 1944– III. Wohlforth, William Curti, 1959–

    JZ1313.B34 2007
    327.1'1209–dc22   2007021646

10 9 8 7 6 5 4 3 2 1
16 15 14 13 12 11 10 09 08 07

Printed and bound in Great Britain by
Antony Rowe Ltd, Chippenham and Eastbourne

Contents

List of Tables and Maps

Acknowledgments

This volume is the product of a workshop on Hierarchy and Balance in International Systems that took place at Dartmouth College, October 18–20, 2003. We are grateful to the Department of Government for hosting the workshop and to the John Sloan Dickey Center for International Understanding for sponsoring the workshop.

Biographies

William J. Brenner is a doctoral candidate in the Department of Political Science at Johns Hopkins University.

Daniel Deudney is Associate Professor of political science at Johns Hopkins University. His most recent book is *Bounding Power: Republican Security Theory from the Polis to the Global Village* (2007).

Arthur M. Eckstein is Professor of History at the University of Maryland at College Park. He is the author of three books, an edited book, and some 45 articles, mostly dealing with Roman imperial expansion under the Republic, and Greek perceptions of that phenomenon, but ranging into the ancient historical foundations of political science – and as far afield as American culture in the 1950s. His latest book is *Mediterranean Anarchy, Interstate War, and the Rise of Rome* (2006).

Victoria Tin-bor Hui is an Assistant Professor in Political Science at the University of Notre Dame. She is author of *War and State Formation in Ancient China and Early Modern Europe* (2005), which won the 2006 Jervis-Schroeder Award from the American Political Science Association and the 2005 Edgar S. Furniss Book Award from the Ohio State University's Mershon Center for International Security Studies.

Charles A. Jones studied philosophy and history at Cambridge. Originally a specialist in the political history of international business he taught international political economy at the University of Warwick before moving to Cambridge to teach international relations theory in 1998.

David C. Kang is Associate Professor of Government, and Adjunct Associate Professor and Research Director at the Center for International Business at the Tuck School of Business at Dartmouth. Kang is author of *China Reshapes East Asia: Power, Politics, and Ideas in International Relations* (forthcoming). He received an A.B. with honors from Stanford University and his Ph.D. from Berkeley.

Stuart J. Kaufman is Professor of Political Science and International Relations at the University of Delaware. His previous book is entitled, *Modern Hatreds: The Symbolic Politics of Ethnic War* (2001).

Richard Little is Professor of International Politics at the University of Bristol. He is a former editor of the *Review of International Studies* and a former president of the British International Studies Association. He is the co-author with Barry Buzan of *International Systems in World History* (2000). His most recent book is *The Balance of Power in International Relations: Metaphors, Myths, and Models* (2007).

William C. Wohlforth is Professor of Government at Dartmouth College. He is the author of *Elusive Balance and Perceptions in the Cold War* (1993) and editor of *Witnesses to the End of the Cold War* (1996) and *Cold War Endgame* (2002).

1

Introduction: Balance and Hierarchy in International Systems

William C. Wohlforth, Stuart J. Kaufman and Richard Little

The balance of power is one of the most influential ideas in international relations (IR). No theoretical concept has been the subject of as much scholarly inquiry and none is more likely to fall from the lips of foreign policy analysts and practitioners. This continued fascination with the balance of power is understandable, for it appears as central to scholarly debates about the basic properties of international systems as it is to policy debates over responses to US primacy in the early 21st century. Yet it has never been systemically and comprehensively examined in premodern or non-European contexts – and therefore it has never been considered in the context of previous cases of unipolarity. Balance-of-power theory and policy analysis thus rest on profoundly unbalanced empirical foundations. Almost everything we think we know about the balance of power is the product of modern European history and the global experience of the 20th and early 21st centuries.

This book redresses this imbalance. We present eight new case studies of balancing and balancing failure in premodern and non-European international systems. Our collective, multidisciplinary and international research effort yields an inescapable conclusion: much of the conventional wisdom about the balance of power does not survive contact with non-European evidence.

Given the foundational role of balance-of-power thinking in the evolution of the academic study of international relations, it is vital to be clear about the specific aspects addressed here. Fifty years after Ernst Haas (1953) identified eight different definitions of 'balance of power,' the concept remains so fiercely contested that the unmodified term is too ambiguous to be meaningful. To clarify our goal, some explanation is needed.

Consider this deceptively simple statement from the 2002 United States National Security Strategy document: 'We seek ... to create a balance of power that favors human freedom' (Bush, 2002). Haas (1953) identified four different ways of using the 'balance of power,' and all four are apparent here. First, as is made clearer elsewhere in the document, the statement is *descriptive*, identifying an international distribution of power in which the United States is the dominant state. Second, it is *prescriptive*, indicating that this particular state of affairs (American pre-eminence) should be maintained. Third, it is *normative* or *propagandistic* associating American pre-eminence with the moral good (human freedom). Finally, it is implicitly *analytical*, with the 'balance of power' representing the central mechanism in the operation of the international system; that is it assumes that creating 'a balance of power that favors human freedom' is the critical step in promoting the goal of freedom. These different uses of the phrase are usually intertwined because for propagandistic purposes they are mutually dependent, even though they are analytically distinct.

The element of propaganda is very evident in Bush's use of balance of power terminology because he wants to convince his audience that all the great powers favor freedom and have formed a grand coalition against those elements of the international system that are opposed to freedom. It follows that the other great powers should not be concerned about US pre-eminence or by its decision to enhance its capabilities because they are all part of a common coalition. Unsurprisingly, other great powers do not share this assessment. For some of them, American pre-eminence represents a serious problem with the established balance of power. The French Foreign Minister Hubert Védrine asserted in 1999, for example, that 'the entire foreign policy of France...is aimed at making the world of tomorrow composed of several poles, not just one' (cited in Walt, 2002).

What makes the debate about the balance of power so complex is that scholars, like statesmen, are also in dispute about what is meant by the balance of power. Some scholars, as Haas (1953) noted, consider 'the balance of power' to be virtually identical with the notion of power politics or with the international struggle for power – in short, they consider it identical to realism. Other complications arise when the focus is on the contemporary system because unipolarity is such a recent development and indeed is often regarded as unique in the modern world Some realists worry, for example, that US unilateralism is now fragmenting the putative grand coalition in favor of freedom. Though there is no consensus amongst the great powers in favor of

'hard balancing' the United States by establishing a countervaⁱ
itary alliance, it is argued that there is now evidence of the ๖.
powers agreeing on less extreme measures to encourage the United
States to rein in its unilateralism – a phenomenon described as 'soft
balancing' (see, e.g., Pape, 2005; Paul, 2005).

Critics, however, argue that this move represents what Giovanni
Sartori (1970) dubbed 'concept misformation' or 'concept stretching' –
essentially, stretching a term to refer to a phenomenon entirely distinct from the one it previously meant. As Lieber and Alexander (2005)
note, behaviors labeled 'soft balancing' are fundamentally different
from traditional balancing, and are instead 'identical to traditional
diplomatic friction'. From the critics' point of view, the underlying
logical error is to conflate balance-of-power theory's analytical insight
(balancing tends to occur) with a particular descriptive position (that
must be what is happening now). Balance of power terminology is particularly prone to such concept stretching because the term was already
so elastic and diverse in meaning, but such stretching creates the risk
of turning the concept into what British statesman Richard Cobden
labeled it almost two centuries ago: 'a chimera: It is not a fallacy, a
mistake, an imposture – it is an undescribed, indescribable, incompre-
hensible nothing' (quoted in Haas, 1953: 443).

The aim of this book

Once we distinguish among these uses of the term balance of power, the
purpose of this book can be stated succinctly: to assess the central analytical and descriptive claims of systemic balance-of-power theory. Haas
(1953: 449–50) notes that some scholars, such as Spykman (1942), use
'balance of power' descriptively (as the Bush Administration did for propaganda reasons) to refer to a 'balance of power' in favor of some state –
in other words, to refer to some form of hegemony. That is clearly the
minority position however; for most American scholars trained in the
Cold War era it refers descriptively to equilibrium, or relative equality of
power between two or more states. Analytically, according to a careful
review by Levy, the core notion of balance-of-power theory is 'that hegemonies do not form in multistate systems because perceived threats of
hegemony over the system generate balancing behavior by other leading
states in the system' (Levy, 2004: 37). Theory based on this notion is the
one we term *systemic* balance-of-power theory.

We focus on systemic balance-of-power theory because of its central
importance to international relations theory and practice. As Levy and

Thompson note in another review, its central claim 'has been one of the most widely held propositions in the field of international relations' (2005: 1–2). Indeed, the assumption – made most explicitly in Waltz's seminal *Theory of International Politics* (1979), but widely held by realists (Levy, 2004; Levy and Thompson, 2005) – is that this proposition is universally valid across time and space. Furthermore, this view that balance is the historical norm is the source of the widespread expectation, among scholars and practitioners alike, that states will soon begin balancing against the United States; and of the assessment, most starkly stated by Waltz (2000a: 56), that 'the present condition of international politics is unnatural.' Even liberal institutionalists and constructivists (Nye, 2003; Lebow, 2004), when arguing for restraint in US foreign policy, cite the expectation of counterbalancing by other states as a reason for their prescription.

The purpose of this study is therefore to test the logic and universality of balance-of-power theory against premodern evidence: the analytical statement that hegemonic threats tend to evoke balancing behavior as the dominant response in international systems; and the descriptive statement that 'balances' of power (as distinct from hegemonic or unipolar distributions of power) are as a result the most common state of international systems. Nicholas Spykman and George Bush notwithstanding, we distinguish theories of hegemony as competing with theories of balance. Far from attacking realism, however, these analyses offer an assessment of balance-of-power theory largely from within the realist paradigm, assessing how, why and how frequently the alternative outcomes of balance and hegemony have historically emerged.

'Balance of power' theories that assert that the balance is associated either with peace or with war represent an entirely different literature that we do not address here. Again, Haas (1953) notes that both claims have a long pedigree. Both have been examined recently in a literature pitting an application of Organski's power transition theory (Organski and Kugler, 1980) to all state dyads (associating dyadic imbalances of power with peace) against the 'balance of power' assertion that parity in power is associated with peace for all state dyads (see, e.g., Tammen *et al.*, 2000; Lemke, 2002; Moul, 2002). While we have doubts about the appropriateness of applying the balance-of-power idea in this way, we merely note here that such an application constitutes a fundamentally different theory from the ones we examine, considering a different dependent variable (peace rather than balance) and a different independent variable (dyadic rather than systemic distribution of capabilities).

We examine the issues of systemic balancing in a series of case studies of international systems with which most scholars of international relations are barely familiar: the Iron Age Fertile Crescent, Warring States China, pre-Columbian Mesoamerica, Ancient India, Greece and Persia, ascending Rome, and the early modern East Asian system. We focus on these cases because such a focus is the *only* way the largest claims of systemic balance-of-power theory can be tested. Balance-of-power theory was originally developed to explain the modern European international system on the basis of evidence from that system. Therefore, while further studies based on that evidence – for example, certain recent process-tracing studies (see Wohlforth, 2003) – can be used to disconfirm the theory, or to confirm its applicability in the European context, it cannot be used to confirm the theory's applicability to any other international system, including the contemporary one.

Since evidence from the contemporary system is inconclusive – we do not yet know what sort of 'balance,' if any, will exist 20 or 50 years from now – the only way to test the theory is with evidence from systems separate from the modern European one and its contemporary successor. We must, in short, broaden the empirical domain in which such theories are tested. The chapters that follow demonstrate that the cases we study *were* all interstate systems to which many international relations theories *do* apply. Most particularly, Waltz's overall hypothesis about interstate systems applies: 'hegemony leads to balance,' Waltz (1993: 77) writes; and it has done so 'through all of the centuries we can contemplate'. Since the claims of systemic balance-of-power theory are transhistorical, they can only be tested transhistorically.

This is our objective. Following the pioneering efforts of English School scholars such as Wight and Watson, and building on a growing emerging body of scholarship on the international politics of non-European international systems (Buzan and Little, 2000; Cioffi-Revilla, 1996; Cioffi-Revilla and Landman, 1999; Kaufman, 1997; Modelski and Thompson, 1999; Wilkinson, 1999, 2002), we bring new evidence to bear on the central problems of balance and hierarchy. The cases in this book collectively survey a large swath of known human history to assess whether the core claims of systemic balance-of-power theory are accurate: that 'balance' understood as multipolar or bipolar distributions of power is the typical state of international systems, and that this has remained so historically because states in such systems engage in balancing behavior in response to hegemonic threats. Against these hypotheses we test the competing notion of hegemonic stability – the notion that hegemony or hierarchy is the typical state of the international system – associated both with scholars such as Gilpin (1981) from the realist camp and with English School theorists such as Watson (1992). In the conclusion we test these raw empirical claims against a larger quantitative database that covers the majority of known international history.

Theorizing international systems

Beyond simply assessing outcomes, however, our case studies focus on assessing competing theoretical claims about the causes of these outcomes. When balanced – multipolar or bipolar – systems remain stable (i.e., durable), what are the causes of this stability? When they collapse into hegemony or empire, what are the causes of the hegemonic rise? Because our authors represent a diverse set of theoretical traditions, we collectively draw on a large toolkit of concepts that might help explain these outcomes.

Definitions

We begin with Bull and Watson's (1984: 1) definition that a group of states comprise a system when 'the behavior of each is a necessary factor in the calculations of others.' Recognizing that systems are not always simply anarchic, however, we reject the North American tendency, among rationalists (Lake, 1996) and constructivists (Wendt and Friedheim, 1995) alike, to understand anarchy and hierarchy as mutually exclusive. Instead, we use as a starting point Adam Watson's (1992) notion of degrees of hierarchy, ranging from pure anarchy through hegemony, suzerainty and dominion to a single empire. All of our cases involve situations in which there were hierarchical relations among some units, and anarchical relations among others. Moreover, some were characterized by a relatively clear hierarchical order among *all* units comprising the system. Highlighting only the purely anarchical elements of each system would cause us to overlook the most interesting and important features of our cases – the nature of Ming suzerainty over Vietnam and Korea, for example, or the ever-changing nature of Assyrian control over neighboring Babylonia. Explaining the propensity of each system towards balance or its opposite demands that we consider degrees of systemic hierarchy within anarchy, just as Watson proposed.

The Roman Empire is considered the archetype of a situation in which a single empire dominates an entire international system.

However, even the Roman Empire faced neighbors outside its hierarchical control, ranging from the Pictish tribes of Scotland to the larger German tribes and the highly advanced Parthian Empire. If that system is classed as simply 'anarchic', then nothing is excluded by the term, so it has no analytical meaning. Our rule of thumb has to be that if a single unit achieves political-military domination over most of an international system, that system is primarily hierarchic rather than anarchic, and is classified as such. The extent of hierarchy, its different types, and the longevity of different types of hierarchies are the key issues addressed in the chapters that follow.

This conceptual approach – looking for systems that may be mostly rather than entirely hierarchical – is consistent with a useful distinction made by Michael Doyle. International systems theory, Doyle (1986: 40) writes, typically takes 'hegemony ... to mean controlling leadership of the international system as a whole'. Following Doyle, we define it as effective control by one unit over the foreign policy of another. The value of this shift is that it turns the question of hegemony from a question of yes or no to a more useful question of more or less: over *how much* of the system does a state exercise hegemony? This move avoids fights over definitional matters and shifts analytical focus to the empirical question of the shape and behavior of the system. It also opens up the possibility of systems characterized by dual or multiple hegemonies, which might differ from bipolar or multipolar systems that include a large number of small, independent actors.

Second, how do we classify the varied units whose interaction constitutes the system? Part of the difficulty in understanding systems, ancient or modern, is merely determining *what* the units are, not only their mutual relationships. After 1990, for example, should Hezbollah be considered a unit in the international system (acting, e.g., as Israel's main adversary to the north); or should it be understood as part of the Lebanese state, or simply as a tool of Syrian or Iranian policy? Similar questions are ubiquitous in ancient systems as well, concerning the Chaldaean tribes of southern Babylonia, the colonies of Greek city-states, Rome's client kingdoms, or the republics within India's Vajjian confederacy, among others. Our rule of thumb is to consider as international actors those that acted autonomously in interstate interactions, especially if they controlled military force.

The logic of balancing

Given the early stage of our endeavor, we do not attempt to offer a complete theory that explains variation in the balancing propensity of systems. Instead, we draw on a toolkit of hypotheses drawn from a variety of theories. An encouraging aspect of this project is that, though we approach the subject from different theoretical perspectives, we generally found it necessary to mix and match concepts in a way that bodes well for future theoretical synthesis. Thus in explaining the stability of the early modern Asian state-system, Kang incorporates the raw distribution of power (a la neorealism), commercial and material interests (liberalism), the effects of Chinese identity (the key constructivist concern) and the notion of systemic hierarchy (a central English School insight). Little, in contrast, focused on showing the value of English School insights, finds that neorealist logic is also useful for explaining some dynamics. Following Victoria Hui (2005), we organize the theoretical approaches according to the overall effect of the factors they identify, distinguishing those emphasizing 'the logic of balancing' from those emphasizing 'the logic of domination' which leads to hierarchy. We begin with the logic of balancing.

Neorealist theory. The starting point of both the logic of balancing and the logic of domination is the standard realist proposition that because states pursue power as a means to security, they frequently tend to expand (Morgenthau, 1978; Mearsheimer, 2001; Layne, 2006). Indeed if international anarchy does generate a security dilemma, the most sensible way to address the resulting insecurity is to expand a state's territory, as both buffer and power base, by any means necessary. Mearsheimer's (2001: 238) summary makes the point succinctly: 'great powers strive for hegemony in their region of the world' – meaning, for ancient systems confined to one region, they strive for systemic hegemony. Furthermore, this tendency applies to second-rank powers as well: they, too, have an incentive to 'bandwagon for profit' (Schweller, 1994) to expand their power – not to mention to establish good relations with neighboring larger powers. This process alone provides a robust explanation for why empires tend to rise in so many times and places.

Naturally, as neorealist theory emphasizes, the rise of any given great power poses a threat to the security of others (Jervis, 1978). In a balanced multipolar system, this creates little problem, as great powers can maintain their relative position through a system of compensation (Gulick, 1955: 70–2). However, under unbalanced multipolarity – that is, when one great power emerges as a potential systemic hegemon – its growth in power poses a potential threat to the independence of all the other states (Mearsheimer, 2001). Under these conditions, balance-of-power theory suggests that great powers, and indeed many lesser powers, should band together to balance against the rising potential hegemon.

According to an insightful typology suggested by Jack Levy (2003), there are at least four distinct systemic balance-of-power theories in common use. The theory may be unconditional, applying to any and all states systems (e.g., Waltz, 1979), or it may be conditional, applying only to contiguous state-systems lacking offshore balancers. This distinction is not important for our study: most of the systems we examine are contiguous most of the time, so evidence from them is pertinent to both the conditional and the unconditional versions. More important is the distinction between balance of power and balance of threat (Walt, 1987) versions of the theory. These different logics yield quite different expectations about state behavior, and so require additional discussion.

The key issue is what constitutes balancing. Keeping in mind that we are examining systemic rather than dyadic balance-of-power theory, we assert that a state is balancing in this sense only if its action is aimed at checking a potential systemic hegemon. As Christopher Layne (2004: 106) observes, 'the concept of balancing expresses the idea of a counterweight, specifically, the ability to generate sufficient material capabilities to match – or offset – those of a would-be, or actual, hegemon.' External balancing, then, is alliance making or other substantive interstate cooperation that is aimed at preventing hegemony. If a state allies with the potential hegemon against a regional rival, this is not 'balancing' against the regional rival, but bandwagoning with the potential hegemon (Walt, 1987). For a systemic balance of power to be maintained, states must put aside secondary disputes when faced with the common threat of a single rival that might conquer and destroy them all. Only this behavior can lead to the outcome of balance predicted by the theory. This hegemonic threat will inevitably be the most powerful state in the system, not necessarily the state most threatening to any particular rival: systemic balancing theory is, therefore, balance-of-power theory, not balance-of-threat theory.

The other type of balancing Waltz mentions is internal balancing, enhancement of a state's power in response to a potential hegemon. In Waltz's rendition of the theory, internal balancing encompasses emulation: when lesser powers adopt technologies, institutions and practices from the leading state to compete more effectively. The theory expects emulation to increase with the probability of hegemony. Theorists of hegemony note a similar phenomenon, observing 'a historical tendency for the military and economic techniques of the dominant state or empire to be diffused to other states in the system' (Gilpin, 1981: 176; cf. Cipolla, 1965; McNeill, 1963). However, while hegemonic theories see such processes as undermining hegemons after their rise, balance-of-power theory would expect them generally to work against the emergence hegemony in the first place.

In assessing balance-of-power theory, we adopt the broadest approach most favorable to the theory, which means considering both *outcome* and *process*. In the European context, most scholars see the outcome as roughly balanced but question whether it is the result of the causal processes identified in balance-of-power theory – that is, alliance formation, internal balancing, and emulation. Hence, insisting that the theory predicts outcomes looks like an attempt to insulate it from empirical disconfirmation. In our cases the brute outcome over and over again is hegemony, not balance, so refusing to examine balancing processes would amount to instant disconfirmation. We thus go on to see whether that outcome occurred *despite* balancing processes. That is, the theory might be wrong about the outcome but right about the basic processes the threat of hegemony elicits. Those processes may simply have been overwhelmed in our cases by causes exogenous to the theory.

Recognizing the insights of collective action theory regarding states' temptation to pass the buck or to bandwagon in the face of hegemonic threats, balance of power theorists have suggested two ancillary hypotheses to account for variation in states' responses. First, whether a given state chooses to balance or pass the buck depends in large part on geography (Mearsheimer, 2001). The potential hegemon's neighbors are more likely to balance than are states further away, because contiguity lowers the costs and raises the benefits of balancing. By exploiting the military advantages of the defensive, a state can balance against a possible offensive by its potentially hegemonic neighbor relatively cheaply, while its incentive to do so is high because as a neighbor, it is the most likely victim of hegemonic expansion. Distant states, in contrast, can rely on those incentives to force states neighboring the potential hegemon to pay the costs of balancing. Moreover, balancing is more expensive for them because they have to pay to move their forces in range of the distant potential hegemon.

Second, states that are very weak will hide from or bandwagon with the potential hegemon. The greater a state's relative power (defined as the capability to balance the hegemon), the more likely it is to balance. Only the weakest and most geographically vulnerable states, whose marginal contribution to containing the hegemon is negligible, should bandwagon. For stronger states, bandwagoning materially increases the probability of hegemony and thus the possibility that the state might lose its sovereignty. The strongest regional actors are the most likely to be able to balance. States whose power falls in the middle of this range should prefer to balance if the threat is high, but may not be able to. If not, they can be expected to follow ambiguous hedging strategies that allow them to cooperate with the potential hegemon even as they encourage other states to pay the costs of balancing it.

System Expansion. Another factor that helps maintain the balance of power is the introduction of new powers into the international system (Dehio, 1962; Thompson, 1996; Buzan and Little, 2000). As Dehio pointed out, the balance of power in modern Europe was maintained by the repeated introductions of marchland powers – Russia and the US, most notably – to balance against the rise of states in the system's core. In systems that have land borders, this can be expected to be a systematic process: as states annex marchland states, bordering tribes that may previously have been geographically outside the system will be exposed to pressure from the neighboring empire. That pressure creates incentives for the tribes to emulate the empire by forming state structures (Waltz, 1979; Buzan, Jones and Little, 1993), thus expanding the boundaries of the system further into previously irrelevant areas. At the same time, groups in the geographic region that had previously not loomed as necessary in the calculations of states in the system might come to be so, thus 'entering' the system functionally. The effect is to create obstacles to an empire's further expansion, if not re-creating a genuine balance of power.

Particularist Identities. Some constructivists (e.g., Kaufman, 1997) and English School theorists (Jackson, 1990) argue that particularist unit identities, and international norms that respect them, can be an important element in the maintenance of a balance of power. Clearly people attached to their own local identity are likely to resist imperial control more fiercely than are people with no such attachment. Empires that conquer such people are therefore likely to face frequent rebellions, be relatively unstable, and as a result are relatively unlikely to succeed in achieving hegemony. If international norms respect such identities, then the effect should be stronger. Robert Jackson (1990) argues, for example, that international acceptance of the norm of national self-determination, in addition to the strength of nationalist sentiment itself, was a critical factor driving the dissolution of European colonial empires (and of the collective European hegemony in Asia and Africa) in the second half of the 20th century.

Government type. Though royal autocracy was by far the most common type government across the ancient world, the democracies and oligarchies of Greece, Republican Rome, and some of the more or less 'republican' states of India, provide enough variety in those cases to make it possible to consider the effects of government type on international systems – and *vice versa*. However, as Deudney (forthcoming) notes, ancient democracies and republics were invariably small, inherently vulnerable to imbalances of power when confronted with imperial adversaries. Deudney asserts that ancient republics could compensate for their small size and power through 'co-binding' – forming stable confederations that enable them to aggregate their power to defend themselves against the encroachment of expansionist neighbors. Nevertheless, to the extent that the component republics maintained their independence, collective action problems in their co-binding would still remain.

The logic of domination

Hegemonic Transition Theory. Though most realists subscribe to systemic balance-of-power theory, the logic of realism does not require this conclusion. In *War and Change in World Politics* (1981), Robert Gilpin proposes a realist theory of international systems that places the concept of hegemony at the center of analysis. Offering a cost-benefit analysis approach similar in many ways to the later neorealist-neoliberal synthesis, Gilpin argued that it would repeatedly occur that states would seek to expand and achieve hegemony because the benefits of doing so would, at least at first, exceed the costs. In short, Gilpin endorses the offensive realist insight about the benefits of military expansion but not the logic of balancing.

The reasons for this conclusion are multiple. First, Gilpin (1981: 55–84) theorized, advances in transportation, communications and military technology would diminish states' 'loss-of-strength gradient', making it easier for expansionist power to seize and hold new territory, reducing the costs of hegemony. Second, military expansion tended in the past to yield multiple economic benefits: economies of scale in providing security, the internalization of externalities (such as tolls levied on trade), and methods of overcoming the problem of diminishing returns by increasing inputs. Third, power and wealth in agricultural societies followed directly from the control of agricultural land so, *ceteris paribus*, larger states were necessarily stronger and richer. As a result, Gilpin (1981: 111) writes, 'World politics was characterized by the rise and decline of powerful empires...The recurrent pattern in every civilization of which we have knowledge was for one state to unify the system under its imperial domination'. *The English School.* A core proposition of the English School and of constructivism is the centrality of ideas to the behavior of any international system. Thus English School theorists emphasize that a key reason for the stability of the European balance of power was the fact that it was normatively approved: this is, indeed, the source of contemporary assumptions that the 'balance of power' is somehow good. Butterfield and Wight insisted, therefore, that there was no balance-of-power system in the ancient world because the idea of the balance of power did not exist. Similarly, Adam Watson's (1992) magisterial survey of international systems places great emphasis on the ideas concerning hegemony or equilibrium that animated different interstate cultures.

This work suggests the hypothesis that the propensity of any system of states towards balance or hierarchy is a function of the ideas that animate the culture of the international society they form. From this perspective, Alexander Wendt's constructivist argument about varying cultures of anarchy is much less bold than the English School upon which it draws, for the latter not only posits but claims to have identified stable *hierarchical* cultures of anarchy – ruled out by Wendt in deference to Waltz's rigid dichotomy between anarchy and hierarchy. A stable hierarchy, by contrast, might arise in an international society with a cultural system demanding that one polity – even perhaps not the strongest one – serve as leader.

In their sweeping consideration of these issues, Buzan and Little (2000) (relying on Watson, 1992) emphasize the English School view that the typical result is some form of hierarchy. International systems, English School theorists point out, typically show a substantial degree of hierarchy, whether in the form of hegemony, suzerainty, or full-fledged empire. One explanation for the emergence and stability of interstate hierarchy is material capabilities. The larger the underlying inequalities among great powers – size, population, natural resource endowments, potential for military power and economic output – and the more these inequalities lead to clear distinctions among ranks, the more likely hierarchical patterns are to emerge and remain stable.

Collective Action Theory. Collective action theorists would doubt even the modified hypotheses about balancing promoted by contemporary neorealists. Balancing, from this perspective, is a collective good which should be chronically under-provided in an anarchical environment (Olson, 1965). Those states for which the threat is more distant may be inclined not only to pass the buck to frontline states, but even to bandwagon with the rising state, seeking compensation instead of blocking the opponent's expansion (Christensen and Snyder, 1990; Mearsheimer, 2001; Schroeder, 1994). Frontline states, if faced with overwhelming force from the rising state, may choose to bandwagon as well, submitting to a milder form of hegemony instead of risking annihilation. These competing systemic incentives, combined with the temptations created by local rivalries, will tend to interfere with the balancing process, rendering it slow and inefficient. The result may be to allow one state to gain enough power to reach hegemony before its rivals coalesce to stop it.

A related and reinforcing factor is uncertainty about the identity and gravity of the hegemonic threat. Decades of cumulating research on decision-making would predict pervasive uncertainty *ex ante* concerning such issues that would exacerbate the other system- and unit-level barriers to balancing (e.g., Gilovich, 2002; Kahneman *et al.*, 1982). Furthermore, in an international system as conceived by offensive realists, all great powers can be expected to aspire to hegemonic status. As a result, there should often be multiple hegemonic threats, so any move aimed at balancing against one may end up benefiting another. The situation is most obvious in cases in which a hegemon arises as a challenger to a previous hegemon: efforts to balance the old hegemon may pave the way for the rise of the new one. This effect may be exacerbated by geography: since distance attenuates threat, states may reasonably choose to align with a stronger but more distant power against a slightly weaker but closer (and more immediately threatening) one – and find that they have enabled the hegemonic threat to overcome its most powerful rival.

Finally, as Hui (2005) emphasizes, the strategic challenges that face balancers provide strategic opportunities to aspiring hegemons. Expansionist powers can exploit collective action problems by offering selective incentives for some potential balancers to buckpass or bandwagon instead – feeding and benefiting from their temptation to 'bandwagon for profit' (Schweller, 1994). Such opportunities suggest that, for a state that has the potential to achieve hegemony – that is, under conditions of unbalanced multipolarity – when balancing behavior is most needed, divide-and-conquer tactics are most likely to be effective.

Unit type. A variable of some importance – in different ways in different systems – is unit type. The four main types of units in ancient systems, Buzan and Little (2000) note, were empires, city-states, and nomadic and sedentary tribes. Obviously unit type matters enormously for the type of interactions they have, though not always in obvious or simple ways. Contrary to stereotype, tribal peoples, even nomadic ones, did sometimes maintain diplomatic relations with empires: one nomadic king of the Scythians even offered a marriage alliance to the Assyrian king. Similarly, unit types change in various ways: city-states could grow into empires (Babylon, Rome), or break off from them; nomadic tribes could create empires (the Medes) or conquer them (Manchus in China).

Theoretically, unit type is critical because the existence of at least one effective empire is a necessary condition for the emergence of hegemony in premodern systems. Furthermore, to the considerable extent that unit type correlates with power, the prospects for balancing a growing empire critically depend on the existence of other empires of comparable size. Given collective action problems, coalitions of city-states and tribes are likely to fragment over the long haul when confronted with an empire larger than any of them singly: as Wohlforth (1999) emphasizes, an alliance or coalition does not change the structural distribution of power in the system.

A related variable, potentially applicable to any unit type, is state disunity. As Hui (2005) argues, expansionist powers can use divide-and-conquer tactics not only against enemy coalitions, but also against enemy states (or tribes), bribing officials or playing factions off against each other to weaken and destroy target states. Thucydides's repeated references to city-states being captured by 'treachery', for example, suggests one way this can happen, especially in situations in which siege warfare plays a prominent role.

Administrative capacity. Since the rise and fall of empires is so centrally important to what we want to explain – the balancing propensity of systems – we also consider in detail the causes of such rises and falls. One factor of considerable importance is the social technology for state administration: empires grow larger and more stable when their rulers develop more effective techniques for governing them (Kaufman, 1997; Buzan and Little, 2000). Related is the physical and social technology for communications: the more quickly rulers can move people and messages across space, the more space they can control. One key implication is that when effective new administrative technologies are developed, international systems can change rapidly as empires exploit the new opportunity to grow.

This concept is relevant to two key variables in international relations theory. The first is Waltz's notion of 'internal balancing', and

Hui's (2005) broader related concept of 'self-strengthening reforms'. According to neorealist theory, if a powerful state engages in some major reform that increases its ability to generate and mobilize power, then its rivals should be expected to emulate that reform in order to maintain a balance of power. However, as institutionalist theorists pointed (Olson, 1965) out decades ago, there are likely to be internal political barriers to reforms that enhance state power: such reforms inevitably come at a cost to important actors inside the state who therefore have strong incentives to resist them (Buzan, Jones and Little, 1993). More broadly, various institutionalist literatures point out that increasing returns, path dependence, barriers to collective identity change, and other domestic-level institutional lags tend to raise the real costs and thus lower the supply of domestic self-strengthening reforms, and therefore of internal balancing (North, 1990; Powell and DiMaggio, 1991; March and Olsen, 1989; Schweller, 2006). Systemic theory can point out that states may be forced to adapt or perish; it cannot specify which will be the outcome, so we must look inside the units to help explain it.

A second, related effect of administrative capacity is on the cumulativity of power in the international system, a concept sometimes considered as an element in the offense-defense balance (Quester, 1977). A recent literature debates the degree to which conquest 'pays' in the modern system, with some scholars (Bunce, 1985; Brooks, 1999) arguing that in modern times, conquests cost more to maintain than they yield in benefits to the conquering state, while others (Liberman, 1993, 1996) maintain the opposite. But the same issue – and the same variability – existed in ancient times, as some empires were more effective than others at overcoming what Gilpin (1981) called the 'loss-of-strength gradient' and converting conquests into additional power. In general, we should expect that the more effectively states can exploit conquered resources to enhance their power – that is, the more power is cumulative in the system – the easier it will be for one state to overturn a balance of power and establish hegemony.

Less important factors

Geography. Geography is making its way back into international relations theory. Mearsheimer (2001), most notably, relies heavily on 'the stopping power of water' in constructing his theory. One could consider several hypotheses about location. One likely geographical effect is that states less threatened by rising powers will typically be those more geographically isolated from them. A second possible hypothesis, worthy of further exploration, is that major mountain and water barriers will tend to form state boundaries that are relatively difficult to breach.

But one immediate insight from looking at history's *longue durée* is that the effect of geography always interacts with social and physical technology. The 'stopping power of water' notwithstanding, maritime empires date back at least as far as the Minoan Empire of the second millennium BCE. Similarly, while Little finds that the Hellespont and the Aegean posed an important barrier to Persian expansion into Greece, the Romans turned the whole Mediterranean into 'Our Sea' and used it as a communications route as important as their vaunted road network. As another example, city-states thrived among the Sumerians of the Mesopotamian flatlands, and also among the Hellenes of mountainous Greece, and the former were arguably as resistant to incorporation into empires as were the latter. Compared another way, while mountainous Greece might have interfered with Greek unity, mountainous Iran did not prevent the Medes from achieving unity. The effects of geography may be important, but they are not simple, and show no consistent effect in our cases.

Economic incentives. David Kang's study highlights trading relationships, but Buzan and Little's economic sector of analysis is largely absent in our other analyses. This might seem surprising – Buzan and Little (2000: 234) emphasize, for example, the significance of the Assyrian silver trade in the ancient Middle East. And indeed, states in resource-poor Mesopotamia always had strong economic incentives for political-military expansion – as did the resource-poor city-states of Greece, early Rome (situated on a trade route from whence it derived its prosperity), and many others. The conclusion the authors come to, more implicitly than explicitly, is that the political-military incentives for imperial expansion were so strong that economic incentives hardly made a difference. Furthermore, the economic incentives varied less than did the political-military environment: the resources were always desirable, but not always equally conquerable. While economic variables are of undeniable importance, their exploration will have to await a future study.

International Organizations. One major school of thought in international relations theory, neoliberal institutionalism, in conspicuously absent from this survey. This is not due to bias on our part, but rather to the fact that neoliberal institutionalism is a quintessentially modern theory, placing at the center of analysis variables that did not become important before the 20th – or, at best, the 19th century. Premodern international relations occurred in the absence of institutionalized regimes for international trade, monetary relations, and conflict management. Since we found no important ancient international organizations, we do not attempt to apply this theory to those cases.

Theoretical summary: propositions to assess

While the chapters in this volume can be said to 'test' only the core assertions of balance-of-power theory – that balancing is the dominant reaction to hegemonic threat, and that the result of such behavior is systems that remain balanced – they do examine and assess a larger number of theoretical propositions developed above. As above, we group these propositions according to their systemic effect according to Hui's (2005) classification of the 'logic of balancing' and the competing 'logic of domination'.

The logic of balancing

Outcome Hypothesis: A balance of power, defined as a multipolar or bipolar distribution of capabilities, is the normal, ubiquitous state of all international systems. Unipolar or hegemonic systems will be inherently unstable, as balancing processes push the system back to bi- or multipolarity.

Propositions about Process

1. Unbalanced multipolarity – concentration of power in a system leader – causes competing powers to engage in internal and external balancing to check the rise of the hegemonic threat.

a. Diffusion of advanced military, economic and administrative techniques should enable rivals successfully to emulate the innovations of potential hegemons.

b. States nearer the threat are more likely to engage in balancing than are more distant states.

c. More powerful states are more likely to engage in balancing than are weaker states.

2. Should unipolarity or hegemony emerge, balancing processes (alliances, internal balancing, emulation, etc.) will emerge in tandem with the relative decline of the dominant state's capacity to enforce its pre-eminence.

3. Imperial expansion causes the size of the international system to expand, bringing in new opponents to aspiring hegemons and ensuring the maintenance of the balance of power.

4. Systems characterized by units with strong group identities and cultural norms valuing independence will tend to reproduce balancing dynamics.

5. Democratic and republican forms of government are incompatible with systemic hierarchy; such states engage in 'co-binding' to form lasting confederations to maintain systemic balance.

The logic of domination

Outcome Hypothesis: System leadership, in the form of a systemic hegemon or a unipolar distribution of power, is the normal, ubiquitous state of international systems.

Propositions about Process

1. States seek systemic hegemony because of the multiple economic and security benefits conferred by hegemonic status.

2. Systems characterized by a single collective identity or by cultural norms of deference to a system leader will tend toward a stable hierarchical structure.

3. Incentives for the hegemon's rivals to pass the buck or to bandwagon enable the rising hegemon to employ divide-and-conquer tactics to impede balancing efforts.

4. Uncertainty about the identity and severity of the hegemonic threat, especially in the context of multiple potential hegemons, impedes efforts to maintain a balance of power.

5. Unit types that are inherently small in size, such as city-states, will be disadvantaged in efforts to balance against larger empires.

6. Advances in administrative technologies increase the ability of larger states to absorb smaller ones, making power more cumulative and increasing the likelihood of systemic hierarchy.

7. Within states, narrow interests and institutional rigidities make it difficult for rivals to emulate the self-strengthening reforms implemented by potential hegemons, impeding efforts at internal balancing.

Findings and implications

The obvious characteristic shared by all of the systems studied in this volume is that all, at one time or another, were unipolar or hegemonic in structure. This might seem to indicate selection bias in the study's design, but it is not so – every one of these hegemonic systems emerged from an earlier multipolar system. In fact, the historical progression of several of these ancient systems is not unlike that of the modern international system, which evolved from the classical European balance of power into the bipolar system of the Cold War period, and then the unipolar post-Cold War era. The fundamental implication of the scholarship presented in this volume is that this evolution is historically typical, and the unipolar outcome is not necessarily, by historical analogy, an unstable one. As we detail in the conclusion, a survey of 7,500 years of the history of international systems shows that balanced and unbalanced distributions of power are roughly equally common. There is no iron law of history favoring either a balance of power or hegemony.

While we must be cautious in applying findings from ancient or early modern history in contemporary conditions, we cannot responsibly ignore those findings either. Statements that systemic unipolarity is 'unnatural' or even unusual simply reflect a Eurocentric ignorance of premodern and non-Western history. Unipolarity is a normal circumstance in world history. Furthermore, the logic of balance-of-power theory suggests that balancing behavior is relatively unlikely in conditions of unipolarity (Wohlforth, 1999). If states wish to maximize their chances of survival, they cannot do so by challenging the sole superpower directly – since, by definition, the lone superpower in a unipolar system has the capability to crush any likely opposing coalition. Rather, rivals to the sole superpower are safest if they engage in buck-passing or bandwagoning, or at most in surreptitious and indirect opposition that falls short of efforts to construct a true balance of power.

Overall, we conclude, the contemporary unipolar system is best understood not by assessing the logic of balancing, or balance-of-power theory; but by considering the logic of domination, and hegemonic stability theory. For realists, the strategic risks of a hegemonic foreign policy are best understood not from the perspective of a fictional balance of power, but from consideration of the possibility of overexpansion, as discussed by Robert Gilpin (1981), Paul Kennedy (1987), Jack Snyder (1991), and others. The sustainability of the hegemon's position is a function of its ability to maintain its economic and military advantage, of its effectiveness at administering or governing the areas it tries to control, and of the legitimacy of its position according to the norms of international society. The tactical competence of its efforts, similarly, is best assessed according to whether the hegemon is successful at dividing and ruling its adversaries, rather than allowing itself to be drawn into expensive and counterproductive boondoggles.

On some very important dimensions, our ancient and early modern evidence cannot provide insights. The prospects for co-binding among modern republics are fundamentally different from those facing their ancient forerunners. The opportunities for using modern international institutions to promote international cooperation find no real parallel in ancient times. And since the contemporary international system is global, we can rule out the possibility that geographic expansion of the system will contribute to the emergence of a new balance of power, as it did so many times in the past. But we confidently state that the contemporary unipolar distribution of power is not unprecedented, and lessons about how unipolarity operates can be learned from premodern and non-western history.

2
Balancing and Balancing Failure in Biblical Times: Assyria and the Ancient Middle Eastern System, 900–600 BCE

Stuart J. Kaufman and William C. Wohlforth[1]

On the first floor of the British museum stands a 3,000 year old monument known as the 'Kurkh Stele.' It portrays the Assyrian King Shalmaneser III above an inscription written in his voice, which includes this passage:

> I approached cities of Irhulenu, the Hamatite ... I razed, destroyed and burned Qarqar, his royal city. An alliance had been formed of these twelve kings: 1,200 chariots, 1,200 cavalry, 20,000 troops of Hadadezer, the Damascene; 700 chariots, 700 cavalry, 10,000 troops of Irhulenu, the Hamatite; 2,000 chariots [and] 10,000 troops of Ahab the Israelite; ... [and others]. They attacked to war and battle against me (Grayson, 1996: 23).

With corroboration from other sources, historians of the period are confident that the battle of Qarqar actually did occur in about 853 BCE, that the alliance mentioned in the inscription represented a concerted effort to balance the rising power of Assyria, that it held together for several years, fighting repeatedly to thwart Assyrian expansion, and that it and all other such efforts ultimately failed to stop Assyria from establishing an empire encompassing nearly the entire international system of the time. Biblical names and Iron Age technology notwithstanding, these events relate directly to this book's central task of explaining systemic transitions from balance toward hegemony and back again. As Chapter 1 argues, for centuries International Relations (IR) scholars have posited that the systemic tendencies featured in balance-of-power theory are central to such transitions. Our collective purpose in this volume is to assess whether this is the case in international systems other than the familiar modern European one and its contemporary successor.

Accordingly, this chapter answers an important question IR scholars have never thought to ask: How important were balancing tendencies in accounting for the 300-year trajectory of Assyrian dominance over the Middle Eastern international system in Biblical times? We begin by showing that a case that seems so remote in so many ways is truly probative for balance-of-power theory. In the second section, we present a theoretically informed narrative of Assyria's rise that allows us to assess the role of the theory's core causal mechanisms in accounting for systemic outcomes. In the third section, we summarize and discuss the implications of our main finding: that the fundamental forces driving systemic outcomes in the ancient Middle East lie outside current renderings of balance-of-power theory, and, indeed, mainstream IR scholarship more generally. We conclude with a discussion of these other causes and their implications of systemic theories of IR.

Case and theory

Given a case featuring unpronounceable names and diplomatic documents on stone tablets, the connection between the case and the theoretical debates at issue does need to be demonstrated. In the subsections that follow we describe the ancient middle eastern system, establish its connections with balance-of-power theory, derive specific hypotheses to assess the explanatory importance of balancing processes, and discuss the evidentiary challenges it presents.

The ancient, middle eastern system and balance-of-power theory

At the start of the 9th century BCE, Assyria lay at the center of an international system comprising several other large states, some powers of middle rank, and many smaller ones, that modern scholars would recognize as multipolar (see Map 2.1). To the north in what is now southeastern Turkey, the kingdom of Urartu, which would become Assyria's most powerful rival during its rise, was soon to form. To the south and southeast were Babylonia and Elam, great powers but generally inferior militarily to Assyria. To the west, a string of neo-Hittite city-states and small kingdoms, led by Carchemish on the upper Euphrates, controlled southeastern Anatolia and northern Syria. Further west and south were numerous Aramaean city-states, most importantly Arpad and Hamath in the north, Damascus in the south, and the related Hebrew kingdom of Samaria-Israel on both sides of the Jordan River, plus the rich but weak Phoenician and Philistine city-states of the Levantine coast. Egyptian power was confined mainly to the Nile River valley and only intermittently played a role in the geopolitics of southwestern Asia.

The sources leave no doubt that these actors constituted an anarchical system. Non-state entities did play important roles: the main Chaldaean tribes in the 'sealand' area of southern Babylonia were autonomous power centers, and various tribal peoples in what is now Iran represented a continuing threat to Assyrian power in the east. But polities with armies and bureaucracies that controlled territories – state-like enough to be called, for convenience, 'states' – dominated the system. Indeed, the social institutions and communications technology that are necessary for states' interaction to constitute a system were more developed in this period than they had been in the Amarna system that preceded it, and the Amarna already met the basic definition of an interstate system discussed in Chapter 1 (Cohen and Westbrook, 2000; Liverani, 2001; Bull and Watson, 1984).

In many respects, moreover, the ancient middle eastern system in Biblical times represents a most likely case for balance-of-power theory – that is, if the theory works anywhere, it should work here

Map 2.1   The Assyrian Empire, c. 860 BCE

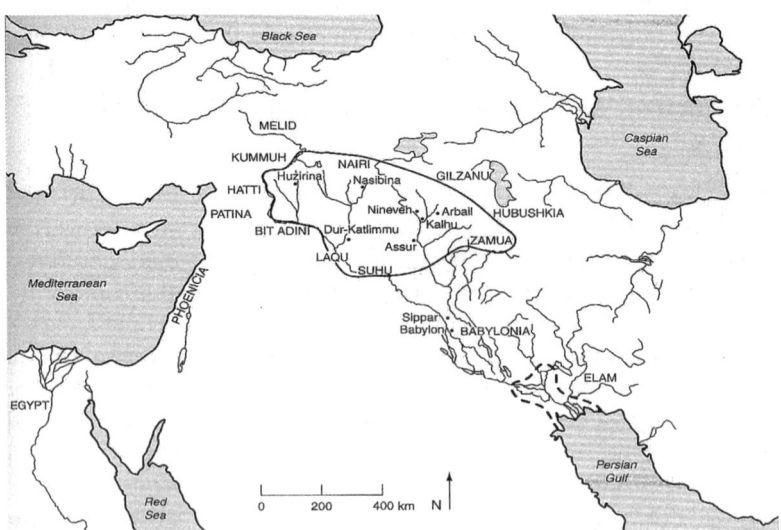

Source: Liverani (2001) reproduced with permission from Palgrave Macmillan.
Note: Dashed line indicates the ancient shoreline of the Persian Gulf.

(Bennett and George, 2005). There were no 'offshore' powers to confound the theory's predictions; few non-material restraints on the use of force; control of territory was the key to power; there was a clear hegemonic threat for decades; and the system experienced dramatic variation in the theory's key variables. Key here is that Assyria was clearly the strongest power on the scene, but the size and resource endowment of its homeland were comparable to those of its major rivals (Cohen and Westbrook, 2000; Brinkman, 1991). It was thus a hegemonic threat, but one that could be balanced. In addition, Assyria's behavior and ideology left no doubt about its expansionist intentions, so both balance-of-power and balance-of-threat theory yield identical predictions of balancing. And its power fluctuated dramatically, opening up windows of opportunity for potential balancers to rein it in. No matter how one construes balance-of-power theory, its predictions should apply to a contiguous multipolar system whose leading state had the means and the manifest intent to create hegemony.

Hypotheses, measurement and evidence

Chapter 1 identifies the causal mechanisms balance-of-power theory predicts will figure centrally in explaining the dynamics of international systems over the *longue duree:* alliance formation, competitive emulation, and self-strengthening reforms, all driven by the logic of security-seeking under anarchy. No matter how one formulates it, the theory yields three core hypotheses: (1) that these balancing processes will present increasingly significant barriers to expansion by the system's most powerful and/or threatening actor; (2) that, if balancing nonetheless fails, the resulting unipolar system will be short-lived; and (3) that balancing processes will play a central role in bringing the system back to a bi- or multipolar equilibrium (Waltz, 2000b).

Evaluating these hypotheses requires measures of the leader's share of system capabilities, a challenge given the limited evidence available. For our case, two rough-and-ready measures are most salient: rising indicators of Assyrian capabilities (increased territory, access to resources, military capability, and extractive capabilities); and fewer rival great powers able to resist. The same measures apply to other actors: with estimates of their general size and military capacity, we can assess the system's polarity and the predicted degree of balancing. And, we need to able to determine roughly the degree to which other actors actually engaged in balancing behavior, including not just alliances and war-fighting, but also domestic self-strengthening reforms and emulation.

Researchers have amassed enough evidence about the international system of the 9th–7th century BCE Middle East to permit us to evaluate these core hypotheses. Archeological research yields crucial evidence on the size, location, and technological level of settlements, demographic patterns, and resource endowments (Brinkman, 1997). Studies of the military and political organization of contemporary polities, and their culture, ideology and administration, yield estimates of emulation and self-strengthening reforms (e.g., Brinkman, 1984; Lipinski, 2000). The most valuable textual sources are Assyrian and Babylonian royal chronologies and 'eponym lists', chronological lists of officials holding a symbolic annual title, after whom each year was 'named' (Grayson, 1996; Millard, 1994). These texts establish basic chronology for most key events, often mentioning the most important military campaign launched in each year.

Next in importance are thousands of letters and other documents from royal (mostly Assyrian) archives that offer a fair amount of detail about Assyrian state administration, as well as the occasional treaty text. Royal inscriptions, while intended for propagandistic purposes, are useful for providing a general outline of events, most notably which states lined up on which side in various military campaigns, where armies marched, and what political outcomes resulted (Grayson, 1996; Grayson, 1991a; Brinkman, 1991). Numerous reliefs of scenes of battle – the favorite subject of Assyrian artists and their royal patrons – offer great detail about the sorts of weapons available at different times and to different armies, along with hints about their tactical use (Saggs, 1963; Yadin, 1963). Finally, when crosschecked against other sources, the Hebrew Bible offers additional evidence, especially about events in the area of the Levantine coast.

The evidence obviously does not permit finely grained tests. We lack good *ex ante* measures of power, and textual evidence on perceptions and intentions is scanty. The Assyrian origin of much of the evidence creates bias, and leaves some important gaps in knowledge about the internal properties of other states. Yet we do know enough to subject balance-of-power theory's core propositions to a completely fresh empirical evaluation. We consider a 250 year span, the equivalent to the period from the War of the Spanish Succession to the Cold War. If we had no prior knowledge of that period in modern history, even a rough outline would be probative for our theories. As it turns out, the 9th–7th century BCE were no less turbulent.

The middle eastern international system, 883–612 BCE

The subsections that follow track Assyria's rise from being the most powerful state in a multipolar system to unipolar status (883–824), its subsequent decline and the reemergence of a balancing order (827–746), a renewed resurgence to systemic hegemony (745–727), and the shift from stable Assyrian dominance to collapse (727–612). Each summarizes the evidence concerning the salience of balancing processes as opposed to other causes of system change.

Rise to partial hegemony: 883–824

In the early 9th century Assyria comprised roughly the northern half of modern Iraq (Map 2.1). King Ashurnasirpal II (883–859) set the stage for Assyria's later expansion. Most of his early campaigns aimed at establishing or enforcing Assyrian suzerainty over neighboring hill tribes to the north and east. In the north, one factor explaining his success in these campaigns was undoubtedly the undeveloped character of the Urartian state, which had not yet achieved the rank of a great power. In the south, Ashurnasirpal defeated Babylonia for suzerainty over at least one key disputed area along the middle Euphrates. And in the west, he forced his near neighbors Bit Adini and Carchemish not only to provide tribute, but to join him in a demonstration march all the way to the Mediterranean.

While Ashurnasirpal faced little balancing, Assyriologists disagree over the degree to which his policy was expansionist enough to warrant it (cf. Paley, 1976 and Liverani, 1992). Rhetorically, Assyria's hegemonic ambition was unambiguous, as Ashurnasirpal's self-proclaimed titles included, 'king of the world, ... subjugator of the unsubmissive, who rules the total sum of all humanity' (tr. in Paley, 1976: 126). Ashurnasirpal's inscriptions are remarkable in part for the detail with which he recorded his atrocities, such as flaying rebellious leaders, burning captured men and women alive, and displaying the corpses, decapitated heads, and skins of flayed leaders around the defeated cities (Roux, 1964: 241). These grisly details clarify the choices facing neighboring leaders threatened by Assyrian expansion. Bandwagoning meant submission to Assyria's often onerous demands for tribute and troops. But balancing efforts that failed could mean excruciating death. In later years wholesale exile of large portions of the defeated population, as happened most famously to the ten 'lost tribes' of Israel, also occurred.

But in practice, the size of Ashurnasirpal's empire was not clearly unprecedented, and in the later part of his reign he was quite restrained: he launched only a few military campaigns in his last 17 years of rule, instead of the annual offensives launched by more aggressive rulers – including his own first seven years.

Assyria's behavior under the next monarch, Shalmaneser III (858–824) was much more clearly expansionist. In his first full year on the throne he repeated his father's march to the Mediterranean, though this time he had to fight his way there. Bit-Adini allied with Carchemish and several neo-Hittite city-states to the west to oppose him, but Shalmaneser defeated the coalition, and the neo-Hittites, joined by Arpad, paid tribute to him. Bit-Adini did not submit, so Shalmaneser destroyed and annexed it.

States to the west and south now identified Shalmaneser as a threat, and a dozen of them led by Hamath, Damascus, and Israel formed the balancing alliance described above (Grayson, 1996: 11, 35). The resulting battle of Qarqar (853 BCE) was large by any standard: the Assyrian account lists over 50,000 troops and 4,000 chariots among the enemy force. While the Assyrians claim to have won on the battlefield, there were no political consequences of their victory: they do not report receiving any surrenders, annexations or tribute. Balancing in the west was successful, this time. Both sides returned for battle again in 848 and 845, but in 845, Shalmaneser reports having mustered a 120,000-man army – huge even if one assumes significant exaggeration. Shalmaneser again claimed victory, but this time perhaps with reason, as the coalition never again took the field against him (Grayson, 1991a: 262).

When Damascus next faced an Assyrian attack it did so alone: after Shalmaneser crossed the Euphrates in 841 and 838, he reported no resistance before he reached Damascene territory, which he ravaged on both occasions. The rulers of Tyre, Sidon, Israel and other local potentates hurried to offer tribute to the conquering Assyrian (Grayson, 1996: 48, 67). With the balancing coalition gone, virtually all of Syria, Lebanon and Israel submitted to Shalmaneser (Finkelstein and Silberman, 2001: 201–2). Assyria now controlled the vital trade routes to Anatolia and the Cilician plain – whence came its supplies of key commodities, especially iron and silver. And some previously powerful enemies, Carchemish and Bit-Adini, had been permanently removed from the rolls of Assyrian adversaries.

To the north, Urartu was enough of a power at this time that it was the target of Shalmaneser's first campaign, in which he captured a 'fortified city of Aramu the Urartian', erected two towers of (decapitated) heads outside it, burned dozens of unfortified towns, and raided deep into Urartu's hinterland (Grayson, 1996: 8). This was a raid, however, not a real assertion of control. It was followed by a devastating sweep in 856 through the Urartian heartland, and another major attack in 844. Near the end of Shalmaneser's reign, however, his field marshal launched a series of attacks against a new, apparently tougher Urartian monarch, Sarduri I – founder of Urartu's greatest dynasty – which did not get past the border areas (Barnett, 1991: 338; cf. Piotrovsky, 1969: 48). Protected by the formidable barrier of the Taurus Mountains, Urartu was gaining strength. Urartu's transformation from a tribal society to a state appears to have been a case of emulation under pressure from Assyria as the Urartians adopted numerous practices from their more powerful southern neighbor, including the Assyrian cuneiform script and language for Royal inscriptions (Kuhrt, 1995: ch. 10). Similarly, Shalmaneser's defeat of Aramu ironically paved the way for the accession of a more effective Urartian dynasty.

While Assyrian armies expanded relentlessly to the west and east, and were locked in continuing combat with Urartu to the north, Babylonia never made the slightest effort to gain ground in the border areas by balancing against the Assyrians. Indeed, Assyrian relations with Babylonia were harmonious throughout Shalmaneser's reign: Shalmaneser had treaties with two successive Babylonian kings, and ordered the sculpting of a relief depicting him grasping hands as an equal with his Babylonian counterpart. Shalmaneser's only two recorded campaigns in Babylonia in his 36-year reign, in 851–850, were to help a Babylonian king put down a rebellion (Grayson, 1996: 267). The Babylonians' quiescence may have been a consequence of their reliance on Assyrian support in defending against the expansion of the Chaldean tribes who were threatening the cities of southern Babylonia. In any case, Babylonia's policy at the time was unquestionably bandwagoning with the stronger Assyria.

The overall reaction to Shalmaneser's expansionism represents a case of highly inefficient balancing, leading to Assyrian hegemony over much of the system, including Babylonia and most of Syria. Shalmaneser's initial march to the Mediterranean provoked the expected balancing response, first by a frontline coalition led by Bit-Adini and Carchemish, and later by the remarkably durable Damascus-Hamath coalition. Urartu fended off Assyria's assaults in the north and developed its state institutions in part as an internal balancing response, but Babylonia preferred to bandwagon with Assyria, as did some key states in the west, especially Arpad and (after the Battle of Qarqar) Israel. These defections were important, because Shalmaneser's difficulty in subduing Hamath and Damascus – and his losses on the northern frontier – suggest that additional allies for the Syrians might have been decisive: a bit of opportunistic bandwagoning apparently made the difference between Assyrian victory and defeat. Furthermore, Shalmaneser's annexation of Bit-Adini and Carchemish gave Assyria permanent control over both banks of the Euphrates, providing a lasting boost to its power projection capability. Assyria's inability to hold and administer the tributary states, however, caused it to lose most of Shalmaneser's conquests in the next decades.

Decline and balancing: 827–746

In the last years of Shalmaneser's reign, starting in 827 BCE, a massive revolt shook the foundations of the Assyrian state. Led by Shalmaneser's son Assur-da'in-apla, the former capital cities of Assur and Nineveh, along with 25 other cities rebelled against the monarch. It took Shalmaneser's younger son Shamshi-Adad (827–746) five years, first as crown prince and then as king, to put down the revolt, and even so he had to turn for help to the Babylonian king. The entirety of Shalmaneser's conquests now had to be retaken. Shamshi-Adad started in the north, where the Urartians had been assiduously winning supporters. In a series of three campaigns he and his field marshal reasserted Assyrian suzerainty over the northern borderlands.

The key balancing coalition emerged neither in the disputed north nor in the west, now largely written off and no longer paying tribute, but in the south. In 814 Shamshi-Adad invaded Babylonia to assert Assyrian predominance there. The new Babylonian king assembled a broad coalition including Elam and Aramaean and Chaldaean tribesmen to resist the Assyrian invasion. Shamshi-Adad won the day, claiming to have inflicted some 18,000 casualties on the enemy coalition, which fell apart (Grayson, 1996: 188). Still, the war was not over: Assyria had to launch two more campaigns against the Babylonians and their troublesome Chaldaean allies before the region was secure.

The northern frontier was next. Adad-nirari III (810–783) sent three early expeditions against tribal peoples under Urartian influence in western Iran; and overall, he campaigned 11 times against just three of the key targets in the Urartian sphere – the Medes, Mannaeans and Hubushkia (Millard, 1994: 57–8). At the same time, Urartian King Menua was making important gains in the southeastern Anatolian regions that controlled the metals trade – gains Adad-nirari was unable to prevent. Urartu also expanded north to the Araxes river, placing it in control of all of eastern Anatolia as well (Millard, 1994: 57–8; Barnett, 1991: 342–3).

In the southwest, Assyria defeated a coalition of Syrian states led by Arpad, reopening the road to Damascus. A decade later (796), a coalition including Damascus and some smaller northern Syrian city-states launched an attack on pro-Assyrian Hamath; Adad-nirari intervened and defeated the coalition, marched all the way to Damascus, and forced his way in – a feat that had eluded his grandfather Shalmaneser. All of Syria, Phoenecia, Israel, the Philistines, and Edom in Transjordan offered tribute to the victor. Arpad, Hamath and Damascus having neglected to unite, balancing had failed again.

It was a similar story in the southeast. Adad-nirari repeatedly invaded western Iran, forcing the Medes, Persians and others of the region to pay tribute; and he repeatedly probed into the region between Babylonia and Elam. Finally, toward the end of his reign he entered Babylon and removed the Babylonian king, continuing his campaign against the troublesome Chaldaean tribes in the south (Grayson, 1991a: 272–3). No balancing coalition seems to have formed, and Assyrian armies penetrated anywhere they wanted to go. Adad-nirari lacked, however, the means to administer what he conquered, so Assyrian control again proved ephemeral almost everywhere.

The period from 782–745 is poorly documented, but what evidence there is clearly shows a pattern of continuing Assyrian weakness, though not catastrophic decline. Urartu continued its rise to power, especially in the northeast, despite receiving the lion's share of Assyria's military attention. Five campaigns in the north created enough breathing space on that frontier for Assyria to reenter Syria and compel Damascus to renew its tribute payments (Millard, 1994; Grayson, 1996). But plagues and revolts frequently prevented Assyrian kings from undertaking military campaigns at all, and three campaigns against relatively nearby Hatarikka indicate 'that Assyria's area of influence was diminishing' (Grayson, 1991a: 277). Sardur II of Urartu claimed in an inscription to have defeated an Assyrian army in battle (Grayson, 1996: 246). One successful campaign against Arpad yielded an unequal treaty of alliance, retaining the Assyrian foothold in northern Syria. Arpad quickly abrogated the treaty, however, aligning instead with the rising Urartians.

The source of Assyrian weakness at this time seems to have been dysfunctional domestic institutions. Assyriologist H.W.F. Saggs (1984: 82) refers to the period as one of 'Weak kings and overmighty governors.' Saggs argues that provincial governors were 'becoming almost local dynasts' (1984: 82; see also Grayson, 1991a: 278–9). One governor of Suhu on the middle Euphrates not only made inscriptions boasting of his achievements – achievements ordinarily attributed to the king – he even dated those achievements by his own years in office, without mention of the king: actions tantamount to claiming independence. This situation undoubtedly contributed to revolts, and, more generally, to Assyrian military weakness. It finally led to a revolt by the governor of Calah, and the installation of a new ruler who would address these problems.

Resurgence and empire: 744–705

The new ruler, Tiglath-pileser III (744–727), reformed the deteriorating institutions of Assyria and inaugurated the decades of Assyria's greatest expansion. Both efforts pointed to the same result: the conversion of Assyria from an unevenly effective superpower into a more con-solidated empire incorporating scores of neighboring peoples. The system now shifted decisively from unbalanced multipolarity to clear unipolarity.

The administrative changes amounted to a social revolution: the old nobility, which had held regional governorships sometimes as heredi-tary possessions, was replaced by a set of officials appointed by the king. Furthermore, the provinces were reduced in size – reducing the governors' resources for any potential uprising – and the king main-tained a number of traveling inspectors to check up on administration throughout the empire. He set up a network of post roads with pony express-style posting stations, and created a particularly effective intel-ligence network in Urartu (Saggs, 1984: 85–6). These reforms enabled Tiglath-pileser vastly to increase the amount of territory under direct Assyrian administration, and thereby to expand the reach of Assyria's armies.

The most important foreign effort to balance Assyria came early in Tiglath-pileser's reign. Arpad, just west of the upper Euphrates, orga-nized a coalition including Urartu and several neo-Hittite states in southeastern Anatolia. Tiglath-pileser invaded the area in 743, defeat-ing an army led personally by King Sarduri of Urartu, and reducing some of the neo-Hittites to tributary status. Arpad held out longer, but in 740 it surrendered and Tiglath-pileser incorporated it into the Assyrian Empire as a province (Grayson, 1991b: 74–5; Tadmor, 1994: 256). The next time Assyria fought in the west, the opposing coalition seems to have been much smaller: most of the region's key powers – notably Damascus, Israel/Samaria, Hamath, neo-Hittite states of the north such as Carchemish, and Urartu – apparently chose to buckpass (Lipinski, 2000; Grayson, 1991b: 74–5).

The Syrians and Phoenicians were soon to regret that decision. In 734 Tiglath-pileser marched through the newly submissive areas to capture the Philistine city of Gaza. Alarmed, Damascus rebelled against Assyria, leading a coalition including Samaria/Israel, Tyre, and a few others. Judah, an Assyrian tributary, came under attack, prompting it to appeal for Assyrian help (Mitchell, 1991: 31; cf. Saggs, 1962: 109). Tiglath-pileser was happy to oblige, and by 732, the coalition was completely defeated: Damascus was reorganized as an Assyrian province; Israel lost its rich northern districts, also to an Assyrian province; and Israel was joined as tributary by most of its neighbors – Phoenician and Philistine city-states and the Transjordanian kingdoms of Ammon, Edom, and Moab (Grayson, 1991b: 77–8).

Urartu remained 'the major foreign power with which Tiglath-pileser III had to contend' (Grayson, 1991b: 74). The contest, however, was an uneven one. As noted above, the first confrontation between the two came in 743, when Tiglath-pileser defeated an Urartian army marching to the aid of Arpad, apparently in an ambush (Saggs, 1962: 107). A few years later, attention turned to the mountainous border region between the two powers, where Tiglath-pileser invaded the border state of Ullubu in 739, reorganized it as an Assyrian province, and transported to it a new population from further southwest. He followed up in 735 with a campaign in the heartland of Urartu itself, defeating the Urartians outside their own capital, Turushpa on Lake Van, though he failed to take the city. In the aftermath, he annexed additional territories to Assyrian provinces in the north (Grayson, 1991b: 76). Tiglath-pileser subsequently had few problems with Urartu.

With Assyria's last true peer competitor subdued for the moment, and both Babylon and Elam quiescent, Tiglath-pileser remained active in the south, campaigning in the mountains of western Iran southeast of the Assyrian heartland. He defeated numerous tribal peoples, created new Assyrian provinces, and expanded older ones. Other states in the region not directly targeted quickly offered their submission, most notably Ellipi (north of Elam) and Mannea (southeast of Urartu). Indeed, in 737 Tiglath-pileser marched even further, forcing the Medes east of Ellipi to pay tribute and penetrating all the way to the border of Elam (Grayson, 1991b: 79–80).

Assyria's southern expansion did not end there. When a Chaldaean leader named Mukin-zer seized Babylonia's throne in 732 Tiglath-pileser marched south, captured Babylon, and ravaged the territories of the rebellious Chaldaean tribes. He capped the campaign by 'taking the hand of Bel' – that is, assuming the kingship of Babylonia personally.

Unable to unite behind an alternate leader, the Babylonians accepted his rule and that of his son (Grayson, 1991b: 79–80).

As in Shalmaneser's time, balancing failures again played an important role in the rise of Assyria. In the southwest, no substantial balancing coalition emerged: Hamath, Damascus and Israel failed to coalesce with Arpad after the Urartian defeat of 843, so they were defeated and annexed separately. In the southeast, neither Elam nor Urartu tried to balance Assyria by supporting tribal neighbors like Ellipi and Mannea. And in Babylonia, Mukin-zer failed even to unite his own Chaldaean people against the Assyrians, let alone the native Babylonians, so again Tiglath-pileser succeeded in dividing and conquering.

Tiglath-pileser's reign marked the emergence of a unipolar system. Assyria was now the direct ruler of virtually the whole Fertile Crescent, from the Galilee and Damascus to Babylon and the shores of the Persian Gulf (Map 2.2). No power or combination of powers could counterbalance Assyria's formidable capabilities. Yet Assyria's material capabilities were still limited by the small size and limited productivity of its heartland, its imperfect administrative capacity, and the con-

Map 2.2   The Assyrian Empire, c. 730 BCE

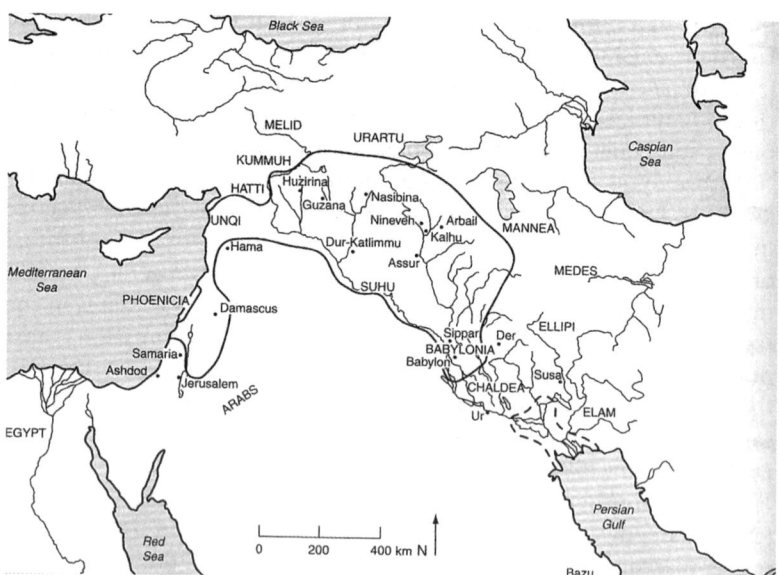

Source: Liverani (2001) reproduced with permission from Palgrave Macmillan.
Note: Dashed line indicates the ancient shoreline of the Persian Gulf.

strained base of its army's manpower (Oates, 1991: 182–3; Oates, 1968: 42–66; cf. Liverani, 1988; Parker, 1997). Its overall resource base does not appear to have been much larger than those of its chief rivals. Thus while Assyria was the sole superpower, it was a vulnerable one, offering other actors numerous opportunities to try to bring the system back into balance.

The succession from Tiglath-pileser's son Shalmanesar V (727–721) to Sargon II (721–705) was accompanied by civil unrest – probably a result of Sargon's status as a usurper. With the imperial center thus weakened, the marchland powers seized the opportunity to foment rebellions among the buffer states and dependencies. Upon accession, Sargon therefore faced three distinct military challenges that reveal much about both the power and latent vulnerability of the empire he ruled, and provided his rivals with the best opportunity to rebalance the system that they would have for a century.

To the south, the Babylon-Chaldaean-Elam coalition reemerged. At the outset of Sargon's reign, the Chaldaean Merodach-baladan secured a formal alliance with Elam and with Elamite support seized the kingship of Babylon in 721. He thereupon welded together Aramaean and Chaldaean tribes into a united anti-Assyrian force, and coordinated strong anti-Assyrian movements not only in Elam, but also in northern Arabia. He even approached distant Judah, apparently 'motivated by common antipathy to Assyrian encroachments' (Brinkman, 1991: 17). An Assyrian force was ordered southward in response to the challenge in Babylon, but it was blocked by the Elamites. Both Assyrian and Babylonian records claim victory, but subsequent records on all sides show no further Assyrian action against Babylon or Elam for another decade, suggesting that the engagement was a defensive victory for Elam (Brinkman, 1991: 28–9; Grayson, 1991b: 88, 98; James, 1991: 692).

Sargon then shifted his attention to the west, where Egypt was supporting Hamath's attempt to forge an anti-Assyrian coalition in alliance with Arpad, Samaria, Damascus, and other kingdoms in Syria-Palestine. In 720, Sargon brought his army to bear throughout Syria, defeating the coalition (including the Egyptians at Raphia), reconquering Gaza and bringing Hamath under direct provincial rule. After routing the Egyptians, Sargon established a garrison at the border, and the Pharaoh elected to pass the buck and pursue détente with the Assyrian king (Brinkman, 1991: 89; Mitchell, 1991: 343).

Sargon's most pressing challenges, however, lay to the North (Urartu) and West (Mushki/Phrygians). His response began in 719, when he battered Urartu's erstwhile Mannaean allies into submission. However, King Mita (Midas) of Mushki now entered the fray, piecing together an anti-Assyrian alliance among the kingdoms of North Syria. There ensued a complex duel between Sargon and his two main antagonists, Mita and Rusa I of Urartu. While the two kings did eventually cooperate against Assyria, Sargon was nonetheless able to concentrate forces against each in turn. The Assyrian first campaigned in North Syria to crush Mita's allies. Then, in a series of campaigns between 717 and 713, he focused on Urartu, retrieving lost territory, adding new domains to the empire, and ultimately dealing a permanent blow to Urartan power, uprooting and transporting many of the defeated peoples to Syria.

By 710, then, Assyria could at last concentrate on the Elam-Babylon-Chaldaean challenge to the south. The Assyrians launched a major southern campaign in 710, first striking against Elam. This attack prompted many northern Babylonian cities to defect to Assyria, paving the way for a concentrated and successful thrust against Merodach-baladan and the Chaldaean tribes in and to the south of Babylon. After

Map 2.3   The Assyrian Empire, c. 705 BCE

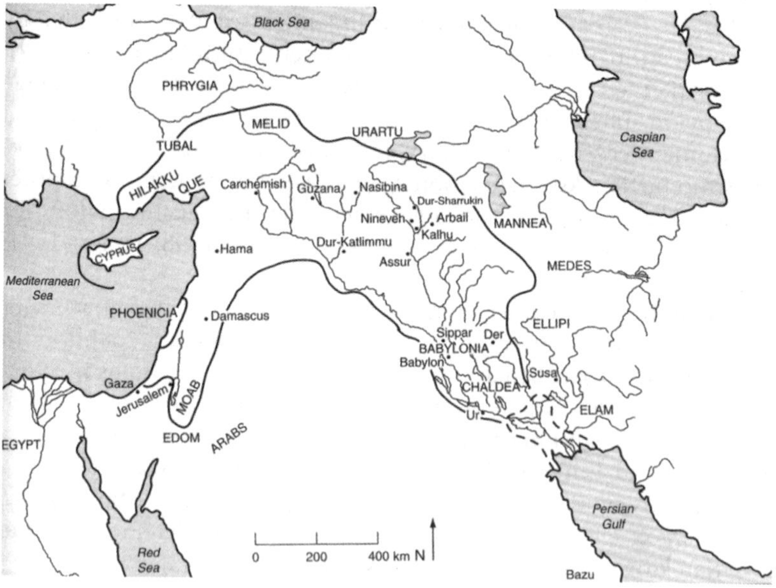

Source: Liverani (2001) reproduced with permission from Palgrave Macmillan.
Note: Dashed line indicates the ancient shoreline of the Persian Gulf.

his success in the south, Sargon once again swung to the northwest, taking the offensive around 709–8 against the Mushki and their allies, eventually securing a cordial alliance with Mita.

When Sargon died in 705, the major threats appeared to have been eliminated, and the empire's territory had been expanded in every direction (Map 2.3). Elam and Urartu had been dealt punishing blows, while Egypt and Mushki had elected to bandwagon under pressure. Assyria's interior location, unmatched military power, superior intelligence and, arguably, effective strategic leadership had again thwarted every attempt at opposition by borderland states.

Again, however, a key explanation for Assyrian success lay in its opponents' failure to pursue effective balancing strategies. Urartu and Mushki clearly would have benefited if they had cooperated more effectively against the common Assyrian threat. And while the Assyrians were focused against them, the Chaldaeans and Elamites could have attacked from the south and east, dividing Assyrian energies and gaining territory for themselves. Assyrian predominance was to continue for another century because of these failures.

Ascendancy to collapse: 704–612

Even with Sargon's victories, Assyria's military primacy was unable entirely to tame Babylonia, whose resistance was based less on military power than on its leaders' skill at claiming legitimacy to undermine the unity of Assyria's governing elite, as well as asymmetric guerilla warfare (Brinkman, 1984; Cole, 1996). When in 703, Merodach-baladan again raised a rebellion with the same cast of characters – Elam, Aramaeans and Chaldaeans – Sargon's successor Sennacherib (704–681) responded with military repression, defortifying and devastating the Aramaean and Chaldaean areas, encompassing nearly all of southern Babylonia.

Sennacherib then shifted his attention to a new goal: the conquest of Egypt. While Assyria encroached on Egyptian positions and courted Arab tribes near the Egyptian border, Egypt supported a rebellion in Palestine. In 701, Hezekiah of Judah (perhaps in cahoots with Merodach-baladan) organized a rebellious alliance of coastal cities, including Sidon in Phoenecia, supported by Egypt (Grayson, 1991c: 120–2; II Kings, 18: 17ff.). Sennacherib put down the rebellion, chased out the Egyptians, and laid siege to Jerusalem. The city was spared as the Assyrians were forced to withdraw to put down yet another rebellion in Babylon – Merodach-baladan's last attempt. Sennacherib reduced Babylon's autonomy, modifying the previous dual monarchy by placing his son on the Babylonian throne. Elam then took over the reins of rebellion in Babylon, resulting in a series of campaigns from 694–689 in which Sennacherib struck first at Elam and then unleashed his vengeance upon Babylon itself. He sacked and flooded the ancient city, defiled its sacred monuments, expelled or executed the rebellion's ringleaders, and thenceforth ruled Babylon directly as an imperial province (Saggs, 1984; Brinkman, 1991).

No sooner had Sennacherib fallen victim to regicide in 680 than stirrings of rebellion in Babylon got underway again. The new king, Esarhaddon (680–669), reversed his father's coercive policy and switched to appeasement, investing huge sums in rebuilding Babylon and pursuing a carefully differentiated policy toward the Chaldaeans (Porter, 1993; Holloway, 2002). The initial stirrings of rebellion were dealt with swiftly and efficiently, and with cooperation from the now-bandwagoning Elam. Assyriologists attribute the shift to three factors: a recognition that the previous policy of deterrence had manifestly failed; an awareness of the potential threat of a newly belligerent people to the east, the Medes, against whom Elam could be useful as a buffer; and the desire to concentrate forces for the conquest of Egypt (Brinkman, 1991: 40–1; Grayson, 1991c: 123).

Esarhaddon was now free to concentrate on a faded but still formidable Egypt. His second attempted conquest, in 671, was nominally successful, but Assyria proved unable to install a local administration that could survive the departure of the main army. Egypt ultimately succumbed to Esarhaddon's successor Ashurbanipal (668–635) in 667. Stretched out over a 1,300-mile line of communication and supply and lacking the manpower to maintain a major armed force on the Nile, the Assyrians nonetheless managed to install a client dynasty of pharaohs who remained faithful to Assyria to the end.

The mid-7th c. BCE marks the territorial high point of the Assyrian Empire (Map 2.4). Not only was Egypt now in the Assyrian orbit, but the empire had also expanded to the northwest. There were indications, however, that the empire was facing increased external challenges. By 657, Cimmerian tribesmen were menacing Syria; states that had been bandwagoning, such as Lydia in western Anatolia, now began to hedge their bets; and notwithstanding early successes in the northeast, Assyria was losing ground in the area, especially to the Medes, many of whom had previously been vassals (Brinkman, 1984; Brinkman, 1991: 53).

The revealed weakening of Assyria's position was followed by intensified balancing behavior. The appeasement policy towards Babylon and Elam collapsed. Elam took advantage of Assyria's distraction in Egypt to

Map 2.4   The Assyrian Empire, c. 640 BCE

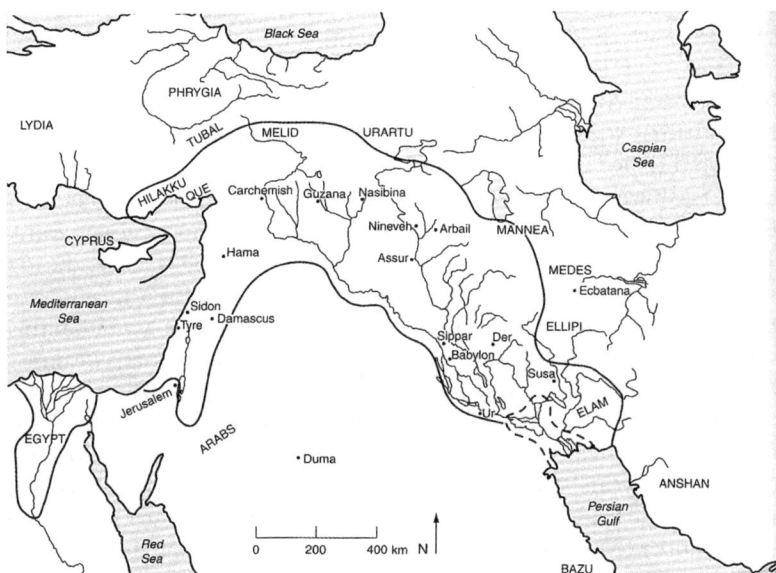

Source: Liverani (2001) reproduced with permission from Palgrave Macmillan.
Note: Dashed line indicates the ancient shoreline of the Persian Gulf.

attack Babylonia in 665 and lay siege to Babylon. The Elamites were quickly chased off, but nine years later they were back as part of the 'Great Rebellion' of Babylonia (led by Ashurbanipal's brother, to whom Esarhaddon had given Babylon's throne), along with a number of Arab princes. Ashurbanipal first defeated the Elamite army, then put down the rebellion in Babylon, and then implemented a final solution to the Elamite problem not unlike Sargon's against Urartu 65 years before. Between 648 and 644, the Assyrians conducted two major campaigns against Elam involving massive devastation from which it never recovered.

Though Ashurbanipal emerged from the Great Rebellion victorious, historians reckon that his empire never recovered from this blow. Slowly what had been a problem of maintaining the empire and managing systemic hegemony metastasized into the threat of a full-blown coalition to bring down the Assyrian state. In Babylonia, alternating Assyrian policies of deterrence and appeasement nurtured group identity and institutions, as happened in so many other imperial contexts (see, especially, Brinkman, 1984). The result was to produce a latent, asymmetric power, combining the imperial history and legitimacy of the Babylonians and the military manpower of the Chaldaeans. Even direct rule of the country by Ashurbanipal as King of Babylonia did not suffice: he was unable to pass on his authority to his Assyrian successor; the next effective Babylonian king was the Chaldaean rebel Nabopolassar. Meanwhile, Assyrian pressure helped hammer the Medes from a tribal society to a major kingdom in North Iran, centered in cities and skilled in war (Kuhrt, 1995).

After Ashurbanipal's death, Assyrian hegemony began to unravel. In 626 Babylon shook off the Assyrian yoke, defeating an Assyrian army. There ensued 11 years of war between Babylonia and Assyria, during which Babylonia achieved full independence. Toward the end the Egyptians began aiding their former Assyrian overlords, but whether this was balancing against Babylonia or opportunistic expansion is disputed (Cf. Oates, 1991: 178 and James, 1991: 714). In any case Egypt was too late to turn the tide. Assyria, for its part, was increasingly unable to oppose the Babylonian threat without opening itself up to Median assault. Two years after a battle between the united Assyrian-Egyptian forces and the Babylonians only 200 miles from Babylon itself in 616, the Medes under Cyaxares conquered the former Assyrian capital of Assur. In 612, the new capital of Nineveh fell to the combined forces of the Babylonians and Medes. Haran, Assyria's last stronghold, was taken in 610. Between 610 and 605, the Babylonians neutralized Urartu, marched at will through the Assyrian homeland, and defeated the Egyptians at Carchemish, forcing them out of the Levant.

The final Assyrian collapse is most persuasively understood as resulting from the classic effects of imperial overstretch. These effects did include limited balancing dynamics, as the Medes transformed themselves into an offensive power in part in response to Assyrian pressure. But as Assyriologist Mario Liverani (2001: 388–91) points out, Assyria had almost certainly faced greater pressure in earlier times than the coalition of Medes and Chaldaean 'rebels' that finally defeated it. Assyria was further weakened by a succession war between Ashurbanipal's sons, but this, too had happened before. The additional factor in the late 6th century BCE, Liverani argues, was the demographic and economic exhaustion of the Assyrian homeland. As the Assyrian population increasingly engaged in unproductive building tasks in the cities – and the countryside became depopulated – Assyria had become irremediably dependent on tribute for basic foodstuffs. Lacking local supplies, rebellion meant it could no longer feed its armies. Thus among the modern classics of international relations theory, causal mechanisms highlighted in Gilpin's *War and Change in World Politics*, rather than those Waltz brought to the fore in *Theory of International Politics*, carry most of the explanatory weight.

Summary and conclusions

Table 2.1 summarizes our findings. Only the reigns of expansionist Assyrian kings are assessed, as only they are most relevant to the theory. We code balancing efforts as successful (B) when the balancing coalition remains in existence at the end of the reign; in most cases, this means the stable acquisition of minor allies by Urartu. When coalitions are defeated or collapse for other reasons – resulting in most cases in submission of some alliance partners to Assyria – the pattern is coded as ineffective balancing (I). Allying with or sending tribute to Assyria is coded as submission or bandwagoning (S). When states under attack by Assyria fail to acquire allies, we code their behavior as simple self-defense (D); these can equally be understood as cases in which the potential alliance partners buckpassed – e.g., Elam's failure to back Mukin-zer's rebellion in Babylonia against Tiglath-pileser III.[2]

The overall picture is a mixed one for the theory. While most – 14 of 24 patterns coded – involve balancing *efforts*, ten of the 14 balancing efforts were ineffective. Some of these efforts, such as the Qarqar coalition against Shalmaneser III and the Bablyonian-Chaldaean-Elamite coalition that opposed his son, were quite impressive in sub-regional scope, but they were never broad and enduring enough to alter systemic outcomes. Thus the expected behavioral pattern holds – balancing is the most common policy in response to expansion – but the outcome is not a balanced system. Instead, for the 70 years following the death of Sargon, the dominant pattern in the international system was of submission to Assyrian hegemonic power.

The implications are thus mixed but unfavorable to strong versions of balance-of-power theory. On the favorable side, balancing processes did occur in roughly the manner expected by the theory. Balancing under multipolarity correlated with the rise of Assyria's power and threat. Most of the great conflicts of the age were between Assyria and the larger opposing coalitions. These included the conflicts of Shalmaneser III against the Qarqar coalition; Tiglath-pileser III against the Urartu-Arpad alliance; Sargon II against Merodach-Baladan's Babylonian-Chaldaean-Elamite coalition; and finally, the Babylonian-Median alliance that brought the Assyrian Empire down. When Assyria was weak or passive, the alliances fell apart and their members returned to fighting each other.

Table 2.1   **Summary of Balancing Behavior in Key Periods**

Years	Assyrian ruler	Area	Acts	Key events
858– 824	Shalmaneser III	N	B	Urartu internal balancing, acquires minor allies
		SW	I	Qarqar coalition collapses
		SE	S	Babylonia quiescent client
823– 811	Shamshi-Adad V	N	B	Urartu defends itself and minor allies
		SW	B	Most Syrian states stop paying tribute
		SE	I	Babylonian-Chaldaean-Elamite coalition loses
810– 783	Adad-Nirari III	N	B	Urartu acquires more allies
		SW	I	Successive small Syrian coalitions broken
		SE	S	Babylon submits to Assyrian invasion
744– 727	Tiglath-pileser III	N	I	Urartu-Arpad coalition quickly broken
		SW	I	Successive small coalitions quickly broken
		SE	D	Mukin-zer fails to acquire allies, loses
721– 705	Sargon II	N	I	Belated Urartu-Mushki coalition broken
		SW	I	Syrian coalition quickly crushed
		SE	I	Merodach-Baladan and Elam too passive, lose
704– 681	Sennacherib	N	S	Urartu a minor ally
		SW	S	Most of Syria quiet when Judah rebels
		SE	I	Elam backs failed rebel Merodach-Baladan
680– 669	Esarhaddon	N	S	Urartu still minor ally
		SW	D	Egypt defends itself when invaded
		SE	S	Babylonia and Elam bandwagon
668– 635	Ashurbanipal	N	S	Urartu still minor ally
		SW	S	Egypt a client after conquest
		SE	I	Elam backs Great Babylonian Rebellion, fails

Codes for Area and Acts:
Area – locale of key Assyrian neighbors
N   – Northern neighbors of Assyria, i.e. Urartu (and Mushki)
SW   – Southwestern neighbors of Assyria, in Syria and Egypt
SE   – Southeastern neighbors of Assyria, i.e. Babylonia and Elam
Acts – overall assessment of policies pursued by states in each region
B   – Effective policy of balancing
I   – Ineffective balancing
S   – Submission to or bandwagoning with Assyria
D   – Self-defense without balancing

Also, as hypothesized, once Assyria passed the threshold to unipolarity, balancing correlated with Assyrian weakness, as balance-of-power dynamics once again became feasible. For example, Merodach-Baladan's first and greatest rebellion in Babylonia coincided with the disorder in Assyria attendant on Sargon's usurpation of the throne. Assyria's narrow resource base and tenuous authority in Babylonia combined repeatedly to create the impression of vulnerability to rebellion, leading to repeated failed attempts to reestablish a balance.

But the big picture is negative for the theory, for the balancing processes it expects to be central to system dynamics were actually of secondary importance. While balancing was common, it was extremely inefficient, even when the Assyrian threat should have been obvious to all. The collective action problem overrode balancing imperatives, and other concerns appeared to put aside fear of hegemony so frequently as to call into question the theory's utility.

Israel, for example, with its important chariot force, defected from the Qarqara coalition after the death of King Ahab. And the opposition to Tiglath-pileser III, the Assyrian king who overturned the balance of power, was one long tale of buckpassing: Hamath stood aside from the Arpad-Urartu coalition early in the reign; Damascus and Israel avoided involvement with Hamath in the Azriyau rebellion that followed; Judah opposed Damascus and Israel when they finally did resist Tiglath-pileser; and Elam and many Chaldaean tribes stood aside when Assyria subdued Babylonia. Partly because these key actors failed to balance, Shalmaneser was able to expand Assyrian hegemony, and Tiglath-pileser could annex numerous Assyrian rivals. These events show how collective action theory undermines the robust prediction of balance-of-power theory that balancing processes should present increasingly significant barriers to expansion whenever the concentration of power in one state threatens hegemony. There is no way to make these events compatible with any robust version of balance-of-power theory.

Later events are equally difficult to explain in balancing terms. The general rebellion that greeted Sargon II's accession to the throne provided a golden opportunity for a grand balancing coalition, but Merodach-Baladan's formidable Babylonian-Chaldaean-Elamite coalition does not seem to have lifted a finger against Assyria for most of the decade when Sargon was busily annihilating his adversaries to the north and west. This decision turned Assyria's central location from a liability into an asset, and led eventually to Merodach-Baladan's own defeat and the secure establishment of Assyria's system-dominating empire.

From Sargon's time onward, events unequivocally demonstrated Assyrian dominance rather than any significant degree of systemic balance. After Sargon marched through Urartu in 714, Assyria never again faced significant opposition from it; on the contrary, Urartu now bandwagoned with Assyria, remaining a reliable minor ally until the Assyrian collapse. The system could almost be termed hegemonic at this point, as the only autonomous 'major' powers were Elam and Egypt, both weak reeds. Sennacherib's campaigns against Elam and Babylonia in 694–689 then essentially eliminated Elam as a serious problem, leaving Egypt as the sole surviving marchland power: the threshhold for full hegemony was now reached. Finally, even Egypt was eliminated as an autonomous actor: after Ashurbanipal left Egypt in 663, the next dynasty of Pharaohs was one he appointed, and its 'final success depended as much on Assyrian patronage as on its own resources' (James, 1991: 710). The Egyptians then acted as minor allies of Assyria until after the fall in 610. Thus when the Medes arose as a new marchland power, they were the only one: Elam was by now a shadow, and Urartu and Egypt minor allies of Assyria. The system was clearly unipolar for a century, and met the more stringent requirements of hegemony for half of that period.

The core hypothesis of balance-of-power theory is therefore disconfirmed. Gross outcomes are totally inconsistent with the theory. The inefficiency of balancing is not just a quibble but goes to the heart of the theory's portrayal of system dynamics. So inefficient was balancing that the threat of Assyrian hegemony did not produce balance but a unipolar structure and eventually complete hegemony. And that structure – while clearly prone to rebellion and hence requiring nearly yearly Assyrian military campaigns – was not short-lived but lasted nearly half the system's lifespan. Furthermore, Assyria achieved this from a comparatively narrow resource base.

The evidence suggests that factors outside the purview of balance-of-power theory drove gross systemic outcomes. In other words, not only is the central tendency toward balancing much weaker in this case than standard renderings of the theory would imply, but the theory appears to be highly misleading as an explanation of systemic patterns. At least in this case, if one wants to understand large-scale system dynamics, balance-of-power theory is not the place to start. Instead, two other variables are central to the Assyrian case.

First is *social technology*. Before Tiglath-pileser III, Assyria could not administer its conquests. Vassals and even governors repeatedly rebelled, and so Shalmaneser III's successors were unable to hold what he had conquered. Under the Sargonids, however, the situation improved in the west, allowing Assyria to establish a stable empire stretching from the Mediterranean to the Zagros. Empire was the fruit as much of the bureaucracy as of the army. Where trouble remained, especially in Babylonia, Egypt, and the Taurus and Zagros Mountains, the key limitation was not the diminution of military force with distance; they simply found no way of ruling what their armies conquered. It is perhaps not surprising that the administrative problems were worst in the countries with long histories of political independence (Egypt and Babylonia) and the ones in mountainous terrain where communications were slow.

This finding buttresses an important line of research. Some theorists (e.g., Van Evera, 1999; Mann, 2003) have argued, especially with regard to the modern international system, that it is expensive to maintain political control over hostile populations, especially in an age of nationalism; or that it is economically more beneficial to trade with a prosperous neighbor than to forcibly extract resources from a repressed province (Rosecrance, 1986). Others (esp. Liberman, 1996) have argued, in contrast, that even in modern societies, conquest and occupation pay. Ultimately, the degree to which annexation pays is likely to vary over time. The implication of our research is that one important factor that might help explain the variance is social technology (Kaufman, 1997): the greater a state's ability to administer conquered territory, the greater is the likely payoff from annexing it. That administrative capability, in turn, is in part a function of communications technology: states with domesticated horses, or railroads and telegraphs, can *ceteris paribus* administer larger territories than those without.

The second key omitted variable is the *size* of the system. If administrative advances made the Assyrian imperium possible, it was the expansion of the international system – *not* balance-of-power dynamics – that finally overthrew it. Urartu emerged in an area that had never before been home to a developed state largely in response to the early growth of Assyrian power (Zimansky, 1985). Assyrian power eventually proved sufficient to cow, if not to rule, even Urartu and Egypt, and to annihilate Elam, but repeated Assyrian expeditions into the Zagros finally spurred the tribes of the region to unite under the leadership of the Medes, while the annihilation of Elam simply removed an obstacle to that consolidation – and to the unification of Babylonia under Chaldaean leadership. The Medes and Chaldaean rebels therefore faced an exhausted and overstretched Assyria that was finally vulnerable to their efforts.

As Kaufman (1997) has argued, great powers' incentives to expand their power creates incentives to absorb other states around them, large and small, leading to a reduction in the number of great powers (i.e., potential alliance partners) in the system, and ultimately, perhaps, to hegemony. What counteracted this tendency in Europe, according to Ludwig Dehio, was a countervailing tendency for the geographical boundaries of the system to expand. William R. Thompson (1992: 129) summarizes Dehio's argument as follows: 'if Europe had been a closed system, some great power would eventually have succeeded in establishing absolute supremacy over the other states in the region. But the system was never entirely closed. Immediately before a would-be continental hegemon could unify the European region by coercion, counterweights on the eastern and/or western wings of the continent emerged to deny a hegemonic victory by introducing new, extraregional resources into the struggle for regional supremacy.' In sum, the maintenance or reestablishment of a balance of power might depend on the timing of the entrance of new actors into the system.

We conclude, therefore, that while one assertion of balance-of-power theory is accurate – states frequently balance against emerging systemic threats – balancing is frequently fatally slow and inefficient. In the ancient middle eastern system, balancing processes are thus not the chief or even a particularly salient explanation for the episodic failures of hegemony and returns to systemic balance. As shown throughout this volume, unipolarity and hegemony are normal configurations of international systems. To explain transitions between balance and hegemony, systemic theory must be expanded to include key additional variables, especially the ability of would-be hegemons to administer what they conquer, and the opportunity for geographic expansion of the international system to permit the introduction of new great-power actors. These factors – originally part of the classical balance-of-power writings – have been systematically excluded from the theory in recent years. Our major conclusion is that excising these variables from the theory sapped its power to account for its most important explanandum.

Notes

1   The authors are grateful to Professors Mario Liverani and J.A. Brinkman for thoughtful comments and bibliographical advice.
2   The only ambiguous case is that of the southwest at the time of Sennacherib: while Egypt did attempt to balance against Assyria by backing the rebellion of Judah and the coastal cities, the previous mainstays of opposition to Assyria, such as Damascus and Hamath, remained passive, so the overall behavior is coded as submission (S).

3
The Greek City-States in the Fifth Century BCE: Persia and the Balance of Power

Richard Little

The Greek city-state system is often treated as an 'analogue' of the contemporary international system (Reus-Smit, 1999: 40). Among English School scholars, Wight (1977: 73) describes it as the 'most complex and highly organised' states-system prior to the contemporary one, and Watson (1992: 47) suggests that for several centuries, 'aspects of Greek practice served as models for the European society of states'. Neorealists also refer back to the Greek city-states. During the Cold War, for example, Waltz (1979: 66) acknowledged the continuing relevance of Thucydides' account of the Peloponnesian War between Athens and Sparta, even in an era of nuclear weapons and super powers; and Gilpin (1981: 227) doubted whether contemporary students of international relations understand anything about international relations that was not already known to 'Thucydides and his 5th century compatriots'.

Despite this common interest in the Greek city-states, when attention is focused on the role of the balance of power in this era, the neorealist and English school positions start to diverge quite substantially. From a Waltzian perspective, in any anarchic system, a balance of power will emerge as an unintended consequence of strategies pursued by independent units that are striving to survive. The strategies ensure that the anarchic structure of the international system is constantly reproduced. As a consequence, for Waltz, anarchy is an extremely resilient and transhistorical structure that has persisted throughout world history. It follows that neorealist theory should be able to account for the behavior of the Greek city-states.

By contrast, although English school theorists, acknowledge that a balance of power can potentially form in any anarchic international system, they view these balances as precarious and transient sources of order. Anarchy is viewed as a rather fragile structure that has not often been sustained in world history for any length of time.[1] But English school theorists also identify an institutionalized balance of power that formed first in the European international society and is much more effective than a systemic balance at reproducing anarchy. This institutionalized balance of power is defined by an intersubjective agreement established amongst the great powers to sustain a system of independent states and it is identified by the rules underpinning the international society and the terms negotiated at major European peace conferences.[2] Earlier states-systems, according to the English school, failed to conceive of an institutionalized balance of power. Butterfield (1966: 13), for example, insists that the balance of power 'did not exist in the ancient world' and that 'more than most of our basic political formulas, this one seems to come from the modern world's reflections on its own experience' (cf. Wight, 1977: 66).

The Greek city-state system, however, poses a problem for both English school and neorealist theorists. From the English School perspective, the problem is its durability: the Greeks preserved some degree of independence for well over half a millennium, and some historians have attributed this resilience to a reasonably effective balancing process. Strauss (1991: 198), for example, concludes that 'a balance of power, however imperfect, did operate in the classical Greek world. It was difficult for any one polis to win hegemony because the other poleis could be counted on to balance rather than bandwagon'. Waltzian neorealism, on the other hand, has trouble explaining the periods of hegemony or near-hegemony in the system, first under Persian influence and later under Roman domination.

We cannot survey the whole history of the rise and fall of the Greek city-states within one chapter and so the focus here is only on the 5th century. This was a crucial era in Greek international relations because of the growing ties between the Greeks and the Persians and the impact of the Persians on the balance of power in Greece. There is also much more information available about the 5th century than previous centuries, primarily because of the histories provided by Herodotus (485–425) and Thucydides (c. 460–400). The tendency to rely so heavily on these two works, however, has meant that there has been a systematic bias in assessments of both the Persian invasion of Greece and the Peloponnesian War, with the former being viewed from a Greek perspective and the latter from an Athenian perspective. But there is a growing awareness of the need to take account of bias when relying so heavily on a specific text.[3] Silences become particularly important. The failure of Thucydides to report on the Peace of Callias between Persia and the Greeks has led to endless speculation.[4] Just as important is the absence of any references by Thucydides to the Persians from 425/4 to 413/2.[5]

There are three main sections in the chapter. The first identifies the principal features of the Greek states-system. The second and longest section centres on the evolving relationship between Persia and the Greek city-states. The final section discusses why the balance of power failed to prevent the Greeks from falling under the hegemonic influence of the Persians and it concludes that this period generates anomalies for both the neorealists and the English school.

Essential features of the Greek city-state system

Geographical factors had a profound effect on the political development of Greece. The mainland is extremely mountainous (75 per cent of the land mass) and this made communication by land difficult and isolated communities from each other. On the other hand, nowhere is more than 40 miles from the sea and boats provided the easiest and most effective mode of transport for the Greeks. The shortage of raw materials also ensured that Greece was drawn into the emerging trade system during the course of the second millennium BCE. Interacting city-states (*poleis*) began to be established in the 8th century with the development of urban centres that took political responsibility from the surrounding rural communities. The resulting Greek city-states system is not a unique development, although it is one of the most extensively studied.[6]

About 1,500 different city-states formed in Greece in this period, although the maximum number that existed at any point in time was probably never more than 1,200. Most of these city-states were little more than fortified villages, and although there were middle rank city-states, such as, Megara, Aegina, and Sicyon, most attention is paid to the city-states at the top of the power ranking. Five city-states – Thebes, Athens, Corinth, Argos, and Sparta – are identified as the great powers on mainland Greece, although there were similar sized cities on the East of the Aegean Sea and on the larger islands, such as Syracuse on Sicily. Most of these cities had populations of between 30,000–50,000 people (Starr, 1986: 46). Because of their size, however, Athens and Sparta, were different from the other city-states. Athens controlled all of Attica, an area of 2500 square kilometres, with a population of over 300,000 people (Cohen, 2000: 13). Sparta was even more distinctive.

Although it controlled an area three times the size of Attica, it lacked a major urban centre and was made up of fortified villages; and whereas Athens was a politically unified territory, the area under Spartan control remained independent except for foreign affairs. Throughout the 5th century, Athens and Sparta outclassed all the other city-states. Most could only raise a few hundred hoplites and one or two warships whereas Athens and Sparta could each raise 9,000 hoplites.[7]

Most city-states were divided politically between the poor who favored democracy and the rich who favored oligarchy. Prior to the 5th century, tyrants often governed the city-states (and they did so again in the 4th century), but the 5th century was characterized by a constant struggle between oligarchic and democratic forces. Civil war was endemic and each faction was willing to sacrifice their freedom and independence in return for external support. Hansen reports that at times more than half of the poleis lacked autonomy and were subordinate to another state.

Nevertheless, from the neorealist perspective, the Greek city-state system provides an almost archetypal example of an anarchic system, with its members locked in highly competitive relations with each other. As Plato noted 'Every state is in a natural state of war with every other, not indeed proclaimed by heralds, but everlasting'.[8] There was, moreover, a universal appreciation of the systemic power structure and abundant evidence of external and internal balancing strategies. According to Starr (1974: 3), a primitive form of political intelligence operated across Greece because 'leaders of each state needed to know what the other constituents of the Hellenic state-system could do and intended to do at any critical point.' The leaders were aware of the number of ships and hoplites being supplied by each city-state. Moreover, the evidence suggests that the Greek city-states constituted an anarchic political system from a fairly early stage in their development. By the 7th century, for example, wars between city-states were fought by heavily armed soldiers, known as hoplites, who were organized to fight in a phalanx formation. Once one city-state adopted this strategy, the others quickly followed suit (Cartledge, 1977; Halladay, 1982). Raaflaub (1991: 575) also argues that once the advantages of empire has been demonstrated by Athens in the 5th century, Sparta and Thebes 'did not hesitate to imitate it'. This is clear evidence of internal balancing, with military strategy being emulated or imitated throughout the system.

By the same token, external balancing was a ubiquitous feature of the system, with states using alliances to enhance their security. For example, Plataea, a small city-state located only eight miles from Thebes, was determined to resist Theban pressure to join the Boeotian League. Plataea therefore turned first to Sparta, and then to Athens, ultimately forming an alliance with the latter in 509 (Amit, 1973: 63–4).[9] Thucydides and Herodotus provide numerous examples of alliances of this kind.

The English school can make a reasonable case that the Greek city-states constituted an international society. Both Wight (1977) and Watson (1992) insist that the Greek city-states formed a distinct cultural unit reflected in 'common language, common theatre, architecture and religious observances' and that this common culture provided the basis for a nascent international society, identified by the existence of panhellenic institutions, a primitive diplomatic system, and 'rules of war and peace, of mediation, and of communication' (Watson, 1992: 50). The boundary of the international society, moreover, is seen to be open and responsive to developments at the world society level. So Macedonia under Alexander I (498–454 BC), despite his unwilling collaboration with the Persians against the Greeks, pursued a systematic policy of hellenization. Alexander eventually persuaded the Greeks to allow Macedonia to participate in the Olympic Games, suggesting that the boundary identifying the Greek states-system could be extended provided that the necessary cultural transformation had taken place.

There is, however, an important difference in the way that the English school and the neorealists assess the Greek city-states. Neorealists tend to treat the Greek city-states as a closed system, whereas the English school see the Greek city-states as an international society that also forms a subsystem within a broader international system that embraced the Persian or Archaemenid Empire.[10] Wight (1977: 73) was particularly interested in the relationship between Persia and the Greek city-states because he recognized that the city-states were dominated 'to an unparalleled extent' by the neighboring 'world empire'. For the English school, the Greek city-states and the Persian Empire represent two separate international societies, operating within a single international system. Examining the two international entities from a cultural perspective, however, reveals a sharp contrast, for while the Greeks embraced a common culture, Persia, because of its rapid expansion, embraced a variety of divergent and ancient cultures and it represents a classic example of a multicultural empire. Centres of strong culture, as in Egypt and Babylon, were constantly disaffected with the Empire.

By contrast, the Greeks established a boundary around themselves with outsiders identified as barbarians. But the boundary that contains what the English school see as the Greek 'world society' was an open one, so that communities of non-Greeks could be 'hellenized' and brought within the Greek 'world society'. The Greeks became increasingly aware of the potential for cultural transformation as barbarians absorbed hellenic cultural norms and it became apparent that the hellenic culture was 'inherently expansive' (Wight, 1977: 85). The process of hellenization took place to the North in Macedonia and on the Western edge of the Persian Empire. Inevitably, the hellenization of the empire accentuated the difficulties arising from its competing cultures and complicated the task of maintaining the cohesion of the empire.

The Persians and the Greek city-state system in the 5th century BC

During the 6th century, Persia absorbed most of the Middle East and Asia Minor. From around 546 BC, when the Persians conquered Lydia in Asia Minor, the impact began to be felt directly by the Greeks in Asia Minor, and indirectly by the mainland Greeks. Previously, the Asia Minor Greeks had experienced what Forrest (1986: 37) calls 'unoppressive dependence' on non-Greek powers, such as Lydia, which operated from the hinterland of Asia Minor. In 560, for example, the Ionian city-states came under the control of Lydia. Initially, the Persians brought the Asia Minor Greeks under more direct rule, than the Lydians, imposing their own tyrants on the city-states. But after an early revolt by the Greeks, both Cyrus II (559–530) and Cambyses (530–522), opted to give the Greeks more autonomy (Georges, 2000: 17–18). In 514 the Persians moved into Europe, and although they were forced to withdraw from Southern Russia, they succeeded in opening up Thrace to Persian influence. At the start of the 5th century, therefore, there can be no doubt that the Greeks were participating in an international system that embraced the Persian Empire. Given that the Persians far outweighed the power of any single Greek city-state, neorealist theory predicts that the Greek city-states should have engaged in balancing behavior and should have continued to do so throughout the century. As this section will show, although there is evidence of balancing, which initially preserved the independence of the Greek city-states, the long-term consequence of balancing strategies was to undermine the independence of the city-states.

The Persian invasions of the Greek city-states

From a neorealist position, balancing strategies should have started to come into play during the 6th century when the Persians began to loom on the security horizon of the Greeks. But, in practice, even at the turn of the century, the Greeks were still deeply divided about how to respond to the Persians. On one side of the debate, it was argued that the best strategy was to accept Persian influence, whereas on the other side, armed resistance was favoured.[11] In 499, however, there was a major revolt by some of the Greek city-states under Persian rule in Asia Minor and at this juncture the Greeks on the mainland had to make a decision about how to respond. Georges (2000: 19–23) argues that the Ionians were not, in the first instance, rebelling against Persian rule, but against the tyrants whom Darius (who ruled Persia from 521–486) had imposed after he took power. In other words, the revolt does not indicate a move towards a balancing strategy. It was simply an attempt to change the terms of a long-established bandwagoning strategy.

The decision by the Athenians and Eritrians to support this revolt however, caused it to spread, thereby chain-ganging the Asian Greeks into a balancing strategy.[12] The Athenian support, though short-lived, enabled the rebels to sack and burn Sardis, the Persians' regional administrative centre, ultimately providing the Persians with a pretext for the invasion of mainland Greece. The conflict persisted until a fatal naval defeat in 494 off the island of Lade, close to Miletus. The blame for the revolt was pinned on Miletus and the city was destroyed. But the other city-states were treated much more leniently and were given the level of autonomy that they had enjoyed under Cyrus and Cambryses – effectively gaining, according to Georges (2000: 25, 32–3), what they had wanted from the revolt. From this perspective, then, bandwagoning was the preferred strategy of the Asia Minor Greeks.

Although neorealism clearly cannot explain the failure of the Greeks in Asia Minor during the 6th century to develop a consistent balancing strategy in order to maintain their independence, the balancing hypothesis seems able to account for the Greek success in withstanding the Persian invasion of mainland Greece. A closer investigation of the events surrounding the invasions shows, however, that balancing was not the dominant Greek response to the Persian invasion (Balcer, 1995: 248), and that there were other factors, apart from a Greek balancing strategy that preserved their independence.[13] The initial Persian invasion started in 492 and Thrace, Thasos and Macedonia were quickly overrun. But the army needed naval support to provide them with supplies and when the navy was destroyed in a severe storm the army was forced to turn back. In 491, in preparation for another attempt to punish the Athenians and the Eritreans for their participation in the Greek revolt in Asia Minor, Herodotus claims that the Persians sent heralds to the Greek cities demanding their submission to Persia. Although Sparta and Athens refused, many Greek cities submitted, including Aegina, a major rival of Athens.[14] Although the number of invading Persian troops is unknown, it was certainly many more than the 10,000 troops that Athens and its ally Plataea were able to raise for the battle at Marathon.[15] Although the highly disciplined Greek hoplites had better armour and longer spears, the victory by the Athenians was, nonetheless, extraordinary. It not only forced the Persians to withdraw, but, according to Aristotle, it gave the Athenian people political confidence and must have started a reassessment of the balance of power within Greece.[16]

Even if it is accepted that the initial Persian moves were directed specifically at Athens and did not warrant any general balancing response, it is not possible to extend this argument to the next invasion mounted by Xerxes who became the new Persian king, on the death of his father. By 484 BC, the Greeks were aware that large numbers of ships were being built in Persian ports from the Black Sea to Egypt (Pomeroy *et al.*, 1999: 192). The Athenians responded almost immediately with an internal balancing move, building 200 new fighting ships at the urging of Themistocles.[17]

In 481, Persian heralds were moving through Greece encouraging city-states to bandwagon with Persia. Simultaneously, however, under the leadership of Sparta, there was also an attempt to get city-states to ally against the Persians.[18] These efforts gave rise to the Hellenic League, established in 481 by Sparta. It consisted of 31 city-states under Spartan hegemony that joined forces to resist the Persian advance. This is a clear case of external balancing. But given the number of city-states in existence, the League could hardly be said to represent a truly united front. As Balcer (1995: 257) notes, 'hundreds upon hundreds of other Greek poleis remained withdrawn, many openly medizing, as Xerxes' Imperial Army campaigned overland to meet his fleet in Attica'.[19] Among the Greek great powers, Thebes openly sided with Persia, while Argos maintained what Balcer (1995: 234) calls a 'malevolent neutrality' that impeded communications and cooperation between Sparta and Athens.[20]

More significant, attempts to get help from more distant areas, such as Crete, Corcyra and Syracuse, all failed (Forrest, 1986: 44). Xerxes was fully aware of the potential for such aid, so when he decided to extend

Persian power into Europe, he reputedly sent an embassy to Carthage with plans for a concerted attack by the Carthaginians against the Greeks on Sicily and Italy. The Carthaginians reportedly agreed to the Persian plan and, unequivocally, between 483 and 480, like Xerxes, they prepared for a massive invasion against the Greeks in the West. Thus when Athens and Sparta approached Gelon, Syracuse's tyrant, for help, he attached unacceptable conditions to his offer of aid, and the Athenians and Spartans left in high dudgeon.[21]

The Hellenic League met again in 480 in Corinth where the allies agreed to set their differences to one side. It is estimated that the League could muster around 40,000 hoplites and 350 triremes, against modern estimates, of 200,000 troops and 1,000 ships on the Persian side.[22] From a purely numerical standpoint, therefore, many more city-states would have had to join the Hellenic League to come close to matching the forces available to the Persians.

Furthermore, the Greek balancing effort was even less effective than these figures suggest because Sparta, the Hellenic League's hegemon, was not fully committed to preserving the independence of all Greek city-states, or even all the members of the League. Rather, following the defeat at Thermopolae, the Spartans withdrew and abandoned the Boiotans and the Athenians to the advancing Persian forces, hoping to remain secure behind a wall built across the Corinthian isthmus.[23] As a consequence, the citizens of Thespiae and Plataea as well as Athens withdrew in 480 from their cities, which were later destroyed by the advancing Persian army (Amit, 1973: 80).

If the Athenians had surrendered to the Persians and handed over their navy, the Peloponnese would have been extraordinarily vulnerable; but fortunately for the Spartans, the Athenians were determined to maintain their independence and knew that they needed the support of the Hellenic League. As a consequence, they refused the Persian offer in 479 to establish Athens as a semi-autonomous polis within a proposed Persian satrapy. As the war with Persia persisted, therefore, Athens began to play an increasingly important role in the League. First, and most important, they defeated the Persian navy at Salamis, forcing the surviving Persian ships to withdraw to protect the escape route for Persian troops across the Hellespont.[24] The following year, the Greeks brought together the largest army they had ever mustered at Plataea and the Persians were then defeated on land as well as at sea. At the same time, the Hellenic fleet crossed the Aegean and landed at Mycale where they defeated the Persians and began the process of liberating the islands and the Asian Greeks.

Despite the clear evidence of balancing amongst some the Greek city-states confronted by the Persian invasion, there is, in fact, much more evidence of states bandwagoning and joining the Persians. This had been the pattern in 545 when Cyrus turned his attentions to Asia Minor, subduing the Greeks that had established cities on the East of the Aegean. Despite a delegation from Sparta, threatening to punish Cyrus if he harmed the Asian Greeks, there was no united resistance; indeed the Persians soon discovered that the Asian Greeks could be subdued with financial incentives (Balcer, 1995: 63). As Herodotus notes, the Persians attempted to use the same strategy to subdue the mainland Greeks, calculating that 'time, accentuated by bribes – Persian gold diplomacy – rather than the force of arms would win over the recalcitrant Greeks, given their factional character' (Balcer, 1995: 281). But to move into Greece, it was necessary, first, for the Persians to cross the Bosporus or the Hellespont, and both posed severe logistical problems. These problems in supplying the Persian army and navy, exacerbated by revolts in other parts of the Empire, made it difficult for the Persians to wait until their established strategies allowed them to pick the Greek poleis off, one by one. So although the determination of the Greeks who joined the Hellenic League to maintain their freedom certainly played a part in the Persian defeat, perhaps more critical were the logistical difficulties faced by the Persian army and navy (Balcer, 1995: 297, 327–31).

It is, therefore, too simplistic to suggest that Greece was saved by either a systemically produced balance or a coherent balancing strategy self-consciously pursued by the Greeks. As the English school recognize, to the extent that a balance does emerge in an international system, it is at best, a 'fortuitous' feature, and, as a consequence, fragile and unstable.

The formation of the Athenian Empire

Although the Hellenic League involved only a small percentage of the Greek city-states, it did ensure a degree of cooperation between Athens and Sparta during the war with Persia. But the war also confirmed the existence of a significant functional division of labor with the Athenians providing effective leadership at sea and the Spartans on land. In the 6th century, Sparta had been a more significant naval power than Athens, but the conflict with Persia had confirmed for the Athenians that their security required a powerful navy. Their new source of revenue from the silver mines at Larinum, first opened in 482, had also enabled the Athenians to take advantage of new weapons systems. In 483, the first trireme had been launched and it quickly took the place of the much smaller pentekontoras that had previously been the main fighting ship.[25] Athens, with a much larger population than its naval competitors, and now with growing financial resources, was in a position to build its navy based on the trireme. In 480, the Greek city-states were able to sail 200 triremes, requiring 34,000 rowers against the Persians at the battle of Salamis. Within 20 years, Athens had swept aside both Aegina and Corinth, its two major naval competitors, and was able to dominate the Aegean (Amit, 1973: 35).

Neorealist theory predicts that Athens and Sparta should have recognized that they had a vested interest in maintaining their alliance in an attempt to deter a future attack from Persia. But Athens had now also emerged as a competitor to Sparta as the natural hegemon in Greece. Thus when the Athenians started to rebuild their defences, destroyed during the war by the Persians, its allies asked Sparta to intercede, and Sparta agreed to do so. Given how vulnerable the Athenians had found themselves in the war, it is unsurprising that the walls were built anyway. But the request does suggest that the Greeks were primarily concerned about the balance of power within Greece rather than the strategic balance of power that operated between Greece and Persia. Though the Hellenic League survived until 461, it was increasingly troubled as traditional rivalries reappeared (Amit, 1973: 31). The Greek sailors almost immediately after the war came to an end expressed their dissatisfaction with the incumbent Spartan naval commander. Sparta recalled him and although they then sent a replacement, it was agreed in 478 to put an Athenian in charge of the navy.

The following year Athens and dozens of other city-states met at Delos in the Aegean and established a new organization that came later to be known as the Delian League. Its members bound themselves to this organization and to exact revenge for the invasions of Greece by enriching themselves at the expense of the Persians.[26] The initial members of the League primarily came from cities on the Asia Minor coast and the islands in that area, but eventually some 150 states joined the anti-Persian league.[27] Some of the larger states, such as Samos and Naxos, agreed to contribute ships to the League. But the vast majority of the members supplied money annually (the *phoros*) to pay for the construction of new ships and other costs.[28] The Treasury, although administered by the Athenians, was located initially on Delos (and then moved to Athens in 454). The League was established on the basis of alliances between Athens and each member, with Athens agreeing, in return for the financial or material contributions, to lead the League in all military operations, although it was also agreed that decision-making should be conducted on a collective basis, and that the Athenians would respect the autonomy of all the member states.[29]

From a neorealist perspective, the existence of the Delian and Hellenic Leagues clearly ensured that the Greeks were balancing against Persia. After the formation of the Delian League, little is heard of the Hellenic League.[30] But by any reckoning, the Delian League was an extraordinarily successful organization, sweeping the Persians out of the Aegean and the South coast of Asia Minor and securing the autonomy of the Greeks in Asia Minor. Athens benefited enormously from securing control of the seas, expanding its trade and establishing large numbers of colonies. Every year, patrols were sent out and not only kept the seas free from enemy shipping but also kept piracy at bay (Meiggs, 1972: 205–6).

There is relatively little information about the conflict between the Delian League and the Persians. Plutarch observes that the Greeks 'stripped Asia from Ionia as far as Pamphylia entirely of Persian arms' (Meiggs, 1972: 73–5), their operations culminating in the battle in Pamphylia at the mouth of the river Eureymedon in 466 when the Persians were decisively defeated at sea. Meiggs (1972: 86) argues that the battle 'eliminated any serious threat to the Aegean and opened up the way to a profitable offensive in the Eastern Mediterranean'.

There are three possible reasons why the Persians did not respond more vigorously to these developments. First, they were on the fringe of the empire and posed no threat to its overall stability. Second, within a year, Xerxes had died and the new king, Artaxerxes was involved in a succession crisis. Third, taking advantage of this uncertainty, a Libyan prince named Inaros launched a revolt in Egypt around 460, calling on Athens for help. At that time, a fleet of 200 Delian League vessels was attempting to take control of Cyprus. The fleet was diverted to Egypt where the small Persian fleet was quickly eliminated and Memphis put under siege. But Artaxerxes was not about to lose Egypt and he mounted a huge invasion force. After a long period of stalemate, the Athenians were decisively defeated in 454.

Remarkably, the Athenians pursued this conflict with the Persians while simultaneously engaged in what was later labeled the first, undeclared Peloponnesian War (460–445). The origins of this conflict were in the expansion of Athenian power on the Greek mainland, as Athens established alliances with Argos, Sparta's long-time rival, and with Megara, a trading state located between Athens and Corinth. The

Corinthians responded to this threat to their position by forming an alliance with Sparta, and then joining forces with Aegina. By 459, Corinth and Aegina were locked in conflict with Athens and in 457 Sparta was also drawn into the war. Fighting extended into the area of Boeotia that had traditionally operated under the hegemony of Thebes. By 456, Athens controlled the whole region, with the exception of Thebes itself. The hinterland regions of Phocis and Locris joined the Delian League, as did Troezen and Achaea in the Peloponnesus; the island of Aegina was also required to join the League after its defeat. Thus by 451, Athens had very substantially extended the Delian League to embrace land as well as sea-based city-states. At this juncture, Cimon, a pro-Spartan Athenian leader, negotiated a five year truce with Sparta and gave up Athens's provocative alliance with Argos, which went on to establish a 30 year treaty with Sparta.

After nearly 30 years of intermittent conflict, it must have been clear to the Greeks and the Persians that while the Greeks were able to control the Aegean – even while fighting among themselves – and had the potential strength to gain control of the Eastern Mediterranean, the Persians unquestionably had the potential military strength to dominate Asia, including the city-states of the Asian Greeks. Given this assessment, then, it would not be surprising to discover that the Greeks, or at any rate, the Athenians, would have been willing to reach an agreement with the Persians. Neither Thucydides nor Herodotus make any reference to such an agreement, and yet from 449 to 412 there were no hostilities between Athens and Persia.[31] Isocrates, in 380 and Demosthenes in the 350s and 340s make unequivocal reference to such an agreement, called the Treaty of Callias, and it was dated at 449 by Diodorus.[32] If there was such an agreement, then it can be assumed that it was intended to maintain the *status quo* between Athens and Persia in the region.

Historians, such as Meiggs (1972: 152), who believe there was such an agreement in 449, further believe that this deal accounts for a subsequent degree of instability and unrest within the Delian League. Most significantly, in 448, there is no record of tribute being received. In conjunction with this period of unrest, it is also argued that there is evidence that the position of Athens within the League changes from one of hegemon to ruler. Decrees issued at this time make reference to 'cities which Athens rules' and can, as a consequence, denote the point at which the League becomes an empire.[33] The function of the League now shifted to one of deterrence: the Persians could be counted upon to respect the autonomy of the Asiatic Greeks only as long as the League maintained the ability to fight them effectively. But with the immediate Persian threat diminished, it became harder for the Athenians to keep the Delian League intact. Athens resorted to a mixed strategy, maintaining a light hand on the tiller and relying on rules rather than force whenever possible; but using force when necessary to prevent defections.[34]

The Peloponnesian Wars

The balancing strategy pursued by Athens in the context of the Persian invasion inevitably had the effect of disrupting established power relations within Greece itself. In particular, the growth of Athens' naval power had a direct impact on rival naval powers, such as Aegina, and, more particularly, Corinth. It had less impact on Sparta because the power of these two dominant city-states was functionally differentiated,[35] and indeed Athens and Sparta could be considered to have maintained a 'time-honoured alliance'.[36] In 462, when the Spartans called on members of the Hellenic League to provide assistance after a helot's revolt, Cimon, one of Athens most important military leaders, argued that the Athenians must not 'allow Greece to go lame, or their own city to be deprived of its yoke-fellow'.[37] Ironically, it was the Spartans who backed away from the alliance: Athens sent 4,000 hoplites to assist the Spartans, but the Spartans, fearing how they might be used, requested them to return to Attica. This was the context in which Athens formed its alliances with Argos and Megara, leading to the first Peloponnesian War (460–445) discussed above.

Extending its hold on Greece made the Delian League a more effective balancer against the Persians. From the perspective of other Greek states, however, and Sparta, in particular, the growing power of Athens must have appeared ominous, adversely affecting the regional distribution of power. This concern must have extended to the League itself and, in 446, when the truce with Sparta came to an end, Euboea rebelled against Athens and this encouraged the Megarians to defect, killing the entire Athenian garrison. With the truce at an end, Sparta returned to war and invaded Attica. But in 445 Athens and Sparta agreed to resolve their differences and they established a Thirty Years' Peace. Under the terms of this agreement, the Athenians relinquished all the gains that they had made over the previous 16 years. But, in practice, they held on to Aegina, contrary to the peace agreement, because the island's position in relation to the Peloponneseus was considered to be so crucial.[38]

At first sight, the Thirty Years Peace, like the reputed Callias Treaty, should have produced a very stable outcome, with an agreement that reflected and was, therefore, reinforced by the underlying balance of power, with Spartan land power being matched by Athenian sea power. Yet within 16 years, war between Athens and Sparta erupted in 431.[39] Thucydides offers two different explanations for the conflict. From one angle, he provides a detailed multilevel narrative of the events leading up to the war. But he also suggests a second approach, writing: 'For, indeed, I think that the truest cause, though least spoken of, was that the Athenians, in growing to great power and furnishing an occasion of fear to the Lacedaemonians, compelled the latter to go to war' (Thucydides 1.23.6).[40]

Every element in Thucydides' second argument can be disputed. Some authors argue that Athens' power had not been growing prior to the onset of the Peloponnesian War,[41] emphasizing the tenuous and rebellion-prone nature of Athens' grip on its empire. Alternatively, it can be argued that if Athenian power was growing, then balancing behavior should have occurred earlier. Others note in defense of Thucydides' thesis that the Athenians had created new colonies and extended their control within the empire.[42] Furthermore, Sparta contemplated an attack on Attica during Samos's rebellion against Athens in 440, suggesting that they did see Athens as a rival.[43]

Although the putative peace between Persia and Athens largely held after 449 and before the Second Peloponnesian War (431–404) there were minor violations of the peace, as with the involvement in Samos that could have had, very serious repercussions (Eddy, 1973: 106). To a very large extent, moreover, from the perspective of internal balancing, their relative strengths were complementary and seemed likely to give rise to a stalemate. So although any anarchic system will generate a security dilemma, the difference in the Athenian and Spartan portfolios of capabilities ameliorated that problem by creating a situation of defence dominance – neither side could easily defeat the other.[44] But both Sparta and Athens also relied very heavily on their allies.

This brings us back to Thucydides' first argument: as with the First Peloponnesian War, Athens and Sparta, were chain ganged into war. Both constantly feared that their allies might move out of the alliance (Strauss, 1997) and as relations deteriorated, both Athens and Sparta assumed that war was inevitable and began to plan accordingly. Very close to the outbreak of the war Athens violated the terms of the Thirty Years' Peace by imposing a garrison on Aegina and issuing the Megarian decrees, which, among other restrictions, excluded all Megarian merchants from Athenian ports (Cawkwell, 1997a: 27–8). Both moves can be seen as attempts to shore up Athenian security in the event of a war which appeared increasingly likely.[45] Nevertheless, the moves undermined the Thirty Years' Peace, and given that Corinth was already threatening to pull out of Sparta's Peloponnesian League, because of its failure to deal with Athens, it becomes understandable why the Spartans refused to go to arbitration, with the result that they too were in violation of a key aspect of the Thirty Years' Peace. But Athens was also unwilling to compromise because in the closing months before the War, Athens wanted to demonstrate to its allies that her sea empire was unassailable and 'that there was no outside help that could save them' (Cawkwell, 1997a: 36).

If this was the thinking behind Athens' and Sparta's refusal to compromise, then it does indicate that their mindset was too focused on Greece and overlooked the permanent threat posed by Persia and its ability to play them off against each other. There had already been one such attempt, when the Athenians went to the assistance of the rebels in Egypt prior to the Peace of Callias. The Persians had approached the Spartans at the time with an unsuccessful offer to fund an attack on Attica. Indeed, the Spartans also made several attempts at the start of the Peloponnesian War to get assistance from the Persians. The efforts came to nothing, but there can be little doubt that the Persians wished to recover the territory that they had lost at the beginning of the century. The situation, therefore, was fraught with danger for all the Greeks, although the risks were much higher for the Athenians than for the Spartans. There is some evidence that the Athenians attended to this danger, sending an embassy to visit Darius II, the new Persian king, in 424/3 (Lewis, 1977: 76–7). There is, however, no further information available about relations with Persia for the next decade and a radically different set of circumstances exist when Thucydides, for the first time, begins to pay serious attention to the role being played by Persia.[46] Without explanation, we learn that Athens has been supporting a rebel satrap in Caria possibly from as early as 415/4.[47]

Such a move clearly violated whatever understanding (generally identified as the Peace of Callias) the Athenians and the Persians had come to in the past. It is not difficult to imagine what could have happened in the previous years to justify such a provocative act at a time when the Athenians were so vulnerable to a change in balancing strategy by Persia. The most obvious possibility is that the Persians had been encouraging the Asian Greeks to bandwagon with Persia. Athenian vulnerability increased dramatically in 413 when much of its army and fleet were lost in an invasion of Sicily. There was clear evidence of band-wagoning as members of the Delian League (Lesbos, Chios, Euboea, and Erythrae) approached Sparta. Much more ominously, the Spartans approached the Persians. In a series of agreements Sparta accepted that there were no limits to the Persians' claim to the Asiatic mainland.[48]

According to Thucydides, the Persians knew that they could influence the outcome in Greece. However, they provided the Spartans with very little assistance because they also recognized that Sparta had long been committed to the freedom of all Greeks. While desiring to reduce Athenian power, the Persians did not wish to strengthen Sparta.[49] In the end, the Persians won: they gave just enough aid to Sparta to defeat the Athenians, and to prevent a compromise peace between them. Even at this stage, the fate of the Asiatic Greeks had still not been sealed. A balancing strategy pursued by the Greeks collectively might have maintained their independence. Instead, Sparta began a war with Persia, and precipitated another war on the Greek mainland (the Corinthian War 395–387). These conflicts further exhausted the Greeks who eventually agreed to a peace negotiated by the Persians, which affirmed the autonomy of the European Greeks but at the expense of the Asiatic Greeks.

Persia, the Greek city-states and balance-of-power theory

Although Greece is often treated as an autonomous system, the aim of this chapter has been to explore the implications, from a balance of power perspective, of treating the Greek city-states as components of a larger system, focusing specifically on their relationship with Persia. At first sight, this move does not pose a problem for either the English school or the neorealists who have developed two of the most explicit theories of the balance of power. Indeed, the two positions effectively coincide on this occasion because although English school theorists concentrate on how states operate within an international society, relations between Greece and Persia involve the interaction between two international societies and can only be examined, as a consequence, from the kind of systemic perspective that neorealists favor. But whereas neorealists predict that systemic forces can produce a stable balance, English school theorists presuppose that any systemic balance of power will be fortuitous, transient and unstable. Despite these conflicting positions, the details presented in the case study, raise problems for both of these assessments and suggest the need for a more pluralistic approach.

From a Waltzian perspective, the invasion of Greece by Persia should have precipitated a high level of balancing from the Greek city-states. In practice, however, the mainland Greeks 'underbalanced' by failing to provide an adequate response to the threat. One reason for this result is suggested by Schweller (2006), who argues that socially cohesive states with united leaders are the ones most likely to respond to structural or systemic pressures. The ancient Greek city-states were, from this perspective, too divided internally to balance effectively; instead, ruling factions tended to bandwagon with, and accept the hegemony of, an ideologically congenial great power.

The mainland Greeks succeeded in compelling the Persians to withdraw only because of two fortuitous advantages. First, the Persians confronted logistical problems associated with crossing into mainland Greece, and so it was difficult for them to maintain their supply lines. Second, there is evidence that the Persians were overextended at this time and they had to withdraw to consolidate their control over their existing territory. One aspect of this overextension, noted by English School but not neorealist theory, is the multicultural, polyglot nature of the Persian Empire that made regions with distinct identities, such as Egypt and Babylonia, particularly likely to rebel. So despite some striking victories by the Greeks, it is not the case that the Persians withdrew because of an unequivocally successful balancing policy by the Greeks.

Ironically, it was only after the direct threat from Persia had been removed that an effective 'balancing' strategy was initiated with the establishment of the Delian League. This development, however, had the counterproductive consequence of destabilizing the regional balance of power. Regional balancing strategies then overwhelmed the need to sustain a systemic balancing strategy. But what the case study also shows is that Persia had a more comprehensive strategic vision than the Greek city-states. If it is true, for example, that prior to the invasion of Greece the Persians approached the Carthaginians and ensured that the Persian attack on mainland Greece coincided with the Carthaginian attack on Sicily and Italy, then these two dominant hegemons had a global strategy that none of the Greek city-states came close to matching. So, for example, Thucydides was unable to take account of this larger strategic picture when he failed to make adequate provision for Persia's role in the Peloponnesian War. By the 4th century, however, Greek historians looking back on the 5th century had now acquired this broader perspective and either assumed that coordination between Persia and Carthage had taken place, or possessed records of an actual agreement.

In the wake of the Soviet demise, neorealist theorists have become more sensitive to the implications of the kind of unipolar world that the Greek city-states confronted and there is a growing interest in the relations between a multipolar region and an external hegemon. In particular, neorealist theorists have conceptualized the hegemon as an offshore balancer, which has a vested interest in promoting the divisions within a multipolar region.[50] With the onset of the Peloponnesian Wars in the 5th century, the balance with Persia established on the basis of the Delian League began to fragment and the way was opened for Persia to move into the position of being an offshore balancer, which not only enabled Persia to recover the territory lost to the Greeks but also to pursue an interventionist strategy within mainland Greece. The case study demonstrates, therefore, that there is much more scope for variation in balancing responses than can be captured by the Waltzian neorealist model.

For the English School, this chapter raises questions about the definition and extent of international society. English school theorists start from the premise that the Greeks and Persians comprised different international societies, implying that there was no intersubjective agreement about the distribution of power between them, and no significant body of shared international norms. Both of these conclusions are questionable, however. The heralds sent by Persia into Greece ahead of the military, indicates, for example, that Greece and Persia shared at least some normative elements of an international society, at least in the functional *gesellschaft* sense articulated by Buzan (1993), though not in the civilizational *gemeinschaft* understanding promoted by Bull and Watson (1984). Furthermore, the Peace of Callias, if it was indeed an explicit agreement, had to rest on a substantial degree of intersubjective agreement between Athenians and Persians about the distribution of power between them. These facts point to a larger weakness in English School theorizing, as the distinction between a international system and international society is yet to be clarified and developed. That said, a valuable insight of the English School approach is to explain what neorealism can only assume: whom was balancing against Persia meant to defend? The answer is members of Greek international society: the mainland Greeks naturally looked to the Aegean Greeks as part of the international society to be defended; their behavior toward other neighbors such as Lydia – long a part of their international system – was much more instrumental.

What the case study in this chapter demonstrates is that balancing is a much more complex and variable phenomenon than either the systemic or the societal approaches to the balance of power can accommodate. Neither neorealism nor the English school can account for the variations that occurred during the period covered, with the underbalancing that took place when the Persians invaded mainland Greece, the effective balancing that occurred with the formation of the Delian League, followed by the establishment of Persia as an offshore balancer during the course of the Peloponnesian War. Waltz argues that international behavior that cannot be accounted for at the systemic level of analysis must be explained from a foreign policy perspective. The case study here, however, suggests the need for a more pluralistic approach that takes account of the geography of the system, the nature of the interacting states, and the interaction between regional and extra-regional dynamics, among other factors. Neither the neorealist assumption that there is structural pressure to balance in an anarchic system nor the English school assumption that the resulting balance is inherently unstable is open to the wide range of factors that crucially affect the level of balancing that goes on in any international system.

Notes

1   Wight (1977) and Watson (1992, 2007) both argue that hegemony is the prevailing international structure in world history. For a discussion of Bull's assessment of a systemic balance of power, see Little (2007).

2   The English school is not alone in viewing the balance of power in these terms. Kaplan (1957) and Schroeder (1994) discuss the balance of power in terms of rules; while Gulick (1955), Holsti (1991), Osiander (1994), Bobbitt (2002) and Clark (2005) explore the impact of peace conferences on the structure of the international system.

3   Balcer (1995) draws attention to the increasing sensitivity to the Persian Empire.

4   See, for example, Cawkwell (1997b). It is debated whether the peace ever occurred.

5   Cawkwell (1997b: 17) describes the failure to discuss the role of the Persians during the Peloponnesian War is 'a scandal'. Andrewes (1961) suggests that Thucydides failed to recognize the important role that Persia would come to play in the outcome of the war when it started and that he had only begun to insert references to Persia at the start of the war when he was in the process of revising the manuscript. This is, of course, pure speculation.

6   The Copenhagen Polis Centre, established in 1993, has now identified 35 different city-state cultures, which are all seen to have some very similar characteristics (Hansen, 2003).

7   Compare this with the 200 triremes that Athens built in 482. Carthage is estimated to have had the same number in 500 BC (Starr, 1989).

8   Plato, Laws 1 (626a) Cited in Starr (1974: 2).

9   But note the point made by Eckstein in Chapter 4 that small states often have difficult choices to make.

10 This assessment applies primarily to Waltz (1979). By contrast, Gilpin (1981: 38) acknowledges that the 'city-states were part of a much greater system dominated by imperial Persia'.

11 Forrest (1986: 37–8) asserts that 'All Greek states we know of were divided about their response (to the Persian threat).'

12 See Christiansen and Snyder (1990). The decision by the Athenians to support (balance) the Greeks in Asia Minor must have been affected by the growing interest displayed by the Persians in the Black Sea (the major source of grain for Athens) expressed through their support for and the growing influence of Miletus – one of the most powerful of the Greek City-States in Asia Minor. Miletus had effective autonomy and their own imperial sphere, albeit under Persian suzereignty (Georges, 2000: 10–11, 34).

13 In Chapter 4, Eckstein shows how nearly 200 years later, with the rise of the Roman Empire, the smaller Greek city-states continued to confront the problem of how to survive in a world of larger, predatory states. Eckstein argues that they looked to great powers for protection and sometimes turned to external great powers, such as Persia in the 5th century and Rome in the 3rd century. However, while Eckstein associates this response with balancing I associate the strategy with bandwagoning. This divergence suggests that the dichotomy between balancing and bandwagoning is problematic. Waltz's (1979) circumvents but does not solve this problem, however, by insisting that his model applies to great powers and has less to say about smaller states.

14 Amit (1973: 26–7) goes on to report that some modern historians have challenged this as a pro-Athenian account. Any notion that the Persians were intending to conquer Greece is rejected. The aim was restricted to punishing Athens and Eretria and to extend the Persian hold on the islands of the Aegean. All of these aims were achieved, apart from punishing Athens.

15 The estimate of Greek troops is taken from Forrest (1986: 39). Pomeroy *et al.* (1999: 185) suggest that there could have been as many as 20,000 Persian troops.

16 See Forrest (1986: 40–1) for an assessment of the political consequences of the victory at Marathon.

17 It was Themistocles who had argued a decade earlier in 493 that walls should be built to protect Athens' harbour at Piraeus.

18 It is argued that Sparta had been developing an anti-Persian posture for at least a decade. So, for example, although they did not fight at Marathon, they did send troops that arrived after the battle was over, with the excuse that they had been engaged in religious ceremonies which had prevented them from coming sooner.

19 The Greeks failed to take note of the distinction between the Medes and the Persians and continued to make reference to the Medes after the Persians seized power. States or individuals who favored the Persians were accused of medizing.

20 Amit (1973) p. 79. The Boiotian League operated under the hegemony of Thebes.

21 See Green (1996: 82–3). This account is taken from Ephorus, a 4th century historian who wrote the first general history of Greece. Only fragments of his writings remain. Green observes that many modern historians have

queried this account, but he concludes that it has been convincingly defended by Burn (1962).

22   The estimates for the Greeks and the Persians are taken from Forrest (1986: 44).

23   Green (1996: 157–9) argues that the Athenians failed to come to terms with the fact that the alliance ties were 'entirely dependent on the harsh demands of strategy'. Fearing a Helot revolt, a permanent reason for isolationism, the Spartans, he argues, can hardly be blamed for the choice they made.

24   It has also been suggested that on the same day, the Syracusans crushed the Carthaginian advance at Himera. See Forrest (1986: 45).

25   Casson (1994) says the trireme had 170 rowers.

26   Flower (2000) argues that one of the fragments that remain of Simonides poem on the Battle of Plataea written in the 470s makes reference to the Greeks driving the Medes and the Persians 'out of Asia'. He suggests, therefore, that the 4th century theme of the Greeks uniting to invade Persia was present throughout the 5th century following the Persian invasions.

27   Meiggs (1972: 138) gives a figure of 175.

28   In practice, a large reserve built up over time – 6,000 talents before the Peloponnesian War, more than ten times the annual income.

29   See Ostwald (1982). It has been strongly disputed that there would have been any reference to autonomy. Meiggs (1972: 46) argues, for example, that the autonomy of the member states would have been taken for granted. A revisionist view of the Delian League has been mounted by Robertson (1980) who argues that the original alliance consisted of Athens and a few strong islands who banded together to attack sea-based medizing Greeks while Sparta attacked medizers on the mainland. See also Rhodes (1985: 9).

30   Cawkwell (1997b: 115) says that it remains 'a somewhat shadowy affair'.

31   Cawkwell (1997b: 115) talks of a 'cessation of hostilities'. Meiggs (1972: 129) is more cautious and says 'no further League operations against Persia are recorded'. Eddy (1973: 241) says 'for over thirty years there was a kind of Cold War between the two powers, a situation of vague menace, of raids, of small successes, of countermoves, of embassies and threats'. Lewis (1977: 51) questions whether it is appropriate to describe the evidence of 'isolated troubles' as a Cold War.

32   Isocrates (436–338) and Demosthenes (384–322) were two of the leading Panhellenists of the 4th century. Isocrates wanted Greece to unite against Persia. Demonsthenes became much more concerned with the threat from Macedonia. Diodorus of Sicily compiled his history between 60–30 BC. The agreement is considered to have been negotiated by Callias, a wealthy Athenian whose family was closely involved in diplomacy during the 5th and 4th centuries. Hence the putative agreement is known as the Treaty of Callias.

33   Meiggs (1972: 171–3); see also Rhodes (1985: Ch. 4). Wickersham (1994) makes it clear that for Thucydides hegemony and arche or empire are diametrically opposed relationships. There is, however, substantial debate about when or whether it is appropriate to identify the existence of an Athenian Empire. One of the problems is that the key decrees are now

being dated much later. For example, the coinage decree which is often seen to have imposed Athenian currency sometime in the 440s on the other members of the Delian League has been challenged. Figueira (1998) argues that Athens allowed cities to continue with their own tender provided that they also recognized Attic coinage as legal tender. Mattingly (1999) reviews Figueira (1998) and argues that the decree was only established in the 420s and that it did aim to impose uniformity across the empire, but it was a short-lived, over ambitious and counterproductive move. However, it is indisputable that Athens moved the League's treasury to Athens in 454 and was collecting tribute, much as the Persians did. As neorealists would predict, in their attempt to enhance their security, therefore, the Athenians emulated a key aspect of Persian organization.

34   See Meiggs (1972: 412) who concludes 'as the Athenians claimed at Sparta in 432, they made considerably less use of force than imperial powers are expected to use; but they could have made more concessions to the general Greek passion for autonomy without undermining their position.'

35   See Levy's (2001) argument that expansion by a sea-based power is considered to be less threatening than the expansion in power by a land-based power. See also Levy and Thompson (2003).

36   This is how Pomeroy *et al.* (1999: 210) describe the relationship.

37   Flower (2000) sees this as an early panhellenic call for the Greeks to stick together against the ongoing threat from Persia. The helots were the indigenous people of territory that had been conquered by Sparta. They were turned into serfs by the Spartans and presented a persistent threat because they outnumbered the Spartans by seven to one. On this occasion, the revolt followed a violent and destructive earthquake in Sparta.

38   At the start of the second Pelonnesian War, the Athenians expelled the indigenous population of Aegina and replaced them with Athenians, confirming the strategic importance of the island. See Figueira (1991), Lebow (1991: 27–8).

39   There are two highly divergent views. One is that Sparta was determined to destroy Athens' power and the argument is made in its most extreme form by de Ste Croix (1972). At the other extreme is the argument that Athens deliberately engineered the war, made by Badian (1993).

40   This is Eckstein's (2003: 773) modification of Sealey's (1975: 92) translation. Eckstein argues that political scientists rely on Warner's translation of Thucydides' (1972: 49) sentence 'What made war inevitable was the growth of Athenian power and the fear which this caused in Sparta'. By relying on this 'mistranslation' they fail to appreciate the openness and complexity of Thucydides' position, seizing on a conception of inevitability that does not appear in Thucydides.

41   Kagan (1969) argues that Athens' power had not grown between the First and Second Peloponnesian Wars. Lebow (1991: 158–9) argues that Athens had recovered from the disasters of the 440s but that its 'power and reputation were still not where they had been in 450'. This leads on to his main argument that it was not fear of Athens that motivated Sparta to go to war but rather a failure by the Spartan leadership to appreciate the depth of Athens' power.

42   See Figueira (1991).

43 Cawkwell (1997a: 37).
44 In other words, the military forces should have served as defensive rather than offensive weapons systems. See Jervis (1978).
45 The timing of these violations are crucial for this argument to hold water and Cawkwell (1997a: 27–34) goes to considerable efforts to demonstrate that the moves were made close to the end of the period of peace.
46 We know from other sources that Darius II faced the usual succession crisis and his position was not secure for several years. See Lewis (1977: 78–82).
47 See the discussion in Cawkwell (1997a: 15); Lewis (1997: 76–7); and Rhodes (1985: 31–2).
48 See Rhodes (1985: 34) and Lewis (1977: 84–96).
49 Persia's strategy is enunciated by the Athenian Alcibiades who had defected to the Spartans and was now working alongside the Persians. The strategy is discussed by Lewis (1977, ch. 4).
50 See Layne (1997), Wohlforth (1999), and Mearsheimer (2001) for competing assessments of the offshore balancer.

4
Intra-Greek Balancing, the Mediterranean Crisis of c. 201–200 BCE, and the Rise of Rome

Arthur M. Eckstein

In AD 1519 the main geopolitical problem faced by the people of the city-state of Tlaxcala on the high plateau of Mexico was their oppression by their neighbors, the fearsome Aztecs. Then a new force appeared on the Mexican geopolitical scene, a force with which the Tlaxcaltecans eagerly allied in order to balance the power of Tenochtitlan. They helped this new force defeat the Aztec army, and many scholars believe that without the help of the Tlaxcaltecans the defeat of the Aztecs would not have occurred. The Tlaxcaltecans, by balancing against the Aztecs, thus achieved their immediate aim of becoming independent of the Aztecs. Unfortunately for them, the new power on the scene on the plateau of Mexico in 1519 was Hernán Cortés and his army of conquistadores.[1]

Two millenia before these events, the Greek city-states of the Ionian coast of Asia Minor were oppressed by their neighbor the Persian Empire – and also feared Pausanias, the Spartan commander of European Greek forces then operating on the coast. Then a new factor entered the Ionian geopolitical scene. This new force held the promise of both balancing the power of the Persians and dealing with Pausanias; most Ionian city-states joined with it. The Ionian states achieved their immediate aim. Persian oppression, and the threat from the arrogant (and, it was rumored, pro-Persian) Spartan commander Pausanias, was lifted. The voluntary nature of the Ionians' adherence to the new power on the coast was publicly proclaimed by spokesmen for that power (see Thuc. 1.75.2). And the deeply intelligent historian of these events testifies in his own voice that in this case the imperial spokesmen were telling the truth about the original voluntary adherence of the fearful Ionians (Thuc. 1.95.1 and 96.1). The new factor on the Ionian coast was Athens.

The theme of the present chapter is that smaller states have difficult choices to make when they seek to follow a policy of balancing against a hegemon. The problem to be underlined here is that sometimes there are several different strong powers against which smaller states must simultaneously seek to balance if they wish to preserve their independence. In the Tlaxcaltecan and the Ionian cases, the governing elites preferred a rising hegemon to the hegemon they knew – hoping to use the new power on the geopolitical scene in order to create a space of freedom of action for themselves, or at least to lift the oppression of the current hegemon. In Stephen Walt's terms: under threat themselves, these governing elites chose to seek the alliance of what they perceived as the least-threatening great power (Walt, 1987: 17–49). We know, after the fact, that in both these cases the choices made by the weaker polities were highly dubious. But for the governments of weaker states in ferocious premodern anarchic interstate systems – as was the Mexican system in the 16th century CE and the Aegean system 2,000 years earlier – the choices were often between bad and worse.[2] The Tlaxcaltecans and the Ionians acted, indeed, with courage to preserve their independence, for there is no doubt that the Aztecs and the Persians (and perhaps Pausanias) would have taken terrible revenge if the gambit had failed. Unfortunately, the Athenians and especially the Spanish turned out not to be much better. That, however, was a problem for the future: for smaller states in savage premodern anarchies, 'sufficient unto the day is the evil thereof.'

The specific topic of this chapter is the action taken by several weaker Greek states in the power-transition crisis that beset the eastern Mediterranean from 207 BCE, a crisis that intensified after 204, reaching a climax of violence in 201–196. Since about 280 BCE, a *de facto* balance of power among the three greatest Greek states had allowed the second-tier and smaller states to exist relatively comfortably within the eastern Mediterranean state-system. The three great powers were the Antigonid monarchy based in Macedon, the Ptolemaic monarchy based in Egypt, and the Seleucid monarchy based in Syria and Mesopotamia. Each of these dynasties descended from a general of Alexander the Great, ruthless men who had seized whatever territory and resources they could in the chaos following Alexander's premature death; each possessed a militaristic ideology stressing that they were the heirs to Alexander's world rule (see Lévêque, 1968; Walbank, 1993). The *de facto* balance of power among the three great states, a relative peace of exhaustion after ferocious wars among them in the period 323–280, facilitated the ability of middle-sized states to balance (or threaten to balance) with one great power when under pressure from another great power. The medium-sized states also engaged intensely in 'internal balancing' – that is, they themselves were highly militarized.[3] But the severe crisis of the late 3rd century was one which they could not overcome on their own. They therefore took the initiative in calling in an outside power to restore the geopolitical situation. That outside power was Rome. One stated question in this volume is: 'Why did the other states not engage in balancing behavior in order to deflect the growth of the hegemonic threat – in this case, Rome?' The answer I offer is that the Greek states *did* engage in balancing behavior, in energetic and courageous balancing behavior – as was indeed their habit, historically. This balancing behavior of the Greek states, however, was aimed against threats more immediate than Rome; it focused on the immediate threats that existed among themselves.

In modern explanations of the events of this period, too much attention has been paid to the militarism and aggressiveness of the Romans. This is not to deny that the Roman Republic was a highly militarized, militaristic and diplomatically aggressive state; it certainly was. Thus the Romans possessed an ideology which wished Rome to be ever larger and ever stronger; they performed state religious ceremonies and the Senate made allocations of military resources that assumed the likelihood of war every year; they idolized bravery in battle; they brutally sacked cities; they fervently celebrated victories and thanked the gods profusely for them; the primary life experience of the Roman senatorial elite was military, and the elite viewed individual success on the battlefield and the management of war as the primary road to personal authority within the state; finally, the habitual Roman attitude in diplomacy was coercion, not persuasion.[4] All of this constitutes an almost unconsciously aggressive stance towards the outside world – a stance which has been called 'the imperialism of routine' (Veyne, 1975: 794, 805).

Nevertheless, the analytical problem facing those who explain Rome's extraordinary success in the expansion of its power by recourse to this 'imperialism of routine' is that this imperialism of routine, and every single one of the elements constituting it, can also be found in every monarchy, every federal polity, every city-state of every size and political structure in the Mediterranean world, as well as every politically undeveloped tribe on its periphery. That is: the state-system of the Hellenistic Mediterranean – the system of which Rome was only one unit – is a classic illustration of the Waltzian maxim that a highly-militarized anarchy forces all states towards functional similarity (Waltz, 1979: 96–7, 101).[5] The Hellenistic Mediterranean was a harshly competitive system that consistently pushed states of all sizes and all political types in the direction of militarism and expansionism, which in turn set off simultaneous synergistic reactions by other states within the cruel general environment.[6] This militarism held true not simply for the largest Hellenistic states, but also for second-tier and medium-sized states; and it has recently been shown how strongly this militarism held even for small and very small city-states, intent on competing against each other in their own 'mini-imperialisms' along the 3rd and 2nd-century BCE. Aegean coast (Ma, 2000). But if *all* Hellenistic states were (from a modern perspective) exceptionally militaristic, bellicose, and expansionist, then one cannot explain extraordinary Roman success on grounds of what looks to us to be its exceptional militarism, bellicosity, and expansionism. Yet recent scholars have tended to do this.[7] Part of the real answer for exceptional Roman success, as Mommsen saw long ago (1907: 340–5), was that Rome – besides being militaristic, bellicose, and aggressive – also developed an exceptional capacity for inclusion of foreigners, which made her capable of gathering and mobilizing exceptionally large social resources with which to confront the ferocious Mediterranean competition for security and power, a point I will discuss further below. But in this chapter, I wish especially to underline how the origins of Roman success lay partly in one particular aspect of the harsh interstate environment which Rome shared with all other Hellenistic states – namely, the habitual flight of small and medium-sized polities, when facing an immediate threat, to the protection of great powers.

Van Evera has stressed that though the modern state-system is essentially an anarchy, the destruction of states within it is unusual, and he suggests this is a consequence of the inherent strengths of the modern nation-state.[8] Van Evera's point holds true for Europe, North America, and parts of Asia in the modern period, but if we look at the modern Third World, we see something different: many fragile states which have suffered invasion, loss of autonomy, and/or dismemberment.[9] The ancient Mediterranean was in all periods characterized by such a striking fragility of states. In antiquity there were no nation-states, though Rome comes closest in some respects, and leaving aside the often grim fates of smaller states in Classical Greece,[10] the instability of the security of even the most powerful of polities in the Hellenistic age is extraordinary. Carthage went from being an imperial power to the point of physical destruction at the hands of its own mercenary troops in the five years between 245 and 240 BCE. Rome in the 230s and 220s might have disappeared under a tidal wave of Celtic invasion (that was Polybius' opinion: 2.35) – and this had already almost occurred in 386. And of course the Roman system in Italy came close to collapse under the successive blows inflicted by Hannibal between 218 and 213.[11]

The events that led to Rome's permanent involvement in the geopolitics of the Greek East had to do with the suddenly exposed fragility of one of the Greek great powers: between 207 and 200 BCE. the Ptolemaic Empire went from being one of the three great pillars of the multipolar system in the East to the verge of destruction. Simultaneously the other two Greek great powers, Macedon and the Seleucid Empire, led by the vigorous kings Philip V and Antiochus III, expanded their power aggressively, mostly (but not totally) at the expense of the Ptolemies. In sum, we are looking at a classic power-transition crisis in the Greek East, and it disrupted the entire state-system, leading to what Realist theoreticians call a 'hegemonic war' – i.e., a war to restructure the system according to the new realities of the distribution of power.[12] As a consequence of the power-transition crisis caused by the faltering of Egypt, the eastern Mediterranean by summer 201 was ablaze from the frontiers of Egypt at Gaza all the way north to Byantium at the entrance to the Black Sea.

It was clear that *something* was now going to replace the old three-way balance of power in the Greek Mediterranean. Moreover, whatever the details of the new system, it was clear that the new system would in general work to the benefit of the most powerful states. In 201 it appeared that the traditional Hellenistic multipolar system would most likely be replaced by the expansion in power of already formidable Antigonid Macedon and/or the Seleucid Empire. The result would be either a bipolar system in the Greek East, focused dramatically on the might of the Antigonids and the Seleucids, or perhaps even a unipolar system – after a second round of large-scale violence and 'hegemonic war' – with either Antigonid Macedon or Seleucid Syria-Mesopotamia emerging as sole hegemon and the totally dominant power. Things turned out differently, of course. What occurred instead was the intervention of Rome, an intervention which for the moment restored the traditional multipolar system but now on an artifical basis, with Rome as its patron and enforcer. But that the previous systemic balance of power would be replaced by something radically new was inherent in the Ptolemaic collapse. It was a collapse much more sudden and much worse than the decline of the Austro-Hungarian regime before 1914.

Influencing the direction and character of the fundamental systemic change that was under way was possible for individual governments, was possible for leaders of vision, by means of crucial decision-making; but halting that change was not.

The failure of the Ptolemaic state derived from inherent regime weaknesses combined with unfortunate contingent events. Late in the reign of Ptolemy IV (c. 207 BCE), a massive indigenous rebellion erupted in Upper and Middle Egypt. The Ptolemaic government was unable to suppress the rebellion; fighting was extensive and savage (cf. Polyb. 14.12.4). The rebellion resulted from the resentments provoked by Ptolemaic Greek rule over a large indigenous Egyptian population. Polybius adds that it was a mistake for Ptolemy IV to train large numbers of Egyptians for service in his army, even though he was short of soldiers with which to confront Antiochus III and the threat to Egypt posed by the Seleucids, and thus the expedient had been forced upon him: it was the native troops who later led the rebellion (5.107.3). The difficult situation worsened greatly with the premature death of Ptolemy IV himself in 204, and the accession to the throne of his son Ptolemy V – a child of six. The government now fell into the hands of a succession of regents, none of whom had much legitimacy or popularity even in the capital at Alexandria itself, let alone in the countryside. Chaos reigned in Alexandria, with riots and the overturning of a succession of unstable governments by force and *coups d'etat*. By 201 the sphere of control of the Ptolemies was restricted to chaotic Alexandria and the lower Nile Valley, with consequent loss of tax revenues with which to fund the government. Meanwhile the indigenous rebels had officially declared one of their leaders as the new Pharoah, in a traditional religious ceremony presided over by Egyptian priests.[13] The sudden collapse of Ptolemaic power now also began to attract increasing military aggression from the vigorous leaders of the two other great dynasties.[14]

The extent of the crisis within the Hellenistic state-system caused by the collapse of the power of the Ptolemies was made public from winter 203/202 BCE by the military actions of Philip V and Antiochus III (Polyb. 14.1a). The Hellenistic system was in any case an anarchy prone as a system to the use of warfare as the natural means by which states dealt with serious conflicts of interest (see Lévèque, 1968: 279). In other words, Hellenistic states tended to regress towards Waltzian 'functional similarity' in terms of their habitual dependence upon military violence to solve interstate problems.[15] In that sense, the highly-aggressive military actions of Philip and Antiochus were predictable system-level responses to the power-transition crisis now besetting the Hellenistic system. In short, deepening Ptolemaic weakness presented an opportunity within a harshly competitive environment that few regimes would refuse to exploit. Polybius indicates that (c. winter 203/202) Philip and Antiochus arrived at a pact to work together to destroy the Ptolemaic Empire, dividing it up among themselves, and apparently including Egypt itself among the spoils.[16] The Greek historian is emphatic about the political impact which this agreement had when it became known in the wider Mediterranean world: all the Greek states now understood the terrible intentions of Philip and Antiochus (14.1a).[17] And a volume later, after castigating Philip and Antiochus for attacking the faltering Ptolemiac Empire on the grounds that they were taking advantage of a child-ruler, Polybius then stresses the great impact which the news of the pact, news brought by Greek envoys from the weaker states, had at Rome:

> Who among those who reasonably find fault with Fortune
> for her conduct of human affairs will not be reconciled to her
> now when he learns how she afterwards made the kings pay
> the due penalty for their crimes?...For even while the kings were
> still breaking their own faith with each other and destroying the
> kingdom of the child, she alerted the Romans to the situation,
> and very justly and properly visited upon them the very evils
> which they had been designing to bring upon others (15.20. 5–6).[18]

Appian and Justin depict the pact between Philip and Antiochus as a rumor – and some modern scholars have denied that it ever existed, proposing that the Roman Senate (and later Polybius) were misled by the propaganda of cynical Greeks who were intent on protecting their own interests against the aggressions of Philip and/or Antiochus.[19] Even if that were true, for our purposes the point would be the same: in the crisis of 201–200 BCE the weaker Greek states turned to Rome to balance Philip and Antiochus. If they misled the Romans about the pact in order to obtain Roman intervention, that was a measure of their desperation. But I think it is hard to deny the weight which Polybius – our most politically sophisticated source as well as the source nearest in time to the events – gives to the pact. This is especially so in 15.20, where Tyche (Fortune) is depicted as drawing the attention of the Romans to the existence of the pact, leading to the crucial Roman decision of 200 to intervene. Later, in Book 16, the existence of the pact is assumed within the general course of the narrative, as an explanation of decisions by Antiochus' generals to cooperate with Philip V as he campaigns in western Asia Minor in 201 (16.1 and 24). Moreover, shortly after Polybius makes his first emphatic reference to the pact (3.2.8) he castigates historians who make non-existent treaties the centerpiece of their historical analysis (3.26: his target is Philinus of Agrigentum). In a society where ridicule was a powerful weapon among intellectuals, Polybius would not have taken such a chance – not in Book 3 and not in Books 14, 15 and 16 – unless he felt his information was solid.

Many more arguments could be adduced in favor of the historicity of the pact, including a newly discovered inscription which shows Philip in southwest Asia Minor in 201 BCE handing over to Antiochus III a town he had conquered from the Ptolemies.[20] Moreover, there is a major problem with the idea that the Senate was intentionally misled by cynical Greeks: the Rhodians have often been targeted as the main source of the information that 'misled' the *Patres*, but we know that in spring 197 the Rhodians withdrew their naval forces from the Aegean where they were engaged against Philip V, and concentrated them instead off the southern coast of Asia Minor, in order to engage the large fleet of Antiochus III in battle – because they were convinced that Antiochus was coming west to help his ally Philip in the war that was still undecided in Greece.[21] Now for the Rhodians, already at war with Macedon, to undertake in addition a war against Antiochus (a renowned general who had reconquered most of Iran and Afghanistan for the Seleucid dynasty) was a highly dangerous act – the kind of act not taken by a government facing a much larger power unless the decision-making elite believes itself in possession of information which leaves it no choice. This suggests that no one in late 201 and early 200 was intentionally misleading the Senate. It is modern doubts about the existence or scope of the pact between Philip and Antiochus which seem misplaced.

The pact between Philip and Antiochus thus appears to be a phenomenon indicating the depths of the power-transition crisis into which the Greek East had been plunged, both by the collapse of the Ptolemies and the suddenly growing ambitions of the two other great powers. The multipolar system of the eastern Mediterranean was collapsing.

It was natural, of course, that some Greek states were desperate to maintain the current political *status quo*: desperate, that is, to maintain both the current Hellenistic multipolarity and their own relatively comfortable places within that multipolar system. The list of states severely worried about the sudden threat to the system arising from Philip V and Antiochus III – states worried enough to take very strong action against them – includes the Ptolemaic regime at Alexandria (of course), but also the Republic of Rhodes, the Kingdom of Pergamum, and even democratic Athens, a state which for the previous 30 years had pursued a policy of strict neutrality in its dealings with all the Hellenistic great powers. All four of these states were at war with either Philip V or Antiochus III by 201–200 BCE. And all four sent special embassies to Rome in 201–200, urging the Roman Republic to come to their rescue against the depredation of the kings.[22]

A tradition held that the Aetolian league also sent ambassadors on a similar mission of complaint to Rome in these years (sometime between 202 and 200).[23] The historicity of this embassy is disputed.[24] The historicity of the Aetolian appeal is supported by a scene from Plautus' comedy *Stichus* (produced in Rome exactly in 200 BCE), in which Greek envoys from Ambracia (an Aetolian city) take up too much room at a dining table, denying poverty-striken Romans their proper place.[25] If the Aetolian story is true, this would mean that no less than five Greek states came to Rome in 202–200 to complain about actions of the kings.

The reason for the desperation of the Ptolemies, the Rhodians, the Athenians and the Pergamenes (and perhaps we should include the Aetolians) was that the Greek state-system in the late 3rd century did not have the constellation of power capabilities in the eastern Mediterranean to balance, restrain or defeat Philip and Antiochus. There can be little doubt that if the warfare that convulsed the region after winter 203/202 had been limited to the participation of the Greek states, the multipolar system would have been destroyed by the two kings.

The Ptolemaic regime itself was unlikely to put up an effective self-defense for long, and we have already seen why: it was on the point of political and military collapse, with a child on the throne, continual political instability in the capital at Alexandria as one caretaker regime for the child succeeded another, and an extremely serious and widespread native rebellion in Upper and Middle Egypt against Greek rule – complete with the proclamation of an indigenous Pharoah. Indeed, the inability of the Ptolemaic regime to maintain its traditional position as one of the three great Greek powers was the central factor in bringing on the systemic crisis in the East after c. 207. In 201 Antiochus' armies advanced as far as Gaza, seizing the long-time Egyptian provinces of Lebanon and Judaea; and although this was followed by a surprising Egyptian counter-offensive, the result was a smashing Seleucid victory at Panion in northern Judaea in 200, and – once more – a Seleucid advance to the borders of Egypt proper.[26]

The military-political situation regarding other potential Greek balancers of the kings was not much better. In European Greece the Achaean League was an ally of Philip, the Aetolian League a twice-defeated opponent (in 220–217 BCE and again in 211–206), and no individual Greek city-state could stand up to the power of Macedon for long. In 202 Philip campaigned with great success in the northern Aegean: he captured the independent island-city of Thasos and enslaved its Greek population, despite promises not to, evidently in order to finance his further military activities. He also captured important places in the northern Aegean belonging to the Aetolian League: the cities of Lysimacheia, Chalcedon, and Cius (in the latter city he again enslaved the population despite promises not to do it). The Aetolians could do nothing militarily to stop Philip, even though he was now in violation of the sworn peace treaty of 206.[27] No European Greek state, then, could mount an effective resistence against Philip alone, let alone Philip in alliance with Antiochus.[28]

That left as counterweights to the kings only the Republic of Rhodes and the Kingdom of Pergamum, on the west coast of Asia Minor. But these were only second-tier powers; in addition, they were long-term traditional rivals.[29] In 201 Philip suddenly appeared in the south Aegean with a large new warfleet, and he gained significant success. He captured the great Ptolemaic naval base on the island of Samos (with a large part of the Ptolemaic fleet), as well as Ptolemaic holdings along the coast, including the important city of Miletus. Only the extraordinarily threatening situation as it had developed by summer 201 led to a fragile Rhodian-Pergamene rapproachement. But even in combination the two uneasy allies had great trouble militarily containing Philip. Severe naval fighting ended either in Macedonian victories – after Philip's victory over the Rhodians at Lade, Polybius says, the king should have sailed directly for Egypt (16.10) – or in draws. Philip then invaded the territory of Pergamum, sacking the shrines outside Attalus' capital; Attalus did not dare to come out to face him in battle. Philip then marched off south into Caria, conquering as he went. His army was being provisioned by generals of Antiochus (16.24).[30]

Political science research suggests that smaller states are more prone to 'bandwagon' with larger states than to 'balance' against them in order to protect their interests.[31] Why, then, did Pergamum and

Rhodes not 'bandwagon' with the kings, not only to protect themselves but perhaps to share in spoils from the Ptolemies? Part of the answer has been pointed out by Barry Strauss: within the stern Greek aristocratic culture of honor, bandwagoning (which smacked of 'servility') was more difficult for decision-makers to engage in than it is with modern nation-states. That is: cultural characteristics specific to the Greeks made them instinctively tend towards balancing rather than bandwagoning.[32] Yet the Rhodian-Pergamene rapprochement came about only very late. If it had come earlier, perhaps a larger and more effective coalition of resistance, involving other states, could have been organized; but this was impossible, given the ferocity of local rivalries. Indeed, that Pergamum and Rhodes came to an agreement to work together at all is an indication of the severe nature of the threat these two governments believed they faced by spring 201.[33]

Moreover, in summer 197 the Rhodians came to an agreement with Antiochus III as he was advancing west along the southern coast of Asia Minor: in effect they 'bandwagoned' with him, in return gaining Seleucid acquiesence and even military help in their own expansionist efforts against independent city-states in the region as well as against Ptolemaic holdings there.[34] But by summer 197 Philip V had finally been defeated by Rome, and was no longer a geopolitical factor. This, we are explicitly told, is what allowed the Rhodian rapprochement with Antiochus (Livy 33.20.10); when the Rhodians thought that Antiochus was coming west to join with and aid Philip, they had been ready to do battle with him (Polyb. 18.41a.1, cf. Livy 33.20.2-3).[35] That is: the geopolitical problem for Rhodes was apparently not so much Antiochus, but the prospect of Antiochus and Philip together. Thus the Pergamenes and Rhodians worked together against the kings in 201–197 primarily because they thought the long-term situation was simply too dangerous for a bandwagoning policy – as tempting as that might have been in the short term.[36]

Sometime in the summer of 201, therefore, the governments of Rhodes and of Pergamum decided to turn to outside help. They turned to Rome. The Ptolemaic regime in Alexandria did the same; whether this came about in cooperation with Rhodes and Pergamum, or through an independent decision, is unknown. A bit later the Athenian democracy, itself having come under ferocious attack from Macedonian forces under Philip's generals, followed suit in sending envoys to the Romans.[37] The sending of the embassies by the four Greek states to Rome in 201 appears as an act of strategic desperation. As with the Tlaxcaltecans and the Spanish, and the Ionians and

Athens, the Greek polities in the late 3rd century turned to Rome for aid because under the conditions of 201 BCE. Rome was for these states 'the least threatening great power' (if only because of its distance) – in the face of the actions of far more threatening and far nearer great powers. From the point of view of international-relations theory, the actions of the four Greek states were – under anarchic conditions – a classic geopolitical maneuver.[38]

The government at Rome – the Roman Senate and People – decided to answer the pleas from the Greek states in the affirmative, and to intervene in the eastern Mediterranean: diplomatically at first, but with the prospect of military conflict clear. Most modern scholars of Rome assign this act primarily to Roman aggression, one of a long sequence of aggressions that took Rome from a medium-sized state to a world empire.[39] Without in the least denying the militaristic and diplomatically aggressive nature of Roman culture, this seems to me the result of an introverted historiography – a historiography that concentrates on Rome (and Roman aggression) alone. If one raises ones eyes from Rome itself to look at the broader geopolitical field in which Rome existed, to look at the characteristics of that geopolitical field and who inhabited it, the actions of Rome look somewhat different.[40] Theodor Mommsen (again) saw long ago that Rome in 200 was responding primarily to a precipitous dip in the balance of power among the great Greek states, caused by the foundering of the Ptolemaic regime based in Egypt. It is time to reemphasize Mommsen's insight.[41] Yet the amount of information we possess on the crucial Roman decision of 200 also allows us to apply a 'layered' approach, combining classic international-systems theory with specific aspects of Rome's unit culture, and even the impact of individuals.

The background interstate structure is clear. Rome had survived, at times barely survived, in a highly militarized multipolar anarchy, in good part because it developed a militaristic, bellicose, and diplomatically aggressive unit culture. It could not have survived otherwise: 'States must meet the needs of the political ecosystem or court annihilation.'[42] This is why militarism, bellicosity and assertive diplomacy were characteristic of the Roman Republic, but also of virtually all polities in the ancient Mediterranean (and characteristic too of the relatively disorganized tribes on the periphery). Once such militarized and militaristic cultures were in place, they played their own destructive role in state actions and interactions.[43] Even the strictest of international-systems theorists accept that not only the general type of interstate structure (i.e., anarchy) and the specific system within which states exist (i.e., militarized multipolarity), but also the internal characteristics and cultures of states have a significant impact on state conduct.[44] Yet the focus of the international-systems theorists *is* on the overall environment, and the approach is essentially a sociological approach – whereas in terms of any individual geopolitical event, Richard Ned Lebow has rightly stressed that all the underlying structural, systemic and unit-cultural factors favoring a certain outcome might well be present in a given situation, but absent a specific catalyst of action that outcome may still not occur. An anarchic interstate structure, a militarized multipolar system, and a militaristic and aggressive unit culture are all crucially important, but may not in themselves be enough to explain events. Lebow (2000: 614 – my emphases), also argues that with specific regard to decisions to go to war, one should distinguish between:

> situations in which actors are *actively looking for an excuse for war*, and those in which *the catalyst reshapes the way they think about the situation*, making them more willing than they were previously to consider high-risk options because of the greater perceived costs of inaction.

This perspective is useful in examining the Roman decision of 200 BCE. The question is whether the Roman Senate in 200 was actively looking for an excuse for war, war in the Greek East against the great Hellenistic powers, war anywhere – and whether the arrival of the Greek embassies merely provided that 'excuse.'

If one examines the situation confronting the Roman Republic in 200 BCE, and even stressing the militarism of Roman culture as it had developed by the 3rd century, the answer would appear to be: 'No'. In that year Rome had just emerged victorious, but at enormous cost, over Hannibal and Carthage in the Second Punic War – a life-and-death struggle that had left the state and its people exhausted. The general scale of Livy's census figures suggests that the Roman populace had lost almost half its male citizens since the mid-220s; the low number of citizens by 209 reveals, as the epitomator of Livy says sadly, 'how many men the unfavorable outcome of so many battles had carried off from the Roman People.'[45] Hannibal supposedly boasted that he had destroyed 400 Italian towns and killed 300,000 Italians (App. *Pun.* 134); defining 'town' broadly and including civilian casualties, this may not be an exaggeration.[46] The Romans themselves had contributed to destruction in Italy, retaliating against polities that went over to Carthage. Our sources give the impression that by c. 200 all of Italy was devastated; certainly significant regions were, especially in the south, and we know that much good farmland was for sale (Livy 31.13.6).[47] A fair proportion of the Allies had deserted to Hannibal in his years of victory, and had then been punished by Roman armies scraped together to deal with the crisis; such polities will not have been eager or ready for a new major war. The same holds true even for the Allies who had remained loyal: they too had suffered seriously in the long, grim struggle with Carthage.[48] And there was serious new trouble brewing on the Celtic frontier of Italy in these years, with even another Celtic invasion of central Italy in prospect.[49]

Moreover, although this is a highly contentious question, the weight of the evidence suggests that before 201–200 Roman involvement in and concern about Greek geopolitics had been minimal.[50] Wars against Adriatic pirates in 229 and 219 had led merely to informal friendship with a scattering of widely-separated Greek polities on the far north-west coast of European Greece – nothing more formal.[51] When Philip V of Macedon allied himself with a seemingly victorious Hannibal and began attacking the informal Roman sphere of influence on the Adriatic coast, Rome had then established war alliances with several Greek states in 214–205 (including Aetolia and Pergamum). But Roman war aims were limited to keeping Philip busy in Greece so that he would not join Hannibal in Italy (which was the great Roman fear), and Roman commitments to this war were limited; thus Rome's Aetolian allies were left in the lurch and had to make a separate peace with Philip in 206. The war between Rome and Macedon ended in a stalemate and compromise in 205; Roman forces withdrew to Italy, and there is no reason to think that this peace was insincere on either side.[52]

This suggests that although Rome was as bellicose and diplomatically aggressive and expansionist as any other Hellenistic power, it is unlikely that the Roman decision-making elite was looking for a new war in the Greek East in 201–200. To increase Roman power and influence was of course the general stance of the Senate, 'the imperialism of routine', an attitude common to all Hellenistic states. But Rome was originally indifferent to the hegemonic war that had begun in the East in 202 because (1) the Republic was exhausted by the long and terrible war just concluded with Hannibal and Carthage, and (2) Roman overall interest in the eastern Mediterranean, and Roman concrete interests there, were to this point minimal. Indeed, the *Patres* were still uninformed in these years even about the basic geography of European Greece (see Polyb. 18.11.3–11: winter 198/197).[53] To employ Lebow's terminology, a catalyst was therefore necessary to produce the historical outcome of 200. Without it, Rome was unlikely to have involved itself in the politics of the eastern Mediterranean, because Greek geopolitics were not yet central to the thinking of the Senate.[54] Given the disorganized internal structure of the Roman Senate, an institution of about 300 men with multiple groupings, factions, families and personalities in constant and fluid interaction with each other, it was in fact natural that it tended to avoid thinking about long-range problems. This included the problem in the East caused by the collapse of Ptolemaic Egypt. As a group the *Patres* could be quite efficient in a crisis, but in general they tended just to 'muddle through.'[55]

The catalyst that brought the East to the *Patres'* attention in autumn 201 – the *necessary* catalyst – is clear: the arrival of embassies from several Greek states, warning of Philip and Antiochus and the dangers they posed. To employ Lebow's (2000: 614) terminology again, the Greek embassies reshaped the thinking of the Roman decision-making elite: the Senate suddenly perceived that the costs and risks of inaction in the East were more dangerous than the costs and risks of acting forcefully there. The terminology of Thomas Christensen also provides a useful theoretical perspective on what was occurring: after 207 and especially after 202 the sudden weakness of the most vulnerable significant actor in the state-system (i.e., Ptolemaic Egypt) tempted the radical expansion of its rivals (Macedon and Syria), which in turn sent destabilizing shocks and ripples throughout the entire state-system, shocks and ripples that eventually reached all the way to Rome.[56]

That the embassies were the catalyst of the Roman decision was Polybius' own analysis. When he says that Fortune (*Tyche*) 'alerted the Romans' to the conduct of the kings (15.20.6), he must mean, at the secular level, the action of the Greek embassies – for it was the Greek embassies that drew the attention of the Roman Senate to the events in the East. He repeats this judgment a volume later, depicting Philip, campaigning in southwest Asia Minor in autumn 201, as worried because embassies from Greek states were going to Rome to complain about him (16.24.3).[57]

What exactly did the Greek envoys say that caused such a sea-change among the senators? Probably different envoys said different things, but we have already pointed to the main issue. The tradition is strong that the envoys warned the *Patres* that Philip V and Antiochus III, each of whom was already a formidable king in his own right, already famous commanders with access to great military power, had now combined their forces and become allies; they had a pact to destroy the Ptolemaic state, a project which would increase their power even more; and their ambitions did not stop there.[58] Both the Ptolemaic government (Justin 30.2.8-3-5) and Rhodes (App. *Mac.* 4) are named as warning the Senate of these developments; since both Livy and Justin in turn link the Pergamene embassy at Rome directly with the embassy from Rhodes, we should assume that the envoys of Attalus strongly seconded the envoys of the Rhodians.[59]

The Greek envoys must have made powerful and convincing arguments to persuade the Senate of the danger, for the *Patres* were not fools. One argument which envoys may have employed to frighten the Senate was not only the existence of Antiochus III's large navy but that Philip V's own large navy – newly built – had just shown itself an effective force off Asia Minor in summer 201: this was probably about the time that the envoys were dispatched.[60] The envoys from Alexandria, meanwhile, also warning of the Pact, could point to Philip's seizure of the great Ptolemaic naval base at Samos (summer, 201), occurring in tandem with Antiochus' overland invasion of Ptolemaic Coele Syria, Phoenicia and Palestine, to demonstrate the scale of the combined aggression the Greeks of the East were facing.[61]

Some scholars argue that the alarm evidently caused in the Senate by the news of the Pact between the Kings occurred because the Romans did not understand the limited goals of wars among the Greek states.[62] But, as discussed above, such a benign view of the conduct of polities in the warlike and anarchic Hellenistic system of states is not accurate – not in the East and not in the West. And thus while it has been proposed here that Roman senators in 201 did not know in detail the world of the Greek East, one may nevertheless suggest that the Senate acted because it *did* understand the ruthless principles of the militarized anarchy in which Rome existed, both the local environment and the broader one, and that the *Patres* had a fair idea of what the ultimate consequences might be if great expansion of the power of Philip and/or Antiochus was allowed unchecked.[63]

One other important factor in the eventual decision of the Senate needs to be underlined: the Roman experience of Hannibal. From the Roman perspective, the events occurring in the Greek East were events occurring far away. But Hannibal had inflicted enormous damage on Rome and Italy when he struck at the Republic from bases which also had seemed very far away, in Punic Spain. The terrible war Hannibal had initiated in Italy had only just come to an end in the autumn of 201. After that experience, any warning of an overseas threat was more likely to be taken seriously by the Senate. This is made clear in the speech which Livy attributes to P. Sulpicius Galba (consul in 200) as he seeks to persuade a reluctant Roman popular assembly to vote for war. The assembly had already rejected the proposal of the Senate, on grounds of great war-weariness and the feeling that no immediate threat in the East existed (Livy 31.6.3-9): having just emerged from the terrible struggle with Hannibal, the *populus* was not interested in what was essentially a preventive war. In Galba's speech attempting now to change their minds, there is nothing about the riches of the East which would become available as booty, or about the glory of Empire, or the right of Rome to rule. The theme is purely one of self-defense:

> It seems to me, citizens, that you do not understand the question before you. The question is not whether you will have peace or war, for Philip will not leave that matter open for your decision, seeing that he is preparing a mighty war on land and sea. Rather, the question is whether you are to send your legions across to Macedonia or whether you meet the enemy here in Italy. What a difference that makes, if you never knew it before, you found out during the recent Punic War...So let Macedonia, not Italy, have war; let it be the enemy's farms and cities that are laid waste, not ours! We have already learned from experience...Go to vote, then, with the blessings of the Gods, and ratify what the Senate has proposed (31.7.2-3 and 13-14).[64]

With the example of Hannibal held up in front of them, the weary citizens in the end voted as the Senate wished.

The Romans acted because they felt they could act, and effectively; despite their terrible losses in the war they were a powerful (and victorious) state, and habituated to dominating their environment. But they could not know how powerful they were in relation to the great Greek monarchies; and their experience of the first war with Philip V was not encouraging in this respect.[65] So the Senate and People acted also because they felt vulnerable. This sharp sense of vulnerability is one of the mainsprings of Realist theorizing about the conduct of states in an anarchy. The evidence above on the fragility of even powerful states in the ancient world (pp. 5–6) shows why this sentiment existed, and so strongly.[66] It was on this sense of vulnerability that the Greek envoys at Rome in 201–200 played; and indeed, those envoys were at Rome because *their* states felt very vulnerable. In political science terms, the Greek envoys presented the Senate with a 'worst-case scenario' about the kings.[67] The Senate and a very reluctant popular assembly reacted by attempting to put a stop to the shift in power in the East, a shift which would have meant the emergence of neighbors, or (worse) one neighbor, more powerful and threatening than Hannibal and Carthage had ever been.

Polybius thought it was the natural tendency of any large state to respond affirmatively to pleas for help from weaker polities (24.10.11); and he assumed such pleas for help from weak states were a natural part of the interstate system: in a world without international law, which Polybius knew to be his world (see 5.67–68), where else but to the strong could weak states turn when under threat? In part the tendency of the strong to answer pleas for help no doubt arose from militaristic and aggressive unit cultures (such as that of Rome) – but these actions were also, simultaneously, natural responses to the dangers lurking in an anarchic environment: better to protect the weak than to allow the weak and their cumulative resources to fall into the hands of a potential great-power enemy. Yet the Senate did not respond automatically to every plea for help from a threatened state which it received. The Greek envoys, then, had successfully made their point about the kings.[68]

The Greek embassies sent to Rome were, in turn, part of the response by less powerful units within the Hellenistic system to the power-transition crisis initiated by the faltering of the Ptolemaic Empire. Philip and Antiochus reacted to this collapse of the previously-existing Hellenistic balance of power by fiercely attacking the Ptolemaic possessions beyond Egypt, and (it seems) preparing to attack Egypt itself. Rhodes, Pergamum, Egypt, and Athens mobilized to block Philip and/or Antiochus militarily; but their military efforts had only equivocal success (capped by the tremendous Ptolemaic defeat at Panium in autumn 200). Feeling unable on their own to check the surging power of the kings, these states turned to an outsider, the Roman Republic, to provide crucial help.[69] The decision-making elites in these Greek states must have known that the price in terms of eventual Roman patronage over an artificially-restored Hellenistic balance of power, or even in terms of Roman hegemony, might be high. But faced with Philip and Antiochus (or, worse, Philip *or* Antiochus as sole hegemon), it appears that the consequences of Roman intervention were a cost that these governments were prepared to pay; Rome, after all, was geographically quite distant – a fact which would ameliorate

any subsequent geopolitical situation. The Greeks in 201 may themselves have been thinking only in terms of checking or defeating the
kings, and not consciously in terms of balancing them – for 'balancing'
as a concept is rarely explicit in ancient political literature. But from
this distance, it appears that the Greek states were instinctively seeking
such a 'balance' against the kings – as Greek states historically, habitually, and instinctively had done against any rising power. And they
instinctively recognized that every means of balancing a threat has its
costs.[70]

In fact, Athens, Egypt, Pergamum and Rhodes all substantially
benefited both initially and for quite some time through their decision
to associate with Rome in an attempt to balance Philip and Antiochus.
The Ptolemaic regime was saved from Seleucid invasion by Roman
diplomatic intervention (the same Roman embassy that declared war
on Philip V); Athens was defended from a serious Macedonian assault;
Pergamum and Rhodes avoided destruction or submission to either
Philip or Antiochus, and Rhodes took advantage of the changing
geopolitical situation to increase its mainland territories in 197.[71]
Meanwhile, Roman troops, having defeated Philip and at least momen-
tarily overawed Antiochus, withdrew back to Italy (by 194). Any
Roman dominance in European Greece thus became very indirect, and
certainly far less threatening than the structure of domination which
either Philip or Antiochus would have imposed if their plans of
203/202 had come to full fruition. The policy of bringing in Rome as
an external balancer of the immediately threatening kings seemed to
have worked.

The apparent lesson was not lost. Towards the end of the 190s,
Pergamum and Rhodes again felt threatened by Antiochus, who by
that time had reconquered almost all of the ancestral Seleucid holdings
in Asia Minor.[72] When the Great King (as he now styled himself) followed these conquests by an invasion of European Greece in 192 – an
invasion that occurred despite repeated Roman warnings to stay away,
for the Romans wanted Greece as a Rome-dominated buffer zone
between the Republic and the Seleucid Empire – these states all sided
with Rome again. Even the Macedon of Philip V now sided with Rome
against Antochus. This was not only bandwagoning (though it may
have been that), so much as sheer self-defence against the more immediate and direct threat posed by Antiochus. And once more, this policy
brought rich dividends to those who pursued it: the Romans were
eventually victorious over Antiochus, and expanded the power of their
friends. By 188 Rhodes and Pergamum were each twice as large in

territory as they had been in 201, thanks to Roman rewards to their allies. They were not alone: the Achaean League, in the Peloponnese, which under Roman military pressure changed sides from Philip to Rome in 198, sided with Rome again when Antiochus invaded Greece; the result was that Rome allowed them to conquer all the Peloponnese, thereby fulfilling an Achaean imperial dream that had existed for a century. Philip V, while not particularly happy with the extent of his spoils, expanded his kingdom once more towards the south. And then the Romans once more withdrew all their armies back across the Adriatic to Italy (188 BCE) In the two decades that followed, Roman interaction with the Aegean region was purely diplomatic, and even Roman diplomacy occurred only occasionally; the Greeks were mostly left on their own. Once more, then, the policies of the medium-sized Greek states in following Rome as a perceived external balancer against an immediate threat (this time, the threat posed to them by Antiochus III) appeared to have been successful.[73]

In the long run, of course, the story was different: by c. 140 BCE Roman domination had become fastened irrevocably upon the Greek states of the Aegean. There was a third war between Rome and Macedon (171–168 BCE), a war from which Rome once more emerged victorious and which resulted in the abolition of the Macedonian monarchy and Macedon being divided up into four republics; but Polybius indicates that for the Greeks the choice in this war was not between Rome and freedom, but rather between Roman domination and that of Macedon; few states joined with the Macedonians.[74] Nevertheless, the destruction of Macedon now left Roman power – as Polybius says (1.1) – unchallenged and unchallengeable, i.e., without any potential counterweight. If the Greek states had wished to balance Rome, they had missed their chance (because they were too busy balancing Macedon). Because Roman forces then withdrew once again back to Italy in 167, the full implications of the new geopolitical situation were not totally apparent. It was only later, after the crisis of 148–146 BCE, which witnessed yet another Roman war with the Macedonians and then a war between Rome and the Achaean League, that Roman control over the European Greeks became fully explicit. In Macedon it was institutionalized through direct rule by a Roman governor and a permanent Roman army; in Greece proper it was still exercised only indirectly, through hand-picked Greek aristocratic governments which (however) knew they had to obey.[75]

Looking back at the terrible dangers that had confronted these Greek states from Philip and Antiochus in 201–200, however, statesmen in, (say) 188 would probably have pronounced their action in going to Rome in autumn 201 a success in terms of preserving the Hellenistic system. The price of employing the Romans as external balancers was only paid in the next generation, as the Romans made it increasingly clear that they would allow no peer competitor among the Greeks, nor allow any Greek polity to balance against *them*. But real governments in the real world have to accept the maxim that 'sufficient unto the day is the evil thereof.' This makes balancing a hegemon – and knowing *which* potential hegemon one should concentrate on balancing against, and when – extremely difficult.

One last question might be asked by political scientists. If all the states of the Hellenistic Mediterranean were functionally similar within a Waltzian anarchy, why, then, did the Romans and not one of the Greek monarchies end up as the system hegemon? What explains Rome's exceptional success?

The answer has to do with the fact that Rome's competitors, while no less militaristic, bellicose, and aggressive than Rome itself, were different in structure. Rome faced two sorts of competitors: ordinary city-states, and (eventually) Hellenistic territorial monarchies. City-states were, in political science terms, highly integrated – and in that sense they were robust; but they were small in scale. Thus they were able to mobilize large percentages of their citizen-bodies when engaged in war, but the absolute number of men they could put in the field was relatively small, and the result was that they could be overwhelmed; Carthage is a good example of this.[76] Hellenistic territorial monarchies were, by contrast, much larger than any city-state, but – by contrast – they were not well integrated. They could field much larger initial armies than any city-state (in part these were mercenary armies, funded by tax-money); but because the stability of the monarchical regime depended heavily on the military prestige of the monarch, such states could not afford many defeats. The Seleucid state, with its large percentage of indigenous tax-paying subjects who were not tied strongly to the regime, is a good example of this.[77]

The intentions of Rome in foreign relations were little different from those of other Hellenistic polities. But already by the mid-3rd century Rome was both a territorially large *and* a well-integrated state. In the terminology of Raymond Aron, it thus possessed an enhanced capability regarding both the extent and the intensity of its mobilization of resources. The degree of mobilization of resources of which a state is capable in the face of severe competition from other states, says Aron, depends on the structure of its society.[78] Two of the factors Aron lists as affecting the mobilization of resources are significant for us. First, he stresses the number of citizens in relation to non-citizens.[79] This, as we have noted, was a weakness of most ancient city-states. Second, Aron stresses the solidarity of citizens in the face of the inevitable misfortunes of war. This, as we have noted, was a serious weakness of the great Hellenistic monarchies. The weaknesses and fragility of Rome's rivals and potential rivals in terms of social mobilization in the face of war, combined with Rome's own strengths in these aspects, thus form the keys to Roman success. These were crucial factors affecting first the distribution of power within Italy, then eventually throughout the Mediterranean.[80] As Kenneth Waltz says in a typically stark way: 'States are alike in the tasks they face though not in their ability to perform them.'[81]

The Roman Republic of this period was exceptionally large for an ancient city-state in terms of territorial size and population, but its true uniqueness lay elsewhere, in the entire basis of the state. The prestige of the Senate was sufficient by this period so that the state was not shaken to its core by defeats – though it suffered many of them (see Polyb. 3.116 and 6.58). But more important, Rome after the Latin War of 340–338 BCE had replaced ethnicity and geographical location as the basis of membership in the polity with a ladder of purely legal status groups not tied to either ethnicity or geography: non-Roman allies (the *socii*), halfway citizens (the *cives sine suffragio*, with civil rights), full citizens (*cives* with voting rights). No other ancient city-state ever instituted such a system, because of the ferocity of their exclusiveness. And because the Romans were relatively generous in allowing non-Roman individuals and even (very occasionally) whole non-Roman polities to climb up this status hierarchy from allies to half-citizens to full citizens, Rome gained both an enhanced population and an enhanced capacity to win loyalty, or at least acquiescence.[82]

Of course, one needs to add that the power imbalance between Rome and any one subordinate Italian polity was also eventually enormous, so there was a large stick as well as a large carrot.[83] But it was the Romans' exceptional capacity for inclusion and integration that set them apart. Just as the power imbalance between Rome and its subordinate states was far larger than the power imbalance between (say) Athens and her 5th century allies, so the rewards Rome was culturally and politically capable of dispensing to subordinate polities, in terms of imposed local peace but also in terms of the inclusion of local elites within the Roman State, were much greater than any state in Greece could ever offer.[84] In 214 BCE Philip V himself underlined inclusiveness as a great source of strength for Rome, stressing Roman inclusiveness in a letter to the city of Larissa in Thessaly in which Philip sought to end the bitter hostility of the traditional citizens of Larissa to the new settlers he was attempting to place there. Philip had the insight to acknowledge this source of Roman power – yet he had a difficult time convincing his own subjects to pursue it.[85] Inclusiveness, too, was the Emperor Claudius's own analysis of the source of Roman power when, much later, he looked back on the historical development of the Roman state – but then, as Claudius emphasized, he was (like so many others at Rome) a descendant of immigrants himself.[86]

Theodor Mommsen, as I have already noted, long ago found the source of Rome's exceptional power approximately where I am suggesting: he argued that the Romans came the closest among great ancient Mediterranean polities to creating a unified nation-state, with all its robustness.[87] By the time of Cato the Elder (c. 170 BCE) Romans could conceive of Italy and Rome as a collective but a unified entity, with the Romans and the other Italian peoples having a shared history; this is evident from Cato's famous history of Italy, the *Origines*.[88] But the Roman development of an idea of citizenship divorced from ethnicity and/or geographical location actually went *beyond* the nation-state; and if Roman rule in Italy had not been something different from a nation-state, the Romans would not have been able in due course to take the process of integration that they had invented in Italy much further, to include eventually regions far beyond Italy itself. Yet Mommsen was profoundly right to emphasize the exceptionalism of the Roman achievement, in that Rome succeeded in creating a large and well-integrated polity, at first in central Italy and then in most of Italy. This gave Rome the exceptional advantages in scale of resources, and in control over those resources, which any large integrated state would have in competition against large but fragile dynastic empires, or against small and well-integrated but limited city-states or mere tribal groupings. It was from those exceptional advantages – along with militarism, bellicosity, and diplomatic assertiveness – that Roman hegemony in the Mediterranean emerged.[89]

Notes

1 See the 1539 discussion by Francisco de Vitoria in Lupher (2003: 73–4).
2 On the relevance of the grim Realist analysis of anarchy at least to highly competitive premodern state-systems, see Wohlforth (2001). On the brutal nature of the central American state-system, see Hassig, 1999; Smith, 2001. On the nature of the Classical Greek state-system see the essays in Lebow and Strauss, 1990.

3   On militarism as internal balancing, see Waltz (1979: 168).

4   The classic discussion of Rome's militaristic culture is Harris (1979); on the Roman habit of coercive diplomacy, see Derow (1979).

5   Contra, e.g., Veyne (1975: 795) – who sees Rome as unique in its 'imperialist' stance among the Hellenistic states.

6   On such systems and their impact upon the units within them, see now Mearsheimer (2001: Chapter 2).

7   The groundbreaking and exceptionally influential work here is Harris (1979). See, e.g., Raaflaub (1996), or Campbell (2002).

8   Van Evera (1999: 41–5); cf. Waltz (1979: 95).

9   See the grim set of essays in Neuman 1998, and the comments of Waltz (2000b: 37) on these findings.

10 More than 40 Greek city-states were destroyed in the period of the Peloponnesian War.

11 The trauma of such 'near-death experiences' naturally gave the Roman Senate a suspicious attitude towards the outside world, a willingness to believe in the worst-case scenario.

12 On the theory of 'hegemonic' (system-wide) war to restructure a state-system, see, e.g., Gilpin (1988).

13 On the native regime established in Upper and Middle Egypt, see Holbl (2001: 153–9).

14 The extent of the crisis of the Ptolemies after 207 is often not sufficiently appreciated in modern discussions of this period. But the Hellenistic historian Polybius, writing in the next generation, was perfectly well aware of how severe the Egyptian crisis was and what an enormous impact it had, devoting an entire volume of his *History* (Book 14) to a discussion of it. Unfortunately, this volume is almost entirely lost. But 14.1a and 14.12.1–4 survive, and make clear how extensive and detailed his discussion was; and according to a gloss on the Polybian mss., his account of the crisis within Egypt covered an extraordinary 48 quarto papyrus-sheets. See Walbank (1985: 319 and n. 58).

15 See now Ager (2003: 35–50).

16 Sources on the pact are comparatively numerous for an ancient event: Polybius (first of all): 3.2.8, 15.20, 16.1.8–9 and 24.6; cf. 14.1a.4–5; also: Livy 31.14.5; App. *Mac.* 4 (somewhat confused); Justin 30.2.8, cf. Pomp. Trog. *Prol.* 30; Hieron. *In Dan.* 11.13 (= Porphyry, *FGH* 260 F 45); and John Antioch. Frg. 54 (*FGH* 558 F 54: confused).

17 On this passage see the comments of Walbank (1967: 424).

18 The key phrase in Polybius. 15.20.6 is often wrongly translated, as if Fortune 'raised up the Romans' against the kings – which would be a historical fact, not a causal connection drawn between events in the East and the Roman decision to intervene. Hence some scholars think Polybius does not stress the impact of the Greek envoys to Rome who brought news of the pact: see Errington (1971: 348 and 352). But for the correct translation see Passerini (1931: 182 n. 1), supported by Walbank (1967: 474). There are multiple examples in Polybius of the Greek verb *ephistemi* meaning to 'alert' or 'draw attention to,' or even 'to open someone's eyes concerning,' with sharp change of direction in action following the awakening: 2.61.11; 12.25.k.7; 15.9.3; 23.11.4; 27.9.6; 27.10.2; 38.8.4. See Mauerberger (1961:

coll. 1060-61). There are <u>no</u> other examples of Polybius employing εφιστημι to mean 'to raise up against.' See in detail now Eckstein (2005), stressing the importance of this passage for our conception of what Polybius thought occurred on a systemic level in 200 BC.

19 So Magie (1939: 32–44); Errington (1971: 336–54), cf. Errington (1986: esp. 5 and n. 16).

20 See Dreyer (2003). Original publication: Blumel (2000: 94–6).

21 Polyb. 18.41a.1 (a crucial fragment of a larger narrative); Livy (33.19–20) [reflecting that larger narrative: Briscoe (1973: 2)].

22 On the four embassies, see Warrior (1996).

23 Livy 31.29.4, cf. Livy App. *Mac.* 4.

24 See Badian (1958: 211) denying the tradition, Dorey (1960: 9) defending the tradition and Walbank (1967: 530–3) defending historicity and placing the embassy in 202. Following Badian (1958a): Ferrary (1988: 51 and n. 26). Most recent discussion: Warrior (1996: 84 n. 16), who is neutral on historicity.

25 See Plautus's comic play *Stichus* (490–500, but especially 494) produced in 200 BCE.

26 On the course of the war (little known because of the loss of Polybius), see now Holbl (2001: 134–40).

27 Sources and discussion: Walbank (1940: 114–15).

28 See the famous poem of Alcaeus of Messene to this effect: the only thing left for Philip to conquer is heaven: *Anthologia Palatina* 9.518.

29 On persistent Rhodian-Pergamene rivalry in the Aegean throughout the last half of the 3rd century, see Berthold (1984, chapters 4 and 5); cf. McShane (1964: 96–7 and 117).

30 On the ferocious fighting in the southern Aegean in 201, see Berthold (1984: 102–24).

31 See, e.g., Jones (1994: 229).

32 Strauss (1991: 101–2).

33 As Wohlforth (2002: 102 and 107) has pointed out, a focus on local issues and rivalries is one of the reasons that coalition-building to balance a greater general threat is difficult.

34 For sources and good discussion, see Rawlings (1976).

35 The Livian account of Rhodian actions derives from Polybian material: see Briscoe (1973: 286).

36 Attalus I of Pergamum in particular had a bad relationship with Philip, having already fought one war against him – and losing badly (see Eckstein, 2002) – while on the other side the official policy of the Seleucid dynasty of Antiochus was that the rulers of Pergamum (self-proclaimed 'kings' only since c. 230) were in fact rebels who had seized important Seleucid territory.

37 On the crisis between Athens and Macedon which began in early autumn 201, see Warrior (1996: 37–42); Habicht (1997: 194–7).

38 Cf. Walt (1987). Distance: given the primitive nature of ancient technology and the difficulties of power-projection over distance for any premodern state, it is worth thinking of the actual distances involved (which are large enough as is) as four or five times larger subjectively: see Heather (2005: 25).

39 See, e.g., Harris (1979: 212–18); Derow (2003: 58–9).

40 See now Eckstein (2006).

41   Mommsen (1907: 697–700); cf. Raditsa (1972: 564–5). Contrast Harris (1979: 212–18), or Mandell (1989).

42   Sterling (1974: 336).

43   Rome of course had lost against attacking Celtic tribes in 390 – the result being that the city was burned to the ground. It took the Roman state decades to recover from this catastrophe, which left a permanent mark on Roman political culture. On the Celtic sack of Rome and its long-term impact, see now Williams (2001: 140–84).

44   See, e.g., Waltz (2000b: 24).

45   Livy has the census of 263 BC with some 380,000 male Roman citizens (Epitome – Perioche 16); by the end of the first war of Carthage the number had sunk to some 270,000 citizens (Epitome – Perioche 19) and it was about the same just before the second war (Epitome – Perioche 20). But by 209 Livy gives only some 137,000 citizens (Epitome – Perioche 27). The quote: *Per.* 27. In 201 the figures were substantially higher: 219,000 (Epitome – Perioche 29), but still far less than either 20 or 60 years previously. The precise numbers cannot be trusted, but the trend is clear.

46   Cornell (1996: 103 and n. 22).

47   *Ibid.*, 103–11; cf. also Hopkins (1978: 1–56).

48   Serious defections among the Allies during the Hannibalic War: Lazenby 1998a: 44–5. The condition of the Allies c. 200: Cornell, 1996: 103 and 107.

49   The Celtic threat in 201–200 BC: Eckstein (1987: 54–8).

50   In what follows, I agree in general with the classic analysis of Holleaux (1935: 29–305).

51   For a discussion, see Eckstein (1999).

52   On the circumstances of the peace between Philip and Aetolia in 206 and then between Philip and Rome in 205, see Eckstein (2002: 291–5).

53   Contrast Harris (1979: 217), who presents Rome's 'intrusion' into Greek affairs in 200 as the inevitable step, after victory over Carthage, in the implacable Roman advance.

54   The thesis of Holleaux (1935).

55   On senatorial 'myopia,' see Astin (1968); Veyne (1975: 804–9); Eckstein (1987: xv–xxii).

56   Christensen (1993: 329–30). Needless to say, Christensen does not have Hellenistic history in mind in emphasizing the importance of 'the most vulnerable significant actor' – which makes his paradigm all the more interesting.

57   In Livy's Latin tradition (31.1–7), Rome acts in 200 mostly to aid threatened Greek 'friends.' This image of an altruistic Rome is, obviously, edifying propaganda, and even Livy knows it is not the whole story, for Livy 31.7 shows that the Romans also acted to protect themselves from possible long-term attack from the East (see below).

58   Livy 31.2.1; Justin 30.3.5; see Briscoe (1973: 43).

59   See Gera (1998: 62, n. 9).

60   See Griffith (1935: 6–9) who notes that the envoys, to arrive in Rome in the autumn, would have been dispatched while the naval fighting in the Aegean was at its height. The Senate believed that sea-power had been critical a decade earlier to prevent Philip from coming to Italy (*ibid.*, 8–9 and 12–13).

61   Griffith (1935: 6).

62 So Griffith (1935: 6); Magie (1939: 42–3); Errington (1971: esp. 352–4).

63 In terms of an understanding of the harshness of the Hellenistic system, note that Polybius did not expect his primarily Greek readership to find the pact between the kings to destroy the Ptolemies unbelievable: see Austin (1986: 457).

64 On the authentic tradition on which this speech is probably based, see discussion in Briscoe (1973: 20–2).

65 P. Sulpicius Galba, the consul who gave the speech favoring war, had commanded against Philip between 210 and 207, and had not accomplished much; nor did he do very well in the actual fighting that occurred under his command in the new war (in 200–199).

66 This sense of vulnerability is strikingly absent from the international-systems Constructivists, writing mostly in the assumed (indeed, unconsciously assumed) total safety of the United States in the 1990s – and proposing that the main problem with the international system is bad discourse (i.e., words).

67 'The worst-case scenario' and its place in Realist thinking about state decision-making under anarchy: see, e.g., Morgenthau (1978: 208); Van Evera (1998: 13–14). Note that like Hannibal himself (Polyb. 3.8–11), both Philip V and Antiochus III consciously modeled themselves on the world-conquering Alexander the Great: see Walbank (1993).

68 In 264 the Senate hesitated long over the pleas of the Mamertines (Polyb. 1.10.1–11.2); it refused the request of the city of Utica in 240 to come under Roman protecton against Carthage (1.83.11), and the first request of the mercenaries on Sardinia (ibid.); in the 230s it long ignored the Italian merchants subject to Illyrian piracy (Polyb. 2.8.3); it long refused the pleas of Saguntum for help against the rising power of Carthage in Spain (3.15.1). We are, as usual, speaking of a trend.

69 The Athenians in autumn 201 also sent an embassy to Alexandria to ask for aid against Philip. Ptolemy V's government, faced with Antiochus, could provide only vague promises; meanwhile they sent a new embassy to Rome, on behalf of the Athenians (Livy 31.9.1–5; indirectly confirmed by the 'Cephisodorus Inscription,' first published by Meritt, 1936).

70 'Instinctive balancing' by the less powerful Greek states in 201–200: see Schmitt (1974: 83–4). Relative absence of explicit 'balancing' in Greco-Roman thought: see Wight (1977: 24); cf. Mommsen (1907: 790). The calculations of the Rhodians: Berthold (1984: 122–4).

71 On the beneficial impact of the Roman embassy (arriving in Syria in the autumn of 200) in preventing a Seleucid invasion of Egypt, see Lampela (1998: 97–8). On the beneficial impact of the Roman association on the fortunes of Rhodes, see Rawson, 1986. On the beneficial impact on the fortunes of Pergamum, see McShane (1964: 130–1). On the beneficial impact on the fortunes of Athens, see Habicht (1997: 194–204).

72 On Antiochus' extensive conquests in Asia Minor in the 190s, see Ma (2000/2002).

73 On Rhodian gains after the Syrian War, see Berthold (1984: 162–6). On Pergamene gains, see McShane (1964: 143–54). On Achaean gains, see Gruen (1984: 462–75). Increase in the prestige of Athens, an ally of Rome in

this war too: Habicht (1997: 204–19). Antiochus' threat to Macedon: see Walbank (1940: 200–1); Grainger (2002: 225).

74 Full discussion of this Greek attitude and the historical reasons for it: Walbank (2002).

75 Discussion in Kallet-Marx (1995: 11–96).

76 On Carthage, see Ameling (1993). For the example of Tarentum, the major Greek city-state of southern Italy, see Eckstein (2006: Chap. 5).

77 On the poor relations between the Greco-Macedonian military and administrative elite and the indigenous populations within the Seleucid realm, see the comments of Billows (1995: 20–3 and 56).

78 Aron (1973: 51); reemphasized by Rosen (2003: 215–16).

79 Aron 1973: 51.

80 Varied state capacities to mobilize internal resources, and the impact on state power in the interstate world: Aron (1973: 46–7, 50–3, and 131). This type of analysis has recently been employed in a series of important historical case studies: Herf (1990); Christiansen (1996); Friedberg (2000).

81 Waltz (1979: 96).

82 See Strauss (1997: 134).

83 *Ibid.*

84 *Ibid.*

85 *Sylloge Inscriptionum Graecarum* 3: 543, esp. lines 26–9.

86 *Inscriptiones Latinae Selectae* 212; cf. Tacitus *Annals of Imperial Rome* (11.24) – a speech of 48 AD advocating the admission of Romanized Gallic leaders from beyond the Alps into the Senate. The emperor was a descendant of the Sabine Atta Clausus, who migrated with his dependents to Rome c. 500 BC.

87 See Mommsen (1907: 412–30, esp. 428–30; cf. 451–2).

88 See Williams (2001: 95–8).

89 On the inherent advantages of large and well-integrated states (in our age, nation-states) in competition against these other forms of states, see Doyle (1986: 34–47).

5
The Forest and the King of Beasts: Hierarchy and Opposition in Ancient India (c. 600–232 BCE)

William J. Brenner

> A king who thus properly fulfills his duties to maintain justice should try to take possession of countries that he has not yet possessed and should protect those that he has. When he has thoroughly settled the country and built forts in accordance with the teaching, he should constantly make the utmost effort to pull out the thorns.
>
> — *The Laws of Manu*

Introduction: History and hierarchy in ancient India

Discussions of hierarchy in ancient India most often focus on social stratification. If there is a timeless pattern in India, this view holds, it is the caste system and its manifold divisions and patterns of social interaction. The understanding of hierarchy and structure as a reflection of the cleavages of caste, and its devaluing of territory and undermining of temporal rule is exemplified in title of Louis Dumont's ethnographic treatment of Indian society, *Homo Hierarchicus* (Dumont, 1990; see Inden, 1990: 152–3). That the social order of caste necessarily dominates considerations of political order, and its impeding of what custom has understood as a state or a state-system, finds it way into examinations of an 'international' system in the Indian context. Since the treatments of caste and of 'Hindu India' emphasize the permanence of this social structure, the presence of a states-system, let alone a balance of power, would be precluded.[1]

Nicholas Dirks attributes the interpretation of the subservient position of the political leaders to colonialism, and asserts that 'Kings were not inferior to Brahmans; the political domain was not encompassed by the religious domain' (1989: 75; 1992: 59). He continues, 'State

99

forms, while not fully assimilable to Western categories of the state, were powerful components of Indian civilization' (1992: 59). More accurately, the relationship of the Kshatriya varna (a broad caste category) to the Brahmans was one of interdependence. Indeed, the root of Kshatriya itself means 'power' (Stein, 1998: 56). Removing the predominating emphasis on social stratification allows for the examination of patterns of political interaction which can be understood by employing an international system framework.

While the empirical base of ancient India is fertile, it is also unruly, as resistant to ordered understanding and mastery as its inhabitants and environments have been. The evidentiary base is fragmentary and conflicting, preventing a neat, coherent narrative concerning the actors and interactions in what can be understood in terms of a system. The moralistic purposes of the Brahmanic and Buddhist texts should prevent uncritical application of the historical evidence they contain, though they may contain valuable clues. Historians have made exhaustive efforts to make sense of this context through textual interpretation, as well as through archeological and numismatic evidence. While these accounts are on the whole reliable, the secondary source material is also subject to occasional biases which litter Indian historiography.[2]

One of the most cited sources of balancing in the ancient Indian context is the *Arthasastra* (the 'Science of Politics') by Kautilya, who was probably a Brahman and a minister to Chandragupta Maurya, founder of the Mauryan Empire (c. 321–232 BCE).[3] As a mirror of princes text, the Arthasastra has both didactic and descriptive elements. Modern international relations scholars tend to focus on one of Kautilya's prescriptive concepts, the *mandala* framework, also known as the 'circle of kings' or 'circle of enemies.'[4] This abstract framework, perhaps derived through historical experience, presents the practice of statecraft as largely the function of spatial adjacency (N.N. Law, 1920: vi). Those states, or polities, that are closest to the kingdom are enemies, the next ring potential allies, and so on. The idealized concentric circles of the mandala represent the equilibrium and balance sought, though the ultimate goal of hegemony, and not equilibrium, can be presumed.[5]

Beyond the Arthasastra we see evidence not only of domination and balancing, but also co-binding and hiding, with geography and variation in government type and unit structure playing clear roles. The highly differentiated topography of the Subcontinent presented a physical context that allowed for forms of resistance to hierarchy that were an alternative to balancing, some of which were ultimately more effective than balancing in resisting hegemony. In the period under examination, from the emergence of territorial based polities around 600 BCE to the decline of the empire of Ashoka (c. 232 BCE), there is evidence of balancing and also of other modes of opposition to hierarchy.

When the opposition came from states with a republican form of government, the key behavior was co-binding, a distinct form of coalescence developed by small ancient republics. When the opposition came from 'forest polities,' embedded, autonomous units, the dominant strategy was a mixture of hiding and raiding dependent on the dense forest topography. Decreasing the emphasis on similarity of unit structure and increasing focus on functional similarities, it is argued, presents the opportunity to understand interaction among structurally dissimilar units in a systems framework. This consideration of different unit types then demonstrates the limits of the neorealist assertion that emulation and socialization are necessary outcomes in international systems.

This chapter begins with a brief treatment of the state of nature and the emergent state-system in ancient India. This provides both a context and set of clues as to the prevailing modes of behavior through an examination of ideals. The next section examines the period through the balance-of-power framework, focusing on like units without respect to mode of governance. The following section adds depth to this analysis by outlining some of the tenets of republican security theory and applying them to republican polities of the period. This discussion highlights particular strategies of opposition to domination associated with this government type, especially the strategy of co-binding. The last section emphasizes the connection between topography, unit structure, emulation, and the conception of an international system. With an appreciation of each of these approaches, the full dimensions of opposition to hierarchy in this historical context is revealed. In examining the diverse range of forms of potentially violent opposition to hegemony, the study infuses the empirical base and begins to refine existing theoretical frameworks in study of international relations, steps that have become especially important since the attacks of September 11.

State of nature and state-system in ancient India

Conceptions of the state of nature can be found in the various religious traditions of ancient India, presenting one set of referents in determining the relevant range of political forms and behaviors. The Vedic conception of kingship and the associated state of nature arises from, and can be understood in the context of, narratives of divine origin and ordination. 'According to the Brahmana canonists the discipline of the life of the householder under the protection of the state is necessary for the attainment' of the ends of life, virtue, wealth, pleasure, and liberation (Ghoshal, 1959: 10). This understanding of divine ordination of kings complements the emphasis on the social dominance of the Brahmans. The social order is a reflection of the divine order, which seeped into the earlier understanding of the state and potential states-system in ancient India.

Another characterization of the state of nature is associated with the role of political authority in perpetuating and preserving *dharma*. Dharma can be understood as 'the eternal and necessary moral law, the code of righteousness; the term is used to denote both truth and righteous conduct' (Drekmeier, 1962: 8). The role of political authority includes preserving the conditions under which dharma can be realized: '[*Danda*] the power of sanction and coercion [was] the means, dharma the end.' Laws were god-given with the Brahmans as its custodians, the secular rulers its protectors. The danda functions to 'ensure compliance with dharma; though dharma depends on danda, dharma is the higher power,' which underscores the interdependence of the Brahman and Kshatriya varnas (Drekmeier, 1962: 10). The restraining power of the king is necessary to avoid life under *matsyanyaya*, the 'law of the fishes' with the 'greater fish eating the smaller' (see Ghoshal, 1959: 373). This condition of society in the absence of danda is one of aggression and injustice (Stein, 1998: 62). The idealized alternative is a universal ruler 'possessed of the whole earth bordered by the ocean' (Singh, 1965: 137). Another characterization of the state of nature highlights this predilection for hierarchy: 'the earth without a king is like the forest without the king of beasts' (Ghoshal, 1959: 391).

Alternative accounts of the state of nature and rule, more amenable to republican (or at least elective) forms of government, can be found in Buddhist cosmology. According to the Pali Canon, there is a pristine state of nature which is fouled by the acquisition of private property and the acquisitiveness and strife that follows. Thereafter, 'beings gather together and, lamenting the appearance of the four evils [theft, censure, lying and violence] decide to select a person ... who should censure that which should rightly be censured ... and they agree to give him in return a portion of their rice....' This individual is referred to by three phrases, one of which is *Mahasammata* – 'one who is chosen by the multitude' (Ghoshal, 1959: 63). It should be noted, however, that while the Buddha had an affinity for republican forms of government, he sought primarily to affect society from the outside in order to ameliorate its ills, in effect 'contracting out' of society (Warder, 1970: 31). This tradition of excepting oneself from society, for good or ill, may provide a cultural referent to an alternate form of opposition to hierarchy, one particularly relevant to the Indian historical context.

Though there is some ambiguity about how state-like the various political forms were in ancient India, the makings of a states-system are evident by the 6th century BCE, in the sense of sovereign entities engaged in increasing levels of interaction, and eventually transitioning from a condition of anarchy to a system-wide hierarchy. Distinct functionally similar units can be identified as comprising a system, and the text of the Arthasastra betrays a clear preoccupation with territoriality. This territoriality represents a shift: according to R.S. Sharma, polities (*ganas*) in the Rig Vedic period 'seem to be nomadic and migratory,' while 'the post-Vedic ganas are described as settled on fixed territory' (R.S. Sharma, 1968: 115). Broader population growth and settlement patterns between roughly 1000 and 500 BCE began to erase the natural boundaries presented by space, and 'underdeveloped areas no longer acted as buffer zones between emerging states, preventing neither the outbreak of hostilities nor the absorption of weaker polities in more powerful ones' (Erdosy, 1995: 110). The ephemeral nature of sovereignty was matched by as yet unattainable ambitions to universal rule. In the *Vishnu Purana* the Earth mocks these rulers, urging them to drop their pretensions, laughing at and pitying the petty kings (Embree, 1977: 260).

It is in this post-Vedic period that we see the emergence of a system from what had been a conflict prone but unsettled mix of political forms to a system of territorial entities with administrative structures that allowed the absorption of rivals and centralization of power (Erdosy, 1995: 120). From state of nature to state-system, the stage is set for a competition for domination and efforts to oppose it. While focusing on an early period in history presents evidentiary limitations, that we can trace the emergence of a system and the interaction of its units from their origination presents a significant advantage in assessing certain assumptions central to neorealism, particularly emulation and its corollary socialization. Buzan, Jones and Little note that emulation should not be expected in circumstances where a condition of low interaction capacity provides no compulsion for units to conform (1993: 74–5). Tracing the interaction of polities from a pre-systemic condition to a full system allows us to see if the neorealist assumption of structurally induced unit likeness holds.

The 'sixteen powers,' the rise of the Magadha and the advent of Empire

This account begins with what have been described as 'pre-state political formations' located in north of the subcontinent, which 'evolved from what are often referred to as "tribal kingdoms"' around 600 BCE (Stein, 1998: 59–60; see Thapar, 1966: 50). At the time of the Buddha (c. 500 BCE), the system was composed of 16 major states which had 'many different types of government, in particular some were monarchies, others republics.' These 'states were frequently at war, and several of them sought universal hegemony' (Warder, 1970: 29).

Historians Hermann Kulke and Dieter Rothermund provide a useful breakdown of the transformation into three phases (1998: 55). The first phase 'was characterized by the transition of the small semi-nomadic tribes (*jana*) of the period of Vedic migration to a large number of tribal principalities of a definite area (*janapada*).' A commonly used term for these polities is *mahajanapada*, meaning 'great community' (Stein, 1998: 59). While these polities retained their tribal names, increasingly the ties were based more on social and economic ties than kinship bonds (Keay, 2000: 50). The 'sixteen mahajanapadas' are discussed in the Buddhist and Jain texts, and though the identities of the states differ between the two, each has the number of major states as 16 (Raychaudhuri, 1997: 85).

Elements of an international system or states-system can be discerned: sovereign, functionally similar, like units, interacting under anarchy. This defines the second phase, competition among the mahajanapadas, which ends in the third phase, in which one unit (Magadha) 'annexed a few major principalities and established hegemony over the others' (Kulke and Rothermund, 1998: 55). Sources identify one important unit among the 16 to be the Vajjian Confederacy, of which the Licchavi and Videha republics were the dominant members (J.P. Sharma, 1968: 169).[6] Indeed the Vajjian Confederacy and the Licchavis are often used interchangeably as labels for the unit. One account represents the Vajjian Confederacy as a 'state' as well as a 'union of several clans' and its treatment as a corporate actor fits with a traditional account of balancing (Majumdar, *et al.*, 1953: 56). See Map 5.1 for the approximate location of these actors.

There are conflicting accounts of what has been termed the 'rise of the Magadha.' Magadha was one of the kingdoms which ascended in power, along with the kingdoms of Avanti, Vatsa, and Kosala. These kingdoms (as distinguished from their republican counterparts), grew 'more powerful than the rest' and followed a 'policy of expansion and aggrandizement at the expense of their neighbors' (Majumdar, *et al.*, 1953: 57). Of these, the kingdom of Magadha ultimately prevailed to establish paramountcy in a struggle with the major and minor powers, gaining 'imperial status' and centralizing control over the region, and then transforming into the Mauryan Empire (Sandhu, 2000: 164). Concerning the 'rise' of the Magadha, and the imposition of a hegemony, material advantages have been noted, including geography and natural resources. Magadha is characterized by one source as a 'compact kingdom protected on all sides by hills,' gifted with 'rich soil' and 'gold-bearing streams' (Majumdar, *et al.*, 1953: 59). The emergence of the polities in the eastern Gangetic plain, and the rise of the mahajanapadas has been attributed by some historians to the introduction of iron implements in 7th century BCE, 'which enabled the people to clear the jungle and

Map 5.1 Northeast Indian Kingdoms and Republics, c. 600–450 BCE

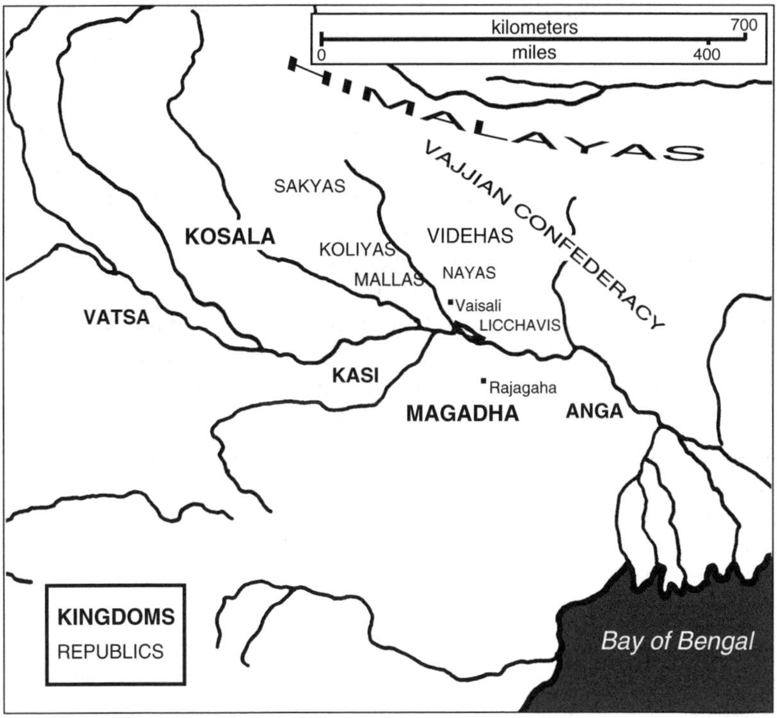

Sources: K. Schmidt, J.P. Sharma

reclaim fertile land.' While discounting the broad material, economic bases as an explanation for the differential development of the rival polities, Kulke and Rothermund do emphasize the important role of iron: 'it seems that … iron was mostly used for the making of weapons and Magadha may have had a strategic advantage due to its access to the deposits of iron ore….' (Kulke and Rothermund, 1998: 55–6).

The expansion of Magadha began in the latter half of the 6th century BCE, under its ruler Bimbisara, with the annexation of Anga, a kingdom, and 'several smaller neighboring republics' (Sandhu, 2000: 166). Kulke and Rothermund state that given its proximity to the iron deposits and trade routes, it was 'no accident' that Anga was targeted (1998: 56). Bimbisara is also said to have entered into matrimonial alliances with other powers, including the Kosalas. Ajatasattu, the son of Bimbisara, continued the conquest and annexation. The Kosalas were separated geographically from the Licchavis and Videhas by the Sakyas, Mallas, and other republican polities. The Kosalan king Vidudabha, sought the destruction of the Sakya republic. Accounts of the Kosalan king's motives vary, but 'the only reliable fact is that Vidudabha conquered and absorbed the Sakyas,' in spite of 'strong opposition from the side of the sturdy Sakyas, … [in which] there was severe fighting and great loss of life' (J.P. Sharma, 1968: 203–5).

Apparently around the same time, Ajatasattu of Magadha was at war with the 'the Licchavis and their Vajjian [republican] confederates,' though the connection between these struggles is not clear (J.P. Sharma, 1968: 94). Sources indicate that Kosala also fought as 'part of a common movement directed against the establishment of the hegemony of Magadha,' and one has Ajatasattu suffering a defeat at the hands of the Kosalas (Raychaudhuri, 1997: 188; Majumdar, *et al.*, 1953: 59; Kulke and Rothermund, 1998: 54). Kasi, which had a long history of warfare with Kosala, was united with Kosala (B.C. Law, 1973: 127). Expansion did not save Kosala, however: while the sequence of events is unclear, 'when the curtain rises again, Kosala has been absorbed into Magadha' (Rhys Davids, 1935: 182).

The conflict between the Magadha and the Vajjians (or Licchavis) was a major conflict between the two strongest actors in the system. The range of explanations as to the cause of the conflict, from psychological to systemic, and from a contest over resources to a battle of distinct and necessarily antagonistic domestic political systems, resonates with some prevailing narratives in international relations theory (See J.P. Sharma, 1968: 132–4). One account in the Jain literature ties the conflict to a mineral mine on the boundary between the territories, while another from the Pali texts indicates that Ajatasattu 'was jealous of the [Vajjian]-Licchavis of Vaisali on account of their national solidarity and numerical strength.' (B.C. Law, 1973: 204). Another infers resentment on the part of the Magadhan rulers, of 'deep rooted hatred' of the Confederacy due to past humiliations.[7] There is also evidence of balancing behavior: shifting alliances, and examples of counter-hegemonic coalitions. More generally, the Arthasastra can provide some indication that geographic counterpoise had some currency in ancient Indian statecraft. We can also recognize, as Doyle notes concerning the balance-of-power system of 18th century Europe, that if there was a system it did not do much to provide its members with security or to prevent the rise of a predominant power (1997: 193).

As an example of balancing and alliance behavior, Sharma notes that according to Jain sources 'the Licchavis were on good terms with the Mallas and the tribal [kingdoms] of Kasi and Kosala.' He continues that 'these four are always referred to as a group in the Prakrit texts,...' and this supports the contention that 'the Licchavis actually did form a league together with these peoples to face common dangers during troubled periods' (J.P. Sharma, 1968: 121). Another account has Ajatasattu facing the 'combined republics' who were 'a powerful opponent with a large reserve of well-trained warriors at their disposal.' According to this, the 'republics realized that [Ajatasattu] was a threat to them all and that the independence of the whole of eastern India was threatened.' Consequently, the 'republican chiefs assembled and resolved to stand united against [Ajatasattu] and resolutely oppose him' (Sandhu, 2000: 167–8). Balancing thus apparently occurred independent of government type.

The combined strength of the Vajjians meant that Magadha could not defeat them militarily, and required 'diplomacy and intrigues' to divide the Licchavi-led Confederacy (J.P. Sharma, 1968: 132). The conflict is referred to as a protracted war, but there is also mention of use of a 'proxy campaign' which 'took three years to implement and become effective.' This source emphasizes an effort to 'create dissension among the various classes of the land...' and turn the Licchavis (and here the distinction between this designation and the Vajjian Confederacy is confusing) 'into a divided society with internecine conflicts and loss of social cohesion' (Sandhu, 2000: 167). Another source indicates that it took ten years for the Vajjians to be overcome (J.P. Sharma, 1968: 132).

What is suggested by the sources was a combination of undermining the Confederacy, followed by a military defeat. According to one source, 'the [Licchavis] were in such disarray that they could not even decide as to who should advance to confront the enemy approaching the capital' (Sandhu, 2000: 167). Whether the emphasis was on dividing the Confederacy, or undermining the individual units is unclear. More clear is the disappearance of the Vajjian Confederacy, though the Licchavi republic, having submitted to the Magadhan suzerainty, seems to have survived and reappears in the historical record following the fall of the Mauryan Empire (J.P. Sharma, 1968: 134–5).

The period following the reign of Ajatasattu and the rise of Magadha is characterized by 'grave uncertainty' (Keay, 2000: 69). Of the series of successors, not much is known. One, Shishunaga, defeated the Prayota dynasty of Avanti, removing a major threat to the Magadha (Kulke and Rothermund, 1998: 56). Following a series of intrigues, Mahapadma, the founder of the Nanda dynasty emerged. The Nanda dynasty consolidated control over most of the northern and central subcontinent. The successors of Mahapadma, his sons, were eventually overthrown by Chandragupta Maurya (c. 321 BCE).

The circumstances which led to Chandragupta Maurya's accession are unclear. Once in power, the Mauryan ruler consolidated control over the territories once occupied by Alexander in the northwest, and Bindusara (son of Chandragupta Maurya) extended the empire into the south. Scholars have presented the Arthasastra as a fairly accurate description of the Mauryan Empire's administration, with the mandala balancing framework derived from the period of the mahajanapadas (Kulke and Rothermund, 1998: 60). The Arthasastra sets out the qualities of a king, and the requirements for the effective administration of empire, including extensive instructions on the employment of spies. These precepts are directed at both external enemies (which remain abstract) as well as the internal administration of empire. Interestingly, and relevant to later discussion, Kulke and Rothermund make the observation that Kautilya actually 'paid less attention to clandestine activities in the enemy's territory than to the elimination of "thorns" in the king's own country' (1998: 61).

The empirical record improves somewhat with the record of the rule of Ashoka (268–232 BCE). The rule of Ashoka is elevated in Indian political history as a period of unity, enhanced by Ashoka's conversion to Buddhism, a precursor to the association of pacifism with Indian identity (one very much at odds with the course of Indian political history). The conversion purportedly took place following the conquest of Kalinga. The slaughter so shocked the emperor, that he proclaimed in one of the famous rock edicts (which provide the evidentiary base) that further conquest would be made only in spiritual terms. The events are said to have triggered Ashoka's conversion to Buddhism and led to the establishment of an 'empire of dharma,' where righteousness and not violence would be the main source of influence (Wink, 1984: 275).

It is uncertain how far Ashoka's rule actually extended, however. The rock edicts provide an account of administration of Ashoka's empire, in which the geographic area of the former mahajanapadas remained under direct rule while outlying areas were ruled by princes, with these provinces divided into districts. To Kulke and Rothermund (1998: 66), this and other evidence about 'the spatial extension of the Maurya empire [indicates] its "All-India" dimensions and that it marked the apex of the process of state formation which had started in the sixth century BC.' André Wink, in contrast, asserts that a relatively 'centralized imperial administration may have existed in a limited region around the Maurya capital,' but that 'it cannot be shown that there was anything like imperial-political unification of the Indian peninsula in [Ashoka's] time....' (1984: 275). The discrepancy in characterizations of the extent and unity of Ashoka's reign highlights the problems presented by the fragmentary evidentiary base. The empire of Ashoka can be, and has been, portrayed as a golden age of imperial unity under enlightened rule, and this interpretation can just as readily be dismissed as a founding myth of modern India.

The evidence, unfortunately, also does not provide a clear account of the decline of the Mauryan Empire. Accepting it as a extensive, centrally controlled empire, though, the successors to Ashoka could not maintain control of the provinces, culminating in the assassination of the last Mauryan emperor, Brihadratha, by the general Pushyamitra Shunga in 185 BCE. Among the many factors cited in the decline of Mauryan Empire are succession after Ashoka and differential rates of economic development among cities and rural areas and different regions (Thapar, 1997: 211–12). Others have pointed to the fecklessness of the dharma in maintaining a vast far-flung empire.[8] Another view emphasizes the challenges presented to any rule over the geographic extent of the Subcontinent (Seneviratne, 1981: 325). Graham Chapman writes: 'The empire of this period, given the distribution of the population, the wild jungles, the difficulty of transport particularly north to south, must be the exception to be explained, not the norm whose absence requires explanation' (Chapman, 2000: 21). Whatever the course of his empire and its fall, the lion pillar of Ashoka remains as an emblem of India; though throughout the course of Indian history the forest, as will be discussed below, has not been accommodating to the king of beasts.

Fish story: The ancient Indian republics and republican security theory

While the application of the balance-of-power framework, irrespective of the units' government type, provides some insight into counter-hegemonic strategies, obscured is the significance of republicanism and republics as political forms. Daniel Deudney has provided a correction of the long ignored traditions associated with republican models of restraint of power, and their foundational role in both the realist and liberal traditions in international relations (Deudney, 2007). Overlooking distinctions in government type occludes potential differences in unit behavior, in this case the reaction to attempts to achieve hegemony.

While the evidence on the subject is fragmentary, sometimes suspect, and usually difficult to interpret, it is possible to assess some aspects of Deudney's republican security theory for the ancient Indian case. J.P. Sharma is the author of the most comprehensive and sober account of the ancient Indian republics.[9] He notes that the 'existence of these republican states in the 6th century BCE in northeastern India was ... by no means a bolt from the blue, but rather was the result of gradual progress with a long history behind it, going back at least to the days when the earliest hymns of the [Rig] Veda were chanted.' (J.P. Sharma, 1968: 62). There was, however, a break in that evolution, as: 'It is not unlikely that some of the early Vedic aristocracies had become monarchies while others moved eastward in order to retain their individual freedom and principles of popular government' (J.P. Sharma, 1968: 5).

The evolution of autocratic governments compelled movement to another geographic area, where the evolution of these latter republican forms proceeded. According to one source, the republics tended to have settled in the hills, while the monarchies settled in the lowlands. The larger states became more concentrated in power, and the republics one by one were absorbed (Schmidt, 1995: 16). Rather than disappearing, many of these republics seem to be hiding, advancing their political forms while nestled in protective enclaves, for a time resisting the advances of the more autocratic kingdoms until succumbing to conquest: the big fish eats the little fish.

The first of these 'little fish' was the Sakya republic. While there have been doubts expressed about the sovereignty of the Sakyas, according to J.P. Sharma: 'the Sakyas were an independent republican tribe, though bordering on the Kosalan kingdom, was distinct from it' (182). Similar controversy surrounds the designation of the polity as a republic. After surveying the contending arguments, however, Sharma concludes that 'there is little doubt that the Sakyan state was a non-monarchical political community' (189). Concerning the topography in which the Sakyas were settled, sources give reference 'to the great forest and hills in connection to the Sakyan capital, [and] suggest that their territory stretched right into the Himalayas and that there was forest north of it' (J.P. Sharma, 1968: 195). While the Sakyas had some measure of protection given their location, to the west and south was the kingdom of Kosala, which ultimately annexed the territory, and if the reports are to be taken as fact, the Sakyas were massacred at the hands of Vidudabha and their capital 'razed to the ground' (J.P. Sharma, 1968: 182).

While the Sakya republic was the first of these republics to be absorbed, the Licchavis lasted the longest and resisted the Magadha in the form of the Vajjian Confederacy. The durability of the Licchavis may be, though tentatively, tied to a number of factors. The Licchavis formed a government 'in which neither a single ruler, nor even a few, but a considerable portion of the population was vested with the final power and ultimate authority of the state.' It is this representation, the government composed of Kshatriyas and not fully democratic in nature, as such 'suggests a picture not unlike Athens in her heyday or Rome during her Republican period' (J.P. Sharma, 1968: 98–9).

Part of the Licchavis' strength and durability we may attribute to its size. In terms of area it was the largest of the republics. According to Sharma, it compares to Sparta, the largest Greek polis (3,360 square miles). The population in the area under the control of the Licchavis 'might have been in the region of 200,000–300,000'. The Licchavi territory was bounded by mountains in the north, and rivers in the south, east, and west. The area occupied by the 'United Vajjis' included the territory of the Licchavis in the southwest corner, the Videhas in the north, and the Nayas around northern fringes of Vaisali, the Licchavi capital. This collocation of the republics is significant in our assessment of the relative durability of the Licchavis, as well as the nature of the Vajjian Confederacy (J.P. Sharma, 1968: 97, 100, 103).

This interpretation has the Vajjian Confederacy as a more or less permanent association of republics. J.P. Sharma writes that the Vajjian Confederacy was 'the most powerful republican Confederacy,' but there was no fixed number of members (1968: 84, 94). Indeed, according to evidence from the Jaina scriptures, it 'is not improbable that some Kasi-Kosalan chiefs threw in their lot with the Confederacy after Vidudabha came to power...,' widening participation in the association to kingdoms – though the membership of the Confederacy is in other sources limited to republics (J.P. Sharma, 1968: 84). It seems accurate then to label the Vajjian Confederacy as a security confederation, and possibly, an aspiration to 'permanence and closeness and by locking together of their exercise of certain fundamental powers' (Lister, 1999: 3).

Ancient republics in the midst of harsh security environments, whether in India or elsewhere, faced a dilemma. In order to maintain their governance based on representation and restraint of power, they were required to maintain a relatively small size (due to the communications requirements of a deliberative polity). Deudney (2007) outlines what he identifies as the 'iron laws of polis republicanism.' The first law concerns the small size of republics and its consequences (either expansion or conquest and incorporation), and the second law concerns the disintegration of power restraints as republics grow in size. These propositions are supported by the ancient Indian evidence: most non-monarchies of the Vedic era were transformed into monarchies; while the Buddhist-era republics were ultimately conquered by them.

The potential foreign policy practices outlined by Deudney (hiding, balancing, dominating, and co-binding) also provide a useful typology for examining the ancient Indian republics. Frequent mentions of foothills, rivers, and forests in association with the geographic locations of these republics, and the example of the eastward migration of the peoples of the Vedic era non-monarchical polities, suggest the use of topographic barriers to insulate the republics from invasion. Concerning balancing, as witnessed above, there are suggestions that the republics did participate in balancing, and formed alliances with monarchies as well as republics.

In addition to the hiding suggested by the material, another highly significant practice was co-binding. Co-binding 'entails republics joining together with other republics in various forms of unions (alliances, leagues, confederations, and federations)' (Deudney, 2007: 57). Broad representation by member republics in a Vajjian council is evident (J.P. Sharma, 1968: 147). The Videhas, while not as powerful as the Licchavis, are also listed as a dominant member of the Confederacy. Words attributed to the Buddha treat the Vajjians as a corporate entity with regular assemblies. In a widely noted account, representatives from the Magadhan kingdom consulted with the Buddha concerning their king's desire to attack the Vajjians. The Buddha responds that the Vajjians are strong and cannot be defeated militarily, and attributes their strength to their form of governance.[10] Republics did have at least short-term advantages in their ability to develop and draw on the martial attributes of their citizenry. A statement attributed to Ajatasattu referring to the 'Vajjians who are so powerful and strong,' supports the interpretation of the association as more than a contingent alliance (Walshe, 1995: 230).

The evidence therefore suggests that the Vajjian Confederacy was an example of co-binding republics. What stands out in this example is that, as Deudney mentions, republics were normally isolated from one another – requiring topographic insulation or succumbing to their larger rivals. This, in most cases, would preclude co-binding of republics. In the strongest interpretation of the material, we have not only an example of co-binding, but of the intentional relocation of republican (or proto-republican) polities hiding and collocating, resulting in a powerful union that successfully resisted its autocratic neighbors, at least for a time. A weaker interpretation would still tend to support Deudney's conception of the iron laws of ancient republics.[11]

The relative strength of the Vajjian Confederacy, prior to its final succumbing to the Magadha, may then be attributed to some measure of protection due to topography, but as much or more to the concerted resources of the confederated republics. In league with other republics the formidable military strength of the Licchavis and the Confederacy for a time blocked the military advances of the mighty Magadha. When the Vajjian confederates were defeated, it was not due to outright military defeat, but due to an effort to undermine the unity of the league and, we can suppose, its individual members.

The Arthasastra (Kangle, 1972: 454) devotes a chapter to 'Policy Towards Oligarchies' – with 'oligarchies' translated from *samgha* which is one of the terms associated with the republics. The section begins by stating that the 'gain of an oligarchy is best among gains of an army or ally... [f]or, oligarchies being closely knit are unassailable for enemies.' Accordingly, one 'should win over those of them who are friendly with conciliation and gifts, those hostile through dissensions and force.' The section goes on to outline the measures by which secret agents and other methods can be used to sow dissension. The Buddha relays the same assessment when he advises the Magadhan representatives that if the Vajjians maintain their republican ways, 'they will never be conquered by king [Ajatasattu] by force of arms, but only by means of propaganda and setting them against one another' (Walshe, 1995: 232). These textual clues align well with the account of the Magadhan defeat of the Vajjians through a divide-and-conquer strategy, with these lessons reflected in both Buddhist and Brahman texts. We find evidence of this strategy in the Kosalas absorption of the Sakya republic, the first of the republics to fall. There is mention in the source material of efforts aimed at 'fermenting dissensions among the inhabitants [of the Sakya republic]' (J.P. Sharma, 1968: 204). Rather than the relative efficiency of their system, the triumph of the kingdoms over the republics may be best understood in terms of ruthlessness and vulnerability, respectively.

Another factor emphasized in republican security theory is the role of topography in influencing the nature of political organizations, and the types of units and systems that are tenable in certain contexts (See Deudney, 2000a and Deudney, 2007). One observer, Hemchanda Raychaudhuri, noted 'the love of local (Janapada) autonomy and the aspiration for imperial unity...,' as characteristic of the ancient period, and concludes that the 'predilection for local self-rule was in part fostered by geographical conditions' (1997: 164). Particularly relevant in the Indian case is the role of forests (as well as other inaccessible stretches of territory) in fostering, and perhaps shaping opposition to imperial unity. In addition, as the next section suggests, physical environments may have a role in supporting the presence of distinct types of actors or systems, which provide a further set of experiences to enrich our understanding of hierarchy and opposition in the historical and physical contexts of the Indian subcontinent.

'Permanent Enemies' and the 'Circle of Anomie': Unit structure, topography and hegemony

As part of their discussion of ancient and classical international systems Buzan and Little emphasize the inadequacy of the like-unit conception of systems (Buzan and Little, 2000: 230). The admission of forms of opposition to anarchy, as units in the system, that do not fit the like units assumption is critical to our understanding of the ancient Indian international system. The presumption of emulation and socialization as necessary outcomes, with the balance of power providing a regulative mechanism, fails to capture the range of patterns of interaction and resistance to power consolidation.

From ancient times to the present some groups have disassociated from society and resisted central rule. These include what have been designated as 'wild tribes' and 'forest kingdoms' as well as the bandits and outlaws that are found up to the present. Recalling the formative early role of cattle raiding for Vedic era kings (R.S. Sharma, 1968: 115), we witness the functional similarity of legitimate polities and criminal bands, a connection Charles Tilly among others has highlighted.[12] One scholar has recorded the 'close affinity between bandit and king' in Southern India, and concludes that in this tradition despite 'the threat he poses to settled life, the bandit is no less part of the social order than his mirror-image, the king' (Shulman, 1980: 303–4; Floris, 1962: 468). In his study of the adaptation of the wild tribes to colonial rule, Frederick Robinson makes note of the references to the 'plundering and predatory tribes' throughout the historical literature of India. While their representation has been marginal, the 'existence of such peoples and their relation to historically prominent polities has long been observed' (1978: 1).

As with the balance of power and republican security theory frameworks, Kautilya provides useful insight. The Arthasastra records: 'The land, whose frontiers have many forts (beyond them) and are never devoid of robber-bands or Mleccha forest tribes, is one with permanent enemies....' (Kangle, 1972: 354).[13] Characteristically, the Arthasastra meticulously catalogues and details how best to acquire the land and make use of the groups to enlist in support of attacking other enemies. The wild tribes, as well as forest dwellers, are both a menace and a resource to co-opt for further conquest. In campaigns against forest troops, the Arthasastra councils, forest troops should be utilized – 'let the Bilva-fruit be destroyed by the Bilva-fruit' (Kangle, 1972: 411). The mention of *mlecchas* should be elaborated. 'Mleccha' is often translated as 'outsider' or 'barbarian,' as well as applied to undesirables who do not speak Sanskrit (Parasher, 1991; Thapar, 1971: 409–10). In this capacity it has been used to refer to invaders from outside of the Subcontinent, but also is applied to those who reside within its geographic confines but outside of the authority of the ruler.

The concern with these 'mlecchas' is demonstrated in a number of other sources. The *Dharmasutra of Apastamba* (c. 450–350 BCE), a legal code book, states that a 'king [truly] provides protection only when there is no fear of thieves in the villages or wild tracts of his realm...' and prescribes that towns should be protected from thieves for up to nine miles on all sides, and villages up to a couple of miles (Olivelle, 1999: 69). The *Laws of Manu* (of around the 1st or 2nd century CE) also records this concern. After settling his country the king 'should *constantly* make the utmost effort to clear out the thorns.' The thorns include thieves and forest bandits. If a king collects taxes without punishing thieves 'his kingdom will be shaken and he will lose heaven' suggesting the problem was more than a passing law enforcement concern (Doniger and Smith, 1991: 225, emphasis added).

Secondary accounts support the prominence and importance of these actors. These include references to 'the presence of numerous petty Rajas holding their courts either in some forest region, mountain fastness, or desert tract away from the main currents of political life....' (Raychaudhuri, 1997: 74). T.W. Rhys Davids refers both to elements of the police forces of Koliya (one of the smaller republics) 'with a bad reputation for extortion and violence' and the jungle 'infested from time to time by robbers....' (1997: 21). This emphasizes the overlap in kind between legitimate authorities and those on the fringes of society. The latter were 'permanent enemies,' not geographical-positional contingent enemies, but perpetual adversaries whose structure and relationships were largely influenced by topography.

Emphasis on the role of jungles and forests as insulators accompanies the frequent association of both forest tribes and bandits as a common concern. The Sanskrit word *jangal* is the origin of 'jungle' and refers generally to uncultivated land, having taken its more specific connotation later (Gold and Gojur, 2002: 242–4). In addition to Kautilya's 'circle of enemies,' what can be termed a 'circle of anomie' is evident. Here deviations from society are realized not only in norms of behavior but in forms of political association; with extraction and protection as common functions of both states and criminal bands. 'Contracting out' of society, a feature of ancient Indian conceptions of the state of nature, manifests as a constant feature of this literal and figurative landscape.

The evidence suggests a set of relations among units that is not represented in the circle of enemies framework. The symmetry of the mandala framework is ill-matched with the asymmetric responses of these actors. If the forest polities, and the associated bands of marauders, were as prominent as is argued here, the pattern would be more of a moth-eaten authority than the balance of the mandala. This is more than a deviation from an abstraction – or 'flecks' of anarchy in a hierarchic order like Waltz's hierarchy flecked anarchic system (1979: 114) – but a fundamental condition fostered by the largely permanent topography. The forest tribes, 'well entrenched in jungle fastness' were, according to one interpreter of Kautilya, 'well organized and brave, practically autonomous and without scruples in matters of looting and killing' (Parasher, 1991: 133). Their use as military allies and spies suggests their relationship to the ruler was at times symbiotic, but the strong interest of these actors in plunder suggests a pattern of predation (Parasher, 1991: 135).

The rock edicts of Ashoka (the 'Beloved of the Gods') also present evidence of this relationship. Some historians attribute Ashoka's 'empire of dharma' less as idealistic and more as a realistic policy; one that recognized the prohibitively high cost of maintaining an empire on the Subcontinent through coercion (Kulke and Rothermund, 1998: 67). The purported righteousness of Ashoka's policy reflected a concern for legitimation of his rule without resort to forceful subjugation. Ashoka's entreaties, however, were not successful in subduing the *atavi* (or forest tribes), who severely tested his patience and tolerance: 'The Beloved of the Gods [Ashoka] believes that one who does wrong should be forgiven as far as it is possible to forgive him,' the edicts relate. 'And the Beloved of the Gods conciliates the forest tribes of his empire, but he warns them that he has power even in his remorse, and he asks them to repent, lest they be killed' (Thapar, 1997: 256).[14]

Romila Thapar (1981), who emphasizes the unity of the empire, notes that it should be understood as a differentiated system, where there existed greater and lesser authority of a metropolitan state which expanded in search of resources. However we interpret the whole of the empire, the role of the atavi as part of a system of cooperative exchange is not supported by the available evidence. Though the Arthasastra indicates that forest tribes did align with centralizing powers in certain conflicts (seemingly against other forest peoples), their overall posture is antagonistic and autonomous. The position of the 'mlecchas' as outside society has been noted by one interpreter, who concludes that during the time of the empire it 'is quite clear that the separateness of the forest from a civilized society had come to be regarded as fundamental' (Parasher, 1991: 133). Gerard Fussman characterizes the Mauryan Empire as having a 'centralizing will,' if not full success in exerting that will. The forest tribes, Fussman concludes, were likely treated in the same manner as the British Raj, 'tribes were left alone as long as they did not disturb the peace of the Empire' (1988: 71).

Concerning their potential role in the decline of the Mauryan Empire, the evidence suggests that the forest tribes often did disturb the peace, resisted incorporation, and resorted to predation and banditry. Thapar characterizes them as an irritant preying on trade caravans and agricultural settlements, but not a mortal threat to central rule (Thapar, 1981: 415). A more dire assessment portrays the threat presented to Ashoka's rule as substantial and persistent. The mention of the atavi in the edicts, according to Kulke and Rothermund, gives the 'impression that Ashoka regarded these tribes as the most dangerous enemies of his empire' (1998: 66). Overall, their effect might best be characterized as a painful if not crippling thorn in the lion's paw. Regardless, the manifestation of opposition to hierarchy in a strategy distinct from balancing is clear.

Evidence of this relationship of constant antagonism and occasional alliance with topographically insulated actors persists through the course of Indian history. Inscriptions by Samudragupta, son of Chandragupta I, in the 4th century CE, like those of Ashoka, may be read to 'indicate that the "forest dwellers" of these two mighty empires of Indian antiquity had preserved their nearly unlimited autonomy' (Kulke, 1997: 245). In peninsular India, similarly, the *Bedas*, a forest-based community of warriors, figure prominently in the Karnataka inscriptions written between the 9th and 12th centuries CE (Guha, 1999: 56). The early 16th century monarch of the peninsular empire Vijayanagar, Krishnadevaraya, composed maxims which include the following: 'Minding the (small) faults of the forest chiefs who have not extensive power is like trying to clean a mud wall by pouring water over it.' (Guha, 1999: 56).

The presence of these polities was also a common problem for the Mughals, Marathas, and British in their attempts to consolidate their empires. Sumit Guha characterizes the nature of the 'forest states' relations with central authorities, local rulers, and, later, colonial rule.

> [The forest polities] were aware of, and exploited the strategic inaccessibility of their lands. For them, the forests were not a refuge, but a base for tribute collection. Though unable to face the full strength of larger agrarian powers when it was deployed against them, the forest peoples had the capacity to deny their enemies the fruits of victory, both tactically and strategically: tactically in that their mobility and local knowledge allowed them to escape from disadvantageous situations; and strategically in that their capacity to terrorize the agrarian population and damage the bases of production made mere military victories sterile and valueless. (Guha, 1999: 81).

This survival strategy of symbiosis and predation by forest dwellers is manifested in the early modern period in the north by the Bhils.[15] The Bhils of Khandesh (c. 1700–1850), as recalled in a study by Guha, 'formed part of the great central Indian block of forest peoples.' As Guha notes, for the Bhils, in 'times of scarcity, taxation crossed the hazy boundary into robbery' (Guha, 1996: 134, 143).

Reflecting their identity as occupiers of unoccupied land, in more recent times these peoples often described themselves as *jangli*, or wild, and also as *janglijati*, 'wild castes' or 'forest castes...,' and they 'thought their power continuous with untamed wildness.'[16] Reflecting their unruliness and lack of socialization the British labeled the forest dwellers as 'rude tribes.' As Akhileshwar Pathak (2002: 73) notes, though, '[t]he rude tribes did not live in the forests. Rather, the tribes who lived in the forest were "rude".'[17] The persistence of these patterns of resistance, over the better part of two millennia, marks not an exception to hierarchy nor an example of insurgency, but an alternative strategy – raiding and hiding, relying on inaccessible topography – that is of equal if not greater significance to balancing in opposition to hegemony. Their persistence also demonstrates a limit to the socialization effect hypothesized by neorealism: these forest polities resisted for centuries the 'tendency toward sameness' in structure and behavior expected by Waltz (1979: 127). Separation and formative deviation was realized while maintaining the necessary level of interaction to be considered part of the system. While balancing presumes processes of emulation and socialization as necessary precursors, the ancient Indian system exhibits processes of disassociation and dissimilation, of partial disengagement from the system and taking on forms unlike the dominant units.

Conclusion: hierarchy and opposition in ancient India

The preceding examination of ancient India raises questions concerning key formulations and assumptions in neorealist theory, as well as the examination of international systems in diverse historical and geographical contexts. While there is evidence in the Indian case of processes expected by neorealism, such as balancing and mutual emulation, these aspects alone provide an incomplete account of the range of responses to consolidation. The Vajjian Confederacy long resisted Magadhan domination not by emulation but through a strategy – co-binding – particular to the republican form. In the end, however, balancing and co-binding were both defeated by a divide-and-rule strategy, with apparent similarities to that applied by Qin some centuries later (see the chapter by Hui in this volume). The result was the system dominated by the Mauryan Empire, in which resistance took the form of the hiding-and-raiding strategy of the forest polities. These irregular actors of no mean significance exploited the topography of India's forests to make this strategy workable. Utilizing the insulation of natural barriers, while maintaining significant interactions, ultimately served to be the most effective and enduring strategy in resisting hierarchy. The concealment of these types of actors in practice has been matched by their obscurity in discussions of international relations. To reflect on the contemporary condition presented by the threat of Al Qaeda is to recognize that such alternative patterns of opposition, and the emergence of systems characterized by dissimilar units, should not be considered mere historically bound and irrelevant aberrations.

Notes

1 George Modelski's (1964) study of 'foreign policy and international system in the Ancient Hindu world,' is indicative of this trend. Exceptions to this tendency include Rosen (1996) and Watson (1992: Chapter 7).

2 Colonialism, nationalism, and Marxism are among the filters that may distort interpretations of Indian history, but these biases have been well charted and are navigable. See Subrahmanyam (2003), and Inden (1990).

3 Concerning the uncertainty surrounding Kautilya's identity, see Kangle (1965: Chapter 4); Goyal (2000); and Ramaswamy (1994: 4).

4 See Kangle (1972: Book 6). An earlier translation is also useful, see Shamasastry (1961). Indian language terms have been added minus diacritical marks.

5 Some international relations scholars have cited Kautilya simply as evidence of the presence of balance-of-power thinking in ancient India (Doyle, 1997, 163–4); while others have used the Arthasastra to argue for the prevalence of balancing across space and time (Seabury, 1965: 1–18).

6 Names of key figures and polities have been standardized, following Sharma (1968) and then Kulke and Rothermund (1998). Where alterations have been made in direct quotes these are placed in brackets.

7 J.P. Sharma (1968: 132). An admonition issued by Ajatasattu, was related in the *Digha Nikaya* of the Buddhist Pali Canon. The king is said to have stated that 'I will strike the Vajjians who are so powerful and strong, I will cut them off and destroy them, I will bring them to ruin and destruction.' See Walshe (1995: 231, 16.1).

8 On the relationship between Buddhism, the empire of dharma, and the effectiveness of Ashoka's rule, see Basham (1982: 131–43).

9 The emphasis on the prevalence and democratic nature of ancient republican polities has shown the influence of secular nationalist discourse in India. The touting of democratic trends evident in India prior to colonial rule reinforces the artificiality of rule by outsiders, and diminishes the role of the institutions of outside rulers in favor of the realization of a wholly indigenous political tradition. While a number of authors are seen as 'guilty of imposing twentieth-century democratic ideas and institutions on early

Indian polity,' J.P. Sharma's detailed account belies the idea that the republics were just primitive forms of tribal representation (See J.P. Sharma, 1968: 2, 11).

10 In the *Digha Nikaya*, the Buddha states: '[As] long as the Vajjians meet in harmony, break up in harmony, and carry on their business in harmony, they may be expected to prosper and not decline' (Walshe, 1995: 232).

11 Even a more modest interpretation would refute an earlier treatment of Kautilya and the 'circle of enemies.' Paul Seabury (1965: 4) cites the Arthasastra as evidence of the universality of the balance of power – highlighting its prevalence in this distinct and distant historical context – in order to support his strict delimiting of constitutionalism (limitation and direction of powers) to the domestic sphere.

12 Charles Tilly (1985, 169–91) has compared states to organized crime, characterizing states as protection rackets, and suggesting that there is a continuum along which states and criminal organizations lie. On cattle raiding and warfare in the Vedic era, see R.S. Sharma (1968: 115).

13 This quote is translated in the Shamasastry translation as '[t]hat land on the border ... giving shelter to bands of thieves, [Mlecchas], and wild tribes ... is a land with a constant enemy' (Shamasastry, 1961: 323).

14 This passage has been translated by others, perhaps trying to maintain the image of Ashoka as purely invested and consistent with the teachings of the dharma, as imploring the forest tribes not to kill, rather than as a threat; but the more menacing translation 'is used by nearly every scholar.' (Fussman, 1988: 50)

15 For a discussion of the Bhils, see Guha (1999: 142–5); and Hardiman (1994).

16 See Skaria, 2003: 295; Skaria, 1999; Gold and Gojur, 2002: 13.

17 This association of environment and acquired or attributed identities may also be evident in the case of another group that has made use of forests to sustain itself, the Chechens. General Mikhail Yermolov, who led a campaign in the 19th century to suppress the Chechens labeled them 'congenital rebels.' The campaign eventually succeeded, for a time at least, by burning the forests that provided sanctuary. See Weir (2002).

6
The Triumph of Domination in the Ancient Chinese System*

Victoria Tin-bor Hui

Kenneth Waltz challenges IR scholars to 'look farther afield... to the China of the warring states era... and see that where political entities of whatever sort compete freely, substantive and stylistic characteristics are similar.' (Waltz, 1986: 329–30) Indeed, the term China or *Zhongguo* originally referred to 'central states' in the Spring and Autumn and Warring States periods: *zhong* means central and *guo* means states. The *zhongguo* system offers IR scholars a most-similar case to evaluate Eurocentric balance-of-power theories. Similar to the early modern European system, the ancient Chinese system experienced disintegration of feudal hierarchy, prevalence of war, conditions of international anarchy, emergence of sovereign territorial states, configuration of the balance of power, and attempts at universal domination. Like their counterparts in Europe, domination-seekers in the *zhongguo* system faced seemingly insurmountable obstacles: the balance of power, the rising costs of expansion, the barriers of geography, and the difficulty of consolidating conquests. However, unlike the fate of Charles V, Louis XIV, and Napoleon, the state of Qin overcame such countervailing forces by self-strengthening reforms, divide-and-conquer strategies, and cunning and brutish stratagems. First, Qin built up its power and

*This chapter is based on Chapter Two 'The Dynamics of International Politics in Ancient China,' *War and State Formation in Ancient China and Early Modern Europe*, Cambridge University Press, 2005, 54–101, © Victoria Tin-bor Hui 2005, with the permission of Cambridge University Press. An earlier version of this analysis was published in *International Organization* in 2004 as 'Toward a Dynamic Theory of International Politics: Insights from Comparing the Ancient Chinese and Early Modern European Systems,' vol. 58, no. 1, pp. 175–205, with the permission of Cambridge University Press.

wealth by simultaneously enhancing its administrative-extractive capacity. It was then capable of mobilizing the wherewithal of war, winning victories on the battlefields, consolidating conquests, and extracting additional resources from subjugated populations. Second, Qin employed divide-and-conquer strategies to isolate enemies and weaken balancing alliances. Third, when Qin estimated that it could not challenge a formidable enemy or a united alliance in a direct confrontation, it would turn to stratagems such as 'feigning and dissembling to deceive the enemy' and 'using bribes, gifts, and other methods to induce disloyalty and cause chaos.' (Sawyer, 1998: 19) This chapter examines how Qin achieved universal domination through such measures.

Introduction to Qin's rise to domination[1]

The ancient Chinese system emerged from the ruins of the prior Zhou feudal hierarchy. After conquering Shang around 1045 BC, the Zhou king directly ruled vast areas that he could effectively control. At the same time, the king enfeoffed his sons, relatives and high officials to defend distant strategic points. Each enfeoffed lord would move to the designated area with his whole lineage and build a garrisoned city-state called *guo*. In the beginning, the Zhou king's authority was buttressed by both his position as the head of an extended lineage and his control over far superior economic resources and military strength. Over time, however, blood ties between the Zhou king and feudal lords became distant. At the same time, the balance of capabilities gradually shifted in favor of *guo* because the centrally located Zhou court had little room for expansion while feudal units could expand into uncharted surrounding areas. The Zhou hierarchy eventually crumbled in 770 BC. A disastrous attack 'marked the definitive end of the political and military dominance of the royal house.' (Lewis, 1990: 47) In the subsequent Spring and Autumn period (770–453 BC) and Warring States period (453–221 BC), *guo* were independent of the Zhou court. In diplomatic meetings, all heads of *guo* treated one another as equals despite their differences in feudal ranks. Historians of ancient China typically date the beginning of the multistate era in 770 BC. However, the disintegration of feudal hierarchy is not the only criterion for dating the onset of system formation. Barry Buzan and Richard Little suggest that 'a set of states that cannot pose each other military threat fail to constitute an international system.' (2000: 80) The means of communication and transportation meant that it was not until around

659 BC that various states came to acquire mutual awareness. Co-incidentally, Chu repeatedly attacked Zheng from 659 to 653 BC and Qi responded by mobilizing a northern alliance which invaded Chu's territory in 656 BC. I thus date the onset of the ancient Chinese system in 656 BC.

For three centuries from 656 to 284 BC, the ancient Chinese system was remarkably stable. Ambitious domination-seekers rose but fell, and attempts at domination were made but checked. (See Maps 6.1 to 6.3.) In the early Spring and Autumn period, Chu, a southern state, was the first to emerge hegemonic. As Chu sought expansion into the central plain area in the early to mid-7th century BC, it was checked by a Qi-led alliance. Qi soon declined as a result of internal power struggles. But Jin then emerged to check Chu in 632 BC. In the ensuing century, the Jin and Chu camps were engaged in a tug-of-war and unable to sub-jugate each other. The two sides finally reached a peace agreement in 546 BC. But this Jin-Chu balance did not last long. Wu, Chu's south-eastern neighbor, rose in power and managed to capture Chu's capital in 506 BC. Wu, in turn, suffered from over-expansion and was even conquered by its own southeastern neighbor Yue in 473 BC. But Yue soon stayed out of great-power competition and focused its attention

Map 6.1   Ancient China in the Middle to Late Spring and Autumn Period

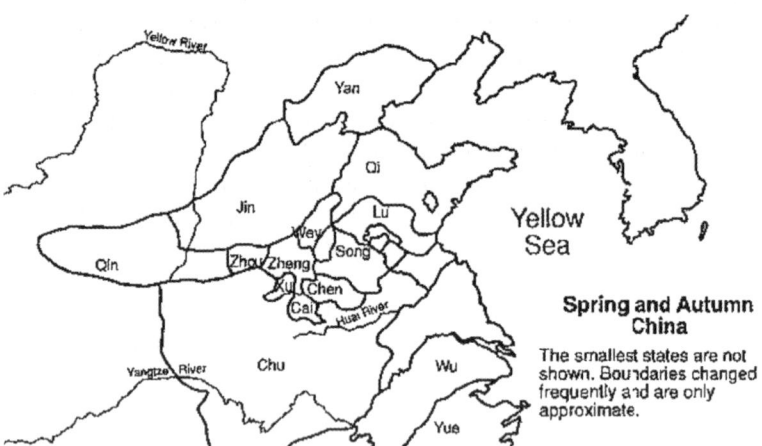

Source: Reprinted from Creel (1970a), *The Origins of Statecraft in China* (Chicago: University of Chicago Press), 204, c. 1970 Herrlee G. Creel, with the permission of the University of Chicago Press; reprinted from Victoria Tin-bor Hui (2004), 'Toward a Dynamic Theory of International Politics: Insights from Comparing the Ancient Chinese and Early Modern European Systems,' *International Organization*, 58 (1): 187, with the permission of Cambridge Univesity Press.

Map 6.2   Ancient China, c. 450 BCE

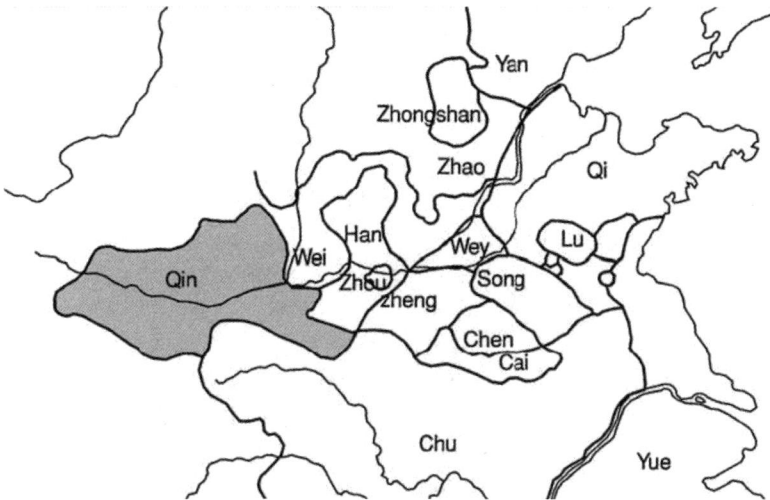

Source: Rui Gao (1995), *Zhongguo shanggu junshishi* (Beijing: Academy of Military Sciences), map 20. Reprinted from Victoria Tin-bor Hui (2004), 'Toward a Dynamic Theory of International Politics: Insights from Comparing the Ancient Chinese and Early Modern European Systems,' *International Organization*, 58 (1): 187, with the permission of Cambridge University Press.

on neighboring weak states. Another great power Jin was split by three ruling clans into Han, Wei, and Zhao in 453 BC. In the ensuing Warring States period, Wei was the first state to emerge hegemonic and it attempted to subjugate its neighbors. But Wei's expansion into Zhao in 354–352 BC and Han in 344–340 BC brought about Qi's interference and decisive defeats. Qi's own attempt at domination, in turn, was thwarted by an anti-Qi alliance in 284 BC.

In those early centuries, the ultimate unifier Qin was 'a minor factor in interstate wars.' (Lewis, 1999: 618) Qin was weaker than other great powers and generally pursued a defensive foreign policy. From 656 to 357 BC, Qin initiated only 11 (or 7 per cent) of 161 wars involving great powers.[2] In the Spring and Autumn period, Qin even performed the role of 'the balancer': Qin was actively sought by both Jin and Chu during their prolonged rivalry from 632 to 546 B; Qin also saved Chu from Wu's conquest in 505 BC. In the early Warring States period (c. 419–385 BC), Qin lost large tracts of strategic territory on the West bank of the Yellow River to the then hegemonic Wei.

Map 6.3   Ancient China, c. 350 BCE

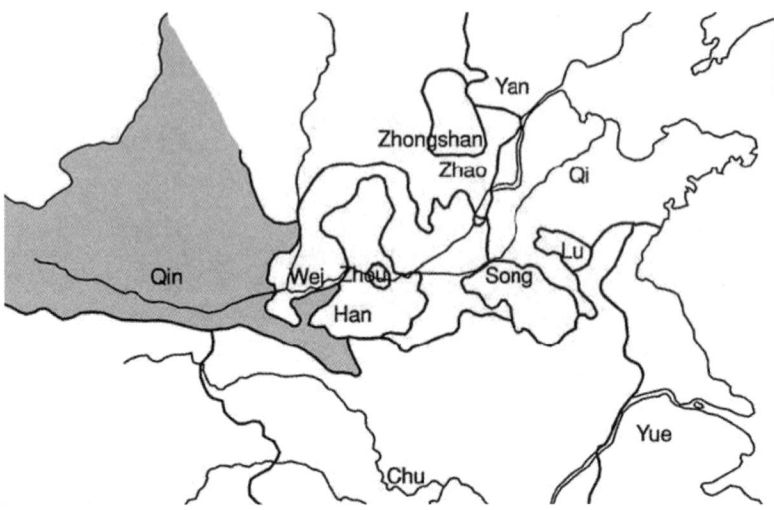

Source: Rui Gao (1995), *Zhongguo shanggu junshishi* (Beijing: Academy of Military Sciences), map 23. Reprinted from Victoria Tin-bor Hui (2004), 'Toward a Dynamic Theory of International Politics: Insights from Comparing the Ancient Chinese and Early Modern European Systems,' *International Organization*, 58 (1): 188, with the permission of Cambridge University Press.

This scenario was gradually altered under Duke Xiao (361–338 BC). Beginning from 356 BC, Qin's new minister Shang Yang launched the most comprehensive self-strengthening reforms known in ancient Chinese history. Duke Xiao's original motivation for reforms was probably defensive – to enhance Qin's security against Wei and to restore Qin's place among great powers. However, as Qin's relative capability improved, Duke Xiao and subsequent rulers switched to an aggressive policy of opportunistic expansion. From 356 to 221 BC, Qin initiated 51 out of a total of 95 wars involving great powers (or 54 per cent). Qin scored 47 victories out of these 51 wars (or 92 per cent) and further won three out of five wars in which it was the target. Qin completely pushed Wei out of the West bank of the Yellow River by 328 BC. Qin also proceeded to seize territory on the East bank of the Yellow River from its immediate neighbors Wei, Han, and Chu. Qin decisively defeated Chu in the wars of 312–311 BC and 301–298 BC. Qin then annihilated the core forces of Wei and Han and pushed them out of the great-power status in 293 BC. Qin's ascendance to hegemony was formally recognized by Qi (which became the strongest power after

Map 6.4   Ancient China, c. 257 BCE

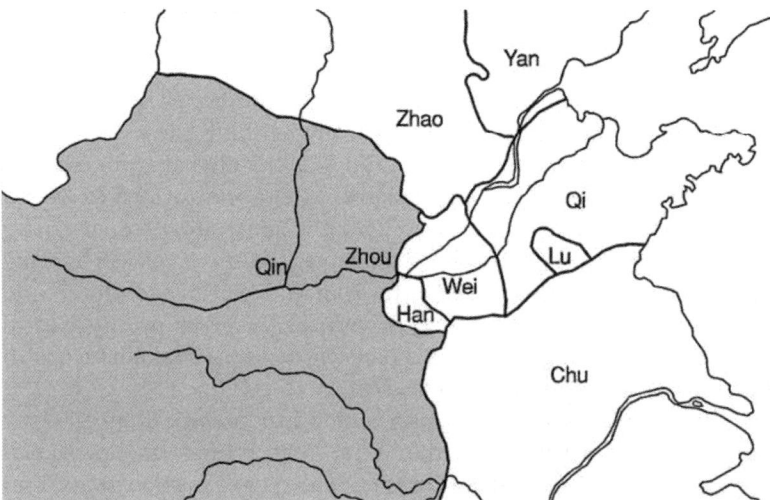

Source: Rui Gao (1995), *Zhongguo shanggu junshishi* (Beijing: Academy of Military Sciences), map 26. Reprinted from Victoria Tin-bor Hui (2004), 'Toward a Dynamic Theory of International Politics: Insights from Comparing the Ancient Chinese and Early Modern European Systems,' *International Organization*, 58 (1): 192, with the permission of Cambridge University Press.

devastating Wei in 341 BC) in 288 BC when rulers from both states jointly assumed the title of emperor. Qin soon ascended further from bipolar hegemony to unipolar hegemony after Qi was nearly conquered by an anti-Qi alliance in 284 BC. Qin moved on to deal severe blows to the remaining two great powers Chu in 280–276 BC and Zhao in 262–257 BC. By 257 BC, all other states had lost their great-power status and Qin controlled about half of the system. (Compare Maps 6.3 and 6.4.) Qin launched the final wars of unification in 236 BC and established a universal empire in 221 BC.

Overcoming the balance of power

As IR scholars would expect, when Qin's relative capability rose and became increasingly threatening to its neighbors, other states responded with the balance-of-power strategy. However, IR theorists often overlook that the balance-of-power strategy may be countered by its opposite – the divide-and-conquer strategy. In the ancient Chinese system, the critical period from the late 4th to the mid-3rd century BC was the age of *hezong* and *lianheng* strategies. The *hezong* strategy followed the rationale of the balance of power by calling for the uniting of weaker states to resist the strongest. At the same time, Qin also developed the *lianheng* strategy which sought to forestall and break up *hezong* alliances by playing the various states off against one another with threats and bribes, and then bring overwhelming force to conquer them seriatim. The terms *lianheng* and *hezong* were based on the geographical locations of the major states. As Qin was located to the far West of the ancient Chinese system, the ideal alliance pattern to balance against Qin's eastward advance was to form a vertical bulwark linking Yan and Zhao in the North, Han and Wei in the center, and Chu in the South, hence *hezong* or vertical. To break up this North-South axis, Qin sought to form a *lianheng* or horizontal alliance with Han, Wei and Qi. (See Map 6.3.)

In the competition between the *hezong* and *lianheng* strategies, the former suffered a dismal record in terms of both the formation of balancing alliances and the defeat of Qin. Qin's 51 expansionist wars from 356 to 221 BC met with only eight allied responses. Five of the anti-Qin alliances were defeated by Qin's forces or dissolved by Qin's *lianheng* strategy. Although Qin was defeated by the other three alliances, the defeats were not decisive and could not block Qin's rise to domination. Events surrounding the first *hezong* alliance of 318–317 BC already bode ill for the balance-of-power mechanism. First, the alliance was formed very slowly and reluctantly. After losing the hegemonic status in 341 BC, Wei began to form an alliance against Qin as early as 334 BC. But other states were suspicious of the once-expansionist Wei. Wei itself wavered between balancing and bandwagoning. Second, when the alliance was finally formed, it was not composed of all the six states which Qin eventually conquered. Qi was the then hegemonic power and probably did not regard Qin as a threat. Chu and Yan joined the alliance but did not contribute troops. Third, allied forces did not have unified command. While the armies of Han, Wei and Zhao still outnumbered those of Qin, allied forces fought separately, thus giving Qin an opportunity to divide and defeat them one by one. Fourth, the alliance disintegrated quickly. After a speedy defeat, Wei unilaterally left the alliance and made peace with Qin in 317 BC. Moreover, Qi took advantage of Wei's and Zhao's defeat by Qin and attacked them in the hope of making easy territorial gains.

After repeated onslaughts by Qin, Han and Wei joined forces in 294–286 BC and 276–274 BC. In both wars, however, the uncoordinated armies of Han and Wei were divided and defeated. In between these two attempts, the badly embattled Han and Wei sought an alliance with Qi, Zhao, and Yan in 287 BC. But the conflicts of interests among allies allowed Qin to dissolve the alliance before it even set off. By 241 BC, Qin had seized so many pieces of territory that it encircled Han and Wei and shared borders with Qi. But Qi still refused to participate in an alliance with Zhao, Chu, Han, Wei, and Yan. Moreover, allied forces continued to have no unified command. Worse, after Qin launched a surprise attack on Chu's camp at night, Chu left the battlefield without notifying its allies. As it was hopeless to fight Qin without Chu, the rest of the allied forces also retreated.

Anti-Qin alliances managed to win three times. Unfortunately, in each of these instances, allies failed to hold together to decisively defeat Qin. In 298–296 BC, the allied forces of Qi, Han and Wei forced their way to the strategic Hangu Pass (which provided an easy passage to cross the Yellow River) and compelled Qin to return some pieces of territory to Han and Wei. But Qi, the strongest power at the time, was discontented because it contributed the most efforts but gained nothing. Qi soon made peace with Qin so as to seek its own territorial ambitions. In 259–257 BC, Chu and Wei helped to relieve Qin's siege of Zhao's capital Handan. However, allied forces had become very fearful of Qin and did not pursue Qin's retreating army. At the end of this war, Qin managed to push its territory far beyond the Yellow River into the central plain and occupied about half of the territory in the system. Against the backdrop of dismal balancing efforts, the alliance of 247 BC was uncharacteristically promising and had the potential to check Qin's seemingly ineluctable rise to domination. When Qin laid siege to Wei's capital Daliang, Wei secured assistance from Chu, Han, Yan and Zhao. Remarkably, allies placed their forces under the unified command of a Wei general who had lifted Qin's siege of Zhao in 259–257 BC. Moreover, the commander-in-chief pursued Qin's retreating army to the East bank of the Yellow River. Faced with unified resistance, Qin resorted to the stratagem of estrangement: It bribed Wei's high officials to spread the rumor that the commander, a brother of the king, had ambitions to take over the throne. After Wei's king dismissed the commander in 246 BC, the last hope for the *hezong* strategy also vanished.

The *hezong* alliance of 247 BC illustrates that it is important to examine not just the weakness of balancing efforts, but also the strength of Qin's divide-and-conquer strategy and the ruthlessness of Qin's stratagems. Qin actively sought to overcome the balance of power by forestalling *hezong* alliances from being formed and by breaking up already formed ones. To facilitate the divide-and-conquer strategy, Qin 'was never reluctant to lie in diplomatic meetings, to acquire information on other states by espionage, and to bribe key figures in the courts of other states into collaboration.' (Hsu, 1997: 5) As Qin's rise to domination was successively resisted by Wei, Qi, and Zhao, it is instructive to examine in greater details how Qin divided and then conquered these once-hegemonic and great powers.

In 344 BC, Qin had scored some important victories over Wei. But Wei remained the strongest power and planned an allied preventive campaign against its rising neighbor. To avert this potentially devastating attack, Qin's Shang Yang requested an audience with Wei's ruler Marquis Hui. Shang Yang appealed to the Marquis's vain glory by suggesting that he should assume the title 'king' and subdue the more worthy targets Qi and Chu rather than the weaker Qin. Marquis Hui soon convened an international meeting and proclaimed himself 'King Hui.'[3] However, except for Qin which feigned support, other great powers boycotted the meeting. King Hui thus attacked Han, the weakest among great powers. When Qi intervened on Han's behalf, Wei was so devastated that it lost the hegemonic status to Qi in 341 BC. Shang Yang seized this golden opportunity and invaded Wei in 340 BC. But he was not confident that Qin could win against such a formidable power in a direct confrontation. Wei's army was commanded by Prince Ang, an old friend during Shang Yang's previous stay in Wei. Shang Yang then captured Prince Ang by pretending to offer a peace agreement and inviting the prince to Qin's camp to negotiate the terms. Without a commander, Wei's army was easily defeated and Wei was forced to cede territory. By resorting to a stratagem which exploited friendship and trust, Shang Yang achieved the unimaginable reversal of the Qin-Wei balance of relative capabilities. In the following decades, Qin inflicted defeats after defeats on Wei.

With the fall of Wei, the most formidable obstacles to Qin's eastward advance in the late 4th century BC became Chu in the South and Qi in the East. Among various great powers in the early Warring States period, Chu had the largest territory and the richest natural resources. Even worse for Qin, Chu was allied with Qi which became the strongest power after 341 BC. To defeat these formidable rivals, Qin proceeded to break up the Chu-Qi alliance. In 312 BC, Qin's chief minister Zhang Yi promised Chu's King Huai (328–299 BC) 600 *li* of territory if Chu would break the alliance with Qi.[4] Chu took the offer but Qin ceded only 6 *li*. The infuriated King Huai launched two poorly planned campaigns against Qin but was severely defeated. As a result,

Chu not only did not receive the promised territory, but further lost 600 *li* plus two cities. In 280–276 BC, Qin made a surprise invasion into Chu's heartland and seized the western half of Chu's core territory.

Qin was also astoundingly successful at playing its immediate neighbors Chu, Han, and Wei off against one another. Qin pursued a strategy of allying with Chu when it attacked Han and Wei, and allying with Han and Wei when it attacked Chu. To make peace with Chu, King Zhao married a princess to Chu's King Huai in 305 BC and returned a piece of territory in 304 BC. The Chu-Qin alliance then invaded Han. Han sought help from Wei and Qi to punish Chu in 303–302 BC. When Qin-Chu relations went sour, Qin invaded Chu in 301–298 BC. This time, Wei and Han were happy to watch Chu suffer. But Qin soon turned around to make peace with Chu again in 295 BC. Qin then invaded Han and Wei in 294–286 BC and even annihilated their 240,000 core troops in a major battle in 293 BC.[5] To preempt the severely embattled Han and Wei from mobilizing a *hezong* alliance, Qin married another princess to Chu's king in 292 BC and offered the title Eastern Emperor to Qi in 288 BC. When Qin turned around one more time to make a crushing attack on Chu in 280–276 BC, Han and Wei planned to join Qin to deal a further blow at Chu in 273 BC. To prevent imminent conquest, Chu sent an emissary to convince Qin to attack Han and Wei instead.

To deal with Qi, the strongest power from 341 BC on, Qin manipulated the interplay of the *hezong* and *lianheng* strategies. Qin first broke up the Qi-Chu alliance and scored a series of major victories over other great powers. After catching up with Qi, Qin placated Qi by offering King Min the title Eastern Emperor in 288 BC. After Qi conquered the prosperous state of Song in 286 BC, Qin exploited the widespread jealousy among other great powers. Qin encouraged Yan (which became Qi's dependent in 314 BC) to lead an anti-Qi alliance in 284 BC. As Qi's defense along the Qi-Yan border was very weak, Yan's army easily marched into Qi's heartland. At the same time, the armies of Qin, Han, Wei, and Zhao attacked from the West. With the combined forces of five states, Qi's armies were annihilated, the king was slain, and the entire state was occupied with the exception of two fortified cities Ju and Jimo. Although Qi managed to restore independence in 279 BC, such a dramatic defeat led Qi to switch to an isolationist policy. Qin further bribed Qi officials so that Qi would not engage in military buildup or lend any assistance to Qin's targets.

After Qin emerged as the unipolar hegemon, 'the age of diplomatic maneuver' based on the manipulation of the *hezong* and *lianheng* strategies gave way to 'the time of "total war"' marked by military prowess (Lewis, 1999: 638). By then, Zhao was the only great power left still capable of resisting Qin. Zhao's King Wuling (325–298 BC) had earlier concluded that it would be too difficult to approach Qin from its East because the only two passes which allowed easy passage across the Yellow River (Hangu and Wu Passes) had fallen into Qin's control. King Wuling secretly planned an operation from the northern frontiers. To attain that strategic position, Zhao had to first seize the region from northern nomadic tribes. For that purpose, King Wuling developed a highly mobile light cavalry on the model of northern nomads in 307 BC.

Unfortunately, this plan died with King Wuling in a succession struggle. His successor King Hui (298–266 BC) even missed a golden opportunity. When Qin poured massive armies to capture Chu in 280–276 BC, Qin's own territory was vulnerable to a Zhao attack. Although Zhao was at war with Qin in 282–280 BC, Zhao agreed to a cease-fire agreement in 279 BC and stayed neutral throughout the conflict. After Chu was decimated, Qin, not surprisingly, attacked Zhao. With a strong army developed by King Wuling, Zhao could hold its defense from 262 BC to 260 BC. Failing to defeat Zhao by force alone, Qin tried the stratagem of estrangement. Qin bribed high officials in the Zhao court to spread the rumor that the commander-in-chief Lian Po could have easily defeated Qin's forces but he was avoiding combat. After Zhao's King Xiaocheng (265–245 BC) dismissed Lian Po, the new commander Zhao Kuo changed the defensive strategy and launched an offensive against Qin's siege forces. In the famous battle of Changping in 260 BC, Qin's commander Bo Qi 'allowed Zhao's forces to advance in the center, encircled them on the flanks, cut their supply lines, and seized the fortifications they had left behind.' (Lewis, 1999: 640) Qin reemployed the same stratagem several decades later in its war of unification against Zhao in 236–228 BC. For four years from 236 to 232 BC, Zhao was still able to resist Qin. Zhao's forces even won two major battles in 233 and 232 BC. Qin thus resorted to estrangement to remove the able commander Li Mu in 229 BC. Zhao fell the following year.

Why did the balance-of-power strategy fail – and why did the divide-and-conquer strategy work?

Why did the balance of power have such a dismal record in the ancient Chinese system? Waltz argues that the balance of power should prevail 'wherever two, and only two, requirements are met: that the order be anarchic and that it be populated by units wishing to survive.' (Waltz, 1979: 121) The anarchical nature of the *zhongguo* system is amply demonstrated by the prevalence of war and diplomacy. Is it then possible that the Chinese *guo* did not seek survival, perhaps because they shared a common identity and welcomed unification? The reality is that the vanquished states mobilized their whole (adult and teenage, male and female) populations and fought to the bloody end in the final wars of unification. Could it be that the *zhongguo* did not understand that balancing would give them a better chance at maintaining survival? In light of various military alliances and other diplomatic efforts in the Warring States period, it would be incredible to claim that ancient Chinese statesmen somehow did not understand the logic of the balance of power. After all, previous domination-seeking states had been successfully checked – Qi in 284 BC, Wei in the mid-4th century BC, and Chu, Jin, and Wu in the Spring and Autumn period.

If the *zhongguo* sought survival and were experienced balancers, then why were they indifferent to mutual cooperation during Qin's rise to domination? Worse, why did they repeatedly follow the opposite strategy of bandwagoning with Qin? Although ancient Chinese strategists did not have a term for 'the collective action problem,' they understood that conflicts of interests would severely hinder balancing against Qin. As Zhang Yi, the mastermind of the *lianheng* strategy, observed, if even blood brothers would kill each other for money, then the impracticability of *hezong* was obvious. (Sanjun daxue vol. 2, 1976: 142) During Qin's ascendance to domination, the six states which Qin eventually conquered fought bitterly to seize territory from one another and from weaker states. Of the 95 wars involving great powers in the period 356–221 BC, as many as 27 (or 28 per cent) involved mutual attacks among the six states. (Fifty-one of the remaining wars were initiated by Qin.) This systemic phenomenon of mutual aggression offered Qin many opportunities to seize territories with minimal efforts. As states could rarely do well in two-front wars, Qin would invade its targets when they were engaged elsewhere. For example, Qin recovered lost territory from Wei when Wei was preoccupied with Zhao and Qi in 354 BC and then Han and Qi in 341 BC. Qin also started the war of unification against Zhao when Zhao attacked Yan in 236 BC.

The six states not only fought among themselves, but also solicited Qin's help in doing so. All of them wavered between the *hezong* and *lianheng* strategies. Indeed, the *lianheng* strategy had two meanings: In addition to Qin's divide-and-conquer strategy, the term also referred to efforts by Qin's targets to seize territorial gains from one another in order to compensate for their losses to Qin. The latter policy is analogous to what Randall Schweller calls 'predatory buckpassing.' (Schweller, 1998: 192–3) Qin's immediate neighbors Chu, Han and Wei would bandwagon with Qin to make territorial gains from each other and from other states. Moreover, on a few occasions, the six states would even take advantage of their neighbors' recent defeats by Qin. For example, Qi attacked Wei and Zhao in 317 BC after the first *hezong* alliance was defeated by Qin in 318 BC.

The fact that all great powers pursued opportunistic expansion also created the systemic phenomenon of multiple threats, which further complicated the balance-of-power mechanism. During the critical decades from 356 BC (when Qin began to launch self-strengthening reforms) to 284 BC (when Qi suffered near annihilation), it was not obvious to statesmen of the time that Qin was the main threat to their survival. Qin was originally a victim of Wei's aggression and had legitimate claims to recovering lost territory and securing defensible borders. After Wei's downfall, Qi became the most conspicuous threat. The situation of multiple threats thus allowed Qin to manipulate the interplay of the *hezong* and *lianheng* strategies to bring down its hegemonic rival with the help of other states.

In addition, the long drawn-out process toward unification further weakened the balance-of-power mechanism. Eric Labs points out that balancing 'would be less likely or late' for states that made 'incremental, repeated, and localized' expansion compared to states that made a conscious bid for hegemony. (Labs, 1997: 12, fn. 38) As Qin seized territory in bits and pieces over the course of 135 years, it was not obvious to any single generation of rulers among Qin's targets that their survival would ultimately be at stake. It was not until Qi's demise in 284–279 BC that statesmen were first alerted to Qin's rise to domination. By then, however, Qi, Yan, Wei and Han had already lost their great-power capabilities.

It may be argued that, when survival became increasingly at stake, Qin's targets should be able to overcome the collective action problem and engage in more effective balancing. This view overlooks the insight that weaker states generally pursue bandwagoning rather than balancing. (Labs, 1992; Schweller, 1998) It also fails to understand the disjuncture between the motivation to survive and the capability to resist domination. After Qin took over about half of the territory in the system, even the combined capabilities of all the six states would not match that of Qin. It is thus not surprising that Han Fei, who witnessed the last decades of the Warring States period, had little faith in the balance-of-power strategy. As Paul Goldin expounds on his view, 'Joining the *lianheng* alliance means prostrating oneself before the might of Qin, and states that routinely prostrate themselves find their territory pared down until nothing is left. On the other hand, joining the *hezong* alliance means rescuing impotent states that are about to be annexed by Qin, and states that routinely rescue their impotent neighbors find their own strength weakened until their armies are defeated.' (2001: 152)

Improving national strength

While IR scholars focus on the balance of power, ancient Chinese states-men tended to emphasize the importance of national strength as the foundation for long-term success in international competition. They generally believed that *fuguo* (economic wealth) and *qiangbing* (strong army) reforms, which involved reliance on one's own strength, were superior to balancing alliances, which involved reliance on others' capabilities. The early hegemonic rivals Chu and Jin first established a tight relationship between self-strengthening reforms and ascendance in relative capabilities. As this relationship was proven again by the next generation of hegemonic rivals Wu and Yue, it became a well-accepted regularity in ensuing centuries. As Chen Enlin[6] puts it, 'the reality showed that any state that had successfully implemented *fuguo qiangbing* reforms also became militarily strong.' (1991: 18) Because Qin was 'relatively backward economically and politically' in the early centuries (Yang, 1977: 10), it was also 'relatively weak and passive in wars' (Gao, 1995: 389).

Nevertheless, late development allowed Qin's theoreticians to draw from the large repertoire of coercive tools that had been accumulated through previous centuries. Shang Yang, who masterminded Qin's self-strengthening reforms from 356 BC on, borrowed heavily from Wei. IR scholars often presume that excellence in international competition rests on revolutionary innovations such as those introduced by Revolutionary and Napoleonic France. But excellence also rests on 'the ability to appropriate aspects of the rival solution and to make them subordinate parts of one's own approach.' (Unger, 1987: 176) While individual elements of Qin's policies, strategies and stratagems were not new, Shang Yang adapted old models to changing circumstances and 'put them into practice more systematically than had any of his precursors.' (Lewis, 1999: 611)

In his efforts to build up *qiangbing* or a strong army, Shang Yang borrowed from Wei the mass infantry formed of peasant-soldiers and a professional standing army formed of elite soldiers. To encourage valor among all ranks, Shang Yang introduced a system of rewards and punishments that was designed – to borrow from Douglass North and Robert Thomas – to 'bring social and private rates of return into closer parity.' (1973: 2) Compared with other reform programs, Qin's rewards were far more substantial (honors, lands, houses, servants, and other material reward) and its punishments far more severe (torture, death, and collective punishment). Moreover, unlike other systems of rewards and punishments which were introduced only in the course of major battles and abandoned as soon as fighting subsided, Qin's system of rewards and punishments was fully institutionalized with the *Qin Law* and a twenty-rank honor system.

The basis of *qiangbing* (military power) was *fuguo* (economic wealth). To maximize wealth in the pursuit of power, Shang Yang introduced an agriculture-for-war policy. Borrowing from Wei, Shang Yang granted rationally divided grids of land to all registered households and imposed high taxes in return. As such land grants became *de facto* private properties, peasants had strong incentives to improve productivity. The Qin state also promoted productivity by building irrigation projects and providing assistance in farm tools and technical advice. Although Qin's *fuguo* as well as *qiangbing* measures were based on Wei's, Shang Yang's package surpassed Wei's with an institutionalized system of handsome rewards and harsh punishments. Peasants who surpassed farming quotas would be rewarded with tax exemptions, but those who failed to fulfill quotas would have themselves and their dependents taken as government slaves. With a population that became 'diligent in production and courageous in war,' 'the country became rich and strong.' (Yang, 1977: 42)

IR scholars may wonder if Shang Yang's agriculture-for-war policy faced the so-called classical trade-off between guns and butter. In the age of national conscription and national taxation, the men of agriculture and warfare were one and the same. So how did Shang Yang solve 'the difficulty... of combining both intensive agriculture and frequent warfare'? (Duyvendak, 1963: 50) This trade-off should be particularly acute for Qin which had a relatively sparse population compared with other states. Shang Yang's solution was to encourage immigrants from neighboring Han, Wei and Zhao by giving them lands and houses with tax exemption for three generations. It is noteworthy that this policy allowed Qin to achieve *relative* as well as *absolute* gains. As the *Shang jun shu* (*Book of Lord Shang*) understands it, because this immigration policy drained peasant-soldiers from neighbors, 'this way of inflicting damage on the enemy [was] just as real as a victory in war.' (Duyvendak, 1963: 272)

After laying down basic military and economic measures in the reform program of 356 BC, Shang Yang introduced a second round of administrative reforms in 350 BC. Unlike balance-of-power theorists who pay little attention to state capacity, ancient Chinese reformers generally viewed administrative capacity as the basis of power and wealth. Indeed, the implementation of *fuguo qiangbing* reforms typically 'entailed the development of new administrative organs for effective local government throughout the territory of the state, practices for registering and policing large populations, and methods to measure and allocate land.' (Lewis, 1990: 9) Building on Wei's two-layered system of commanderies and counties, Shang Yang added two administrative layers of townships and villages. This measure represented a final step toward direct rule, giving the Qin court the capacity to penetrate the society down to the village level. Shang Yang used the unprecedented capacity to tighten the policy of household registration which formed the basis for military service, land tax, and corvée. Members of the Qin population were registered when they reached the height of 4 feet 11 inches (about 16 to 17 years of age); from then on, they were obliged to fulfill military and corvée obligations and to pay full taxes until they retired at age 60. (Yates, 1987: 231) Shang Yang further proceeded to systematize universal military conscription by grouping village households into units of five on the model of five-man squads in military organization. As eligible villagers could be easily mobilized as squads and platoons, 'virtually an entire country could go to war.' (Sawyer, 1994: 76) In addition, to ensure that the central court was in full control of all human and material resources, officials at all levels had to submit annual reports on 'the number of granaries ..., the number of able-bodied men and of women, the number of old and of weak people, the number of officials and of officers, ... the number of horses and of oxen, the quantity of fodder and of straw.' (*Shang jun shu*, trans. Duyvendak, 1963: 205) With the ability to engage in *total* mobilization of national resources, Qin's power and wealth reached a new height.

Minimizing emulation by other states

It may be argued that efforts at self-strengthening are elusive, because 'states tend to emulate the successful policies of others' and engage in what we call an 'arms race.' (Waltz, 1979: 124) Indeed, before Qin's rise, domination-seeking states would always be surpassed by new ones which borrowed from and improved upon successful models of previous powers. So why did other states not pursue even more comprehensive self-strengthening reforms and cleverer strategies and stratagems to overtake Qin? At the minimum, why did the six states not imitate Qin's self-strengthening reforms and clever strategies to resist Qin?

In understanding the emulation problem, it is important to realize that the pursuit of *fuguo qiangbing* reforms was a systemic phenomenon not unique to Qin. Qin's ascendance from relative weakness to hegemony in the period 356 to 284 BC was eclipsed by the growth of Qi – just as balancing against Qin was eclipsed by balancing against Qi. When Qin's Duke Xiao introduced Shang Yang's comprehensive reforms in 356 BC, Qi's King Wei also launched reforms to build up Qi's strength. Because Qi was traditionally a stronger power, it enjoyed the initial upper hand. In 353 BC, Qi defeated Wei, the then hegemonic power. In 341 BC, Qi further annihilated Wei's core forces and seized the hegemonic status. In ensuing decades, Qin gradually reversed its relative power *vis-à-vis* Han and Chu as well as Wei. But it was not until at least 316 BC, when Qin doubled its size by conquering the non-Sinitic states Ba and Shu, that Qin caught up with Qi. Qi recognized Qin's equal status when rulers of both states jointly proclaimed themselves emperors in 288 BC. But Qi soon surpassed Qin after conquering the prosperous Song in 286 BC. At that stage, however, jealousy of Qi tilted the Qi-Qin competition in Qin's favor. An anti-Qi alliance almost annihilated Qi in 284 BC.

After Qin emerged as the unipolar hegemon, why did other states not emulate Qin's self-strengthening reforms? Again, the context matters. All other states had pursued some variants of self-strengthening reforms by the turn of the 3rd century BC. In the early 5th century BC, Wei, Zhao and Han developed progressive institutions during a bloody civil war which carved up Jin. Around 445 BC, Wei kicked off the new wave of self-strengthening reforms by systematizing preexisting practices. In the 380s BC, Chu introduced some of Wei's reform measures. In 355 BC, Han systematized bureaucratic rules for appointing and appraising officials. After Qi's invasion in 314 BC, Yan secretly carried out self-strengthening reforms while feigning allegiance to Qi. Later in 307 BC, Zhao created the light cavalry on the model of northern nomadic tribes. In short, during Qin's early ascendance, all other great powers introduced various elements of self-strengthening reforms such as the mass army, national taxation, household registration, hierarchical administration, and so on. Although no other reform programs matched Qin's in terms of comprehensiveness and institutionalization, other states were able to use their increased national strengths to pursue their own opportunistic expansion in the shadow of the Qin-Qi struggle for supremacy.

Such a background is important. States which had recently pursued self-strengthening reforms and had already experienced rise and decline would find it more difficult to pick up renewed strengths to play the game of catching up. For Qi, the dramatic defeat by the Yan-led alliance in 284 BC caused it to withdraw into isolationism. Other formerly self-strengthened great powers did not fare much better. The relatively weak Yan achieved the great-power status only in the course of fighting Qi and lost the status after it was driven out of Qi in 279 BC. The once-hegemonic Wei had been pushed out of the great-power status in 293 BC. The originally weaker Han had similarly become Qin's easy prey after 293 BC. The once-largest Chu had been alternately weakened by Qi and Qin after it was deceived into breaking up with Qi in 312 BC. Chu further lost to Qin the western half of its core territory in 279 BC. At the end of the Yan-Qi war in 279 BC, therefore, Zhao was the only great power that had pursued self-strengthening reforms but had not started on the road to decline.

In understanding the puzzle of missing emulation, it is also important to keep in mind that there may be a disjuncture between motivation and capability. As in the balance of power, the pursuit of self-strengthening reforms is not simply a function of the desire to survive. As Jon Elster points out, 'when people are badly off their motivation to innovate... is high. Their capacity or opportunity to do so, however, is the lowest when they are in tight circumstances.' (1989: 18) Qin's rulers and strategists seemed to understand this rationale. To further weaken other states' motivation and capability for renewed resistance, Qin engaged in massive brutality and bribery. In 268 BC, a strategist Fan Sui proposed to Qin's King Zhao the policy of attacking people as well as territory. He argued that Qin should aim at not just territorial expansion, but also 'the destruction of armies on such a scale that rival states would lose the capacity to fight.' (Lewis, 1999: 639) Before Fan Sui articulated this policy, Qin's commanders had already begun mass slaughters of defeated armies. Qin is recorded to have killed over 1.5 million soldiers of other states between 356 and 236 BC. While these numbers are likely to be exaggerated and should not be taken as absolute battle death figures, they nevertheless present a picture of ruthless brutality in Qin's pursuit of domination.[7] As the six states lost more and more territories and peasant-soldiers, it became increasingly difficult for them to engage in meaningful buildups. Han and Wei, in particular, became so frightened that they increasingly followed a policy of appeasement – ceding territory without fighting. As Stephen Van Evera observes, '[w]ar is a trial of strength. If its results were foretold, the weaker could yield to the stronger and achieve the same result without suffering the pain of war.' (1999: 14–15) In Han's and Wei's calculation, if they fought Qin, they would most likely lose and suffer further devastating losses of territory and troops; even if they happened to win, they would still suffer from exhaustion. (Zhang and Liu, 1988: 94) After the last hope for *hezong* vanished in the 240s BC, therefore, further resistance was no less suicidal than appeasement. To further weaken the motivation for resistance, Qin also bribed high officials in the courts of other states so that these corrupt officials would convince their kings to befriend Qin.

If Qin was so astoundingly successful at using stratagems to defeat more powerful foes when it was relatively weak and prevent other states from catching up when it was hegemonic, why did other states not emulate Qin? Although the stratagems of bribery and deception are very simple and obvious, they can be effective as long as individuals have desires for power, profit, and pleasures. As the *Sunzi* suggests, 'if [the enemy] seeks benefit then tempt him.' (trans. Lewis, 1990: 124) For self-indulgent individuals, it would not be difficult to entice them with 'the allure of beauty, and debauch them with scents, music, and sexual delights.' (Sawyer, 1998: 231) Moreover, bribery of high officials could cripple armies because states were not unitary actors as assumed by realists. As Han Fei, an observer of the late Warring States period, pointed out, the interest of the ministers and the interest of the ruler were diametrically opposed. (Goldin, 2001: 151) Indeed, even kings should not be treated as synonymous with their states, because the self-interest of the ruler did not always coincide with the national interest of the state. (Goldin, 2001: 152) In ancient China where power struggles were common and victorious commanders had the capability to threaten the throne, a ruler's personal interest in staying in power in the short term could diverge from the public interest of national survival in the long term. Thus, the stratagem of estrangement was repeatedly effective whenever insecured kings were suspicious of competent generals and high officials were at odds with their rulers and with one another.

Reducing the costs of war

Qin's superiority in both strength and stratagems allows us to understand another puzzle: why did Qin not suffer from overextension? Wars – even when victorious – are extremely costly. As the *Sunzi* calculates, 'when you send forth an army of a hundred thousand on a campaign, marching them out a thousand *li*, the expenditures… will be one thousand pieces of gold per day.' (trans. Sawyer, 1998: 127) In the same manner, the *Wuzi* (named after Wu Qi, Wei's famous general who seized large tracts of strategic territory from Qin between 413 and 385 BC) advises that: 'any state that constantly engaged in warfare would simply exhaust itself and, irrespective of its victorious record, ultimately be vanquished.' (Sawyer, 1994: 308) Wei indeed lost the hegemony in 341 BC and then the great-power status in 293 BC. Qi, in turn, experienced exhaustion from the conquest of Song in 286 BC and then a dramatic defeat by a Yan-led alliance in 284 BC.

However, while Wei and Qi engaged in costly direct confrontations with enemies, Qin largely avoided such occasions during its ascendance to domination. When IR theorists discuss the costs of war, they often overlook the ancient Chinese wisdom that such costs are subject to manipulation. As the *Sunzi* argues: 'to win all of your battles is not the highest skill. To bring the enemy's army to submit without combat is the highest skill. Therefore the best is to attack his stratagems and deliberations, the next best is to attack his system of alliances, the next best is to attack his army…' (trans. Lewis, 1990: 116) Thus, the divide-and-conquer strategies and ruthless stratagems discussed above helped to overcome not only the balance of power, but also the rising costs of expansion. In general, Qin's costs of war were much reduced by avoiding overwhelming alliances and multi-front wars, making friends with target's enemies, making tactical peace with secondary targets to isolate prime targets, launching surprise attacks when targets were unprepared, seizing moments of opportunity when targeted states were preoccupied with other states, and threatening weakened states to cede territory without fighting at all.

It is most remarkable that, although Qin's ascendance was successively blocked by Wei, Qi and Zhao, Qin did not have to defeat the first two with its own troops. Wei was brought down by Qi. Qi, in turn, was toppled by a Yan-led alliance. It was only in its confrontation with Zhao that Qin had to fight a formidable foe in battle. The experience of Zhao further shows that stratagems were useful not just on the diplomatic front, but also on the battle front. In an age when victory hinged on forging the multitude of five-man squads into an integrated entity to strike at the decisive moment, 'forcing a change in commander could reverse previous defeats, even result in complete victory.' (Sawyer, 1998: 99) Qin deployed this tactic against not only Zhao in 260 and 229 BC, but also Wei in 340 BC and an anti-Qin alliance in 247 BC.

It is also noteworthy that Qin rarely relied on overwhelming army strength to secure victories. As the *Sunzi* understands it, army strength is 'a question of dividing up the numbers.' (trans. Sawyer, 1994: 187) For example, in a battle with Han and Wei in 293 BC, Qin's troops were outnumbered by 240,000 allied troops. But as Han's and Wei's armies fought separately without unified command, Qin's commander could defeat them one by one. In the direct confrontation with Zhao in 262–257 BC, Qin mobilized only its standing army plus male populations aged 15 and above from the nearby Henei commandery. Classical texts record that Zhao lost 450,000 troops in 260 BC. While this figure is most likely exaggerated, Zhao apparently engaged in massive – if not total – mobilization to fend off Qin's aggression. For Qin, mobilization on a comparable scale occurred only in the final wars of unification. Even in the last war against Chu in 226–223 BC, Qin originally sent only 200,000 troops. It was only after an initial campaign went badly that Qin more than doubled its troops in a subsequent campaign.

Overcoming offensive disadvantages and seizing offensive advantages

It is sometimes argued that Qin could achieve domination because it enjoyed offensive advantages. Stephen Van Evera suggests that conquest is easier if there are no major 'oceans, lakes, mountains, wide rivers, dense jungles, trackless deserts, or other natural barriers that impede offensive movement or give defenders natural strong points.' (1998: 19; 1999: 154) However, any topographical map of the Chinese continent can show that the area of the ancient Chinese system is marked by significant geographical barriers including the Qin Ranges, Taihang Mountains, Yellow River, Yangtze River, Dan River, and Huai River. If there were no *systemic* geographical advantages in the ancient Chinese system, did Qin nevertheless enjoy some *dyadic* geographical advantages *vis-à-vis* its targets? Mark Lewis indeed points out that 'Qin enjoyed a splendid geographic situation that combined productivity and security. It was accessible from the East only through the Hangu Pass and from the southeast through the Wu Pass.' (1999: 596) However, as Zhao's King Wuling saw it, such a splendid location would still be vulnerable to an attack from the poorly guarded northern frontiers. Even more notably, various natural barriers along the Yellow River originally belonged to Qin's neighbors. Qin even lost strategic territory on the West bank of the Yellow River to Wei in the period 413 to 385 BC.

Qin's ultimate success at universal domination calls of theories of offense-defense balance. Although m offense-defense balance treat geography as a 'hard cor states cannot change or evade' (Glaser and Kaufman, strategists in ancient China believed that geographical could be overcome and geographical advantages could noted earlier, Qin used cunning stratagems against Wei to recover lost territory on the West bank of the Yellow River. Moreover, although theories of offense-defense balance argue that 'terrain that slows or channelizes movement, or that strains logistics, strengthens the defense more than terrain that does not' (Glaser and Kaufman, 1998: 65), Qin's experience reflected the ancient Chinese wisdom that difficult terrain could be exploited. For instance, when Qin planned to strike a fatal blow at Chu in 280 BC, Qin contemplated among the alternative routes of (1) the easily accessible but heavily garrisoned central plain, (2) the similarly guarded Yangtze River valley, or (3) the rough but practically unguarded Qin Ranges. Qin's decision was to send expeditionary forces to climb the unguarded mountains to catch Chu off-guard, and then send reinforcements and supplies downstream on the Yangtze River. In 278 BC, Qin successfully seized the western half of Chu's territory including its capital. The experience of Zhao was no less remarkable. Zhao was originally separated from Qin by the Yellow River and the steep Taihang Mountains. With such formidable geographical barriers, Zhao was relatively free of Qin's encroachment well into the early 3rd century BC. However, Qin slowly approached Zhao on the central plain by seizing pieces of territory from Han and Wei. By 262 BC, Qin encircled Zhao and was ready to launch a full-scale invasion of Zhao.

It may be argued that Qin was blessed with a peripheral location which facilitated domination. Robert Gilpin, for instance, points out that 'the ultimate beneficiaries of efforts to change international systems have more frequently than not been third parties on the periphery of the international system.' (1981: 52) A peripheral state is supposed to have more room for expansion, fewer fronts to defend, and lower involvement with warfare in the center. It is true that Qin enjoyed these advantages while Han and Wei were locked in the center and Qi had no peripheral frontiers for easy expansion. However, Chu, Zhao, and Yan also shared Qin's advantages. (See Map 6.3.) Moreover, the peripheral location is a two-edged sword – it also lengthened the distance of expansion. As Charles Glaser and Chaim Kaufman argue, 'distance favors defense. If the attacker must travel a considerable

Van Evera is wrong to argue that 'the outcomes of battles and wars reveal the shift toward the offense.' (1999: 181) He is also wrong to think that 'Qin conquered all of China in a rapid campaign lasting only 9 years at the end of the Warring States period (230–221 BCE).' (*ibid.*) Such a view completely overlooks the difficult struggles and maneuvers which had begun over a century earlier. Overall, Qin's success involved seven generations of rulers through 56 wars involving great powers (51 initiated by Qin and five initiated by other states) in the course of 135 years (356–221 BC). When Qin first emerged from relative weakness in the mid-4th century BC, the obstacles it faced were considered insurmountable by statesmen of the time – and similar obstacles continue to be regarded as insurmountable by current IR theorists. In the end, what allowed Qin to roll up the system was not some offensive advantages, but superiority in statecraft.

Consolidating conquered territories and maximizing extraction

Dissolving balancing alliances, avoiding direct confrontations, and scoring victories on the battlefields were significant markers of excellence in international competition. Nevertheless, to achieve universal domination, there were still the challenges of consolidating conquests and making them pay. Throughout world history, conquests often drained national resources rather than provided additional revenues. Stuart Kaufman argues that 'administrative capability' has been a critical 'limiting factor' for system consolidation. (1997: 174) In this regard, it is significant that China developed the centralized, bureaucratic state two millennia ahead of Europe. (Creel, 1970b) As Richard Walker remarked, 'without this background of development,' 'the unification of China... could never have taken place.' (1953: 35)

As early as 686 BC, Chu turned a newly conquered city-state, Shen, into a *xian* or 'an administrative district governed by an official appointed by and responsible to the central government.' (Creel, 1970: 132) In ensuing centuries, Chu absorbed more and more conquered territories as *xian*. With rudimentary centralized administration, Chu not only could consolidate conquests, but also extract handsome revenues in terms of military service, land tax, and corvée. Seeing Chu's success, Jin and Qin copied Chu's practice. In the late Spring and Autumn period, Jin established another form of directly administered district, the *jun*, in 'newly conquered, relatively under-populated, frontier regions.' (Lewis, 1999: 614) At the onset of the Warring States period,

Wei reorganized the whole country – core as well as conquered territories – into a two-tier structure of *jun* (commanderies) and *xian* (which evolved from dependent districts to counties). By the time Qin rose to domination, the *jun* and *xian* were standard administrative units. When Qin advanced eastward, it could readily incorporate preexisting *jun* and *xian* into its own administrative hierarchy.

Qin's ability to roll up a whole international system was also aided by the policy of gradual, piecemeal encroachment. As discussed earlier, piecemeal encroachment weakened the awareness of Qin as a threat and alleviated the obstacle of distance. This policy also allowed Qin to adjust territorial expansion with its gradual growth in relative capability. By the time Qin launched the final wars of unification, Qin had already consolidated more than half of the territory in the system. Moreover, the sovereign territorial states in the last decades were no longer the same entities as when they were hegemons and great powers: Han and Wei had been reduced to the size of single commanderies, and Chu and Zhao had been reduced by about half compared with their size at the turn of the 3rd century BC.

Although Qin followed gradualism for over a century, it sought to sweep through the system as fast as possible when it launched the final wars of unification in 236 BC. Qin's strategists seemed to understand that targeted states should now know that death was imminent and so would be highly motivated to engage in military buildups and form *hezong* alliances. To simultaneously achieve speedy victories and minimize last-minute resistance, Qin again complemented its overwhelming strength with handsome bribes. In the face of imminent death, therefore, Qin's targets could only rely on 'self-help' – in the literal sense of self-reliance. Fighting alone, the six states were defeated one after another. Qin conquered Han in 230 BC, Zhao in 228 BC, Wei in 225 BC, Chu in 223 BC, Yan in 222 BC, and Qi in 221 BC. The state of Qin established the Qin Dynasty in 221 BC.

Conclusion

As a most-similar case, the ancient Chinese system challenges IR scholars to rethink Eurocentric theories. Balance-of-power theorists are correct to argue that the balance of power is a transhistorical phenomenon, but they are wrong to presume that balancing is normally effective. In the *zhongguo* system, Qin achieved universal domination by the shrewd combination of self-strengthening reforms, divide-and-conquer strategies, and brutish stratagems. Qin's ascendance was backed by military, economic, and administrative capabilities. While other states did form balancing alliances against Qin's conquests, they also pursued their own opportunistic expansion and had conflicts of interests among themselves. Qin further weakened the balance of power by diplomatic and strategic maneuvers. As a result, anti-Qin alliances came about very slowly and infrequently, they did not have enough members to overpower Qin, they rarely had unified command, and they readily disintegrated. With weak balancing, Qin's rise to domination was only slowed down but not checked. Confronted with the failure of balancing in the *zhongguo* system, some IR scholars retreat to the position that Qin's targets must be uniquely incapable of balancing or that conquest must be inherently easy in this system. Such a presumption is not warranted. Instead, scholars should reconsider the Eurocentric belief that the balance of power is immutable.

Notes

1 For selected sources on ancient China, see Chen, 1991; Gao, 1995; Hsu, 1965; Lewis, 1990, 1999; Lin, 1992; Sanjun daxue, 1976; Sawyer, 1994; Yang, 1986; Zhang and Liu, 1988. For more extensive sources, see Hui, 2005, ch. 2.

2 All quantitative indicators are based on Hui (2005: appendices II and III). Wars in which Qin was the target are not counted among these 11 wars.

3 At the time, rulers with Zhou lineage still retained their feudal titles such as 'marquis' and 'duke.' The non-Zhou states of Chu and Yue were exceptions. Soon after Wei's move, other Zhou states – despite their boycott of Wei this time – also acquired the title 'king.'

4 One *li* is roughly equivalent to 0.3 mile or 0.49 kilometer. There is no agreement among historians whether 600 *li* referred to 600 square *li* or 600 *li* on one side.

5 By the 3rd century BC, Qin pursued a policy of killing enemy soldiers *en masse* so as to prevent defeated states from recovering. Classical texts record hundreds of thousands of battle deaths in major battles. Ancient Chinese data typically reflect 'orders of magnitude' instead of absolute figures (Lewis, 1999: 626). But such data may be 'less inaccurate than thought' because states of the period were certainly capable of mobilizing very high per centages of their male population, particularly when threatened with extinction. (See Sawyer, 1998: 559, fn. 38).

6 Chinese names follow the Chinese convention of beginning with surnames.

7 For a discussion of battle deaths, see Hui (2005: chs. 2 and 3, appendix III).

7

'A Republic for Expansion': The Roman Constitution and Empire and Balance-of-Power Theory

Daniel Deudney

The Roman legacy and the balance of power

Ancient Rome looms far larger in the modern Western political inheritance and historical imagination than any other ancient or non-Western system. For medieval and early modern Europeans, the sprawling monumental ruins of imperial Rome served as the inescapable and ubiquitous marker against which they measured their decline and then their progress. For the Roman Church and Holy Roman Empire, the late Roman Empire served as a source of legitimacy by descent. Many of the landmark works of medieval and early modern thought wrestled with the Roman legacy and its meaning (Millar, 2002). For Augustine, the sack of Rome by barbarian armies served as the template for the vanities and futilities of human aspiration. For Machiavelli the early Roman Republic offered a model for political renewal held up against the decadence of the Roman Church (Sullivan, 1996). For Montesquieu (1965 [1734]) and the Enlightenment, Roman militarism served as a model against which the progress of the moderns could be measured. And Rousseau launched the counter-Enlightenment with an appeal to the rustic virtues of the early Romans. For the American founders the collapse of the republican constitution exemplified a problem to be solved. For two millennia no serious thinker of the first rank could afford to write without an interpretation of the Roman political experience. These interpretations have been integral to the development of Western politics and theory, making Rome not the story of another civilization, but the first chapter in the story of Western civilization. Even in the 19th and 20th centuries, as the preoccupation with things Roman began to slip to the margins of Western thought, major theorists such as Marx and Weber offered substantial treatments of the Roman historical experience.

Roman legacies are also deeply woven into the fabric of balance-of-power theory. For the first systematic theorists of the balance of power in the early modern period, the Roman Empire was of central importance. In first conceptualizing and theorizing about the modern European state-system as a distinctive political arrangement, theorists pointed to the 'universal monarchy' of the ancient Romans as the antithesis of the plural 'republic of Europe' constituted by an array of power restraints, among which was the 'balance of power.' To the friends of the 'liberties of Europe' any assault or subversion of the balance betrayed an aspiration to re-erect the Roman imperium, and defenders of the balance and the plural political order it underpinned were continuously battling the persistent claim, inherited from Roman antiquity and its medieval ghosts, that the peace of Europe depended upon the unification of Europe into one empire.

The Roman experience also played a central role in modern theorizing about the domestic or 'interior' balance of power and its role in underpinning limited constitutional government. For the modern republican enemies of monarchical and absolutist government, the experience of the death of the Roman Republic at the hands of ambitious generals such as Julius Caesar served as a dominant historical reference point for the argument that the imperial enlargement of states in pursuit of security posed a grave threat to internal limited government. The conclusion drawn from the Roman record was that external expansion was deeply problematic for the preservation of an interior balance of power supportive of political liberty and limited government, and the overall prospect for republican government seemed bleak, as the absence of external expansion and thus small size entailed insecurity and vulnerability, while large size and the external security it provided produced an internal concentration of power fatal to popular political liberty. Such arguments about large size, the interior balance of power, and political liberty played a central role in the theory and practice of the American founding, and it was the founders' claim to combine large size with republican government through federal union that was the basis for their bold assertion that the American constitution was a 'new order of the ages' capable of ushering in a new era of strength and security for free government.

Despite the extensive role played by the Roman experience in forging the key concepts of international theory, 20th century international theorists have largely ignored Roman history and the implications of Rome's ascent to regional universal Empire. International theorists during the Cold War were avid students of Thucydides, and looked to the three decades of the Peloponnesian War as an early case study of bipolar system dynamics and democratic-totalitarian rivalry (Fliess, 1966; Lebow and Strauss, 1991). But international theorists have virtually ignored the several century rise of Republican Rome to unrivaled dominance in Mediterranean world as a case study in the failure of balance of power-based plural state-systems. Only in the last few years has this neglect begun to diminish with a rise of interest in the precedents to American unipolarity and the consequences of American Empire for constitutional limited government (Todd, 2002; Johnson, 2004).

For students of comparative international system theory, the extant historical record of Roman expansion provides far more written material than is available for any other ancient state-system. Several major ancient histories of crucial periods of the Roman ascent, most notably those of Polybius and Livy are largely extant, as are works by many other ancient political writers, and this written record has been augmented and interpreted by several centuries of classical scholarship and archaeology (Walbank, 1954). Despite its relative abundance, the historical source material has many gaps and tells the story of Roman expansion almost entirely from the Roman side. Even more limiting is the fact that ancient writers placed great emphasis on the deeds, words, and characters of key historical figures presented as models for emulation or condemnation, with relatively little analysis of broader political structure, and even less about economics and military logistics. Despite these significant limitations, the extant historical record provides a rich array of empirical information about the failures of balance-of-power practices to halt the seemingly inexorable rise of Roman imperial power.

Explaining Roman success

The question of why Rome, of all the many polities in the Mediterranean basin in ancient times, came to dominate all others has been a topic of perennial fascination and serious analysis since ancient times. The explanation offered in the 3rd century BCE by the Greek historian Polybius – that Rome's internal constitution was the basis for its success – remains the most compelling overall explanation, but is incomplete in several important ways. This domestic regime-centered explanation, while hallowed by time, is cast in terminologies non-congruent with the conceptual categories of modern social science, neglects several system-level and material-contextual factors, and gives little attention to the limits and weaknesses of Rome's adversaries.

The argument of this chapter proceeds in two main steps. In the next five sections, I survey five stages or periods of Roman expansion, summarizing the key features of each period. Stretching from the founding of Rome as a village in 753 BCE through its territorial zenith under the emperor Trajan in 117 CE, to its collapse in the west in the middle of the 5th century, the pattern of Roman expansion is roughly broken into five periods, each examined in a section: (1) conquest of Italy; (2) the Punic Wars with Carthage for control of the Western Mediterranean; (3) the absorption of the Hellenistic kingdoms in Greece and the Eastern Mediterranean; (4) a mopping up and filling in during the late Republic and early Principate; and (5) three episodes of substantial expansion during the Principate (conquest of Britain, Dacia, and Mesopotamia). During the later imperial period, conflict at the northern and eastern frontiers and wars of imperial succession shed light on the sources and limits of Roman power.

In the second part of the chapter, I consider four clusters of factors which taken in combination provide a multi-faceted explanation for Roman success. The first cluster of factors concerns the system level factors: the distribution and diffusion of technological capabilities, the fluidity of the system's borders, the bellicosity of the interactions among the actors, and the roles of international institutions and practices, most notably counter-hegemonic alliances. The second cluster of factors concerns the socio-economic foundations of military and organizational capability in ancient polities, specifically the status of the agriculturalists who made up the bulk of the populations in ancient polities, and the double-edged role of urbanization in shaping military efficacy. The third cluster of factors concerns five Roman domestic regime characteristics, specifically the 'mixed' or balanced constitution, the proto-democratic character of Roman political institutions, the relative 'stateness' of the Roman Republic, the capabilities of the Senate as a guiding force in Roman statecraft, and Roman practices of hegemonic alliances and assimilation of defeated adversaries. The final section contrasts these features of the Roman polity with those of its typical adversaries (monarchical Empires, tribal confederations, and city-states) and argues that each had structurally rooted weaknesses.

Roman expansion in Italy

In the roughly five centuries between the customary date of the founding of the village of Rome by the brigand Romulus (753 BCE) and the outbreak of the First Punic War (264), Rome came through a lengthy sequence of wars to dominate almost all of the Italian peninsula (Livy, 1960, 1982). Italy before its unification by Roman arms was a geographic rather than a political unit, inhabited by a highly diverse array of peoples with varied levels of political organization. The peoples of the peninsula included numerous autonomous Greek colonial city-states along the southern coasts, native tribal peoples in the rugged interior, notably the Samnites, the urbanized Etruscans of Tuscany, and the tribal Celtic peoples of the Po Valley in the far north (Alfoldi, 1965; Scullard, 1967; Ellis, 1998; Salmon, 1967). In the course of Roman expansion in Italy, Rome never faced a general counter-hegemonic alliance of adversaries, and its expansion was a gradual and piecemeal process stretching across several centuries (Cornell, 1989).

The immediate vicinity of Rome, the plain of Latium, was inhabited by many other towns and villages of Italic peoples of Indo-European origins. Like many of its neighbors, the town of Rome was initially ruled by petty kings, possibly of Etruscan origins. After rule under seven such rulers, the Romans ejected their last local king, Tarquinius Superbus in 510 and established what they referred to as a *res publica*, a form of government which proved superbly fitted to survive and prosper in its environment of nearly incessant petty warfare with its neighbors. This political arrangement, initially an oligarchy, was given a substantial democratic component in the wake of a general military strike of the lower classes, the plebs, who provided the manpower for the Roman army (Raaflaub, 1986). With plebian rights protected by a class of elected officials known as the tribunes, who could veto the action of any magistrate deemed abusive of popular rights, and its voice heard in a series of assemblies (which elected all public magistrates, and decided all acts of war and peace and all matters of taxation), the political constitution of the early Roman Republic maintained a high degree of public support and loyalty among its citizens (Taylor, 1966; Millar, 1998).

Machiavelli (1970 [1531]: 17–18) observed that Rome was a 'republic for expansion' in contrast to the republics of Sparta and Venice, which were 'republics for preservation.' While it may be doubted that the constitution was designed *for* expansion, the Republic developed several approaches which were highly effective. During the first and most lengthy phase of the conquest of Italy, Roman practices toward defeated adversaries were distinctive. Although Roman policy toward states viewed as particular transgressors, particularly perceived acts of betrayal or revolt, could be harshly savage, the general pattern was quite enlightened by ancient standards. Unlike Athenian hegemony under Pericles and his successors, Rome permitted the ruling groups in defeated polities to remain in power and to enjoy nearly complete internal autonomy, and did not impose direct taxation. In return, alliances with any state but Rome were prohibited, and the allies were required to provide substantial levies of troops to be employed and commanded by Roman generals. In this way Rome turned defeated enemies into protected clients. As a result of these arrangements, the Italian allies had little motivation to rebel against Roman hegemony and Rome was able to tap the military manpower of all Italy without the burdens of direct administration (Crawford, 1992: 31–56).

The Romans were also relatively assimilative of other peoples. During the expansion in Latium, the inhabitants of defeated towns gained full Roman citizenship. The early Romans also appear to have been adept at incorporating the religious practices and rituals of their neighbors. As Roman power expanded across larger areas in Italy, the Romans on occasion offered the populations of particularly loyal towns and cities a diluted form of citizenship, *civitas sine suffrergio* (citizenship without voting). It is notable that the largest revolt of the Italian allies against Roman rule, in the Social War of 91, occurring at a point when Rome had become effective master of the Mediterranean world, did not aim to seek independence from Roman rule, but greater inclusion in the Roman polity, and its culmination was the extension of *civitas sine suffrergio* to a wide strata of the upper classes across Italy (Gabba, 1994; Sherwin-White, 1939).

The Punic Wars

The climax of the struggle for dominance in the Mediterranean world was a series of three wars between Rome and the Phoenician city-state of Carthage, which was located near the site of the modern city of Tunis in Northern Africa (Warmington, 1960; Lancel, 1997). Prior to this struggle, the Western Mediterranean had been marked by the presence of two subsystems, one centered on Carthage and its far-flung trading network, the other on Rome's Italian territorial dominion, and they coexisted without major interaction (Whittaker, 1978). In the First Punic War (264–41) Rome wrested Sicily from Carthaginian control. In the Second Punic War (218–201), widely seen by both ancient and modern historians as the climax of the struggle, war was waged over the entire Western Mediterranean for 17 years. This war culminated in the expulsion of Carthage from the Iberian peninsula, the imposition of a substantial indemnity, and the reduction of Carthage to its immediate original territory. In the Third Punic War (149–46), more a massacre than a war of even near equals, Rome besieged Carthage itself, razed it to the ground, and killed or enslaved its entire population (Livy, 1965; Goldsworthy, 2000).

The First Punic War was the first occasion Roman power had been deployed beyond the Italian peninsula. At the outset of the war, Sicily was a complex patchwork of Greek and Carthaginian colonial cities with a long history of conflicts, and restive under a recently imposed Carthaginian hegemony. Rome was drawn into conflict through its alliances and the request from its protectorates for assistance against the encroachment of rival powers. This war was notable for marking the beginning of Roman naval activity. Previously lacking naval capability or experience, the Roman navy reportedly built a fleet of ships modeled after a shipwrecked Carthaginian vessel. Its first fleet, comprised of several hundred vessels, was destroyed in a battle, and substantial losses were also incurred from storms, but Rome replaced what it lost and eventually defeated the main Carthaginian fleet, which combined with victories of Roman armies in Sicily, led Carthage to sue for peace and to withdraw from Sicily. This struggle points to both the Roman capacity for emulation of new technologies and its formidable resource base which enabled Rome to keep fighting despite severe losses.

With both sides anticipating a fuller clash, the Carthaginians sought to recoup their position through the conquest of the tribal peoples in the hinterlands of the Iberian peninsula, where Carthage had long established coastal trading outposts. In a struggle marked by great savagery, roughly the western half of the peninsula was brought under Carthaginian control (Scullard, 1989). From this base, Hannibal the legendary commander and scourge of Rome, invaded on land across Southern Gaul and boldly crossed the Alps, arriving in the Po Valley with an army of hardened veterans, a contingent of war elephants, and an assortment of Gallic allies gathered along the way. Thus began the greatest military ordeal of the Roman Republic (Lazenby, 1998b). Catching the Romans by surprise, Hannibal defeated a Roman army, killing a consul, at the northern edge of Roman territory, and then proceeded into Rome's heartland on the peninsula where he ambushed and annihilated a Roman field army at Lake Trasimene (217). Now ranging at will across Italy, Hannibal annihilated a second Roman field army of 70,000 men at Cannae (216), marking one of the three greatest defeats of Roman arms prior to the collapse of the Empire in the West. Unwilling or unable to move against the city of Rome itself, Hannibal apparently hinged his hopes for victory upon the defection of Roman allies and clients. But with a few exceptions, defections did not occur, and Hannibal was forced after some 15 years of living off the land in

Italy to return to Africa where he was defeated at Zama by Publius Cornelius Scipio, (subsequently 'Africanus'). Even while suffering staggering losses in the Italian theater, Roman armies were making major advances against Carthage in Spain, where Roman armies defeated several Carthaginian armies, and were welcomed by substantial numbers of Iberians as liberators from the recently imposed heavy hand of Carthage. At this key juncture of Roman vulnerability, Carthage formed an alliance with the king of Macedonia, Philip V. Unfortunately for Carthage, however, Philip's aims were limited to the reassertion of control over the Illyrian coast (on the Greek side of the Adriatic Sea), where Rome had advanced, largely as a side-effect of fighting pirates based there. Philip sent no assistance to Hannibal, either in Italy or after his retreat to Africa, and this alliance, which in principle could have been a decisive counter-hegemonic alliance against Rome, must be classified as a limited aim, jackal alliance.

Looking beyond the details of this pivotal struggle, a broader lesson about Roman statecraft can be drawn. It appears that the Roman practice of imposing hegemonic alliances on defeated adversaries in Italy may have played a decisive role in this conflict (Errington, 1972: 4–5, 62–90). Despite the shock of Hannibal's sudden appearance and string of battlefield victories, he was unable to evoke significant defections from Rome's Italian client allies, and Rome was able to replenish its armies (Reid, 1915: 87–124). In contrast, the Roman general Scipio was able to evoke widespread rebellion of the tribal groups in Carthaginian dominated Eastern Spain who chafed under harsh and exploitative direct Carthaginian rule and Carthage's dependence on mercenaries made raising additional armies burdensomely expensive. In addition, the outcome was heavily shaped by Rome's greater resource base (Mommsen, 1911).

Whatever the causes of its outcome, the war with Hannibal had a transformative effect on Roman conceptions of where its security interests lay. The speed with which Hannibal had entered Italy, the great distances he had traversed to do so, and the fact that he had nearly brought Rome to its knees, drove home the lesson to the Senate that Roman security was potentially threatened by states anywhere in the Mediterranean Basin. The brief and ineffective alliance between Carthage and Macedonia had not affected the outcome of the war, but it did mark the full joining of the subsystems of the Western and Eastern Mediterranean. No longer would Rome confine itself to Italy and its immediate environs, but felt compelled to concern itself with developments everywhere in the Mediterranean world.

The absorption of the Hellenistic East

The pattern by which Rome came to dominate the lands of the Eastern Mediterranean was significantly different from its epic struggle with Carthage. The lands to the east of Italy were the seats of highly developed kingdoms and city-states, and were far wealthier and more populous than the lands of the Western Mediterranean. The Greek city-states of Southern Italy had been gradually absorbed prior to the Punic Wars, and the experience of Pyrrhus's campaigns (282–75 BCE) and the role of Macedonia during the Second Punic War had demonstrated to the Senate that Roman security was potentially affected by developments in Greece. (Pyrrhus, the King of Epirus, was invited to Italy to protect the Greek city-states from Roman encroachments, marking Rome's first conflict peoples from the developed Eastern Mediterranean. Pyrrhus defeated the Romans in two battles, after which he is reported to have said that another such victory would ruin him. The Romans persisted and eventually defeated Pyrrhus, who retired from Italy, leaving the Greeks colonies under Roman rule (Lomas, 1993).) The pattern of Roman expansion into Greece and Asia Minor and beyond occurred over approximately a century and a half, and was initially marked by great reluctance on the part of Rome to annex territory (Gruen, 1984; Sherwin-White, 1984).

Despite the unifying spread of Hellenistic rule and culture in the wake of the conquest of the Persian Empire by Alexander the Great of Macedon during the 330s, the political landscape of Greece and the lands beyond was highly fragmented. Following Alexander's death, three of his generals (Antigonus, Seleucus, and Ptolemy) seized parts of his sprawling domain and established independent kingdoms and dynasties centered in Macedonia, Syria and Egypt (Bevan, 1902). In Greece and the Aegean, the Macedonian hegemony established by Alexander's father (Philip II) had gradually decayed and in its wake had emerged a complex array of independent units, most notably two leagues of city-states, the Aetolian and the Achaean (roughly encompassing the Greek mainland and the Peloponnese respectively) (Freeman, 1893: 95–111, 243–51; Larsen, 1967), the Greek kingdom of Pergamum on the coast of Asia Minor, and the naval-mercantile island city-state of Rhodes. Further east, the Seleucid kingdom, with its capital in Antioch in Syria, and the Ptolemaic kingdom, with its capital in Alexandria, ruled over large politically inert non-Greek populations, and were dependent militarily upon a steady stream of mercenaries recruited from Greece. At the time of Rome's arrival, this constellation of states constituted a fairly tightly coupled state-system with a highly developed diplomacy and incessant limited aims warfare (Watson, 1992: 69–76).

Despite its inexorable trajectory, Roman advances in the east never evoked a general counter-hegemonic alliance and indeed Roman advances were as much welcomed as resisted (Livy, 1976). Part of the reason for the absence of general resistance to the Romans was that the Greek and Hellenistic states looked at each other – rather than the distant Romans – as the main threat to their security (Eckstein, 2006). Rome became extensively involved in the east through its standard practice of establishing alliances with various friendly powers. Although commonly cast in the prevalent diplomatic language as alliances between equals, these links were understood by the Romans to constitute a permanent client-patron relationship, essentially an externalization of the pattern of extra-constitutional but pervasive relations which marked Roman society and politics (Badian, 1958b; Braund, 1984). As a result of these treaties, Rome was called upon to vindicate the calls of its clients to defend their interests against encroachment by their neighbors, most notably the Macedonians, and then the Seleucids against Rome's allies Rhodes and Pergamum. Despite the intricacy of these diplomatic maneuvers, a rough overall pattern can be discerned. Rome sent armies from Italy, decisively defeated the largely mercenary armies of Macedonia, redistributed lands so as to reward friends and punish enemies, and then withdrew its military forces. Periodic Roman military intervention was accompanied by a continuous diplomatic and propagandistic struggle in which the Romans sought to present themselves to the Greeks as the 'liberator of Greece' from Macedonian encroachment. In the climax of this pattern in the Third Macedonian War, Roman arms virtually annihilated the Macedonian army at Pydna (168) and the Senate imposed a draconian peace abolishing the Macedonian monarchy and dividing the country into four non-monarchical units. A subsequent revolt of the Greek city-states in the Achaean League was crushed and the city of Corinth was sacked (146), at which point the Senate imposed an even more intrusive settlement in which large numbers of prominent Greeks not deemed sufficiently pro-Roman, or otherwise troublesome, were dispossessed, killed or displaced to Italy as captives. Yet despite this unmistakable subjugation of the Greeks, the Romans continued to rule indirectly until after the disruptions and reorganizations of the Roman civil wars.

Further to the east, Roman security interests were less pronounced, but a roughly similar pattern prevailed against even more feeble resistance. After the defeat of the Seleucid monarch Antiochus at Magnesia

(190), the Senate demanded a withdrawal beyond the Taurus mountains in Southeast Asia Minor. Lacking a male heir, Attalus III of Rome's long-time ally Pergamum, simply willed his kingdom to Rome (133) (Hansen, 1947). Mediating a dispute between the Seleucids and Ptolemaic Egypt (168), a senatorial envoy drew a circle in the sand around the Syrian king and told him to decide whether to accept Rome's terms regarding withdrawal from Egypt or wage war before stepping outside the circle.

Although not without bloodshed, the ascent of Rome in the Eastern Mediterranean is overall notable for its relative ease. Roman advance never evoked anything even approaching a general counter-hegemonic resistance. One battlefield victory, which Roman armies were able to provide with clock-work regularity, was almost always decisive. The deeper causes for this easy ascent lay in the dependence of the monarchies upon under-motivated armies composed of scarce and expensive mercenaries and non-Greek levies who had little stake or identification with the royal houses for which they fought. The Greeks themselves remained fatally divided and were always more concerned with the proximate threats of their immediate neighbors or Macedonia than with the distant threat of Rome. The limited character of Roman aims, and the light burden of Roman demands also surely played a role, as did the widespread support Rome garnered from the property owning classes in Greece, always fearful of democratic revolution (Fustel de Coulanges, 1864).

Predatory expansion and civil war

The year 146 BCE, when Roman armies sacked Carthage and Corinth, marked a decisive watershed in the expansion of the military power of the Roman Republic. With Macedonia dismembered, Carthage in ruins, and all other substantial states firmly anchored as client allies of Rome, there was no potential adversary anywhere in the Mediterranean basin that could constitute a first rate threat to Roman power. Yet at this juncture formal Roman rule was confined to a handful of territories outside of Italy, and large areas of hinterland in the west as well as Asia Minor were still outside Rome's network of client allies. The story of how Rome came to capitalize on its position of unequaled paramountcy among the core states in order to fill in and formalize its control constitutes a new chapter in the Roman ascent. In this period the sources of Roman expansion increasingly had more to do with rivalries within Rome than external threats.

The single most important development in this period, commonly delineated by historians as late republican, was the inexorable disintegration of the republican constitution culminating in decades of civil war and the establishment of a *de facto* monarchy by Octavian after his defeat of his last rival, Marcus Antonius at Actium (31 BCE). Although Romans were increasingly fighting Romans during this period, these internecine Roman conflicts carried with them a substantial pattern of external expansion, the fruits of which were a great growth in the extent and the depth of Roman rule.

The underlying cause of the failure of the republican constitution was the success of Roman arms abroad and its implications for the balance of power and wealth among different strata of Romans (Deininger, 1980: 77–99; Pocock, 2003). The fruits of expansion came to be enjoyed disproportionally by the Roman senatorial class. The extensive importation of slave labor produced by Roman victories, combined with lengthy campaigns fought on distant frontiers, combined to undermine the position of the free peasantry, traditionally the backbone of the Roman army. Initial efforts to re-dress this progressive marginalization through redistribution of lands in Italy were aborted by the assassinations of the Gracchus brothers, Tiberius and Gaius, by senatorial reactionaries. Subsequent rounds of conflict between the senatorial faction and various military commanders sympathetic to the popular cause grew increasingly violent and sustained, to the point where pitched battles between Roman armies were fought all across the Mediterranean world. This fascinating story, with its vivid figures such as Sulla, Marius, Caesar, Brutus, Cato, Crassus, Pompey, Antonius, Cleopatra, and Octavian has exercised an enduring hold on the Western historical imagination (Smith, 1955; Syme, 1952), but for our purposes what is most important is that the conquest of additional non-Romans was a recurrent gambit in these struggles among Romans. Politically ambitious generals sought to raise their standing in Rome through conquests abroad. The booty of conquest, traditionally distributed by the victorious general, offered resources to pay off clients in Rome necessary for election to military commands, and the image enhancing opportunity of a major triumphal procession in Rome. Even more importantly, generals cultivated the personal loyalties of the soldiers in their armies through the distribution of booty and forged ties of personal loyalty through long common experiences of hardship. The overall tendency was that the armies of the late republic were increasingly converted into the private armies of their generals, ready to do battle against domestic political rivals.

Perhaps the most outstanding example of this pattern was the Gallic campaign of Julius Caesar (58–49), which produced a great expansion of direct Roman rule in the west, roughly modern France and much of Switzerland. Roman control of the Celtic peoples in the Po Valley of Northern Italy was relatively recent, and Rome had been sacked by the Gauls (390 BCE), leaving a vivid memory of potential vulnerability. Equally important, the restive populations looked to the much larger Celtic populations in the mountains of Helvetia and beyond in Gaul for aid in resisting Roman rule. With the pretext of eliminating this threat at its source, Caesar led his army on a preventive war and predatory military expansion, the result of which was the complete subjugation of the Gauls by Roman arms. This bloody campaign, chronicled in detail by Caesar in his *Commentaries*, witnessed the conquest of a large population of tribal peoples, a high percentage of whom bore arms, by a relatively small Roman army. The key to Roman success was that the Gauls, who fought with great ferocity in defense of their political liberties, tended to be highly disorganized and undisciplined, both in strategically combining their vastly superior numbers, and in the actual execution of battles and their follow-ups. The Gauls were *warriors*, capable of great courage and exertion, but prone to disorder in and after battle. In contrast, the Romans were a highly trained and disciplined body of *soldiers*, who were able to recover from reverses and exploit victories.

Fresh from this extraordinary feat of arms, Caesar, increasingly seen as a threat to the hegemony of the senatorial class, marched his army into Italy, seized control of Rome, and had himself proclaimed *dictator perpetuus*, but was soon assassinated in the Senate chamber itself, thus setting in motion yet another round of civil war (Gelzer, 1968).

After the defeat of the senatorial faction at Phillippi (42), the Republic was effectively dead, and an informal tripartite division of power, known as the 'second triumvirate' was established by Antonius, Octavian and Lepidus. The uneasy peace which ensued is of note in the larger story of Roman unification of the Mediterranean basin because the triumvirate divided the Roman world into three parts, thus posing the possibility that a partition of the type which occurred after the death of Alexander might have brought about a renewed fragmentation and the emergence of a tripolar state-system. Octavian was awarded Italy and the west; Antonius the east and Egypt, while, Lepidus, the weakest member of the clique, was awarded Africa. Antonius decamped to Egypt, never to return to Rome, and took up with the Ptolemaic princess Cleopatra. Rumors that Antonius was increasingly 'going native' and was contemplating a replication of Alexander's campaign into Persia and beyond, helped Octavian's well-conceived propaganda campaign to paint Antonius as a traitor and threat to Rome. After Lepidus' death, Octavian absorbed his domains, setting the stage for the final confrontation between Octavian and Antonius and Cleopatra at Actium. Had the battle not been so decisively won by Octavian, or been avoided, it is possible that the Roman world at this unsettled stage of its formation might have been permanently cleft in two, with a Greek east against a Latin west.

Late expansion, insecure frontiers, and wars of imperial succession

The ascent of Octavian to undisputed mastery of the Roman world marked a watershed in both Roman constitutional development and the course of Roman expansion. Under the honorific title of Augustus, he ruled another 45 years (31 BCE to 14 CE), and in the course of this long reign ushered in a period of much-welcomed peace to the Roman world weary of endless war and civil strife. Although Augustus's armies waged wars in Iberia, Illyria, Germany, Asia Minor, Africa and elsewhere, these were much more limited affairs, apparently designed to fill in and secure Roman frontiers (Gruen, 1990: 375–416). The general theme of Augustus's rule was peace and political reconciliation, not further expansion. To this end, the size of the army was reduced, taxes decreased and veterans generously retired and settled in colonies across the Roman world.

Despite this general aspiration, the fluidity of Rome's frontiers in the far east and the long northern line across Europe posed enduring security problems for which there was no ready practical solution. The complete annihilation of two Roman legions under the administrator Varus at Teutoberg Forest (9 CE) in an ambush by Germans pointed to the dangers both of expanding and not expanding in this direction. Also, the drive of politically ambitious Romans to advance through foreign conquests had been reined in, but not eliminated. But the lesson of the collapse of the republic – that successful generals are potential political rivals – was surely not lost on Augustus and his successors and also helps account for the cessation of Roman expansion. Although Augustus added more territory to Roman rule than any other figure in Roman history, he bequeathed to his successor the advice to keep the Empire within its present frontiers.

During the four and a half centuries between the ascension of Augustus and the collapse of the Roman Empire in the west (conventionally dated 476 CE), the territorial reach of Roman rule was extended on three occasions after the death of Augustus (14 CE) (Millar, 1967). Under the emperor Claudius, Roman armies crossed over to the hitherto distant and politically obscure island of Britannia where they subjugated most of the native Celtic population on the island (43 CE), leaving only the highlands of the far north, thinly populated by a Celtic people known to the Romans as the Picts, free of Roman rule. During the reign of Emperor Trajan, Rome embarked upon its last substantial expansion, first into Dacia, an area corresponding roughly to modern Romania, and then into Mesopotamia and Western Persia, where the vigorous and chronically troublesome Parthian Empire had its seat. This advance in the east was short-lived however, as Trajan's successor Hadrian, having little taste for war, abandoned Roman gains in Mesopotamia. Subsequent predations by the Parthians upon the eastern provinces of Syria and Asia Minor evoked more counter invasions, but Roman power was never extended for long beyond the eastern frontiers of Syria.

Despite these various bouts of expansion at its periphery, the nearly half millennium between Augustus and the collapse of Roman power in the west was marked by two problems that became interrelated and ultimately fatal to the Roman order – the persistence of adversaries beyond the northern and eastern frontiers that posed recurrent major security threats, and the endemic intra-Roman struggle between generals and armies for the imperial mantle. Although the Roman Empire extinguished anarchic 'international politics' in the Mediterranean basin, it remained very much in a larger system which included the vast interior of central and eastern Europe and the states in western Asia. On neither the northern nor eastern frontiers were the Romans ever able to achieve a permanently stable security situation, despite strenuous efforts to do so.

On the long northern frontier across Europe which the Empire sought to stabilize along the southern banks of the Rhine and the Danube, the Romans had to stand vigilant against the recurrent incursions of various tribal Germanic peoples (Luttwak, 1976; Elton, 1996). After the death of Marcus Aurelius and the ascent of his dissolute son Commodus in 180, containment of the Germans became increasingly difficult and demanding. The German peoples across the northern frontiers of the Empire were, as Tacitus famously argued, more like the early Romans in their cultural simplicity and military prowess than were the Romans of the mature Empire (Burns, 2003). Due to their long interaction with the Romans, both militarily and economically along the Rhine-Danube frontier, the political structure and military capabilities of the German peoples evolved in ways which made them even more formidable. Emulating Roman military techniques and increasingly united in larger groupings, the Germans posed a chronic pressure on the Empire which increasingly strained its economic and military resources (Whittaker, 1994). After a series of large raids into Roman territories, Roman power, also sapped by plagues and recurrent civil wars among generals vying for the imperial throne, appeared on the verge of collapse in the middle decades of the 200s. However, under the iron fist of the Illyrian soldier-emperor Diocletian and his immediate successors, notably Constantine, the Roman Empire was roused from its death-bed and reorganized along much harsher and draconian lines (Williams, 1985). So dramatic was this reorganization of the Roman realm that historians refer to the heavy centralized bureaucratic empire as the 'dominate' in contrast to the lighter and happier earlier principate.

But even this increasingly hollow fortress of an empire was eventually overwhelmed in a series of catastrophic military reversals in the middle of the 5th century, as several Germanic peoples, themselves fleeing the onslaught of a people from the steppes of Eurasia known as the Huns, poured into the empire and sacked major cities, including Rome (410 and 455) (Ferrill, 1986). The eastern half of the empire, with its capitol in Constantinople, strategically situated at the maritime 'choke point' between the Black and Aegean seas, and at the juncture of the road running across the Balkans and Asia Minor, held out for a thousand years before its final extinction by the Ottoman Turks in 1453.

In the east, Roman provinces around the shore of the Mediterranean had previously been parts of a long-developed state-system which previously had been imperially consolidated by peoples from Mesopotamia and the Persian plateau. The successor states on the Persian plateau remained potent adversaries which the Romans were unable to subdue, and on several occasions they made extended encroachments on Roman possessions in the east.

The second major baneful pattern of late imperial politics was the recurrent struggles among imperial generals and armies for the imperial mantle. As Rome's military exertions on the frontiers grew, so too did the Roman army. Struggles between Roman generals and their armies for supremacy within the empire were frequent, marked by pitched battles, and often lasted for many years. In many regards, an intensely violent internal anarchy, not durable hierarchy, marked the politics of the later Roman world. Yet it is notable that the contenders in these struggles did not attempt to secede from Roman rule and establish separate states.

The causes of the end of the Roman imperium in the west point to the importance of the factors which led to its ascent, only now these factors were reversed against the Romans. As the army grew in size and internal political power, it became disconnected from the civil population of the empire, and increasingly manned by 'barbarian' recruits from beyond the frontiers. Rome had become much like the earlier Hellenistic monarchies, and like them it ultimately succumbed to agricultural peoples with less predatory internal political structures.

Having identified and surveyed the five phases in the trajectory of Roman expansion and outlined the important features of the different phases, we now turn to an examination of four clusters of factors that in combination provide a multi-faceted explanation of Roman success.

Systemic factors

While the features of the Roman constitution did play an important role in distinguishing Rome from its numerous adversaries, the ways in which these factors came into play was shaped by several broad systemic factors which have received lesser attention in accounts of Roman success. In this section, five factors are examined and five main points made. First, the level of technological capabilities was largely static and evenly diffused, although organizational capabilities were more unevenly distributed. Second, the space within which Rome expanded was, as an 'international' system, highly fluid and unstable. Third, the actors in this proto-system were territorially indistinct and diffuse. Fourth, the interaction of ancient polities was highly violent and predatory and ancient polities suffered from high levels of chronic and acute insecurity. Fifth, the institutions of 'international society' were underdeveloped and the crucial practice of counter-hegemonic alliance formation was largely absent.

First, concerning technology as a factor, the period of Roman expansion was not marked by decisive technological innovations regarding either warfare or its ancillary activities (Delbruck, 1975). On land, infantry warfare, fought along lines largely developed by the Greeks several centuries earlier, was militarily decisive and the core of Rome's power was its large and highly trained infantry force. Cavalry forces served largely in ancillary support roles. At sea, both mercantile and naval activities relied upon multi-tiered rowing vessels (augmented by sails), and naval engagements were essentially infantry battles on water, marked by ramming, boarding, and hand-to-hand combat (Chaniotis, 2005). Due to their cost and technological sophistication, warships were beyond the reach of tribal peoples. With this exception, Rome's rise is not attributable to its technological superiority: it and almost all of its adversaries were on a roughly comparable technological level. Roman superiority was, rather, in its political system, military organization, and economic resources.

There was, however, an overall pattern of political development in the period before and during the Roman expansion which provides a certain unity, namely the diffusion of peoples and technologies toward the west from the older settled and heavily populated areas of the Eastern Mediterranean, where highly urbanized and technologically advanced polities, first in Egypt and the Levant, then Asia Minor and Greece, had emerged long before Rome was founded. The general diffusion of technologies and peoples from east to west was carried mainly by Phoenician and Greek traders and colonists, who established over several centuries an archipelago of littoral city-states in the Western Mediterranean situated on geographically favorable sites. In the longer and larger pattern of Mediterranean development both Rome and its arch rival Carthage were 'marcher states,' deploying forms of life invented at the older core to a peripheral zone populated by diverse peoples at the beginning edge of the processes of intensive agriculture and urbanization.

Second, the borders of the overall system and its subsystems were highly indeterminate. Geographically, the area of the Roman Empire is highly fragmented, with many islands, peninsulas, mountain ranges, and rivers. It lacks a 'core area' of substantial arable land around which a universal state might emerge. Despite the seemingly 'natural' character of dominion in this area in later Roman eyes, no previous political unification of this space had been achieved or even attempted. Nor has this space subsequently been politically unified, particularly after the emergence of Islam and its conquest of the lands on its southern and eastern shores in the 7th century. The central location of Rome and Italy within the Mediterranean basin provided the Romans with the advantage of 'interior lines of communication' and exacerbated the collective action problems of counter-hegemonic alliance formation by surrounding states.

Third, prior to the rise of Rome, the area which Rome came eventually to dominate, the entire Mediterranean basin and its hinterlands, was a series of partially overlapping subsystems rather than a highly interactive state-system. In the east, the interactions (military, political and economic) among the Hellenistic empires and the various city-states was sufficiently dense and recurrent to constitute a 'state system.' In the west, where densities of population and levels of material civilization were much lower, interactions were not extensive or regular enough to constitute a system until the Punic Wars. Further pulling political patterns away from a bounded territorial state model, city-states, typically centered on a coastal city built around some fortified high ground, were settled with populations who had migrated from often distant cities in the Levant or Greece. Enmeshed and dependent on long distant trade, such city-states tended to have spheres of influences into their hinterlands rather than clearly delineated territorial spaces.

These indistinct and partial systems were further disordered and debordered by the long ranges at which occasional military invasions were successfully conducted. Despite the primitive level of communication and transportation technologies, high impact military interactions occurred at remarkably long distances. Perhaps the most spectacular example of such eruptive long distance military predatory interaction was Alexander of Macedon's armed odyssey not just through the vast provinces of the Persian Empire, but also beyond, into the Indus Valley, itself the seat of an ancient, populous, and developed grouping of polities. Further subverting the crystallization of a system, long distance raids and invasions of whole peoples in armed migration for better or more ample lands was a recurrent phenomenon. Whole cities, states and peoples periodically met military catastrophe from peoples that not only had they not been interacting with, but that they had never even heard of. These 'over the horizon' military interactions subverted the crystallization of a distinct system in which counter-hegemonic practices might have developed.

Fourth, the interaction of ancient states was highly violent and predatory. Systems are profoundly shaped by the types of interactions which occur among groups at the largest scale of interaction (Buzan, Jones and Little, 1993). The ancient world was marked by extreme levels of violence among (and within) polities (Finley, 1983). War was an endemic activity. Conflicts were often highly destructive. Decisive battles and sieges produced catastrophic results for the defeated. The basic underlying fact was that 'war paid' – military power could be made to cumulate. 'Knock out blows' sometimes in one battle, sometimes over years of warfare, routinely occurred. Once achieved, military supremacy was routinely ruthlessly employed for the total aggrandizement of the victor. Cities were looted, burned, and razed. Populations were massacred or sold into slavery. Security from violent destruction or enslavement was something which polities could never take for granted.

Fifth and finally, institutions of international society existed in Western antiquity, but were unevenly present and underdeveloped in comparison with early modern Europe. Diplomacy via *ad hoc* emissaries was widespread and there was a widely diffused norm for the safe conduct of such messengers and negotiators, but there were no permanent embassies and ambassadors (Philipson, 1911; Campbell, 2002). The diplomatic capacities of tribal peoples in the hinterland and the west was limited largely to events in their immediate areas and they were unlikely partners in more general alliances. Alliances and treaties of peace and war were extensively employed instruments of statecraft and the Romans displayed a continuously sophisticated use of them.

Although diplomacy and alliances were features of ancient interstate politics, Rome never faced a general 'counter-hegemonic' alliance among the leading states in the system. The patterns of resistance to Roman military advance varied widely, and included frequent cases of 'bandwagoning for profit,' as well as tenacious resistance approaching total war levels of violence. In part the absence of a general organized resistance to Roman expansion was the product of its piecemeal progress and slow pace. It may also have been the product of the absence of a clearly defined or perceived system. Although the large and developed Hellenistic states of the Eastern Mediterranean were aware of events in the west and the Greeks had even on occasion militarily interacted with the Greeks in the west (most notably the Athenian invasion of Sicily and Pyrrhus' intercession in Italy against the Romans on behalf of the Greek colonies there) it does not seem that the diplomacy of these states seriously entertained the possibility that events in that distant area could affect their core interests. The ancient world was a quasi-system populated by a very heterogenous set of polities, many of which lacked essential attributes of stateness.

Farmers, soldiers, and cities

The political and military developments which capture the attention of the historians of word and deed rest upon, and are ultimately bound by, the constraints and opportunities afforded by the mundane world of economic production. In the terminology of historical materialism, the 'superstructure' of politics, and the viability of different 'modes of protection' are powerfully conditioned by the 'forces and modes of production' (Deudney, 2000b: 77–108). The entire edifice of ancient civilization rested upon an agricultural realm that was technologically primitive and stagnant, and highly labor intensive. Where dense populations lived, and hence where economic and military power might be assembled, was, to a first approximation, determined by the presence of arable land. The overwhelming bulk of the population of the ancient world was agricultural, and the relationship between this labor force and control of the land and its surplus had far-reaching social, political, and military implications (Anderson, 1974).

Given that ancient warfare was first and foremost infantry warfare, and given that ancient populations were primarily agriculturalists, the rate of military participation of the agricultural masses was of pivotal importance. Polities, such as Rome in the republican period, which were able to sustain the political and economic enfranchisement of the agricultural peasantry had a superior reserve of military manpower from which to draw. The general pattern of political development in agricultural societies was toward the erection of caste hierarchies based on military predation, in which the agriculturalists were reduced to various forms of politically passive bondage, particularly slavery and serfdom (Garlan, 1975). In the Mediterranean world of the half millennium in which the Roman Republic existed and expanded, this pattern of 'development' was extremely uneven across space. In the ancient polities of the east, where agriculture had been invented much earlier, the complete subordination and consequent political and military demobilization of the peasantry had been achieved in the distant past. The most extreme exemplar of this pattern was Egypt which was ruled by a succession or foreign military dynasts, despite its rich soil and dense population, and hence great latent power potential. In contrast, the tribal hinterlands of the west were still at the beginnings of this trajectory of development, and their polities were socio-economically 'flat' with very high rates of political enfranchisement and military participation (Andreski, 1968). In the five centuries of its life and expansion, the Roman Republic essentially traversed this developmental path. It was able at the beginning to achieve a high level of military participation from its agricultural population, but then gradually its free peasantry was displaced by various forms of bonded labor. The empire created by Italian peasants undermined its own foundations (Hopkins, 1978).

The second socio-economic dynamic with far-reaching implications for military and political capability was urbanization. Floating above and extracting from the realm of agriculture, cities accreted as locus points for the conversion of agricultural surplus into primitive 'manufactured' goods, long distance trade, and elite consumption.

Urbanization was a 'double-edged sword' for military viability. On the one hand, urbanization afforded literacy and the accumulation and transmission of complex bodies of practical knowledge, the creation of complex functionally differentiated political organizations, and technologically advanced complex artifacts such as ships and siege machines, and walls and roads, which together provided urbanized polities with important military advantages.

But these advantages were offset and subverted by another powerful tendency, military enervation. A central argument, advanced in both antiquity and the modern era by a wide array of theorists, was that the 'way of life' of city-dwellers was not conducive to the maintenance of a high level of military skill. Because ancient warfare was primarily infantry battles fought at close quarters and dependent on unit cohesion, and punishingly long marches carrying heavy loads of weapons, armor and supplies, a high military advantage accrued from physical conditioning and constant drilling and training (Goldsworthy, 1996). Thus a widely recurrent pattern in pre-industrial societies was for peoples living in harsh semi-subsistence conditions (as long as they were free) to be militarily superior to peoples enjoying the creature comforts and plying the diverse crafts afforded by cities (Ibn Khaldun, 1967). Like the dispossession of farmers, urbanization was spatially very uneven in western antiquity, being most developed in the east, and least in the west. During the era of its military ascent, Rome was midway on this trajectory, being urban enough to reap its technological and organizational advantages, but rural enough, and rigid enough in its customs and mores, to sustain a high level of military prowess in its population long enough to vanquish and absorb all its neighbors and rivals, before succumbing to such enervation.

'A Republic for Expansion'

It is within these multiple systemic and socio-economic dynamics that the arguments about Rome's domestic regime advantages are best situated as explanatory factors. The answer to the question posed by Polybius as to how it was that Rome came 'to subject the whole known world to her sole rule' lies, for both Polybius (1923: book 6, section 56) and many subsequent historians, in the particular features of the Roman constitution and civic culture. There were five ways in which elements of the Roman constitution and domestically-rooted practices combined to make the Republic particularly successful in the highly competitive anarchic system of the ancient Mediterranean world.

First, Polybius emphasized the particular stability afforded by what he termed, in the language of Greek political science, a 'mixed constitution' which blended elements of the monarchical, the aristocratic, and the democratic (von Fritz, 1954). Polybius' account of the Roman republican constitution as mixed emphasizes the central role of what would later come to be called 'checks and balances,' the arrangement of government authorities in such a way that each part could block action by others, thus forcing all to compromise and reach consensus. Against the backdrop of the incessant factional strife of the Greek city-states with which he was familiar, a structural mechanism for forcing consensus must have looked particularly appealing.

Second, the singular success of Roman arms owed much to the sustained commitment of the ordinary soldier to the Roman cause which can be attributed to Rome's quasi-democratic mechanisms of public accountability (Hanson, 2002: 99–132). The legendary discipline of Roman armies cannot be solely the result of training and drilling, but must also be rooted in a shared interest in Roman success (Nicolet, 1980). Part of this intense loyalty and identification is no doubt attributable to the widespread practice of wrapping acts of policy in the legitimating cloak of particularistic pagan civil religions (Fustel de Coulanges, 1864; Wardman, 1982). But this practice was widespread in the ancient world and therefore it cannot account for any Roman advantages. Although Roman society was oligarchical in many important regards, the common soldier, as voting citizen in the assemblies and as small agricultural proprietor, did have a voice, however diluted, in making Roman policy and sharing in the benefits of Roman victory. Political participation and representation were not, of course, unique in the ancient world to the Roman Republic, since they were present in various forms in the Greek city-states as well as many of the tribal peoples Roman encountered. However, what was distinctive about the Roman Republic was that it was able to extend this sense of shared interest to a much larger population than any other ancient polity (Rosenstein, 1999). The Roman republican constitution possessed quasi-democratic mechanisms of public accountability and decision-making which increased and sustained support and commitment to the regime from the large mass of Romans, thus enabling Rome to more consistently mobilize and sustain popular mobilization for war-making. Around the nucleus of a city-state, Rome as master of Italy had partially evolved into something approximating a nation-state with elements of popular government (Cornell, 1991).

Third, the Roman Republic was in important ways a *state* in the modern sense of an abstract entity not reducible to the actions of a single individual or group, and this distinguished it from both its larger rivals, particularly the Hellenistic monarchies, and the amorphous acephalous tribal polities. The simple fact that republican Rome was not a monarchy meant that it did not labor under the debilitations, idiosyncratic impulses, and succession uncertainties which inevitably attend the concentration of power in one individual or family. Roman policy had a constancy and persistence rooted in its collective decision-making. If someone was not performing with distinction, there was always a replacement ready at hand. The pervasive role of law, courts, and judicial procedures added to this sense that there was a Roman 'state,' a 'res publica,' a 'public thing' not reducible to the interest of any one individual or group.

Fourth, there is the role of the Senate in the conduct of foreign policy. Composed of approximately 300 members in the middle and late Republic, most of them former high magistrates and members of leading families, the Senate did not have the formal powers to declare war or peace, elect officials, or raise taxes, but it did have the formal authority to conduct foreign diplomacy and assign military commands. But the influence of the Senate, particularly after the near disaster of the war with Hannibal, was far greater than its formal powers implied. Although the Senate's internal procedures and deliberations remain obscure, it is clear that it reached decisions through debate and consultation. Because so many of its members had held high military and civil positions, the Senate was a repository of great experience and knowledge. Its size and depth of abilities meant the Senate could simultaneously appoint emissaries, receive foreign emissaries, dispatch commissions, and direct military strategy on many fronts (Harris, 1979).

Fifth and finally, republican Rome's practices of hegemonic confederation and assimilation, described earlier, afforded the Romans considerable advantage. In extending its domestic client-patron pattern of relations to conquered peoples, the Romans were able to increase their military power, reduce administrative burdens, and diminish incentives for revolt. The advantageous Roman practice of extending citizenship rights to elites in conquered cities was also relatively distinctive in a world where criteria for group membership were commonly based on clan 'blood' lineages, and probably reflects the eclectic character of Roman origins as well as the capacity of relatively law-based polities to abstract from particularistic distinguishing features. Rome's practice here contrasts sharply with the Greek city-states, such as Athens and most extremely Sparta, which were fiercely parochial in their citizenship standards.

Monarchical empires, tribal confederations, and city-states

The role of Rome's internal organization in explaining the success of Roman expansion can be further demonstrated by examining the domestic regime-based weaknesses of its adversaries. Although Roman institutions and practices were distinctive, they were certainly not without wide precedent in the polities that Rome encountered and mastered. What ultimately distinguished the Roman Republic was not the particular elements that made up its constitution, but rather the ability of the Romans to combine these elements in ways that other polities could not. Each of these three types of polity that Rome encountered – monarchial empires, tribes, city-states – possessed some of the features of the Roman Republic, but none had all. Each had fatal liabilities and limits relative to the Roman combination.

Monarchical empires, mainly in the Eastern Mediterranean, had sizes, populations, and technologies roughly comparable to Rome's at the time of their collisions, but these empires ruled large polyglot subject populations who were politically disenfranchised and demobilized and disconnected from their rulers in ethnicity, language, and religion. The mass of the population in the agricultural base was dispossessed, political demobilized, and militarily inactive. Often Roman mastery of the large monarchial empires was achieved with relative ease, through what might be termed a *capitation conquest*, in which Roman armies defeated mercenary armies and simply replaced the foreign dynastic house with a Roman governor.

At the other extreme, geographically, developmentally, and in domestic regime type, were the tribal clan-based polities found throughout the hinterlands of the Mediterranean basin, and particularly in the west (Hubert, 1987; Rankin, 1987; van Wees, 1992). These polities were very 'flat' with relatively limited stratification and functional differentiation. Typically territorially amorphous and politically acephalous, they were governed by councils of elders and warrior assemblies which provided a very high level of 'public' accountability and they had extremely high levels of mobilization and support. Although largely ignored by both the republican political tradition and 'democratic peace' inventories, these polities sit, along with Athens and a few other ancient city-states, at the high end of the democracy scale. Their agricultural mass was almost all the population and it was politically enfranchised, militarily able, and readily mobilized.

Their fatal weakness, however, was their relative lack of organization. Fragmented into many local groups, they faced daunting collective action problems in aggregating and applying the capabilities of their warrior-farmer citizens. Their lack of central governmental apparatuses meant they were ill-equipped to conduct complex diplomacy and build alliances. Their lack of military organization and a logistical arm meant they were at severe disadvantage in waging sustained warfare against highly disciplined and well-equipped Roman armies. Against tribal groups, Roman mastery was achieved through a much more extensively violent *corporeal conquest* in which virtually the entire male population appears to have been defeated and either killed or sold into slavery.

City-states, most established as colonies of older Greek or Phoenician city-states in the east, dotted the littoral of the Mediterranean and were the third type of Roman adversary. In the course of its ascent, Rome dominated and absorbed scores of previously autonomous city-states. Typically heavily involved in mercantile activity, they enjoyed high levels of technological capability. Ancient city-states were typically either broad-based oligarchies or democracies, so their motivational mobilization potential was fairly high. The larger and more established city-states tended to have highly parochial political identities. These advantages, however, were counterbalanced by the often severe limitations of their small size, exclusive ethnic and religious make-up, and fractious internal politics. They also tended to engage in endemic petty warfare against each other. As potential counterweights to Roman power, city-states faced severe collective action problems in alliance formation due to their sheer number, individuated characters, and historical conflicts.

This schematic assessment of the three types of Roman adversaries reveals a general pattern. The level of military effort required to master other polities varied greatly and the tenacity of resistance to Roman advance was roughly inversely proportional to size. States with sufficient size, populations, and economic development to potentially counter Roman encroachments lacked the ability to mobilize. Stateless tribal groups with high levels of mobilization potential lacked sufficient size and economic development. With the possible exception of the mercantile imperial city-state of Carthage, Rome never faced a large adversary with both a highly mobilized populace and sufficient size, resources and organizational capacity.

It is notable that Rome's most potent adversary, Carthage, sits partially outside of these three types. Like Rome, Carthage was a city-state which vanquished or absorbed its immediate neighbors to become an imperial state with substantial military capabilities. Carthage had the disadvantage of a relatively weak agricultural base, its immediate arid hinterland lacked a politically enfranchised peasantry. Master of the long distance trade routes in the Western Mediterranean, Carthage's empire was unlike both the eastern Hellenistic monarchies and the Roman proto-national proto-state, in that it was mainly a network of anchored coastal trading fortress-enclaves that did not directly rule their hinterlands. Ruled by a mercantile oligarchy of the descents of colonists from the Levant, and possessed of a severe and elaborate religion which did not incorporate local cults, Carthage did not expand its citizenship. It also tended to rely heavily on mercenaries. Yet once its conflict with Rome commenced, Carthage did show remarkable organizational and strategic capabilities, manifest both in its systemic crash program to replace its losses in Sicily with expansion into the Iberian hinterland and Hannibal's bold strategic gambit of invading Italy from the north.

Conclusion

What overall implications can be drawn from the ancient Roman experience for theories of international systems and the balance of power? The basic fact, long recognized and inescapable in the historical record, is that Romans absorbed the entire array of polities and systems in the Mediterranean basin because the peoples they militarily subdued never aggregated their capacities to resist through counter-hegemonic alliances. There are several strong factors which account for this non-balancing. The barriers to effective collective action both between and within polities were formidable. The borders of the system and many actors in it were indistinct. States lived in, and acted like they lived in, a highly competitive, violent, and precarious condition where wars were endemic and conquest was a recurrent and highly attractive means of gain. Polities might be attacked from any quarter, defeat often meant catastrophe, and levels of trust between polities was low.

Given the absence of effective collective action to preserve the autonomy of the units and the persistence of plural system, the question of Roman success becomes one of explaining why Rome was so consistently successful for such a long time against a very numerous series of adversaries. Here regime factors, operating within broad material context and socio-economic constraints, must be judged to offer powerful explanatory leverage.

Rome's most distinctive trait was its ability for a few crucial centuries to sustain a regime which preserved popular rights – and hence popular support – for strenuous collective disciplines and sacrifices, and to absorb and harness, through patron-client alliances, and citizenship assimilation, the efforts and capacities of conquered peoples. It also had highly competent arrangements of elite statecraft. In contrast, Rome's typical adversaries had profound structurally-rooted weaknesses. Those large enough and state-like enough to be great powers in the overall Mediterranean system were stratified hierarchies with disconnected elites and dispossessed and politically passive agriculturalists, and thus lacked the capabilities to mobilize their latent human military power potential. And as monarchies, their 'executive energy' was highly uneven. Conversely, those tribal polities with flat and accountable political structures were too disorganized to aggregate, direct, and logistically sustain their highly capable and well-motivated warrior-citizens. And city-states, almost all too small to matter much militarily, were too highly individuated, habitually conflictual, and widely dispersed to aggregate on a sustained basis.

The pattern of violent conflict in the Roman world after the consolidation of the Mediterranean basin adds further credibility to this explanation for Republican Roman successes. As Rome passed beyond the proto-nation state and horizontally assimilated space of the Italian peninsula, its relentless success in securing itself from potentially threatening adversaries by conquering them set in motion a process of structural regime change marked by increasing stratification and rural marginalization, and highly violent inter-Roman struggles that culminated in the imperial monarchy founded by Augustus. The absence of a balance of power externally fatally undermined the Roman Republican constitution internally, choking off the well-springs of Roman capabilities.

So great was Rome's power at this juncture that its enervation initially did not threaten its survival. As the engine of imperial expansion slowed and effectively stopped, Rome found itself faced with adversaries at its vast frontier who could not be readily conquered and whose overall situation resembled that of the early Romans. This chronic external security problem necessitated an army so large as to be completely uncheckable by any domestic source, leading to the chronic interior warfare among Roman generals and armies for the emperorship and the spoils it yielded. With these costly internecine struggles, the later empire came to resemble an anarchy as much as a hierarchy. The inability to control the military arm was as much a cause of the death of the empire as it was of the Republic. Disconnected from its agriculturalist base, the empire in the west succumbed to militarily more vigorous peoples at lower levels of political development.

8
Hierarchy and Resistance in American State-Systems 1400–1800 CE

*Charles A. Jones**

After spelling out some implications of recent ethno-history, this chapter examines the two great areas of extensive urbanization and political organization encountered by the Spanish in the Americas in the early 16th century, asking when and to what extent balancing had failed in each prior to the Spanish invasion, and seeking to account for this. It goes on to ask why Aztec and Inca overlordship was followed by Spanish empire rather than a recovery of sovereignty by indigenous polities, incorporating settler-states into local balancing systems or replacing them altogether, as would happen in sub-Saharan Africa within a century of the so-called Scramble of the 1880s.

Empires? Conquests?

Extensive scholarship over the past half-century has been directed toward reasserting the relative autonomy of polities once regarded as unproblematically subordinate to imperial authority in the Americas (Lockhart, 1992: 3–5). This has modified perceptions not only of the Inca and Aztec Empires but also of their Spanish successor. Ethno-historians invite us to regard city-states or other relatively small, ethnically-based polities as the basic political units in Mesoamerica and the

---

*I would like to acknowledge helpful comments on drafts of this paper from the co-authors of this volume and from David Brading and Liselotte Odgård. Liselotte complains that more needs to be said about the texture of international society in the Americas before the European invasions, and she is right. But that must be for another occasion.

Andes. For Mesoamerica, the account which most subtly balances the basic *altepetl* building blocks (or city communities) and the quite complex forms of organization superimposed by the Mexica is that of Carrasco (1999). Summing up what were then recent revisions, almost a quarter of a century ago, George Collier (1982: 8) alleged that 'the underlying and characteristic organization of both civilizations was at this level rather than that of the relatively short-lived empires ... [and] organization at the sub-imperial level lasted well into an era of colonial rule founded upon it.'

This claim has a number of implications. One is that the two major pre-Columbian empires of early 20th-century history books dissolve into societies of polities (*altepetls* (or cities) in Meso-America and *ayllus* (loosely, clans or tribes) in the Andes) periodically and incompletely inundated by empire; revolt becomes less an internal affair than the reassertion of sovereignty barely lost. Joseph Bram (1941: 31) put it nicely, describing the *ayllus* as 'autonomous and indestructible cells of ... Andean social morphology.' Writing of Meso-America, Lockhart (1992: 14) echoed this, affirming that 'at the heart of the organization of the Nahua world, both before the Spaniards came and long after, lay the *altepetl* or ethnic state.' Some of what is normally regarded as internal or domestic affairs comes to be seen as the workings of a submerged or ghostly international society. With such thoughts in mind, Rostworowski (1999: x) declined to use the word 'empire' in the text of her book about the Andes during the period of Inca hegemony, preferring an indigenous term, *Tahuantinsuyu*, meaning 'the four united regions,' while use of the phrase 'Inca realm' in her title suggests compromise with an exasperated publisher. The early chroniclers wrote of the 'Mexicanos' and many since have preferred to write of the Mexica rather than the Aztecs. No group in the period dealt with here called itself Aztec. Indeed, the term was only popularized by William Prescott in the 19th century. Pedro Carrasco (1999: 3), while willing to speak of a Mesoamerican Empire, finds the term Mexica 'awkward' because of its unwanted resonances with the contemporary Mexican republic, and writes instead of the Tenochca Empire, from the name of the capital city, Tenochtitlan. Lockhart (1992: 1), by contrast, prefers to emphasise linguistic commonality, referring to Nahuas rather than Aztecs, feeling that the latter term 'implies a kind of quasi-national unity that did not exist [and] directs attention to an ephemeral agglomeration.'

But if the Inca and Aztec Empires lose definition as their ethnic components swim into focus, so too does that of the late-medieval Hapsburgs (hardly yet, strictly speaking, a *Spanish* Empire): a sprawl of discontiguous and heterogeneous lordships stretching from the shores of Africa to the Low Countries and from the Philippines to the borders of the Ottoman Empire. Or think of Europe itself. Reading Lockhart on Mesoamerica at the beginning of the 16th century (1992: 1), one can without too much distortion substitute 'Europeans' for 'central Mexicans': '[d]ivided into a large number of separate, often warring regional states, each with its own sense of unique ethnic origin, sometimes living under the partial dominance of imperial confederations and sometimes not, the central Mexicans ... were united, to the extent that they were, not by politics ... but by their common language.' Why, then, should not the Spanish, in extending European practice to the Americas, have reached an accommodation with their new vassal states based on loose suzerainty? Why, from another point of view, should we be shy about calling such things empires? The answer is that the Spanish were to be at the forefront of a dramatic change in European imperial theory in the 16th century, a development that would have strong implications for traditional political life in their American conquests.

A second implication of the recent emphasis on sub-imperial polities is that, precisely because of its suggestion of the superficial or incidental character of successive empires, the Spanish conquests cease to be the prominent historical landmarks that they once were. In a thought-provoking meditation on the significance of 1492, Olivia Harris (1995: 9) takes as her point of view the way in which contemporary Aymara-speaking peasants in Northern Potosí, Bolivia, 'did not give the same saliency ... to the moment of the coming of the Spanish'. In place of the conquests, the moment of greatest threat to the continuity of traditional political organization in these two zones is shifted several generations later to the time when, first of all, the Spanish Crown moves from the loose late-medieval style of empire hinted at in the previous paragraph to stricter absolutist forms of control throughout its dominions and, subsequently, following the wars of independence of the early 19th century, power was transferred to creole elites, determined to eliminate the implicit autonomy granted by the European empires to those indigenous groups they had used as auxiliaries in their intermittent 18th-century wars and bent on creating centralized and homogeneous nation-states guided by the ideas and models of post-Revolutionary Europe (Watson, 1984: 132). This displacement of the conquests justifies, in turn, a periodization of *circa* 1400–1800 (as in the title of an important collection of essays on American ethno-history: Collier, 1982) as the truly proto-modern historical era in Mesoamerica and the Andes, and is one reason for treating, within a single chapter, both the local balancing failures of the immediate pre-conquest period and the failure of indigenous states to balance the Spanish following the initial conquests.

Within the context of contemporary politics in the Americas, the recent historiographic trend toward ethno-history arouses residual suspicion because it is so conveniently – even Romantically – consistent with a rising tide of assertiveness among indigenous groups in so many countries, North and South, which it has often been felt to legitimize, and with which it may therefore be thought in some measure complicit. Yet the weight of supporting evidence appears incontrovertible, and however this may be, the new interpretation has profound implications from the perspective of any student of balancing and hegemony in the Americas, since it perceptibly nudges the norm of political organization away from hierarchy and toward anarchy, opening up questions about balancing and hegemony, and oscillations between them, which were long thought closed.

Why was it the Inca and Aztec states that emerged as hegemons, and not their seemingly similar neighbors? Was their ability to impose authority on other polities based more in material or ideological differentiation? Why did those neighbors not emulate the proto-hegemonic states or combine together in coalitions to check their expansion? Why, when the Spanish arrived, did some states choose this moment to switch from bandwaggoning to balancing, in coalition with the newcomers? Why, having seen the stranglehold of indigenous hegemony broken, did these same states not succeed in constraining the Spanish, instead allowing hegemony – and worse – to pass to them? Questions long regarded as settled or impertinent are re-opened by the recent tendency of ethno-history.

To the political scientist, pre-Columbian America offers an additional enticement, though one that leads into an historiographic minefield. While the post-conquest position is clearly complicated, with Spain participating in the European as well as local American systems of states, the pre-conquest systems seem simpler. For here were two systems of states, autonomous from one another and from the Old World throughout the greater part of the century preceding the Spanish conquests. Even allowing for the possibility of Chinese exploration, trade and settlement, abruptly curtailed on the death of Emperor Zhu Zhanji in 1435 (Menzies, 2003), this would appear largely to remove the intriguing problem – common to many chapters in this volume – of system/sub-system interference or indeterminacy, creating near laboratory conditions in which to observe the ebb and flow of empire.

Yet the approaches to these two seemingly exemplary instances of failed balancing are treacherous. The reasons that more is known about the Mesoamerican and Andean political systems are also the reasons why their histories are difficult to read. These two cases stand out from the larger story of European conquest of the Americas because the degree of centralization in each was sufficient for Spanish defeat of the indigenous hegemon to bring an extensive territory and numerous subject peoples into almost immediate interaction with the newcomers, allowing information, including historical accounts, to be gathered. This contrasts with the experience of European settlement along the Atlantic seaboard of North America. There, smaller polities were encountered; small bands of European settlers were often recruited by one or another of the indigenous polities as allies in local balancing systems, but lack of hierarchy or centralization prevented rapidly decisive outcomes and – crucially for purposes of retrospective analysis – obscured the extent of the state-systems concerned, as well as the knock-on effects upon them of such struggles in the form of continental migration and the spread of new technologies and infections. But this very same concentration of power allowed the Aztec and Inca elites, anxious to retain status and sub-imperial authority over other ethnic groups even following their defeat, to transmit to the Spanish versions of the past that had formed part of the ideologies underpinning their own recent dominance.

Worse, each of those histories had been constructed quite deliberately in the first half of the 15th century in order to boost the status of a rising group by occluding its own humble origins and downplaying the status of contemporary rivals. In 1428 the Mexica destroyed all earlier codices and reinvented their past as part of a general ideological revolution. In place of the ancient books, Itzcoatl put in place 'a new tradition conveying an image of the past that would fit the requirements and ideals of the group whose dominance was in the process of rapid expansion' (León-Portilla, 1984: 14). A decade later – in very much the same way, though in a pre-literate culture – Cusi Inca Yupanqui, in naming himself Pachacuti ('... "cataclysm", or "He Who Remakes the World"...'), signaled a new beginning of history after he seized power, not least through a compression and mythologizing of the then memorable past into a narrative of his own accomplishments (Conrad and Demarest, 1984: 111).

Nor were the Spanish passive recipients of these narratives. They had their own rivalries. In a slight variation of the truism that victors write history, we find here versions of the past being passed from one victor to the next upon a bloody and uneven playing field, with distinct factions jostling within each group, Spanish and indigenous, to establish favorable pasts. Yet there is little option but to make the best of it, and begin by providing the most plausible narrative possible of the pre-Columbian century, first in Mesoamerica and next in the Andes.

The Aztec ascendancy

The people known to European history as the Aztecs, and perhaps better referred to as the Mexica, settled in the valley of Mexico in 1325, on the island of Tenochtitlan, which they reached as defectors from the Colhuacán confederation. There they became vassals and increasingly significant military allies of the Tecpanecs of nearby Azcapotzalco, who were at that point the proto-hegemonic power in the central plateau of Mexico, successfully challenging the Colhuacán (León-Portilla, 1984: 17; Nicholson, 1996). The Mexica rose to power in a world where complex patterns of migration and shifting alliance linked a large number of small, ethnically-based and mutually intelligible polities which coalesced and fragmented by turns within a landscape marked by the spectacular ruins of earlier civilizations.

Rather in the manner that the petty states of early medieval Europe looked back upon Rome, many of these American states looked to the Toltec tribute-empire of the 10th and 11th centuries, which had been based about 50 miles to the north of the site of Mexico City, as a model of political organization and a source of legitimacy. To the south, the Maya had sustained a literate culture of a high order over several centuries, bearing marks of Teotihuacan influence. During the final phase of this classical era, between 1200 and 1450, the Cocom lineage had ruled over a quite extensive and consolidated territory in present-day Yucatan, spawning a large number of successor states on its downfall (Fowler and Monaghan, 1996; León-Portilla, 1984: 9–17).

In all probability, claims to a direct link between the Toltecs and late classical Maya civilization are spurious. This is not true of the influence upon the Maya of the highly urban Teotihuacan culture, remains of which – dating from the first to the eighth centuries CE are to be found about 25 miles North-East of Mexico City (Townsend, 2000: 44–53). What matters is that these were peoples for whom the past carried political and ritual significance and who cherished the cultural expectation of a universal state, so that the claim to Toltec lineage of the Mexica ruler, Acamapichtli (1376–1390 or 1396), represented aspiration to or achievement of higher status, even though he and his successors Huitzililuitl (1390/96–1415) and Chimalpopoca (1415–26) would continue to be vassals of the Tecpanecs. Of particular importance for later Aztec ideology was the claim of Acamapichtli to descent from the Toltec god-ruler Topiltxín Quetzalcoatl.

On the death of the Tepanec ruler of Azcapotzalo, Tezozomoc, in 1426, one of his sons, Maxtla, seized power, and the subsequent succession crisis led to a general revolt throughout the recently created tribute-empire. In the war that ensued, the rulers of Tenochtitlan and its twin city of Tlatelolco were both killed. Subsequently, the new ruler of Tenochtitlan, Itzcoatl (c. 1427–1440), working in a loose military alliance with other former Tepanec subject-states, led a successful counter-attack against Maxtla. Of critical importance in this campaign was the assistance of the exiled Texcoco prince, Netzahualcoyotl, who captured Maxtla and personally slaughtered him in an elaborate and bloody public ritual that ended Tepanec power. To deter any attempt at a Tepanec restoration, Itzcoatl next formalized the victorious alliance between Tenochtitlan-Tlalelco, Tlacopan, and Tezcoco, fueling it with a division of the extensive lands and tribute made available by the collapse of Tepanec authority (Townsend, 2000: 71–7). The outcome was twofold. The Mexica achieved autonomy but, in the process, the nobility or warrior class (*pipiltin*) strengthened their position to such an extent that they were able to embark on a policy of expansion, building a tribute-empire of the traditional Mesoamerican kind, though distinguished by much more prominent private landholdings and an exaggerated emphasis on the importance of human sacrifice as a means of propitiating the gods and maintaining divine energy (León-Portilla, 1984: 17–32).

Under Motecuhzoma I (1440–69), the Mexica of Tenochtitlan became the dominant element in the Triple Alliance that ruled what Europeans would later call the Aztec Empire, though a breach with Tlatelolco in 1473 left a dissident population there, separated from Tenochtitlan by nothing more than a broad canal. Leadership of the Mexica, though soon settling upon a single dynasty (not unlike the imperial crown in Europe), passed from one *huey tlatoani* or supreme lord to the next by consensus of the nobility (*pipiltin*). Axayacatl was followed by his brothers, Tizoc (1481–1486) and Ahuitzotl (1486–1502), and his son, Motecuhzoma II (1502–20). The empire continued to expand, though by the beginning of the 16th century the pace had slowed. The Mexica encountered attempts at balancing, notably the sustained resistance of Chalco in the mid-15th century and the series of alliances formed by Mixtec and Zapotec states in the 1480s and '90s to check Aztec expansion to the South, and it may be that by the early 16th century, Aztec power had reached full extension (Townsend, 2000: 94; Hamnett, 1999: 54; Conrad and Demarest, 1984: 61).

Yet internal and external constraints can hardly be said to have contained Aztec power. Toward the end of the reign of Motecuhzoma II, close to 40 tributary provinces and other lesser dependencies stretching from the Pacific to the Atlantic were under his sway, though autonomous states persisted even quite close to the heartland of the Triple Alliance (Soustelle, 2002: xxi; Conrad and Demarest, 1984: 45 and 63).

Generally self-governing, the dependent territories often paid a high price immediately following unsuccessful resistance to the Alliance armies, as thousands of warriors were taken to Tenochtitlan for ritual sacrifice and punitive rates of tribute imposed. But often, it appears, a display of Aztec military might was enough to secure voluntary submission on terms satisfactory to both parties (Hamnett, 1999: 51–3). Thereafter, vassal states were required to supply goods, logistical support, and troops to assist their overlords, and to accept the ultimate supremacy of the imperial courts, while, in return, they were able to gain from the extensive trading networks made possible by what Soustelle refers to as the 'lax confederation' that the Mexica and their allies had established (Soustelle, 2002: 137).

Then, in the spring of 1519, a small Spanish force under Hernan Cortés landed on the East coast of the empire. When Motecuhzoma eventually granted Cortés an audience the Spanish took the opportunity to seize him, and he died soon afterwards in their custody. Motecuhzoma was succeeded by his brother, Cuitlahuac, who drove Cortés and his men out of the city, only to die of smallpox weeks later. A cousin, Cuauhtemoc, followed Cuitlahuac as *huey tlatoani*, defending the besieged city against the Spanish and their Tlaxcaltec and other indigenous allies – by now numerous – but he was finally forced to surrender in August 1521 and was executed not long afterwards on suspicion of conspiracy against the new Spanish overlords.

To sum up, Mesoamerica had been for many centuries characterized by processes of urbanization and state-building that led periodically to the creation of short-lived coalitions, confederacies and empires. This was a world in which bandwaggoning and balancing were both evident in what should be regarded as a society rather than merely a system of states, since its component cities were linked by language, shared customs, beliefs, and institutions (including very specific forms of ritualized warfare). The Mexica became prominent in this international society only after 1426, but their expansion, as the progressively strongest city in a Triple Alliance, was unusually rapid and successful. Though independent enclaves remained, and some coalitions had attempted to check the Aztecs, many states had chosen instead to bandwagon, and were permitted to retain their ruling dynasties and internal self-government. This may properly be called an empire, and it is remarkable for its unprecedented extent in the region and the absence of any really effective contrary force to balance it. Such a force finally emerged only following the intervention of a small Spanish band of adventurers in 1519, and led rapidly to the collapse of the empire. Balancing failure was overcome only after a new actor, from outside the Mesoamerican states-system, intervened, though it must remain a moot point whether a succession crisis or general rebellion might not, before long, have brought down a hegemonic power, already over-extended (Conrad and Demarest, 1984; Townsend, 2000: 114).

The Inca ascendancy

In the Andes, as in Mesoamerica, the properly historical period extends back barely a century before the arrival of the Spanish. Various legends of migration account for the arrival at the site of Cuzco – the city that was to become their capital – of a group of Quechua-speakers, known to history as the Incas (or Inca) after the title of their rulers. There, they encountered an international society of Aymara-speaking successor states of earlier empires, united by language and religion but divided by rivalry and war (Klein, 2003: 12–13). It was within this context that the Incas developed as a local power during the 14th and early 15th centuries. The decisive moment that was to set them on course for large-scale imperial expansion came in 1438, during the reign of Viracocha, when Inca power was challenged by the seemingly more powerful Chanca confederation as it expanded from its base in or near Ayacucho, some 150 miles to the North. In the decisive battle, so the half-mythic story goes, Viracocha fled, but his son Inca Yupanqui was able to rally his troops and defeat the Chancas. He then deposed his father and took the name Pachacuti, becoming the first clearly historical Inca overlord or emperor (McEwan, 1996; Townsend, 2000; D'Altroy, 2002).

Pachacuti entirely reorganized the Inca polity. He tightened the control of Cuzco over local vassal states. He despatched military expeditions to subdue areas to the North, in what are today the central Peruvian highlands, and to the South as far as Lake Titicaca. The Inca authority was established over the Aymara kingdoms of the region during the 1460s. A major revolt by Aymara-speaking polities in 1470 was repressed, and Quechua-speaking colonies and garrisons established in these areas (Klein, 2003: 17). The effect was to create a linear highland empire, *Tahuantinsuyu* or the land of four quarters, close to 500 miles in extent. At its heart, Pachacuti established Cuzco as a formal imperial city, where four main roads (representing the four quarters) met in a central plaza. To hold his conquests together he built royal roads with storehouses and lodges, and created a relay postal system. Further expansion took place under Topa Inca, who succeeded his father, Pachacuti, in 1471. This series of military campaigns accomplished Inca control of the entire Andean region, as the last serious rival, Chimú, was eliminated in 1476. The Inca realm now extended as far south as Bolivia, Northern Chile, and North-West Argentina, and as far north as Ecuador.

In 1493, Topa Inca was succeeded by Huaynu Capac. Campaigning continued in the north, with further gains in Ecuador and the north-eastern Peruvian highland. But diminishing returns had set in. Not only were logistics strained, but the absence of the Inca on his long northern campaign weakened his grip on the empire and its capital, while his presence led to the emergence of a rival court at the northern military headquarters of Tomebamba, in present-day Ecuador.

This division led to dissension when Inca Huaynu Capac died suddenly in 1527, followed within a few days by his son and heir. A succession crisis ensued, leading to outright civil war, as two sons of Huaynu Capac claimed the throne. Huascar succeeded formally in Cuzco. His brother Atahualpa, who had been with the northern army when his father died, disputed the succession and had the backing of the army. The struggle was long and bloody, ending only in 1532, when Atahualpa's armies finally took Cuzco. But as the new Inca followed them south with a large force, he was met by the Spaniard, Pizarro, at Cajamarca. With less then 200 men, Pizarro successfully attacked, capturing Atahualpa himself, in November 1532. Held to ransom by the Spanish, Atahualpa managed to engineer the murder of his rival brother, Huascar, from his prison cell before he, in turn died at the hands of the Spanish in July 1533.

Once again, in the Andes as in Mesoamerica, the arrival of the Spanish brought to an end a period, no more than two or three generations in duration, in which a tribute empire had effectively come to dominate the whole of an extensive settled area which had, as its heritage from earlier confederations and empires, sufficient cultural uniformity – through trade, conventions of warfare, shared religion, and common language – to be regarded as an international society rather than merely a states-system. Once again, it required intervention by an external power, the Spanish, to oust the ruling dynasty. It is true that civil strife, indicative of strains in the empire, seems to have been substantially responsible for Spanish victory, rather than the formation of a local coalition in support of the Spaniards. Yet it is unclear whether the lengthy succession crisis might, but for the Spanish, have given way to a period of consolidation. There is no contradiction between the views, expressed by Herbert Klein, that the Inca Empire had, by the time of the Spanish invasion, 'found its natural limits' and that the Inca state was eliminated 'just as it was beginning to mature' (Klein, 2003: 21 and 18).

Aztec and Inca distinctiveness

In a Mesoamerican world of many *altepetls* or cities, why did Teno-chtitlan, and not one of its materially and culturally similar neighbors, achieve such exceptional dominion in the 15th century? In an Andean world of many *ayllus*, why the Incas? The answers lie quite clearly in the revolutionary changes that took place in Tenochtitlan in and around 1428 and in Cuzco in 1438.

These were the decisive moments of differentiation in each case. Each immediately precedes and helps account for a period of rapid expansion of power. Before them, there was nothing distinctive for others to emulate and no clear and present danger requiring resistance, whether unilateral or cooperative. There is evidence also, prior to 1428/1438 of routine bandwaggoning and balancing activity in more or less anarchic systems. The Mexica defected from the Colcuacán confederacy to join the Tepanec confederacy, later defecting to the Acolhua confederacy based in Texcoco, and finally displacing it from leadership of what became known as the Triple Alliance. Bandwaggoning when weak, balancing when strong, the Mexica were unexceptional partners in the Mesoamerican political dance up to 1428. In much the same way, the Inca rose to power in a system marked by a steady rise and fall of rival polities. To the north, power was relatively concentrated in the Chimu Empire. In the central Andes, a number of polities, probably successor state of an empire centered upon Tiahuanaco, which collapsed in about 1200, jostled for position, the most prominent and aggressive being the Colla and Lupaca, in the Titicac basin. In the period of the initial Inca rise to power, 'the southern sierra was in a chronic state of petty war' (Conrad and Demarest, 1984: 95). So it was to be expected that its growing yet modest power would bring the Inca state into conflict with the more established neighbors, for its growth challenged the authority of the Lupaca, to the south, who had by this time defeated the Colla, and the Chanca to the north, who had 'completely upset the balance of power to the north and west of Cuzco' (Conrad and Demarest, 1984: 110).

Why, then, did what appear to have been routine processes of fluctuating power, confederation, fragmentation, and adjustment suddenly give way to exceptional and sustained expansion of two centralizing powers? In attempting a general account of the causes of imperial expansion and its limits I have relied heavily on the lucid and compelling comparative study by Conrad and Demarest (1984). The roots of expansionism within each state need first to be accounted for, and next the balancing failure explained.

Since there is little to separate rival Mesoamerican and Andean polities of the early 15th century in material or technological terms, and since the normal pattern was only upset after the 1428/1438 watershed, it may be that the answer to the first of these questions is to be found in the ideological reforms instituted by Itzcoatl and Pachacuti. In what did these consist? In each case relatively small changes to established practice and belief had disproportionately profound consequences. In Mesoamerica, the new historians employed by Itzcoatl after the burning of the codices elevated the Mexica god, Huitzilopochtli, into a higher place in the shared Mesoamerican pantheon, more in keeping with the newly victorious state. Now it was claimed that he was associated with the sun, both as the bringer of fertility in spring and summer, and as the source of light and life, associated with the warrior sun, Tonatiuh, who fought his way across the sky each day. Perhaps intended to motivate Mexica warriors, the idea that Huitzilopochtli required the blood sacrifice of warriors captured in battle, became a self-sustaining ideology, according to which the Mexica, as the chosen people of their god, had a sacred duty to save the cosmos from destruction by constant warfare and human sacrifice (Conrad and Demarest, 1984: 38). Each new reign began with a coronation war, in which the designated ruler campaigned to acquire prisoners by whose sacrifice the cosmic security of his government was assured. By the late 15th century this state religion had been reinforced with an extensive educational system, while elaborate ceremonies might require the deaths of thousand men on one day.

This tight linkage between religion, kingship, warfare, and continued good fortune led to human sacrifice on a scale unprecedented in Mesoamerica. Clearly it could not be indefinitely sustained. As the empire expanded it outgrew the area of common culture within which the Mexica understanding of warfare and sacrifice was understood and a measure of reciprocity and acquiescence might be expected. Worse, distant wars were often fought in terrain and by methods not conducive to the taking of suitable prisoners for sacrifice. This led to the Mexica being driven back on devices such as the purchase of slaves, ritualized warfare against vassal states, and the needlessly harsh suppression of revolts in order to maintain the supply of sacrificial victims. And this in turn began to have so substantial an impact on population in the food-producing regions on which the imperial core zone depended, that Ahuitzotl, at the end of the 15th century, was driven to a heroic but counterproductive attempt to bring more fresh water into the Valley of Mexico, leading to a great flood and much destruction of stored crops.

His successor, Motecuhzoma II, fared no better. In what may have been an attempt at consolidation, but perhaps also a way of solving the shortage of sacrificial victims, he set about eliminating enclaves, such as the Tlaxcalans, that had up till then survived in the heart of the empire. But these inconclusive struggles, together with fruitless wars of attrition on far-flung frontiers of the empire and periodic food shortages in the Valley of Mexico, gradually sapped morale and brought the official imperial sun cult into question, while Motecuhzoma II fostered further dissension and factionalism at the heart of empire by imposing sumptuary laws to try to remove the incentives to upward social mobility that motivated warriors, and clumsily intervening in the succession in the Triple Alliance partner, Texcoco (Conrad and Demarest, 1984: 58–9).

The Inca innovations under Pachacuti were in some measure administrative and monumental, but like those of the Mexica they were underpinned by an ideology with expansionist implications. As in Mesoamerica, this ideology was an adaptation of elements common to the larger culture of the region. Like all Andean peoples, the Inca worshipped their ancestors. Even their adoption of split inheritance had precedents (Conrad and Demarest, 1984: 91ff). Their innovation consisted in the combination of a stricter and more elaborate form of split inheritance with belief in the divine origin and status of the imperial family.

The Inca system of split inheritance worked in the following way. Each Inca had access to state resources, including estates and labor, but also amassed a personal fortune. On his death, the office of ruler together with public resources for the support of the state passed to his principal heir, but his personal fortune passed in trust to a collective, the *panaqa*, comprising his remaining heirs and their subsequent heirs. Each *panaqa* managed the estate of a previous ruler, constituting in effect his court, even after death. Indeed, the mummified body of the past ruler was believed still to be alive, and was the focus for elaborate rituals.

On coming to power, Pachacuti had divided the lands around Cuzco into a number of estates, some allocated to the *panaqas* of real or mythological earlier rulers and others to the maintenance of the state. However the system created a strong incentive for each new ruler to acquire personal property, since further estates had been alienated to a new *panaqa* following the death of his predecessor. As ruler, he had access to surplus labor, as a form of taxation, but in a system of reciprocation he was expected to sustain that labor force from his own resources as it cultivated state lands, engaged in road-building, terracing, and other civil engineering projects, or fought in the imperial armies. This created a constant need for new conquests of agricultural land, without which the ruler could not rule effectively, still less ensure the loyalty and wealth of the *panaqa* that would honor him after his death (Conrad and Demarest, 1984: 113–25). Even if this system was less uniform than Conrad and Demarest suggest, it surely contributed to an expansionist dynamic.

In the Andes, as in Mesoamerica, a state religion that created an imperative need for expansion and tribute may have constituted a key point of differentiation, setting the Inca, like Mexica, on the path to empire. By the later 15th century military success had taken the Inca armies to the limit of the terrain that suited their military techniques and lent itself readily to post-conquest exploitation. The populous lands of what is now Ecuador were a step too far. The logistics of the vast linear empire were strained. Its population was ethnically heterogeneous. In any case, the quest of each new Inca ruler for personal estates had effectively to be subsidized by state administrative structures and armies fulfilling their public labor-tax obligation and dependent on the product of state-owned lands, a system that could hardly be sustained. As the end of the 15th century approached, rulers, recognizing this, were driven to appropriate state lands or employ state resources in the reclamation of marginal land, notably by terracing. The first of these reduced the state lands available for the future, since expropriated lands passed to his *panaqa* as part of the private estate of the ruler. Marginal lands, meanwhile, though an addition to the estates of the ruler, may have cost more to bring into cultivation than they would produce. And to cap it all, each new *panaqa* offered a new focus for factionalism among an increasingly restive aristocracy, while the basis for imperial succession, by which office was meant to pass to the most competent son of the primary wife, left ample room for argument.

The succession crisis of 1527, which left the empire effectively divided between Atahualpa, in the North, and Huascar in Cuzco, allowed the latter – whose claim to rule was clearly superior to that of Atahualpa – to try to save the empire from destruction. He did indeed attempt to abolish the imperial ancestor cult, but this step so alienated the vested interests of the *panaqas* as to give Atahualpa, previously isolated with his northern army in Ecuador, unprecedented political leverage at the heart of the empire. This triggered the civil war of 1529–32, in which each claimant enlisted the support of different provinces and lineages, tearing the empire apart (Conrad and Demarest, 1984: 126–7).

Balancing failure in pre-Columbian America

An ideological account of the imperial drive and early successes of the two pre-Columbian empires provides the first element in an explanation of why neither was decisively checked before the Spanish invasions, whether by a balancing coalition, successful emulation by a powerful rival, or internal collapse. Other states, while equally competent and resourceful, may simply have lacked the religious or ideological impetus to expand, leaving the field clear for the two proto-hegemons.

It is quite another matter to explain why, when faced with a militant neighbor, other states did not check its expansion by emulation or coalition. One way to begin to answer this question is to take a step back from what was referred to, at the outset, as an enticement to the political scientist, namely the isolation of each of the two American systems of settled states. This appeared to present in each case a simple model in which a pre-existing anarchic international society failed to prevent the emergence of a hegemon. There is not, prior to the Spanish intervention, the complication of extricating one system from another, sub-system from primary system, and so forth: no French army to fall on Italy as in 1495, no Persian Empire on the flank of the Greek states-system, no continental superpowers ready to intervene in Europe as in the 1940s or South-East Asia a generation later. However, closer examination has made clear that the system/sub-system problem cannot entirely be eliminated. For in an anarchic states-system where there are constant bids for power, emulation of a proto-hegemon may itself result in one's own state becoming a hegemon, whilst to enter into a coalition to balance a proto-hegemon may make one the inadvertent helpmeet of an ally more dangerous than the supposed enemy. Rising powers do not come clearly labeled: 'Beware: hegemon-in-the-making!' To act too early against a rising power is to squander scarce resources, while to act too late is to court annihilation. It is therefore in the period soon after 1428 in Mesoamerica and 1438 in the Andes that balancing was most likely to take place, when the cat was out of the bag, but not yet fully grown.

It has already been seen that there *was* resistance. Sometimes this took the form of emulation, as in the Tlaxcalan development of a rival state-god, Camaxtli. Sometimes it was based in an alternative innovation, as with Tarascan metallurgical innovations (Conrad and Demarest, 1984: 70). Sometimes coalitions of formerly hostile polities emerged; sometimes an existing state or coalition achieved victory against the tide, as did the Tarascans against the Mexica in 1478 (Conrad and Demarest, 1984: 55; Townsend, 2000: 102). So the crucial question is why resistance was not more frequent and more effective.

A possible answer is that the anticipated advantages of bandwagoning generally exceeded the expected costs of balancing. Successive interpretations of both empires have painted the Aztecs and Incas as everything from benign communists to blood soaked and rapacious tyrants. Much hinges on this, for there is arguably less reason to resist incorporation into a loose and lightly-taxed confederation that offers the public goods of a wide trading network and security against external threat than submission to a more centralized empire, of whatever kind. Many commentators have felt that the closing stages of the Cold War bore out this generalization.

A first point to bear in mind is that in the early stages of expansion, when it has just gotten its nose ahead, a proto-hegemon has considerable logistical advantage over its neighbors. The tribute systems established in the Aztec and Inca Empires allowed armies to be recruited, moved, and provisioned with considerable efficiency. The expanding empires had decisive expeditionary advantage, at least in the campaigning season, and this made resistance hazardous.

This said, defensive armies on their own ground had compensating advantages and motivations and, perhaps appreciating this, the Aztec and Inca armies appear to have been more often used to threaten than to engage the forces of surrounding states during the expansionary phase. The Aztec armies generally avoided decisive encounters, preferring ritualistic demonstrations of force that showed the futility of resistance (Hassig, 1992: 145–6). The Inca armies, similarly, were primarily concerned to secure a compliant labor force and preferred negotiation to combat. 'Promises of fair treatment ... were mixed with undisguised menaces and the success of diplomatic negotiations was often due to the presence of huge concentrations close to the border of the coveted land' (Bram, 1941: 33). Subsequent incorporation into either empire, especially when voluntary, brought minimal interference. Hassig (1992: 137) notes the care with which the Aztecs avoided suppression of the customs and rights of tributary states, seldom insisting on dynastic change or a local garrison.

Nor was it entirely unreasonable for polities to heed these 'appeals to reason' if, as many sources suggest, the general experience of the tributary state was positive, with both empires employing systems of indirect rule. Carrasco (1999: 427), in an account of the Aztec Empire that makes scant reference to human sacrifice, is perhaps extreme in his judgment of its benevolence. 'Contrary to what has sometimes been said – he writes – the [Triple a]lliance was not a predatory organization that maintained itself by the tribute from conquered peoples'. This contrasts sharply with accounts of the aftermath of the rout of the Mixtec armies by an Alliance force of some 200,000 soldiers in 1458, when the defeated ruler was killed, a tribute collector imposed to oversee the defeated territories, sacred objects seized from the temples to be held hostage in Tenochtitlan against good behavior of the defeated Mixtecs, and thousands of captives carried off for ritual sacrifice (Townsend, 2000: 95–9). But this harsh treatment was the sequel to the contested conquest of a stubbornly independent rival, and the current consensus appears to be that tributary states did not fare too badly, and gained from the long-distance trading opportunities created by the armies of the Triple Alliance.

The theme of mutual advantage is much more developed in the Andean case. From the very beginnings of Inca expansion, incorporation of a new ethnic group into the empire was preceded by offerings of goods and women. If these were accepted, the recipients became one more tributary state with obligations to provide goods and labor to their overlords. Only if the gifts were declined would force be used, and the existing leadership then displaced (Rostworowski, 2000: 177). Indirect rule left tributary states with considerable autonomy and 'many societies voluntarily joined the powerful new empire' (Klein,

2003: 20 and 19; Rostworowski, 1999: 223). Moreover the promise of reciprocity was believable, since its practice was already fundamental to Inca society, in which, as we have seen, the ruler was expected to complement the labor force made available to him as taxation by feeding and sustaining it, much as Anglo-Saxon kings once showered gifts on those who fought for them.

Balancing failure against the Spanish

Balancing failure in the century before the Spanish invasions has been explained by a combination of factors. Early inability to distinguish the proto-hegemonic state from other threats was followed by a period in which many chose bandwaggoning because the anticipated balance of tribute paid against public goods received looked satisfactory, relative political autonomy was assured, and the costs of resistance looked prohibitively high. However, even if hegemony was not something to be resisted on principle (any more than it is in today's relatively benign unipolar world), there is evidence to suggest that both the Aztec and Inca Empires were becoming more exploitative and tyrannical in the decades immediately prior to the Spanish invasions. This accounts for the divisions that immediately preceded the arrival of Pizarro in the *altiplano* and those that broke out when Cortés reached Tenochtitlan. Indeed, Townsend (2000: 219) reckons the cause of the collapse of the Aztec Empire to have been 'as much an Indian revolt as it was a Spanish conquest', while Hamnett (1999: 55) goes so far as to claim that 'alliances within Meso-America made the Spanish conquest possible'. Far to the south, similar ethnic divisions and balancing behavior were immediately apparent in the Andes following the death of Atahualpa at Cajamarca. There, while the Inca armies rallied against the Spanish, no longer constrained by fears for the safety of their leader, the Xuaxa and Wanka peoples of the Montaro valley gleefully welcomed the Spanish, supplying them for their southwards march to Cuzco from the local royal warehouses (D'Altroy, 2002: 316; Klein, 2003: 29).

If strongly anti-hegemonic attitudes had set in by the early 16th century, as this evidence suggests, then why did newly liberated polities in the Americas, having by and large preserved their governmental institutions and cults through the recent imperial past, not defend their autonomy and identity more effectively against the new hegemon?

It may be objected that the answer is obvious. Smallpox, measles, and other diseases new to the Americas took a dreadful toll. Estimates of American population decline following first contacts with Europeans vary widely, but some run as high as a 95 per cent fall in native population during the century following the invasions (Hamnett, 1999: 6). This led to social dislocation in many areas which, more than sheer loss of numbers, must have inhibited solidarity and effective collective action (Klein, 2003: 47). Within Mesoamerica, which was worst affected by post-conquest demographic collapse, the late Aztec expansion of human sacrifice may have had substantial demographic impact even before this, and their combined effect would prove decisive. Nor was this all. The Spanish possessed horses and firearms. They were taken for gods (a view nicely dismissed as regards the Andeans by Harris) (1995: 13).

These traditional explanations for the surprising ease with which the Spanish were able to prevail cannot be dismissed, but are not sufficient. There were few Spanish; their horsemanship, weaponry and tactics could be emulated, and were as time went by (D'Altroy, 2002: 318–19). They too suffered from disease, and would long constitute a minority throughout the Americas. Especially in the Andes, they were riven by factionalism, fighting among themselves in ways that might have offered opportunities for indigenous groups, as did later Anglo-French rivalries in North America (Conrad and Demarest, 1984: 138). There *was* resistance; there *were* revolts; autonomous enclaves persisted. So why were the weaknesses of the Spanish not more fully exploited? Why were they not driven out or else confined, their settler-states becoming members of anarchic and balanced system of states in the Americas?

If the main premise is correct, and late-imperial oppression had created an anti-hegemonic temper in both Mesoamerica and the Andes, then one commonly proposed explanation clearly fails. This is that the indigenous polities simply acquiesced in a transfer of power, accepting that the Spanish would prove to be benevolent successors to the equally good-hearted imperial powers they replaced, because they promised continued respect for local customs, local nobilities, and the like (Klein, 2003: 29 and 34). This is unlikely given their recent experience of oppression and the iconoclastic behavior of the Spanish.

More plausible are the suggestions that there might be room, in whatever new system, for polities to hide in the borderlands of the settled zones or persist as enclaves, as in the past, or that the Spanish, being so very few, were at first thought less likely to be hegemons than prospective allies in restored anarchic systems. Many ethnic groups that had evaded Aztec or Inca conquest because of their isolation successfully resisted Spanish dominion and even that of the independent successor states of the Spanish Empire. Others settled for quiet semi-autonomy, with varying degrees of success. This is a central point of the recent ethno-historiographic revolution surveyed in the first section of this chapter. Aymara-speaking groups have retained their language and culture to the present day in the Andes. Groups speaking Maya languages have persisted in Guatemala and Southern Mexico. A thoroughgoing modernist must unhesitatingly point to the ultimate lack of sovereignty of these communities; yet, for those who chose to remain in them, they have in large measure continued to encompass the subjective experience of political life.

The second possibility is hinted at by several authors. It is that the Spanish were mistakenly taken for a new middle-rank power. Brian Hamnett (1999: 55) remarks on the ways in which '[r]ival American states sought to take advantage of the small-well-armed band of Castilian fighting men in pursuit of their own traditional objectives'. León-Portilla (1984: 36) suggests that 'the enemies of Tenochtitlan believed the Spanish were siding with them [rather than the reverse] ... not knowing for a while that their foreign allies were the only ones to profit from such a victory'. This view is strongly supported by the speed with which resistance, including balancing coalitions, developed in the Andes as soon as a more accurate appraisal of Spanish power and methods was reached.

In Mesoamerica, indigenous rulers and nobles, whose status was initially respected and even received royal protection, subject to conversion to Christianity, in 1557, did not persist as an independent political force, mainly, it seems, because of particularly severe population decline. Spanish authority was more quickly consolidated than in Peru, as viceregal authority was imposed at the expense of the conquistadors as well as indigenous peoples. Yet even here, the Mixtec states that had long resisted Aztec authority before the Spanish invasion only to submit without opposition to Cortés, reacted to the arrival of Spanish royal officials at district level, challenging traditional leaders and customs, by twice rebelling, in 1528–31 and 1548. But in this region, indigenous population was to fall by 90 per cent during the first century of Spanish rule. Resistance could hardly be sustained (Hamnett, 1999: 72).

Less spectacular was the persistence, even in the Valley of Mexico, of local indigenous states 'long into the postconquest period, with their territories and many of their internal mechanisms essentially intact' (Lockhart, 1992: citing Gibson, 1964). Indeed, Lockhart insists that the government of indigenous states was hardly changed before the middle of the 16th century, and that even following the gradual introduction of Hispanic *cabildos* or town councils over the century that followed, traditional *tlatoani* and nobles dominated office-holding. All true; but to have been of any real political significance, *independence* would have required, at the minimum, the possibility of resort to the legitimate use of force. This was the sticking point. Militarily effective emulation of the Spanish would have meant abandonment of central concepts of religion, honour, and status. Warfare for the nobility in Mesoamerica had been primarily concerned with the taking of high-status captives in battle for subsequent sacrifice. Persistence of this very formal kind of warfare had provided unique opportunities for upward social mobility. 'The Spaniards [by contrast] had no sense of proper behaviour on the battlefield, where they were ready to use crossbows and cannon to kill at a distance, and where they fled their opponents without shame' (Clendinnen, 1995: 269; Hassig, 1992: 137–46). In short, even if many indigenous states, beloved of the ethno-historians, remained well into the 17th century, they had no direct significance for the student of international relations and no traditional motive for fighting the Spanish, since they found themselves in a world without honor.

In the Andes, the persistence of politically effective indigenous authority was greater. Surviving elements of the Inca northern armies continued to harass the Spanish. As soon as Manca, the Inca installed by the Spanish in 1533, realized that he was not sovereign, he began to organize additional resistance. But he was already too late, since the Spanish had exploited anti-Inca feeling to acquire powerful local allies (Klein, 2003: 29). Escaping from Cuzco, Manca besieged the Spanish headquarters there in 1536 and 1537 with a vast army, in excess of 200,000 men. But non-Inca, Aymara forces were split. The Lupaqa joined Manca, but the Colla remained pro-Spanish, obliging the Inca-Lupaqa force to waste time and resources in a joint attack upon them, paving the way for their own defeat the next year by a Spanish expeditionary force under Francisco Pizarro (Klein, 2003: 30). Following this defeat at Chuquito and the lifting of the siege of Cuzco, the Incas withdrew, founding an independent state from 200 kilometers from Cuzco down the Urabamba river, at Vilacabamba. From there, they continued to fight against the Spanish and their indigenous allies. Inca ancestor worship continued, and the Spanish took great pains to hunt down and destroy royal mummies, a process only completed toward the end of the 1550s. So, for a generation, a multistate system existed, to all intents and purposes, with elements in the divided Spanish group allying with this or that indigenous state, while the Inca state persisted, albeit much diminished (D'Altroy, 2002: 319–20).

In the short run, therefore, depopulation and post-imperial rivalries outweighed the considerable strategic advantages of the indigenous polities. Spanish overlordship emerged rather than a mixed anarchy of indigenous and settler states, and by the time that immigration really gathered pace and Spanish rule became intrusive and seriously disruptive of indigenous social and political forms, it was too late for effective opposition to be mounted. Viceroy Toledo's reforms of the 1570s were perhaps the decisive moment in Peru (Klein, 2003: 34ff; Rostworowski, 1999: 224). The pre-Columbian states would become a source of legitimacy for later protests and revolts, as they are to this day, but in a spurious, imagined way. The direct traditions had been broken.

Depopulation, cultural shock, and post-imperial rivalries all played their part in frustrating effective balancing against the Spanish in Mesoamerica and the Andes. One final element must be added to complete the explanation, and this has far more to do with the evolution of political forms in 16th-century Europe than with the European predicament in the Americas directly. For the Spanish to have begun by accommodating indigenous authorities within its structures of local government was, from a European point of view, less a matter of their initial incapacity, and still less of respect for local tradition. Rather it was an extension to the new dominions of 'the purest tradition of medieval Castile, which drew upon centuries of municipal coexistence between Christians, Jews and Moslems' (Perez Collados, 1998: 27). Conversely, the intrusive reforms of Viceroy Toledo and his execution of the last Inca, Túpac Amaru, in 1573, were as much about the consolidation of Spanish monarchical power and state organization as about the politics of the *altiplano*, in *very* much the same way that the Henrican Reformation of the 1530s had been as much about the establishment of English sovereignty as about religious doctrine. The execution of the last Inca – according to a recent historian of the Spanish Empire – 'fitted in opportunely with the perspective of empire that the Spaniards were now adopting'. In the colonial territories there was to be no other authority save that of the king: popes, princes, Incas, were no longer to dictate the limits of Spanish power ... There was henceforth to be one sole empire, ruled over by one sole authority, the Crown of Castile' (Kamen, 2002: 195). Two European states with the same absolutist imperial aspirations; but Charles V and his successors were to receive from their American empire what the Tudors and Stuarts would lack: sufficient wealth to convert aspiration into reality, or so it seemed.

Conclusion

So long as one regards balancing as the norm in anarchic systems, the experience of the most civilized parts of the Americas in the century-and-a-half commencing in 1420 seems anomalous in the extreme. In the absence of thoroughly-administered assimilative empires of the Chinese kind, the state systems in these regions were technically anarchic. Yet they also showed an inclination towards hierarchy as hegemonic powers arose and balancing against them failed. Indeed in Mesoamerica and the Andes, prior to the Spanish invasions, this pattern can be thought of as exemplifying a well-established cycle, stretching back for centuries, in which the archaeological evidence suggests that tribute-empires formed and dissolved with some regularity within relatively homogeneous cultural spaces. Taken together, the available pre-Columbian evidence suggests a persistent oscillation between hegemony and fragmentation in systems of city-states. The final case is more complicated. Demographic catastrophe and technological superiority might have proved incidental, as the Spanish fused local and Iberian practice to impose a quasi-feudal tribute-empire of an almost traditional sort. But deep cultural incompatibility between the conquistadors and their new vassal states, coupled with the new imperatives of contemporary European state formation and balancing, meant that the age-old cycle of American civilization was decisively broken toward the end of the 16th century, as the Spanish embarked on what would prove to be an ephemeral and never more than partly successful experiment in bureaucratic authoritarianism.

9
Stability and Hierarchy in East Asian International Relations, 1300–1900 CE

David C. Kang

For too long, international relations scholars have derived theoretical propositions from the European experience and then treated them as deductive and universal. This book builds on an important new line of research (e.g., Kaufman, 1997; Wilkinson, 1999; Buzan and Little, 2000; Hui, 2004b) that corrects this scientifically indefensible parochialism. However, even this research has paid little attention to a major historical epoch – the Asian international system from 1300–1900. As a result, scholars may still underestimate the challenges a truly unbiased assessment of non-European international history presents to the conventional scholarly wisdom. For, whereas in many of the other international systems analyzed in this book balance-of-power processes occurred but were overwhelmed by other causal forces, in the Asian international system such processes barely registered in historical evidence. If balance-of-power theory is misleading in the other cases, in this case it is profoundly and fundamentally wrong.

Coming to grips with the historical East Asian system is important not only for theory but for contemporary policy analysis. Today's East Asian system is often discussed as if it emerged fully formed – like Athena from the head of Zeus – in the post-World War II and post-colonial era. To date, scholars have rarely described the main features of this system (Fairbank, 1968; Johnston, 1994; Hui, 2004b; Cha, 1998). But if anything, many East Asian countries have been geographically defined, centrally administered political units for longer than those of Europe. To ignore the evolution of these states is at best an oversight; at worst it reveals an unwillingness to engage the reality of East Asia's own dynamics (Frank, 1998; Anderson, 2002). To explain East Asian international relations in the 21st century, we should begin by exploring how the region got to where it is today.

Indeed, discussion of the contemporary global system might also benefit from comparison with this relatively recent example of political-military as well as economic hegemony. As Barry Buzan and Richard Little (2000: 2) write, 'existing frameworks in IR [international relations] are seriously crippled by their failure to build on a long view of history.'

In this chapter I introduce the international system of early modern Asia, assess the role of balancing in the larger pattern of the system's interactions, and provide a theoretical explanation for the absence of balancing dynamics and the system's overall stability based on a logic of hierarchy that contradicts the core assumptions of neorealism.

The chapter is organized into three main parts. In the first, I describe the system and its constituent units. A generation ago, it might have been possible to dismiss the evidence concerning early modern East Asia as not truly probative for IR theory because it was not a 'real' system, the chief actors did not interact enough, or they were not state-like enough. This view is no longer tenable. New research tends to support the contention that this is a system to which IR theory, and balance-of-power theory in particular, ought to apply.

The theory, however, cannot account for behavioral dynamics of this system, which I establish in the second section. Between 1300 and 1900, China's preponderant power never generated balancing behavior. If the system moved toward equilibrium, it was not as a result of balancing processes but rather the outgrowth of domestic Chinese weakness. Other actors did not generally use these windows of opportunity to rein in Chinese power. Instead, Chinese decline led to periods of generalized chaos and conflict in East Asia. When China was strong and stable, order was preserved. Until the intrusion of the Western powers in the 19th century, East Asian international relations was remarkably stable and peaceful, punctuated only occasionally by conflict between countries.

In the third section, I explain this behavioral pattern. The key is that East Asian international relations emphasized formal hierarchy among nations while allowing considerable informal equality. This system was materially based, and reinforced through centuries of cultural practice. With China as the dominant state and the peripheral states as secondary states or 'vassals,' as long as hierarchy was observed there was little need for interstate war. This contrasts with the Western tradition of international relations that consisted of formal equality between nation-states, informal hierarchy, and almost constant interstate conflict.

The system

In a study such as this, which covers a large, relatively understudied region over many centuries, it is important to be self-conscious about the limits and extent of the domain of inquiry. In this section, I delineate the geographical scope of the Asian system, identify the key actors, assess the rough distribution of capabilities, and begin to establish the intensity of interactions among the system's constitutive actors.

Geographical scope

The geographical domain of East Asian international relations studied in this chapter begins with Manchuria in the north, the Pacific to the east, the mountains of Tibet to the west, and the nations of Thailand, Malaysia, and Indonesia running south. This study focuses mainly on the region comprising Japan, Korea, China, and Vietnam. Other countries that were sufficiently involved in the system to warrant discussion include Siam, Indonesia, the Philippines, the Ryukyus, and Malaysia. These countries were the major actors in the system (Table 9.1).

This chapter focuses on the main political units that constituted the East Asian region from the 14th to the late 19th centuries. Some other actors existed, including the nomadic Uighurs and Mongols, and powerful pirate clans, but these will be discussed only in terms of their influence on great power relations. This study does not highlight these non-state actors for the same reason that studies of the European Westphalian system do not focus on Barbary pirates or Catalan separatists (Osiander, 2001; Krasner, 1999). In addition, the time period of this study is restricted to roughly the six centuries from 1300 to 1900 – a period that covers the Chinese dynasties from the end of the Yuan, the Ming, and finally the Qing. China – and East Asia – has millennia of history, and this study no more attempts to explain earlier historical periods such as the 'Warring States' period in China (481–221 BC) than a study that focuses on Napoleonic-era Europe would attempt to explain the foreign policy of 3rd century Visigoths (Hui, 2004b).

The major actors

Political units comprising the East Asian international system of the past millennium have been recognized sovereign entities with power over a geographic area. As Lien-sheng Yang (1968: 21) wrote, 'there is no doubt that China had at least a vague concept of state (*kuo*) by late Chou times (BC 400).' Both Korea and Japan historically have used the

202

Table 9.1 East Asian Political Systems, 1200–1900

	China	Japan	Korea	Vietnam	Thailand	Taiwan	Malaya	Java	Philippines
1200	1279–1368: Yuan	1160–1333: Kamakura	918–1259: Koryo	939–1407: Champa and Nam Viet	1238–1350: Sukhothai		Thai domination	1222–1293: Singosari	
1300		1333–1573: Ashikiga	1392–1910: Choson		1350–1782: Ayuthia			1293–1520: Majapahit	
1400	1368–1644: Ming			1407–1427: Chinese rule 1427–1787: Le Dynasty			1402–1511: Malacca		Majapahit influence
1500							1511–1641: Portuguese Malacca		1571: Spanish colony
1600	1644–1911: Qing	1600–1868: Tokugawa				1662–68: Dutch 1683–1895: Chinese district	1641–1796: Dutch Malacca	1619: Dutch colony	
1700					1782: Chakri		1796: British colony		
1800		1868: Meiji		1802–1955: Nguyen Dynasty and French colony		1895–1945: Japanese colony			1898: US colony

word for 'country' (*kuo* in Chinese, *koku* or *kuni* in Japanese, *kuk* in Korean, *quoc* in Vietnamese; all derived from the same Chinese character) to refer to each other and to China since well before the Sung dynasty. Korea has a long history of sovereignty. Although Korea was occupied by the Han dynasty around 100 BC, the Silla dynasty unified the peninsula in 668 AD, and since that time Korea has existed separately from China and Japan (Kim, 1980: 40; Cumings, 1996: 3). The Korean embassies to Japan referred to the Tokugawa shogunate as *Ilbon kukwang* ('king of Japan'), while the Korean king was known as *Hankuk kukwang* ('king of Korea') (Kim, 1980: 16). These three states together with Vietnam constituted the inner core of the Chinese-dominated regional system. In these four, the Chinese cultural and political influence was direct and major.

There were other states in the system that did not experience the same Chinese influence. Geographically more distant from China, states such as Siam, Java, the Ryukyus, and Burma engaged in extensive relations and interactions with the other states, and followed some Chinese norms and practices in dealing with other states, but were not directly influenced by Chinese culture and politics to the same extent as were Japan, Korea, and Vietnam (Smits, 1999). Although not as tightly incorporated into the Sinocentric system, these states were deeply incorporated into the China centered regional economy. Janet Abu-Lughod (1989: 303) writes, 'From the time the southern Sung first took to the seas in the late twelfth century...the petty kingdoms of the [Malacca] strait...changed from "gateway" to dependency...the Strait area must be conceptualized, at least in part and in the preceding centuries, as a dependency of China.'

Other political actors

In addition to the main political units that conducted international relations, there were other significant political or military actors in the region. Of these, the most important were powerful pirate clans, known as *wako*. The *wako* were never considered a legitimate or alternative political entity, however, and they were never a political threat to Japan, Korea, or China. Indeed, dealing with the *wako* was one of the main factors that caused coordination among these countries – as the analogous problem of piracy eventually was to do among European states in the 18th–19th centuries.

The *wako* had two major periods of activity – the mid-14th century and the early 17th century. *Wako* ('invaders from Japan') were originally petty military families from the western islands in Kyushu. Bands of as many as 3,000 intruders would pillage granaries, attack towns, take slaves in Korea and China, and interrupt trade. *Wako* roved as far south as the Yangtze Delta, Fujian, and Guangdong. The Chinese emperor Hongwu (1369–98) warned the Japanese that he would send forces to 'capture and exterminate your bandits, head straight for your country, and put your king in bonds' unless the *wako* raids were stopped (Elisonas, 1988: 241). The Koreans as well sought the cooperation of the shogunate to repress the *wako*, sending a number of embassies in the late 14th century to Japan. In fact, foreign relations between Japan and Korea at this time were essentially initiated because of the piracy issue (Ha, 1994; Kang, 1997: 25). The Koreans licensed a certain number of Japanese ships each year to trade with Korea; since trade was valuable, the Japanese had an incentive to rein in the *wako* (Elisonas, 1988: 244).

As Kawazoe Shoji (1990: 430) writes, 'the problem of suppressing piracy and the development of the tribute system that accompanied the founding of the Ming dynasty were the common threads running through Japan's relations with Choson, and Ming China.' Official relations between Korea and Japan covered protocols about how to deal with the return of Koreans or Japanese who were captured by pirates or those (known in Korean as 'Pyoryumin') who accidentally landed in the other's country (Min *et al.*, 2000). With the consolidation of the Ashikaga shogunate (1336–1573), the *wako* were severely weakened, and by the early 15th century, the *wako* had become more a nuisance than a threat. However, a century later, a resurgent tide of pirates was afflicting Korea and China. Focused more on China than Korea, this later wave of *wako* pirates attacked Fukien and other southern regions of China.[1] In large part, the resurgence of pirate raids caused the Ming to officially sever relations with Japan in 1621 (Kang, 1997: 2). As the central governments of East Asia became more powerful and exerted great control, the *wako* eventually died out.

Thus, the main actors in the system were national states that conducted formal, legal international relations with each other, and for whom international recognition as a legitimate nation was an important component of their existence. Other political actors such as pirates were a part of the system, but more as a cause of relations than a viable political alternative. Thus, national states of varying size and technological capability existed in an international system based on formal recognition and regulated by a set of norms. As we shall see, from Japan to Siam, and for well over six centuries, this system functioned in essentially the same manner.

The distribution of capabilities

Material power was a major component of the medieval East Asian international system. China was the largest and most advanced country, and had the capability to move armies of hundreds of thousands of troops across water. In balance-of-power terms, it represented an existential hegemonic threat through most of the over half-millennium period discussed here.

China was by far the largest, most powerful, and most technologically advanced nation in East Asia, if not the world. China has historically been the economic, political, and diplomatic center of East Asia, as well as the center of technological innovation and cultural construction for the region. Tables 9.2 and 9.3 show the relative share of world manufacturing and per capita levels of industrialization in 1750. In 1750 China had a per capita level of industrialization equivalent to those in Western Europe, and twice that of the American colonies. China's output far exceeded that of Japan or any other country in the region. Paul Bairoch (1982; cf. Maddison, 1983 and Kennedy, 1987) estimates that China produced almost one-third of the entire global manufacturing output in 1750, while Japan produced less than 4 per cent. Vietnam and Korea were dwarfed by China's size. David Marr (1981: 49) writes that 'despite the well known "march to the south," which brought them to the Mekong delta by the 17th century, the Vietnamese could never boast of controlling more people or resources than a single Chinese province.'

Table 9.2 Per Capita Levels of Industrialization (UK in 1900=100)

	1750	1800	1860	1913	1928	1953	1980
China	8	6	4	3	4	5	24
Japan	7	7	7	20	30	40	353
India	7	6	3	2	3	5	16
United States	4	9	21	126	182	354	629
Developed Countries*	8	8	16	55	71	135	344

*Austria-Hungary, Belgium, France, Germany, Italy, Russia, Spain, Sweden, Switzerland, UK, Canada, United States, Japan

Source: Paul Bairoch, 'International Industrialization Levels from 1750 to 1980,' Journal of European Economic History 11, no. 2 (Spring 1982): 269–334.

Table 9.3   Relative Shares of World Manufacturing (in percentages)

	1750	1800	1830	1860	1880	1900	1913
China	32.8	33.3	29.8	19.7	12.5	6.2	3.6
Japan	3.8	3.5	2.8	2.6	2.4	2.4	2.7
India	24.5	19.7	17.6	8.6	2.8	1.7	1.4
United States	0.1	0.8	2.4	7.2	14.7	23.6	32.0
Developed Countries*	27.0	32.3	39.5	63.4	79.1	89.0	92.5

*Austria-Hungary, Belgium, France, Germany, Italy, Russia, Spain, Sweden, Switzerland, UK, Canada, United States, Japan

Source: Paul Bairoch, 'International Industrialization Levels from 1750 to 1980,' *Journal of European Economic History* 11, no. 2 (Spring 1982): 269–334.

Korea and Vietnam, both part of the Asian landmass and sharing borders with China, were particularly vulnerable to Chinese conquest, had China wished to expand. Chinese military organization and technology also gave it the capability to project power over long distances. Indeed, China ruled Vietnam for almost a 1,000 years, from 112 BC, when Vietnam was invaded by the Han emperor Wu-di, until the fall of the Tang dynasty in 907 (Buttinger, 1958). Chinese military organization has been formidable since ancient times, and China had the military and technological capacity to have expanded through conquest further than it did.

As early as 624, under the Tang Dynasty, emperor Taitsong built a standing army of 900,000 men, the first standing professional Chinese army (Davis, 1996: 131; Capon, 1989). The limiting factor was not technological, but political – a decision by China not to pursue conquest. Although Japan was protected by water, it was a surmountable barrier, and China had the military capability to invade Japan throughout this period. The Chinese invasions of Japan in 1274 and 1281 involved up to 150,000 men and 4,400 Chinese naval vessels (Shoji, 1990: 418). As to China's naval potential, the famous 1405 and 1433 expeditions by the Chinese admiral Zheng He (Cheng Ho) took 62 ships and over 28,000 men as far as Africa, bringing back elephants and other treasure to China (Levathes, 1994). The Ming navy consisted of 3,500 oceangoing ships, including over 1,700 warships. Janet Abu-Lughod (1989: 321) writes that 'no naval force in the world at that time came close to this formidable armada.' When Japan invaded

Korea in 1592 with intentions to conquer China, Hideyoshi took 200,000 men, transported on 300 Japanese naval vessels.

Trade and the level of interaction

The East Asian system, in short, featured smaller states existing under the shadow of a preponderant power with the material wherewithal potentially to conquer all or most of the system. In other words, it was a system primed for intense balance-of-power politics. We would only expect balancing dynamics to come to the fore, of course, if these actors were in sufficient contact with each other to truly constitute a system. I have already mentioned military interactions and below I will analyze political and diplomatic ones. Here I detail another important indicator of high interaction levels: trade.

Far from the West's bringing trade and interaction to a somnolent East Asia in the 17th century, there existed a vibrant East Asian economic trading system well before the West arrived. China and its tributaries had far more interaction with each other than has been traditionally acknowledged. Recent scholarship is finding that trade, both private and tributary, made up a significant portion of both government revenues and the national economies. The system was geographically quite wide, including trade from Japan to Java and Siam. Furthermore, trade with the West (mainly the Portuguese and the Dutch) in the 17th and 18th centuries was at most a minor portion of overall East Asian trade. The countries in this system were part of a thriving, complex, and vibrant regional order. As Janet Abu-Lughod (1989: 317) writes:

> The literature generated both in China and abroad gives the impression that the Chinese were 'not interested in' trade, that they tolerated it only as a form of tribute, and that they were relatively passive recipients...This impression, however, is created almost entirely by a literal interpretation of official Chinese documents ....Upon closer examination, it is apparent that much more trade went on than official documents reveal, and that tribute trade was only the tip of an iceberg of unrecorded 'private' trade.

Lee (1999: 14) notes that 'China since the sixteenth century was even more deeply involved than Japan in trade with the larger world. Few other places produced the commodities that were universally in demand in greater quantity or variety, and few others attracted foreign traders in the same number.' Deng (1997: 254) agrees: 'China is often portrayed as a country isolated from the outside world, self-sufficient and insulated from capitalism...with marginal, if not non-existent, foreign trade. In fact, China needed foreign trade, both by land and sea, as much as many other pre-modern societies in Eurasia.' Table 9.4 shows selected estimates of the quantity of goods traded between China and its vassals during the Ming era.

As Deng (1997: 254) explains, these figures belie the old 'trade as tribute' view (Beckwith, 1992):

> Zheng Chenggong's Ming loyalist regime in Taiwan (1644–83) took part in triangular trade involving Japan, Vietnam, Cambodia, Indonesia, and the Philippines; his fleet to Japan alone comprised fifty ships a year...The total profit from overseas trade each year has been estimated at 2.3–2.7 million *liang* of silver...The tributary system was a form of disguised staple trade. Trade is also shown

Table 9.4   Quantities of Tribute During the Ming Era

Time	Country	Export to China	Quantity	Import from China	Quantity
1393	Korea	Horses	9,800	Silk Cloth	19,000 rolls
1394	Cambodia	Incense	60,000 *jin* (35.8 tons)		
	Siam	Pepper	10,000 *jin* (6 tons)		
		Sapanwood	100,000 *jin* (60 tons)		
1403–1570	Mongolia	Horses	4,000*		
		Hides	100,000		
1406–7	Japan			Copper coins	215×10^5
1411	Malacca			Copper coins	26×10^5
1417	Philippines			Copper coins	30×10^5

*quantities exported yearly

Source: Gang Deng, 'The Foreign Staple Trade of China in the Pre-Modern Era,' *International History Review* 19, no. 2 (May 1997), p. 260.

because of the fighting over the ability by tributary states to pay tribute. Hideyoshi invaded Korea, a Ming vassal state, to force China to allow Japan to resume a tributary relationship, and threatened that a refusal would lead to invasion of China itself.

During the late 16th century, trade between Manila and China was an estimated annual value of 800,000 *liang* of silver (Atwell, 1982). Table 9.5 shows the estimated number of ships that traded each year between China and Japan during the 17th century. Korea-Japan trade – between equals – was essentially pluralistic. *Daimyo*s and rich Japanese merchants were involved, and Etsuko Kang (1997: 28) writes that 'from the fifteenth century Japanese-Korean trade surpassed Japanese-Ming trade in quantity, and it had a greater impact on the daily life of the Japanese in western areas.'

During the Qing period, the Chinese built more than 1,000 ocean-going ships each year. Deng (1997: 283) concludes that, 'pre-modern China's long-distance staple trade reveals a system of international exchange, a prototype of division of labor transcending national/ethnic territories, and great manufacturing capacity with considerable technological advancement.'

Japan was deeply enmeshed in a network of foreign trade with other parts of East Asia at this period. Table 9.6 estimates Japanese silver trade in the mid-17th century. Most notable is how small the Dutch portion of the silver trade actually was.

Table 9.5   Chinese Data for Ships Visiting Japan, 1641–1683

Year	Number of Ships
1641–5	310
1646–51	220
1652–6	259
1657–61	238
1662–6	182
1667–71	185
1672–6	138
1677–81	126
1682–3	53
Total: 43	1,711
Annual average	40

Source: Gang Deng, 'The Foreign Staple Trade of China in the Pre-Modern Era,' *International History Review* 19, no. 2 (May 1997), p. 262.

Table 9.6   Japanese Silver Exports, 1648–1672

Year	Silver exports to China (kanme)	Silver exports to Netherlands (kanme)	Total silver exports (kanme)
1648	1,794	6,222	8,016
1649	5,454	5,341	10,795
1650	6,828	3,940	10,768
1651	4,749	4,896	9,645
1652	5,687	5,719	11,406
1653	3,517	6,191	9,708
1654	8,181	3,848	12,029
1655	4,655	4,002	8,657
1656	5,241	6,190	11,431
1657	2,450	7,562	10,012
1658	11,029	5,640	16,669
1659	19,401	5,960	25,361
1660	20,151	4,269	24,420
1661	25,769	5,544	31,313
1662	12,943	5,960	18,903
1663	5,411	3,672	9,083
1664	16,664	5,572	22,236
1665	8,042	6,880	14,922
1666	7,236	3,977	11,213
1667	4,547	3,574	8,121
1668	3,415	0	3,415
1669	296	0	296
1670	395	0	395
1671	950	0	950
1672	8,964	0	8,964

Note: one Japanese kanme equals 3.75 kgs.

Source: Richard von Glahn, 'Myth and Reality of China's Seventeenth Century Monetary Crisis,' Journal of Economic History 56, no. 2 (June 1996), p. 443.

Sanderson (1995: 153) writes: 'trade with China and Korea became an important part of the Japanese economy...During the fifteenth and sixteenth centuries foreign trade grew rapidly in intensity and trade ventures were extended to other parts of the far east, even as far as the Straits of Malacca.' During the Muromachi bakufu period, it is estimated that annual traffic between China and Japan was never less than 40 to 50 ships annually (Shoji, 1990: 408). Between 1604 and 1635, the Japanese recorded 335 ships sailing officially to Southeast Asia, and even in the late 17th century, 200 ships arrived in Nagasaki every year (Frank, 1998: 106; Klein, 1989: 76; Howe, 1996: 37).

Even during the Tokugawa era, Japanese exports in the 17th century are estimated to have reached 10 per cent of its GNP (Howe, 1996: 40). Indeed, China under the Qing was much more willing to consider private trading relations in the stead of formal tribute relationships. Von Glahn (1996) writes that 'Japanese trade with China grew substantially after the Tokugawa came to power in 1600. The Tokugawa *shogun* Ieyasu aggressively pursued foreign trade opportunities to obtain strategic military supplies and gold as well as silk goods.' Lee (1999: 7) stresses the 'undiminished importance of a trade relationship with China and, to a lesser extent, with Korea and the Ryuku' during the Tokugawa period.

Using reports of Chinese ship captains as given to Japanese officials in Nagasaki during the Tokugawa era, Yoneo Ishii estimates that the junks that carried trade between China, Southeast Asia, and Japan had an average size of between 120 and 500 tons, with some capable of carrying as much as 1,200 tons of cargo. Because of the dynastic transition between the Ming and the Qing during the 1670s and 1680s, direct China-Japan trade was difficult, so many of the junks originated in Taiwan, went to Southeast Asia, and then traveled to Japan. After the Qing court established full control of Taiwan in 1683, it lifted restrictions on shipping to Japan, and trade expanded dramatically (Ishii, 1998: 6–11; Ikeda, 1996). 'During the eighteenth century,' Klein (1989: 67) writes, 'Japanese exports of precious metals over the isle of Tsushima into Korea and China actually surpassed the amounts of silver that had earlier been carried away from Nagasaki by the Chinese and Dutch.' The Tsushima profits from Korean trade during Tokugawa were enough to feed the entire population of Osaka at current rice prices (Toby, 1991: xxviii).

Trade served as a double-edge instrument of system consolidation, for it facilitated not only more intense state-to-state interactions but also the development of domestic state institutions. Southeast Asia illustrates both processes. From roughly 1400 to the 18th century, the expansion of international trade within Southeast Asia, and between Southeast Asia and China, Japan, and Northeast Asia, resulted in a regionwide process of territorial consolidation and centralization of royal authority (Lieberman, 1993). Frank (1998: 97) notes that, 'At least a half dozen trade dependent cities – Thang-long in Vietnam, Ayutthaya in Siam, Aceh on Sumatra, Bantam and Mataram on Javva, Makassar on Celebes – each counted around 100,000 inhabitants plus a large number of seasonal and annual visitors' (Reid, 1993).

As in Northeast Asia, trade in Southeast Asia was regulated by royal monopolies. Thailand (Siam) is a case in point. The Siamese central civil administration had four working departments – Treasury, Palace, Land, and City. Treasury was in charge of overseeing foreign trade, and consisted of royal warehouses, factories, tax and duties collectors, and the 'port master' (Viraphol, 1977: 20). By the early 18th century, the number of Chinese ships calling at Siam had steadily increased. One European trader at the time wrote:

> The Chinese...bring them the most valuable commodities; and, at the same time, allow their own people to disperse themselves unto a great number of foreign parts, whither they carry their silks, porcelain, and other curious manufactures and knickknacks, as well as their tea, medicinal roots, drugs, sugar, and other produce. They trade into most parts of East India; they go to Malacca, Achen, Siam, etc. No wonder then that it is so opulent and powerful... (quoted in Viraphol, 1977: 54).

And, as Cushman (1993: 78) emphasizes, 'Siam's exports should not be seen as marginal luxuries, but as staple products intended either for popular consumption or for the manufacture of consumer goods by the Chinese.'

Evidence on the relative importance of trade with the west suggests, moreover, that relations among Asian states continued to outweigh more sporadic interactions with outside powers. In contrast to Japan's continued incorporation into active trade in the region, Western trade – mainly Dutch and Portuguese traders – was simply never as important as has been believed. The annual Portuguese share of silver exports was usually less than 10 per cent of total exports (Klein, 1989: 76). The Dutch were actually pushed out once the East Asian system stabilized by the end of the 18th century. Indeed, in 1639, the Tsushima *daimyo* told the Korean government that 'because commerce with the Portuguese has been banned from this year, we must seek more broadly trade with other foreign nations besides them, and [the *shogun*] has ordered us to trade with your country even more than in the past.' (quoted in Toby, 1991: 9) Thus, Klein (1989: 70) concludes that 'during the eighteenth century...the East China Sea saw the re-establishment of its traditional self as it more or less retired from the world [European] market.' Numerous estimates complied by researchers on different regions, periods, and markets, show the overwhelming bulk of trade occurring within Asia as opposed to between Asian states and Europe (e.g., Frank, 1998: 101; van Luer, 1955: 125), Klein's (1989: 86) assessment is typical: 'European penetration into the maritime space of the China sea was marginal...weak and limited.'

Thus, the economic system of East Asia was far more integrated, extensive, and organized than the conventional wisdom allows. From at least the Sung era of the 10th century to the end of the Qing dynasty in the 19th century, there existed a vibrant and integrated trading and foreign relations system in East Asia that extended from Japan, ran through Korea to China, and also extended from Siam through Vietnam and the Philippines. So extensive was this regional economic order that it had domestic repercussions such as monetization of the Japanese economy. The Dutch and the Portuguese had less impact than is normally thought. It was only when China began to crumble in the 19th century that this system finally broke apart.

In sum, research on trade patterns indicates a high level of system interaction in East Asia that was relatively independent of the simultaneously developing European system. As Hamashita (1994: 92) contends, it is necessary to see 'Asian history as the history of a unified system characterized by internal tribute/tribute-trade relations, with China at the center.' He stresses that a 'fundamental feature of the system that must be kept sight of is its basis in commercial transactions. The tribute system in fact paralleled, or was in symbiosis with, the network of commercial trade relations, the entire tribute system and interregional trade zone had its own structural rules which exercised systematic control through silver circulation and with the Chinese tribute system in the center.'

Behavior

Behavioral patterns in the Asian system are impossible to reconcile with balance-of-power theory. Most important, there is simply scant evidence of balancing. We do not see alliance-formation against China, notwithstanding large fluctuations in Chinese capabilities that might have offered other states windows of opportunity to at least attempt to diminish Chinese dominance. To be sure, neighboring states did seek to emulate Chinese practices, but there is little evidence that the aim was to build up capabilities in order to match and rein in Chinese power. On the contrary, as I will discuss in more detail below, emulation actually had the opposite effect of ramifying the Chinese-dominated order.

Patterns of conflict, moreover, do not correspond to balance-of-power expectations. As treated in this volume, balance-of-power theory is not a theory of war. Nonetheless, as a theory that explains systemic tendencies toward balance, it would predict that a system as dominated by one state as Asia was by China would be inherently unstable owing to underlying anti-hegemonic systemic forces. The theory expects that a state as dominant as China will likely seek further territorial expansion at the expense of weaker neighbors. This is, after all, why balancing is supposed to be the prime directive of states' foreign policies: to prevent a dominant state from expanding at the expense of the sovereign security of other system members. For this reason, the theory also expects those neighbors to fight to resist Chinese dominance when possible. Neither of these expectations is borne out.

The most striking feature of the system was its comparative peacefulness. The contrast with Europe during the same time period is revealing (Table 9.7).

Overall, war between states was rare, and wars of conquest were even more rare; often centuries separated wars between the main political units. China did not seek to translate its dominant position into a system-wide empire by force of arms. China's last attempted invasion of Japan occurred in 1281. The Qing expeditions against the Korean Choson dynasty in the early 17th century were aimed more at consolidation, demarcation of borders, and reestablishment of the tribute system than with conquest (Han, 1999). For example, Kim (2006) argues that the Qing expeditions against the Choson in the early 17th century were aimed at demarcating the border between the two states, arguing that 'it was the wild ginseng growing in the borderland that initiated the border demarcation between China and Korea.' He quotes Hwang Taiji (the Manchu emperor from 1626 to 1643 who laid the groundwork for the Qing dynasty) criticizing the Choson King Injo in 1631 for his trade policies, saying 'the ginseng prices used to be sixteen liang per jin, but you argued that ginseng is useless and fixed the price at nine liang....I do not understand why you would steal such useless ginseng from us.'

Conflict tended to occur not to check rising Chinese power but rather as order within China itself was decaying. As a Chinese dynasty began to decay, conflict among the surrounding states would flare up, as the central power's attention turned inward. But that peripheral conflict was generally impossible to interpret as directed at reinforcing balance by checking China's potential to recover.

Thus, at the beginning of the era under study, in 1274 and 1281, the Mongols under Kublai Khan, having conquered northern China from the Song, attempted unsuccessfully to conquer Korea and Japan (Curtin, 1972). Eighty years later, with the consolidation of the Ming

Table 9.7   East Asia and Europe over the Last Six Centuries

	Europe	East Asia
1492	Expulsion of Moors from Spain	(1392–1573) Ashikaga Shogunate, Japan (1368–1644) Ming Dynasty, China (1392–1910) Yi Dynasty, Korea
1494	Charles VIII of France invades Italy Beginning of struggle over Italian peninsula by Spain and France	(1467) Onin War, Japan. Beginning of 'The Age of the Country at War'
1526	Bohemia and Hungary under Habsburg rule	
1527	Sack of Rome	
1552	Maurice of Saxony revolts against the Emperor	
1556	German-Spanish division of the Habsburg possession	
1562	French Wars of Religion	
1572	Revolt of the Netherlands	
1580	Portugal united with Spain	
1588	Spanish Armada defeated	(1592, 1596) Hideyoshi invades Korea
1618	Thirty Years' War begins	(1600–1868) Tokugawa Shogunate, Japan
(1618)	Manchus declare war on the Ming	
1630	Countermoves by France and Sweden begin	(1627) Manchus invade northern Korea
1640	Portugal breaks away from Spain	
1642	English Civil War	(1644) Qing Dynasty (Manchu)
1648	Peace of Westphalia	
1652	First Naval War between Britain and Holland	
1667	War of Devolution: Louis XIV against Spain in the Netherlands	
1672	Second War, France against Holland and Spain	

Table 9.7   **East Asia and Europe over the Last Six Centuries** – *continued*

	Europe	East Asia
1672	Second Naval War between Britain and Holland	
1681	Vienna besieged by Turks	
1688	Third War (League of Augsburg)	
1710	War of the Spanish Succession	
1720	Prussia acquires Western Pomerania from Sweden	(1709–29) Chinese intervention in unstable Vietnam
1722	Peter's War against Persia	
1733	War of the Polish Succession	
1735	Annexation of Lorraine to France assured	
1739	Britain at War with Spain in West Indies	
1740	First Silesian War, War of the Austrian Succession	
1744	Second Silesian War	
1755	Britain attacks France at sea	
1756	Seven Years' War	
1774	Crimea annexed to Russia	
1772	First Partition of Poland	(1788) Chinese punitive expedition against Vietnam
1792	France declares war on Austria	
1793	Britain declares war on France, Second Partition of Poland	
1795	Third Partition of Poland	
1799	War between France and the Second Coalition	
1801	Nelson's victory at Copenhagen	
1805	Trafalgar	
1806	Jena	
1808	Insurrection in Spain	
1812	Napoleon's Russian Campaign	
1815	Waterloo	

Table 9.7   East Asia and Europe over the Last Six Centuries – *continued*

	Europe	East Asia
1815	Congress of Vienna	
1823	Absolute rule restored in Spain by France	
1830	July Revolution in France, Polish Revolution	(1839, 1856) Opium Wars in China
1848	Revolution in France, Italy, Germany	(1853) Commodore Perry lands in Japan
1859	War for Unification of Italy	
1864	Denmark's war against Prussia and Austria	
1866	Austro-Prussian War	
1870	Franco-Prussian War	(1868) Meiji Restoration
1878	Congress of Berlin	(1874) Japan annexes Taiwan
1899	Boer War	(1894) Sino-Japanese War
		(1900) Boxer Rebellion, China
1904	Russo-Japanese War	(1904) Russo-Japanese War

Sources: R. Ernest Dupuy and Trevor Dupuy, *The Harper Encyclopedia of Military History: From 3500 BC to the Present*, 4th ed. (New York: HarperCollins, 1993); and Paul K. Davis, *Encyclopedia of Invasions and Conquests: From Ancient Times to the Present* (Santa Barbara: ABC-CLIO, 1996).

Dynasty's control in China in 1368, Zhu Yuan-zhang sent envoys to Annam, Champa, Koryo, and Japan announcing the founding of the Ming dynasty, and revived the policy of political relationships and an international order in which tribute missions were the main envoys between the surrounding states and the Chinese emperor (Shoji, 1990: 424). The sole conflict that might be reconciled with a broad interpretation of the theory occurred centuries later. As the Ming dynasty weakened, the Japanese general Hideyoshi attempted to invade China through Korea in 1592 and 1598, although he failed to take Korea. And, as the Qing consolidated power early in the 17th century, conflict between the surrounding states ceased and relations between states was relatively peaceful for another 200 years.

For centuries the Chinese did face running border battles with the Mongols to the north, at times employing 500,000 troops in an effort to secure their northern front (Johnston, 1994: 234; Van de Ven, 1996: 737). In fact, the only successful invasions of China came from the north – Genghis Khan in 1215 and the Qing in 1618 (Shu, 1995). Despite successful conquest of China, however, change was not as lasting as it might have been. Genghis Khan ruled through the existing Chinese bureaucracy instead of supplanting the existing Sinic civilization. When the Manchus invaded the crumbling Ming dynasty and founded the Qing dynasty 1644, they also adopted Chinese and Confucian practices (Kwanten, 1979; Davis, 1996).

This brings up a final major difference between the Asia and contemporary Europe that suggests the existence of a different systemic logic: in Asia major political units remained essentially the same after war. Boundaries and borders were relatively fixed, and nations did not significantly change during the time period under review. In 1500 Europe had some 500 independent units; by 1900 it had about 20 (Kaufman, 1997: 176). In East Asia, the number of countries, and their boundaries, has remained essentially the same since 1200 AD. With such a large central power in China, other nations did not wish to challenge China, and China had no need to fight.

In sum, the larger behavioral pattern is precisely what balance-of-power theory does not expect: stable system dominance by a materially preponderant state.

The logic of the Asian systemic hierarchy

When China was stable, the regional order was stable. The dominant power appeared to have no need to fight, and the secondary powers no desire to fight. Why? Three overlapping explanations account for the system's stability: the distribution of power and benefits reinforcing Chinese dominance; culture and ideas supporting a stable hierarchy; and the diffusion of Chinese institutions and influence into the domestic politics of the other states comprising the system. The following subsections discuss each of these logics, and then a fourth subsection considers the case of Japan – as the second largest state a crucial test case for the argument.

Power and the cost-benefit equation

For most of the period under review, capabilities were distributed such as to make it very hard if not impossible for a balancing order to emerge. China was simply too strong, advanced and central to counterbalance effectively. For simple realist reasons, therefore, all the usual impediments to balancing were exacerbated. In other words, one benefit of establishing subordinate relations with China was to ensure peaceful relations with China. For example, the Japanese Ashikaga shogunate (1333–1573) sought investiture by the Ming emperor in order to eliminate the insecurity caused by fear of another Chinese invasion. As Shoji (1990: 437) writes, 'in order to [ensure peaceful relations with China], Japan had to become part of the Ming tribute system and thus cease to be the "orphan" of East Asia. For centuries the Japanese had feared attack by the Silla (Korea), and the Mongol invasions had provided real grounds for fearing a Ming attack.'

China's strength also allowed it to provide security benefits to lesser states that agreed to play by the system's rules. Incorporation into the Chinese world provided protection from attack, and left the secondary states free to pursue domestic affairs and diplomacy with each other as they saw fit. For example, in 1592 the Chinese sent troops to Korea to attack Japanese general Hideyoshi's invading troops. (Ledyard, 1988–99; Boscaro, 1975). Jung Yak-yong, a prominent scholar during the 19th century, argued that Choson Korea after the Hideyoshi invasion had little fear of a second Japanese invasion both because Choson elites thought Japan's understanding of Confucianism was deep enough that it would not invade, and also because they knew the Qing would come to Choson's aid in event of another Japanese attack (Ha, 1989).

Other states bought into the Chinese role as system manager. In 1592, for example, King Naresuan of Siam learned of Japan's invasion of Korea, and sent a mission to China in October of that year, offering to send the Siamese fleet against Japan. Wyatt (1984: 104) emphasizes: 'This was no empty gesture. Naresuan understood the interconnectedness of international relations, and he wanted to maintain a balance of power favorable to open international commerce and to China's dominance in an orderly Asian state system.'

But this is only part of the explanation, for it cannot account for failure to balance when China was weak, for China's disinclination to expand further, and more generally for the system's astonishing stability. Another rationalist logic was at work: Trade with China was a key element of international relations in the region. As detailed above, China was a lucrative and advanced market that tended to draw others into the system. Key here is that even 'tribute' was more a hypothetical goal than reality, for the tributary nations gained as much in trade and support as they gave to the Chinese emperor. Tribute in this sense seemed as much a means of trade and transmission of Chinese culture and technology as it was a formal political relationship.

Japan is an important example. During the Song and Southern Song dynasties in China (907–1297), the Japanese economy was monetized because trade with China brought in so much coinage that the Japanese government was forced to legalize the use of coins. As Yamamura (1990b: 358) notes, this 'had profound effects on the political, economic, and social history of Japan.' Despite three separate decrees by the Japanese *bakufu* to ban the use of coins, by 1240 they had allowed the use of coins in all but the northernmost province of Japan. Shoji (1990: 435–6) notes that 'many have since contended that it was the income that could be gained from missions to China that motivated Japanese king Yoshimitsu (Ashikaga shogunate in 1403) to open relations with the Ming...the large gifts of copper coins, silks, brocades, and so forth that the Ming envoys brought to the shogunal court were certainly a major economic attraction. This tribute-gift exchange was in reality simply trade...'

Ideas and culture

In short, being a client state brought economic and security benefits at a cost lower than engaging in arms races or attempting to develop a counterbalancing alliance against China. Sill, the rationalist calculus leaves a lot unexplained. After all, balance-of-power theory assumes rational actors, and the potential for mutually beneficial security and economic relations is frequently overwhelmed by problems of uncertainty and commitment that generate conflict. Indeed, many of the other chapters in this volume detail distributions of power not unlike the China-dominated Asian system that nonetheless witnessed frequent balancing efforts and wars. There are thus strong grounds for according ideational and cultural factors an important causal role in explaining Asian hierarchy.

The traditional international order in East Asia encompassed a regionally shared set of norms and expectations that guided relations and yielded substantial stability. In Chinese eyes – and explicitly accepted by the surrounding nations – the world of the past millennium has consisted of civilization (China) and barbarians (all other states). In this view, as long as the barbarian states were willing to 'kowtow' (to publicly show acceptance of Chinese authority) to the Chinese emperor and show formal acceptance of their lower position in the hierarchy, the Chinese had neither the need to invade these countries nor the desire to do so. Explicit acceptance of the Chinese perspective on the regional order brought diplomatic recognition from China and allowed the pursuit of international trade and diplomacy.

The formally hierarchic relationship consisted of a few key acts that communicated information between actors. Most important was kowtow to the Chinese emperor by the sovereigns of the lesser states. Since there could be only one emperor under heaven, all other sovereigns were known as kings, and on a regular basis would send tribute missions to Beijing to acknowledge the emperor's central position in the world. In addition, when a new king would take the throne in a lesser state, it was customary to seek the emperor's approval, a process known as 'investiture.' Although *pro forma*, investiture was a necessary component of maintaining stable relations between nations. Korea, Japan, the Ryukyus, Vietnam, Tibet, and other nations peripheral to China pursued formal investiture for their own rulers, sent tributary missions, and maintained formal obeisance to China (Smits, 1999).

Kowtowing to China did not involve much loss of independence, as these states were largely free to run their internal affairs as they saw fit, and these nations could also conduct foreign policy independently from China. China viewed its relations with its subordinate states as separate from its internal relations, and generally did not interfere in the domestic politics of tributary states (Son, 1994, 1999). For example, while Vietnam kowtowed to China it also went on to expand its territory in Southeast Asia. With Japan, as with Vietnam's relations with its Southeast Asian neighbors, China always had a policy of non-interference toward its tributary states, as long as its sovereignty was acknowledged and not threatened (Kang, 1997: 6–9). With regard to the Korea-China relationship, Gari Ledyard (2006a) notes that:

> Chinese 'control' was hardly absolute. While the Koreans had to play the hand they were dealt, they repeatedly prevailed in diplomacy and argument...Korea often prevailed and convinced China to retreat from an aggressive position. In other words, the tributary system did provide for effective communication, and Chinese and Korean officialdom spoke from a common Confucian vocabulary. In that front, the relationship was equal, if not at times actually in Korea's favor.

As for Vietnam, a brief Chinese interregnum (1407–1427) was brought about by turmoil in the Vietnamese court. After a ten-year struggle, the Le dynasty lasted from 1427 to 1787, and existed uneasily beside China. Truong Buu Lam (1968: 178) writes that '...the relationship was not between two equal states. There was no doubt in anyone's mind that China was the superior and the tributary state the inferior.

The Vietnamese kings clearly realized that they had to acknowledge China's suzerainty and become tributaries in order to avoid active intervention by China in their internal affairs.' As Marr (1981: 49) notes:

> This reality [China's overwhelming size], together with sincere cultural admiration, led Vietnam's rulers to accept the tributary system. Providing China did not meddle in Vietnam's internal affairs ... Vietnamese monarchs were quite willing to declare themselves vassals of the Celestial Emperor. The subtlety of this relationship was evident from the way in which Vietnamese monarchs styled themselves 'king' (*vuong*) when communicating with China's rulers, but 'emperor' (*hoang de*) when addressing their own subjects or sending messages to other Southeast Asian rulers.

Culturally the Chinese influence was formative. Although both the Japanese and Korean languages are not Sinic in origin (generally they are thought to be Ural-Altaic, with more similarity to Turkish and Finnish), Vietnam, Korea, and Japan have used Chinese characters and vocabulary for over 2,000 years (Taylor, 1976). Although the indigenous languages were used for everyday speech, formal communications were written in Chinese, and it was a sign of education to be conversant in Chinese literature and poetry.

China's long institutional reach

Many of the East Asian states were centrally administered bureaucratic systems based on the Chinese model. Centralized bureaucratic administration in China involved a complex system of administration and governance. Ming-era China was centrally organized into administrative districts down to the province level, with appointments made from the capital for most tax, commercial, and judicial posts (Mote, 1988). In addition, since the Han dynasty, an examination system was used for selecting government bureaucrats, resulting in East Asia's region-wide focus on education. Anyone who passed the exam assured both himself and his family a substantial increase in prestige and income. The states peripheral to China also had developed complex bureaucratic structures. This form of government, including the bureaucratic system, was derived from the Chinese experience. The civil service examination in these countries emphasized knowledge of Chinese political philosophy, classics, and culture.

With the promulgation of the Taiho Code in 701, Japan during the Heian era (749–1185) introduced a Chinese-style government utilizing a bureaucratic system that relied heavily on imported Chinese institutions, norms, and practices (Yamamura, 1990a; Hall, 1968). Japan's university system in the 11th century was based on a curriculum that studied the Chinese classics, as was the organization of its bureaucracy, and the capital city of Kyoto was modeled after the T'ang dynasty capital in China (Shively *et al.*, 1999).

Japan, with perhaps the least centralized authority of the East Asian nations in this study, had a feudal tradition nominally overseen by an emperor. However, all countries in East Asia were essentially feudal in domestic social structure, and Japan was no exception. In addition, the domestic process of expanding centralized political control occurred in Japan just as it did in other countries in the region. Like all countries, Japan saw a waxing and waning of state power over the centuries, with a relative breakdown in central political control during the 14th century, but relatively firm centralized control both before and after. The Japanese emperor himself was a weak and nominal leader of the country. Most importantly for our purposes, Japan had a long tradition of being independently recognized as a single unit in international relations of East Asia.

Korea also used a bureaucratic system borrowed from the Chinese model that emphasized the study of Chinese texts (Lee, 1984). In Korea the examination system was used since the Silla dynasty of the 7th century, although it became fully incorporated into public life under the Choson (1392–1910) dynasty (Kang, 2002: 78–81). Indeed, Choson dynasty court dress was identical with the court dress of the Ming dynasty officials, with the exception that the identical dress and emblems were two ranks (in the nine-rank scheme) lower in Korea. That is, the court dress of a Rank I (the highest rank) Choson official was identical to that of a Rank III official at the Ming court (Ledyard, 2006b).

Although each country retained its own identity, the Chinese influence on family organization, education, culture, crafts and arts, was pervasive. The Sinicizing process included migration of Chinese to the Vietnam region, increased use of the Chinese language, the civil service examination system, the establishment of Confucian schools, the rise of Buddhism, Taoism, and Confucianism, Chinese-style clothing and marriage ceremonies, and a militia based on Chinese inventions and technology (Taylor, 1983; Woodside, 1971; Coedes, 1969).

Thus, the Chinese influence on East Asia was pervasive.

Japan's role

The role of Japan is perhaps the most important to discuss, because for centuries Japan was the second largest country in East Asia, although still considerably smaller and weaker than China. Did the system really encompass Japan? Until the Tokugawa shogunate (1600–1868), Japan followed essentially the same rules as other East Asian countries. The Japanese have traditionally described the world as *ka-I no sekai*, or 'the world of China and the barbarians.' Kazui (1982: 286) notes that 'from the time of Queen Himiko's rule over the ancient state of Yamatai [A.D. 183 to 248] to that of the Ashikaga shoguns during the Muromachi period, it was essentially these same international rules that Japan followed.' In 1370, Prince Kaneyoshi of Japan presented a *hyosen* (*piao-chien*, a foreign policy document) to the Chinese emperor in which he referred to himself as 'subject' (Shoji, 1990: 425). Yoshimitsu's acceptance of Chinese suzerainty became a powerful legitimizing tool for his government (Kang, 1997: 18). Writing about the 15th century, Tashiro Kazui (1982: 286) notes that 'both Japan and Korea had established sovereign-vassal relations (*sakuho kankei*) with China, joining other countries of Northeast Asia as dependent, tributary nations.' Key-huik Kim (1980: 15) adds:

> In 1404 – a year after the ruler of Yi Korea received formal Ming investiture for the first time – Yoshimitsu, the third Ashikaga shogun, received Ming investiture as 'King of Japan.' The identical status assigned to the rulers of Yi Korea and Ashikaga Japan under the Ming tribute system seems to have facilitated the establishment of formal relations between the two neighbors on the basis of 'equality' within the 'restored' Confucian world order in East Asia.

One common misperception in the scholarly literature is that Tokugawa-era Japan (1600–1868) was a closed and isolated nation, that operated outside the East Asian international system. However, in the last two decades, a revisionist view has become widely accepted, one which sees Tokugawa as deeply interested in, and interacting with, the rest of East Asia. There was a change in Japan's international status following its attempts in 1592 and 1598 to invade China through Korea. China essentially de-recognized Japan, forcing it outside the legitimate international order of the time. The Ming in 1621 expelled Japan from the Chinese world system, making it the 'outcast of East Asia' (Kim, 1980: 15).

Japan was forced to find an alternative way to conduct its foreign relations and trade. Although not fully reincorporated into the tributary system, Japan operated by essentially the same set of rules, following the function if not the explicit form of tributary relations with China. The key point is that Tokugawa Japan continued to accept the

Chinese-centered system, even though formal tributary relations were never fully restored. Indeed, after the Hideyoshi invasions of Korea in 1592–1598, the Tokugawa shogunate recognized China's centrality and Japanese-Korean relations as equal. Kim (1980: 15) writes:

> The Tokugawa rulers understood and accepted the Korean position. Japan after Hideyoshi had no ambition for continental conquest or expansion. They tacitly acknowledged Chinese supremacy and cultural leadership in the East Asian world...Although Tokugawa Japan maintained no formal ties with China...for all intents and purposes it was as much a part of the Chinese world as Ashikaga Japan had been.

The Japanese called this new policy the *Taikun* (Great Prince) diplomacy, and some view this as a way for Japan to opt out of the Chinese system, because such a concept did not exist in the Confucian world order. It allowed the Japanese to conduct foreign policy without explicitly recognizing the Chinese emperor as superior, while still not provoking too harsh a response from the Chinese by formally challenging the position of China. However, the Tokugawa rulers remained integrated into East Asia, and made systematic efforts to gather information on regional affairs (Ishii, 1998: 2). Trade was still conducted through Nagasaki, only by private merchants, and indirectly through Korea and the Ryukyus. Although the conventional wisdom was that the Tokugawa shogunate closed itself off from the rest of the world formally in 1633, a policy sometimes referred to as *sakoku*, the reality was that trade with China and the rest of the world continued to be an important part of Japan's economy. The more recent scholarship interprets *sakoku* as merely 'maritime provisions' that were 'simply a part of a sequential process rather than firm indications of new policy directions (Wray, n.d.: 2) As noted previously, Japanese exports in the 17th century are estimated to have reached 10 per cent of its GNP (Howe, 1996: 40). This revisionist view sees Tokugawa foreign relations more as an expansion of state power and regulation in Japan rather than a policy of isolation. Indeed, it has been shown that the phrase *sakoku* did not exist historically, and is not seen in any Japanese sources, public or private, until a translation of a Dutch book about Japan (Kzuii, 1982: 283–306). These countries, even during Tokugawa and Qing, had extensive relations. During the Tokugawa period, the *bakufu* established formal and equal diplomatic relations with Korea, subordinate relations with the Qing, and superior relations with the Ryukus.

Klein (1989: 69) notes that 'by the end of the seventeenth century the Tokugawa regime had succeeded in maneuvering Japan into the center of a regional system of international diplomacy of its own making.' Wray (n.d.: 12) adds that '[Tokugawa] Japan had a distinctive policy for virtually every country or area with which it traded. There were far more Chinese than Dutch ships coming to Nagasaki...' Historians today interpret these maritime provisions more as examples of normal statecraft and the extension of Tokugawa control, rather than paranoia or cowering anti-foreignism. Toby (1991: xvi) argues that Japan under Tokugawa had an 'active state-sponsored program of international commercial and technological intelligence...that enhanced domestic sovereignty and enabled the state to regulate a desired foreign trade.'

Conclusion

Explanations consistent with realism, liberalism and constructivism reinforce each other, generating a basic hierarchical logic in East Asian system so strong that evidence of balancing processes over six centuries is hard to find. Consistent with hegemonic stability versions of realism, China's neighbors recognized the preponderance of Chinese power and accepted it instead of trying to balance against it. As liberalism would expect, the stability of the system was increased by substantial trading links among the major states. And as constructivism would suggest, the system was also stabilized by a complex set of norms about international behavior that was generally observed by the main political units. But both the outcome (stable hegemonic dominance) and the process evidence (no balancing and remarkable stability) decisively contract balance-of-power theory.

The demolition of this regional order came swiftly in the mid-19th century. The intrusion of Western powers and the inherent weaknesses of the East Asian states created a century of chaos. With the Western powers dividing up China and limiting its ability to act, the system broke apart. Japan was able to seize the initiative and attempt to become the regional hegemon. Much of Southeast Asia became embroiled in guerilla wars in an attempt to drive out the Western colonizers, from Vietnam to the Philippines to Malaysia and Indonesia. The two world wars and the Cold War all muted East Asia's inherent dynamism. It was only in the 1990s that the system appeared to begin – once again – to resemble an East Asian regional system that is both powered by and steered by East Asian states themselves.

Yet the causal factors that were important for stability in early modern East Asia remain worthy of attention. That stability was a function not only of power and size, but also of a complex set of norms about behavior that governed international relations between the main political units. East Asia from 1300 to 1900 was economically and politically important, and it was more stable and hierarchic than the European system. This observation is of great theoretical significance: there is a logic of hierarchy that can lead, and has led, to a stable, relatively peaceful hierarchical international system under (early) modern conditions. Further study of the historical East Asian international system should yield additional insights not only into the dynamics of that system, but also about the dynamics of international systems more generally – including the contemporary one.

Note

1 As Elisonas (1988: 250) emphasizes, although called 'wako,' many of the pirates were actually Chinese, located along the coasts of China itself.

10
Conclusion: Theoretical Insights from the Study of World History

Stuart J. Kaufman, Richard Little and William C. Wohlforth

The goal of this volume is to assess the workings of a variety of international systems across thousands of years of time and five continents, in order to learn how they actually worked. The concepts of the balance of power and its opposite, hegemony, involve the most central issues in international politics and international relations theory, and the case studies in this volume focus primarily on these issues. The case studies also, however, address a much wider range of international issues, and therefore offer important evidence on a number of important debates in international relations theory.

In this conclusion, we begin by addressing competing theoretical traditions' assumptions about the frequency of balance and hegemony. We find support neither for the neorealist assertion about the universality of balance nor for the English School claim about the normality of hegemony. We find instead that balanced and unbalanced distributions of power seem roughly equally common. What is universal in international systems, we note, is a mix of anarchy and hierarchy within them: systems vary in the degree to which they are hierarchically rather than anarchically organized.

To the degree systems are anarchical, we next consider the degree to which the logic of anarchy may vary from system to system, and relatedly, the degree to which international norms or international society modify the behavior of states in the system. We find, in Wendt's (1999) terms, that a Hobbesean anarchy is more common in our cases than is a Lockean one, but that a few of the systems do have important Lockean elements, and that a normative structure supportive of the international order does seem to contribute to the stability of such orders, at least in some cases. The last systemic-level factor we consider is geography, finding that while the topography of a system does not have consistently important effects, its size does: the opportunity for a system to expand in size seems almost a necessary condition for it to remain balanced.

We then turn to examining unit-level variables, which turn out not only to drive most state behavior, but also to a large degree the evolution of the systems themselves. Our cases show that not only is military expansion a well-nigh universal behavior, but that such expansion is frequently characterized by myopic advantage-seeking (boondoggling), rather than aimed at long-term system maintenance (balancing), even among rivals to potential hegemons. Uncertainty about the identity of the hegemonic threat sometimes contributes to balancing failure, but this is by no means a necessary condition for balancing failure. The pattern of boondoggling is a major reason why balanced systems routinely break down, and why systemic hegemons frequently squander their advantages.

In the face of the frequent failure of balancing, the key variable limiting the expansion of great powers seems to be administrative capacity – the ability to administer territory efficiently, including newly conquered territory, in order to extract resources and make power cumulative. What matters is the outcome of a governance arms race – who can overcome domestic political obstacles to develop efficient processes of government, assert a plausible legitimating ideology of rule, and avoid the internal disunity that can destroy states, either by itself or in the context of outside pressure. The outcome of this governance arms race, in turn, depends in large part on principles of unit identity. Peoples that cling to their local identity often suffer a sad fate: they are inclined to balance, but not to trust their neighbors, so balancing tends to fail. They then tend to rebel frequently against their hegemonic master, and so face the hegemon's wrath – but not before weakening the hegemon itself, sometimes significantly.

Each of these patterns is explored below.

The balance of power: universal, normal, or rare?

The first and simplest issue this volume addresses is the neorealist assertion that 'hegemony leads to balance ... through all of the centuries we can contemplate' (Waltz, 1993). The evidence we provide is sufficient to reject that hypothesis as a serious assertion about international relations. Every one of the cases studied here ended in the establishment of lasting hegemony by a single power over what had previously been a multipolar balance-of-power system. Assyria destroyed and conquered its rivals Babylonia, Urartu, and others. It was eventually replaced by Persia's two century-long dominance of an even larger area, creating an empire whose expansion the Greek city-states could limit, but whose overall power they could not begin to match. In similar fashion, Rome destroyed all of its Mediterranean rivals, Qin conquered the Warring States system, Magadha united the Indian system into the Mauryan Empire, and the Aztecs and Incas asserted their hegemony over all their regional rivals. Modern China retained its hegemony over East Asia for many centuries. The balance of power is not a universal constant.

On the contrary, the ubiquity of hegemonic outcomes seems to support the contention of the English School (Watson, 1992) that some form of hegemony rather than balance is the norm in international history. If this is right, then not only is the balancing proposition wrong; so is the first assumption of all major American schools of international relations theory – realism, liberal institutionalism, and constructivism – that the international system is axiomatically anarchic. The fact that *all* of our chapters concern hegemony, however, or the transition to it, raises a methodological issue: do we have a problem of selection bias? It could be argued that the systems discussed here are not typical, and that the modern European norm of multipolarity is really more common that these chapters might suggest. Clearly any attempt to generalize about what 'typically' happens in international systems requires a careful assessment of what is typical.

To address this question, we have compiled a data base of 7,500 system-years of international history to try to measure the frequency of different distributions of power in international systems. In this data base, we code polarity in international systems decade by decade from four different parts of Eurasia: the Middle East and Mediterranean from 1500 BCE to 390 AD; East Asia from 1025 BCE to 1850 AD; India from 400 BCE to 1800 AD; and modern Europe and its global successor-system from 1500 to 2000 AD. Most of this data was compiled by David Wilkinson; we added codings for the classical Mediterranean period (400 BCE to 390 AD) and for modern Europe. Details of our codings and adjustments to Wilkinson's codings are explained in Appendix A. This data base assesses a majority of all international history and provides a reasonable basis for comparison.

The full data set is summarized in Table 10.1.

This table summarizes the polarity of international systems for 750 decades, or 7,500 years of time. The data it summarizes are not supportive of the most common thinking about the balance of power.

Table 10.1   Frequency in Decades of Different System Polarities

System	Nonpolar	Multipolar	Bipolar	Unipolar	Hegemonic
Ancient Mideast: 1500–400 BCE		60	6	38	6
East Asia: 1025 BCE–1875 CE	5	107.5	35	85	57.5
South Asia: 400 BCE–1810 CE	17	26	68	73	37
Classical Med.: 400 BCE–390 CE		13	1	18	47
Modern Europe: 1500–2000 CE		41	8	1	
Total Frequencies	22	247.5	118	215	147.5

First, balanced international systems are not the norm: 'balanced' multipolar and bipolar systems are almost exactly as common (365.5 decades)
as are 'unbalanced' unipolar and hegemonic systems (362.5 decades). If
anything, this conclusion is probably overly generous to multipolarity:
some periods Wilkinson codes as multipolar, such as the 10th century
BCE in the Middle East, are characterized by Kaufman (1997) as 'fragmented,' or nonpolar. Stricter coding rules would certainly decrease
the number of multipolar decades in the early periods.

A second generalization is that, the modern system aside, there is little
variation across space in balanced versus unbalanced systems (Wilkinson,
2004). The East Asian system is exactly equally divided between balanced
and unbalanced periods (142.5 decades of each). The South Asian system
is also roughly equally divided between balanced (94 decades) and unbalanced (110 decades) periods. And if our classical period Mediterranean
data is folded into Wilkinson's ancient Middle East data to form a single
two-millenium long series for what Wilkinson calls the 'Central' international system, the same pattern emerges – relative equality between balanced (80 decades) and unbalanced (109 decades) periods.

A third generalization is that, though Wilkinson (2004) concludes
the opposite, there is over the very long haul a trend toward system
consolidation or imbalance over time – or, more precisely, a tendency
for the last centuries of any system to be unbalanced rather than balanced. In the ancient Middle East, sustained unipolarity was very rare
in the 15th through 10th centuries BCE, then shifted decisively toward

unipolarity or hegemony under the leadership of Assyria (9th through 7th centuries BCE), Persia (6th through 4th centuries BCE), and Rome (2nd century BCE through 4th century CE). In East Asia, almost half of the unbalanced periods come in the last seven centuries during the Yuan (13th–14th centuries), Ming (14th–17th centuries), and Qing (17th–19th centuries) dynasties, which included 62.5 unbalanced and only 7.5 balanced decades. South Asia follows the pattern less strongly: its most concentrated period is near the beginning under the Mauryan dynasty (3rd century BCE); but still the last five centuries are more often unbalanced (31 decades) than balanced (20 decades) under the leadership of the Delhi Sultanate (12th–14th centuries) and the Mughal Empire (16th–18th centuries).

The implication of these data is that the Neorealist assertion that 'balances form and reform' is only spottily true. Balances frequently form, but they always break down. Sometimes they break down into fragmented or nonpolar systems, but more often in the last two millennia they break down into unipolar or hegemonic systems. The longevity of these systems is widely variable. Sometimes balances of power last for many centuries, as they did in Warring States China and modern Europe. In other cases, like the multipolar Middle Eastern system of the 6th century BCE, or the Mediterranean balance of the 3rd century BCE, balanced systems are relatively brief interludes between relatively longer-lasting periods of unipolarity or hegemony. Similarly, some hegemonies (such as Alexander the Great's) are extremely brief, while others (such as Rome's or Han China's) last for centuries. With regard to polarity, therefore, what international relations theory must explain is why balanced and imbalanced systems are roughly equally frequent, and why shifts occur from one to the other.

Variations in anarchy and its logic

The finding that balanced and unbalanced systems are roughly equally common disproves the English School assumptions that anarchy is a fragile structure and that some form of hegemony is the most common state of international systems. However, a related insight is firmly supported by our evidence: there is always hierarchy within anarchy, and it is very common for more international relations in a system to be hierarchical than anarchical. As Little points out in this volume, Watson (1992) asserts a conception of international relations in which there is no sharp line between politics within and outside the empire, but rather gradations of control.

This insight is reinforced when we consider that Watson's definition of hegemony – a situation where units are nominally independent, but where the foreign policy of one state is severely constrained by the other – fits the realist understanding of unipolarity (which is the definition used in Wilkinson's data cited above). In sum, a realist's unipolarity within anarchy is the English School's hegemony (a weak sort of hierarchy). Realism's rejection of this notion is based on its odd reification of the legal notion of state sovereignty – odd, that is, for a school of thought that otherwise rejects on principle any role for international law, and asserts its exclusive focus on the realities of power rather than the abstractions of law. The realities of power are that hierarchical relations between nominally independent actors are entirely normal.

For example, while the degree of Assyrian control over Babylonia was often arguable and varied significantly over time, it remains true that for decades Assyria had some degree of control over Babylonia, but that at the same time this critical relationship has to be understood as a part of the international politics of the system, not merely of the internal politics of the Assyrian Empire (which made a clear distinction between 'the Land of Assur and the Yoke of Assur'). Before Rome was hegemonic, the Seleucids and the Ptolemies had to carefully calculate how far they could go in their conflicts with each other without provoking intervention by the superpower. Even the Aztecs, in spite of their well-earned reputation for bloodthirstiness, established a system that was more suzerain than imperial, allowing more autonomy to its subjects than one might expect. Early modern China's relations with its satellites were functionally similar to Rome's with the Ptolemies and Seleucids in the 2nd century BCE (the Emperor expected little more from his neighbors than restraint and an exchange of gifts) even though they were nominally more hierarchical (since he expected that their envoys would kowtow to him and verbally acknowledge his primacy). These relationships cannot be understood without the English School's recognition that anarchy and hierarchy are not mutually exclusive categories in international relations, but rather form a continuum.

A separate question is the 'logic of anarchy' that anarchic systems display (Buzan, Jones and Little). Realists assume, or claim to assume, that international politics is invariably a dog-eat-dog affair of unlimited violence and unending war (Waltz, 1979; Mearsheimer, 2001). English School theorists argue that in some international systems, states may share enough intersubjectively understood norms to constitute an international society (Bull and Watson, 1984). Constructivists define these as simply different possible logics of anarchy: the realist version is 'Hobbesean,' while an international society's logic is 'Lockean.' Though our evidence is not adequate to distinguish Hobbesean from Lockean international systems in every detail, there is one pivotal distinguishing feature that we can measure: the degree to which states in the system accept each other's existence so that state 'death' becomes improbable or rare, especially among major powers, and international relations are to that extent restrained.

Realists would argue that our evidence supports the Hobbesean understanding of anarchy as the transhistorical norm. Assyria, Rome, Qin, Magadha and the Inca annihilated most of their adversaries, and even the 'civilized' Athenians within Greek international society annihilated defiant Melos late in the Peloponnesian War. Persia, early modern China and the Aztecs were more restrained, more often settling for acknowledgment of suzerainty instead of direct rule, but even this could be understood as reflecting sober judgments of limits on their material power: the Persians surely knew they were overstretched, for example, and the Chinese apparently recognized that they probably would be should they attempt to conquer Korea or Vietnam.

While it is clear that most of the systems we discuss were Hobbesean in nature – Eckstein and Hui emphasize this point about Rome and Qin, and the Assyrians were comparably ruthless – English School or constructivist theorists would nevertheless argue that some of the systems did contain international societies (i.e., were Lockean in logic). The clearest example is early modern China, which evolved a widely accepted set of norms and practices which kept the international system remarkably stable, substantially limited the frequency of war, and ensured the continuing survival and autonomy of the smaller state-units. The Aztecs, too, as Jones points out, led an international society, building a system that was more suzerain than imperial in nature. This meant that, like the modern Chinese, they allowed many of their subject peoples continued autonomous existence; and like modern Europe, had rules that limited the ferocity of war (though not the ferocity of treatment of prisoners of war).

A case can also be made for two separate international societies in the Greek-Persian case. Persia, for its part, carefully negotiated the terms of incorporation into its empire of the Ionian Greek city-states, the Egyptians, and the Jews, allowing considerable autonomy to these and presumably other subject peoples. Among the Greeks, Thucydides seems to find Athens's treatment of the Melians remarkable precisely because it violated a longstanding and long-observed norm of treatment of Greek prisoners. Indeed, Thucydides (1951, p. 172) terms the earlier near obliteration of Mytilene 'horrid,' and the point of the Melian story is the degradation of the Athenians' own former moral standards.

Finally, it is worth noting that these cases are not the earliest known international societies: though the case is not included in this volume, the Amarna period system including Egypt, the Hittites, Babylonia and others c. 1500–1200 BCE also had a well-documented system of international norms and generally moderate relations among great powers (Cohen and Westbrook, 2000; Liverani, 1988). While Hobbesean anarchies seem to be the most common sort, then, Lockean anarchies – international societies – are not terribly rare in international history.

Additionally, the evidence seems to indicate a stabilizing effect for international norms: when there exist international norms supportive of the international order, that order appears frequently to be more peaceful and longer-lasting than those that lack such supportive norms. For example, the Assyrians, whose ruling ideology was to a large extent 'my god is better than your god,' lacked legitimacy among subject and neighboring peoples and hence endured as hegemon for less than a century. Their Persian successors, in contrast, gained legitimacy by showing greater religious toleration, and in partial consequence lasted more than twice as long. The strongest case of legitimized hegemony, of course, is the early modern Chinese example, since there a relatively peaceful and stable Chinese hegemony continued, albeit with interruptions, for some five or six centuries. The modern European case illustrates an alternative role for international norms: there, as English School theorists and traditional realists have long argued, it was the balance of power that was normatively favored, and that norm contributed to the maintenance of the balance over the centuries of European multipolarity.

Geography and system size

Ever since the geopolitical speculations of Mackinder, the popularity of geography as an explanatory variable in international relations has fluctuated dramatically. Attention to this variable has modestly increased recently in wake of Mearsheimer's (2001) firm assertion about 'the stopping power of water'. Our cases, however, reveal no consistent support for any specific geographical hypothesis. For those cases in which the stopping power of water is potentially relevant, only one case supports the contention (Greece's resistance to Persia), while four do not. By Mearsheimer's logic, for example, the Mediterranean should have obstructed Rome's conquest of Carthage and later Egypt; instead, Rome turned 'Our Sea' into a highway of control. Similarly, Kang finds that the Sea of Japan did not prevent Chinese hegemony over Japan; and oceans certainly failed to prevent the Spanish conquest of the Aztecs and Incas. At least since the days of Minoan Crete, empires have often found that water provides transportation power rather than stopping power.

Other specific hypotheses about geography similarly fail to find support. One can develop logical arguments suggesting either that marchland powers or centrally-located powers have the better chance of becoming system hegemons, and it turns out that both propositions find roughly equal support. Assyria, Rome, and the Aztec and Inca heartlands were all centrally located. In these cases, geographical centrality divided the growing empires' enemies, an effect that proved more important than the 'two-front problem'. On the other hand, Persia, Qin and Magadha were all marchland powers, exploiting their positions at the edge of their international systems to defeat their rivals in detail. There is no one spatial logic of conquest.

Mountains have no invariable effect, either. While tribal peoples are often limited either to mountains or to lowlands, hegemonic empires have succeeded in controlling both at least since Assyria surmounted the Taurus Mountains to defeat Urartu. Similarly, Rome crossed the Apennines, Alps and Pyrenees, the Aztecs controlled mountainous central Mexico, and the Incas conquered the Andes. Neither does the original base matter: Magadha began in the lowlands of Bengal, Assyria in the plains of Mesopotamia, and the Aztecs in the Valley of Mexico; but Rome emerged from the foothills, and the Incas in the Andes Mountains.

The only important generalization about geography, then, is that successful hegemons develop or find the communications technology to overcome its obstacles. The Romans began as landlubbers but conquered the sea to conquer Carthage, and Caesar crossed the Alps to conquer Gaul. The Incas developed an astonishing road network enabling them to tie together their imperial possessions across hundreds of miles of mountainous terrain. And a succession of Mesopotamian empires achieved similar results in the Fertile Crescent centuries before the Romans came along to take credit for the idea.

What turns out to matter more than topography for explaining international systems is the flexibility of system borders. It may be that a necessary condition for maintaining balance in an international system is flexibility of the borders of that system. For example, Assyria's brief period of hegemony ended only when the Medes organized the uplands of Iran into a new empire outside the previous boundaries of the system: the Medes first balanced and then destroyed the Assyrian Empire. Persia then ran the tables of the old international system, to be checked not only by the Hellespont, but by the Hellenes beyond it in what had been a different international system. And Chinese emperors' hegemony was repeatedly checked not from within the system, but by tribal peoples (such as Mongols and Manchus) from outside it.

System expansion is not, of course sufficient to maintain balance: Rome's world expanded to include the Hellenistic empires of the eastern Mediterranean after it defeated Carthage, but the Romans quickly came to dominate even that larger system. Still, system expansion may be *necessary* for maintaining balance over the long haul: even the modern European balance was maintained only by the repeated introduction of new powers on the flanks, most importantly Russia and the United States (Dehio, 1962). We assess that the rigidity of the borders of the international system contributed importantly to the hegemony of Persia and Magadha, and was a necessary condition for hegemony in every other case we examine.

State behavior: expansion, balancing, buckpassing, bandwagoning and boondoggling

Realist theorists hypothesize three typical behaviors for states in the international system. Offensive (Mearsheimer, 2001) and hegemonic stability (Gilpin, 1981) realists assert that military expansion is the norm. In Mearsheimer's (2001, pp. 34–5) typically stark assertion, 'great powers have aggressive intentions. ... [S]tates do not become *status quo* powers until they completely dominate the system'. Defensive realists (Waltz, 1979; Walt, 1987) argue, in contrast, that the most common state behavior is balancing against great-power expansion. Realist critics of the balancing proposition (Powell, 1999; Rosecrance, 2003) argue that collective action problems systematically interfere with efforts at balancing, asserting that in many cases states may find buckpassing or bandwagoning with the expanding power to be the safer course – or the more profitable one (Schweller, 1994). Our findings show that all of these courses of action are commonly followed, often to the point where they become foolish boondoggles.

First, almost every one of our cases involves, as Mearsheimer and Gilpin hypothesize, an expansionist state with limitless ambitions which defeats and subordinates lesser breeds of expansionists. As Eckstein and Hui emphasize for their cases, 'everyone does it' – ruthless expansionism was so common that it became characteristic of the system itself. This assessment is no less true of the systems that came to be led by Assyria, Persia, Magadha, the Aztecs, and the Incas (and their successors, the Spanish). Interestingly, though, in most of these cases hubris eventually brought forth Nemesis, as expansionism was pursued to self-defeating lengths. Both Assyria and Persia were certainly suffering from imperial overstretch by the time they reached (but never fully pacified) Egypt; and Jones identifies a similar overstretch in the Inca Empire by the time Pizarro appeared. Qin's overstretch is demonstrated by the fact of its immediate collapse after the death of the first Qin emperor, Shih Huang-ti.

The hegemons that endured, in contrast, were the ones that knew when to stop. Most starkly, early modern China consistently resisted any temptation to invade its neighbors, and therefore maintained its preeminence for centuries. The attempted Mongol invasion of Japan famously foiled by the 'Divine Wind' is the exception that proves the rule: the effort was never repeated. Similarly, the greatest Mauryan emperor, Ashoka, announced after a great military victory his conversion to Buddhism and his dedication to virtue rather than expanded power: as clear a statement as is possible that enough is enough. The first Roman emperor, Augustus, made the same judgment, and while his advice was not always followed, it is notable that most of the later Roman expansionist efforts (e.g., central Scotland, Dacia, Mesopotamia) were eventually quickly abandoned.

Countering these rising hegemons were rival powers which usually tried a balancing strategy and uniformly failed. The obstacles they faced, due to the collective action problem, were formidable: it is always tempting to pass the buck to other potential balancers, or to 'bandwagon for profit' by joining the expansionist power. Hui offers the most sophisticated analysis of the resulting dynamics: clever rising powers exploit the collective action problem facing its rivals to counter the balancing strategy with divide-and-conquer tactics. Eckstein points out a reinforcing problem: sometimes it is unclear which of several expansionist great powers is the greater threat – a problem further complicated if the greater threat to a particular balancer is not the same as the greater *systemic* threat.

All of these phenomena played important roles in the failure balancing efforts, with the free-riding problems particularly common. The Aramaean city-states facing Assyria were never able to stand together for long against the superpower, and indeed some called for Assyrian help against their local rivals, providing Assyria with the chance to divide and conquer. Many of the Greek city-states bandwagoned with Persia (as Thebes did) or passed the buck (as Argos did). Qin made divide-and-conquer an explicit strategy against neighbors that frequently bandwagoned with it against Qin's victims, or squabbled with each other while Qin expanded. Brenner and Jones find that the rivals of Magadha, the Incas and the Aztecs faced similar difficulties.

The problem of identifying the rising hegemon was slightly less common in our cases, but very important when it occurred. It is the centerpiece of Eckstein's story: by the time the medium powers of the Greek east no longer needed Rome to balance more immediate threats, they found that no one left could balance against Rome. It is equally pivotal in Hui's story: a crucial stage in Qin's rise came when it joined a balancing effort against then-hegemonic Qi. Only after the defeat of Qi was the Qin threat plain, and by then it was too late. In other cases, this problem of threat identification played a lesser but still important role: Assyria's resurgence under Tiglath-pileser came so quickly that southern and central Syrian states could be excused for failing to perceive its gravity until after the defeat of the Arpad-Urartu coalition – by which time it was too late for balancing. The Aztecs and Incas also rose in the context of the collapse of previous hegemons, so the gravity of their rise, too, was probably not fully appreciated in time. The key finding here is that while balancing is a very common strategy, it is not a dominant one: it often fails, in part because some potential balancers typically choose to do something else.

A related finding is that while Mearsheimer and Gilpin are right that states tend to expand where they can, expansionist moves are frequently unwise because they either disrupt a balancing coalition or represent overexpansion by the dominant power. For reasons of alliteration, we label such unwise expansion 'boondoggling'. 'Bandwagoning for profit' is one subtype of boondoggling. In the Assyrian case, both Israel and Judaea sometimes indulged in this, seeking gains at each other's expense while their northern neighbors were trying to balance Assyria; the result was that Israel became the Ten Lost Tribes. Qin's neighbors repeatedly pursued boondoggles, scrapping for each other's territories while Qin grew and ultimately destroyed them all. A stark example is Wu, which captured its rival Chu's capital in 506 BCE, but overexpanded and was in its turn conquered by its neighbor Yue three decades later. Thebes's decision to 'medize' – to bandwagon with Persia – was also a boondoggle even though Persia lost. This is a characteristic feature of boondoggling: it is unwise regardless of the fate of the larger partner. If the larger partner loses, the boondoggler is exposed to retribution; if the larger partner wins, it is likely to swallow the boondoggler.

Boondoggles by hegemons have the same quality: low benefit in case of success (usually due to overexpansion), but high cost in case of failure. Assyria's conquest of Egypt was a boondoggle, fortunately (for both sides) settled by the rise of an Egyptian regime willing to bandwagon with the superpower after the withdrawal of Assyrian troops. The Assyrian boondoggle of annihilating Elam turned out to be more costly, as it helped open the way for the rise of the Medes, who eventually destroyed Assyria. Xerxes's invasion of Greece was similarly a boondoggle for an already-overextended empire, though its consequences were less dire. Athens's Sicilian expedition during the Peloponnesian war may be the most famous boondoggle of classical history, as Athens did not only lose its army; it gained a new enemy that played an important role in its ultimate defeat.

Roman history is also replete with boondoggles, such as the invasion of Parthia by Caesar's friend Crassus leading to the defeat at Carrhae in 53 BCE, and the invasion of Germany leading to the loss of three legions at Teutoberger Wald in 9 CE. The classic examples of 'successful' hegemonic boondoggles are also Roman: the campaigns of the Emperor Trajan, who annexed Dacia (modern Romania) and Mesopotamia early in the second century CE, only to have his successors abandon both places as too costly to hold.

All of these versions of Realism, therefore, share the same qualities of partial descriptive accuracy but general prescriptive failure. States typically expand, but continuing to do so leads to boondoggles. Other states often try to balance, but are hampered by would-be allies' boondoggles (bandwagoning for profit) or buckpassing. Restraint and cooperation work better, but are less frequently found.

Self-strengthening reforms: administration and legitimation

If balancing is not a dominant strategy, frequently failing due to collective action problems and difficulty identifying the hegemonic threat, why are balanced international systems even as common as they are? Why is the English School not correct that hegemonic systems are the norm? The studies in this volume suggest that the critical variable determining the rise of a hegemon is administrative capacity. As Gilpin noted, conquests tend to generate diminishing marginal returns over time due to a 'rising cost of expansion'. It is this dynamic – states' inability, in essence, to digest their conquests – that tends to limit most states' expansion. Only when great powers develop the ability to administer new conquests and extract resources from them to fuel further expansion – when, that is, expansion becomes cumulative – does hegemony become possible, and indeed likely. Developing this capability is not easy; it requires what Hui has labeled 'self-strengthening reforms,' which may require something akin to a social or political revolution.

But the existence of such administrative capacity is a necessary condition for hegemony. Assyria was unable to hold onto its conquests in the Middle East until Tiglath-pileser III's internal reforms made that possible: the earlier conquests of Shalmaneser III were quickly reversed. Rome rose because it combined the strengths of traditional Republican institutions with innovations that gave it a unique capacity for inclusion of foreigners, enabling it to continue to expand its resource base. Similarly, Magadha was the most administratively durable of the ancient Indian states; and Qin, with the self-strengthening reforms of Shang Yang – economic reforms and military conscription as well as bureaucratic innovations – developed the most penetrating and brutally effective state structure in its international system. The Incas were also remarkable for the sophistication of their system of rule, as was early modern China for its elaborate bureaucracy and extensive political structure.

Realist theory hypothesizes that rival states should emulate such self-strengthening reforms, engaging in 'internal balancing' to match any advances made by a potential hegemon. The various new institutionalist theories, however, posit a host of reasons why this is not likely to be so easy. Mancur Olson-style logrolled political coalitions are likely to block reforms that might increase state power at the expense of powerful domestic interest groups. Path dependencies may mean that the rival state's institutional structure is so different from the system leader that copying the leader's institutions is effectively impossible. (Russia, to take a modern example, is famous for failed efforts to implant western institutions in its very different social climate.) Political and institutional cultures may be an obstacle. And so on.

The evidence generally supports the institutionalist objections, rather than the internal balancing hypothesis. Rome provides the most extreme example: Hellenistic empires and Greek city-states were such fundamentally different beasts that it is meaningless to suggest they 'should' have copied Roman institutions. Babylonia might have had a chance to emulate Assyria's administrative structure, but it was unable to resolve the conflict between old Babylonians and Chaldaean newcomers until the very end of the period of Assyrian hegemony. And while Qin's neighbors did try to emulate its innovations, Hui find that Qin simply did better, successfully implementing 'the most comprehensive military, economic, and administrative reforms known in ancient Chinese history'.

A related factor that may promote either international hegemony or diversity is the political unity of the states in the system. On the one hand, divide-and-conquer strategies can work not only among states in the system but also within them. The histories of most of the hegemons discussed here are replete with examples in which pro-hegemonic factions successfully appealed for assistance from the hegemon against their local rivals. Regime change is a common hegemonic tool, but it works best only where significant political factions are willing to collaborate with the hegemon. The most vivid examples in these cases include Assyria's repeated efforts to place pro-Assyrian leaders on the Babylonian throne, and Qin's bribery of key officials in rival states, but Romans, Persians and others commonly resorted to the same tactics.

On the other hand, political division can also occur within the system leader, weakening the leader and moving the system toward diversity. Qin's rivals repeatedly suffered from this problem, as did Assyria (near the end of Shalmaneser's reign, for example) and Persia. Later Roman history is of course largely the history of one civil war after another as generals competing for the imperial throne, and civil war in China was one of the few factors that could shake early modern China's hegemonic grip on its world. The Inca Empire also had this problem: Atahualpa had just been involved in fighting a civil war against his brother when he marched to face Pizarro. Whether we conceptualize political unity as a function of administrative capacity or as a separate factor, its role is clearly critical.

Another key factor that interferes with the effectiveness of both internal and external balancing is the diversity of units. Systems frequently include different types of units based on different principles of legitimacy and unit identity. The effect is differences in size and methods of rule that may make both internal and external balancing unworkable.

The most obvious problem is size: city-states are necessarily smaller and weaker than are empires. And city-states were what several of our rising hegemons faced: Assyria against the Aramaeans of modern Syria; and Persia and Rome against the Greek city-states. Such smaller units must necessarily form larger coalitions to generate enough military power to balance an empire, and as the number of units in the coalition rises, so do problems of coordination and collective action. Most importantly, though, city-states cannot expand – they cannot emulate empires by increasing in size and scale to increase their capabilities without ceasing to be city-states. Fundamentally, they are not like units.

The main obstacle to city-state expansion is not administrative but ideological – the principles legitimating unit identity. The Greek case is the most famous here: the Greeks simply considered the *polis* to be the most advanced form of social life, and a key marker distinguishing them from barbarians (such as the Macedonians). The idea of joining an empire was what their foreign policies aimed at preventing. A similar dynamic operated among the Aramaeans. Furthermore, for those whose governing ideology insisted on a democratic or republican form of government, such self-rule was generally understood to be possible only in small units such as city-states. Brenner, citing Deudney, notes that republican city-states had the opportunity to form larger leagues in a process called co-binding, but these formations also had limited success: Brenner notes that the Vajjian Confederacy was an early victim of Magadha's expansion; and its Hellenic cousins such as the Achaean League were virtually defenseless against the might of Rome. Thus in at least four of our cases, empires' rise to power was facilitated by some units' commitment to political forms that required small size.

The significance of local identity principles is not, however, ended by the conquest of such units by empires. Though easy to conquer, such units frequently prove difficult to hold because the local population refuses to accept the legitimacy of the empire. In short, peoples with strong local identity principles tend to rebel against their conquerors. Babylonia, with its distinctive identity, repeatedly rebelled against Assyrian rule, a problem Assyria never solved. Persia, too, faced multiple rebellions from those of their subjects with strong local identities – Egyptians and Greeks as well as Babylonians. Rome had to crush Greeks, Jews and other particularistic groups ruthlessly and repeatedly before they finally became docile. The Mauryan Empire never fully controlled the forest polities it encompassed. And the Aztecs finally paid for their oppression of other city-states when Tlaxcallan provided Cortes with a base from which he could operate to destroy their empire. The conclusion here is a melancholy one: though local identities are an important fact characterizing many international systems, small groups' insistence on political expression of those identities is highly costly to them (as well as to their conquerors) when they face systemic hegemons.

Final words

The fundamental finding of this volume is that international life cannot be understood either as typically hegemonic or as reliably anarchic within a balance of power. The basic starting point for any theory of international relations must be Watson's image of time's pendulum swinging between balanced and unbalanced distributions of power – though Watson, too, was wrong about the center point of the pendulum's swing. If we want a theory of the international system that explains the shape and behavior of that system, the central problem of that theory is to explain the motor that drives the pendulum's swing: what is it that makes the pendulum swing from diversity to hegemony and back again?

We think the evidence in this book suggests the outlines of an answer. We find no one dominant factor driving the pendulum, but rather a number of factors pushing in each direction. The location and velocity of the pendulum at any one time seems to be the result of the sum of the forces operating on it, the pushes and pulls in each direction. The most important forces pushing the system toward hegemony are the tendency of states to expand their power, and innovations in administrative capacity that enable states to absorb their conquests, making power cumulative. The most important forces pushing the system toward diversity are expansion of the system to include new players, and local identities that motivate some units fiercely to resist hegemonic control. A factor that can push in either direction is norms of an international society, which can work to stabilize either hegemonic or diverse systems.

If the cases in this book are representative – and we believe that they generally are – then the modal behavior of states in the international system is not balancing, buckpassing, or bandwagoning, but rather expansion continued to the point of boondoggling. This means, on the one hand, that hegemonic stability theorists and offensive realists are right to see expansion (whether security-driven or otherwise) as normal. On the other hand, it means that balancing behavior cannot be expected reliably to counter great states' hegemonic ambitions. Divide-and-conquer tactics routinely trump balancing strategies, paving the way for system-wide hegemony by the leading power. The greater obstacle to hegemony is in states' ability to administer and extract resources from the areas they conquer. While military superiority is the *sine qua non* of hegemony, most cases of a rise to hegemony are preceded by the construction either of an improved administrative or political machinery, or of an elaborate ruling ideology, or both. As long as conquest is limited by the problem of the rising cost of expansion, balance is maintained whether states engage in balancing behavior or not. But once power truly becomes cumulative, a hegemon sooner or later emerges whether its rivals attempt to balance it or not.

The most reliable means of reintroducing diversity in such circumstances is the introduction of new units from outside the previous system. The rise or entrance of new players, from the Medes' opposition to Assyria to British opposition to Chinese regional hegemony, is one of the constants in the history of international systems, and the central reason for a return to political diversity in many of them.

A second means of reintroducing diversity is decay in administrative capability or political unity. While our case studies are primarily about hegemonic rise rather than imperial decline, the implication of our logic is that if a hegemon's ability to administer its subjects erodes, it should be vulnerable to the loss of hegemony due to a combination of internal revolt or civil conflict and attack by remaining independent or autonomous units. Examples of such decay are easy to provide; the history of the succession of Chinese dynasties is replete with them. Hegemonic boondoggling may contribute to such administrative decay, as overstrain on resources caused by imperial overstretch is a common contributing factor in imperial decline.

A third source of international political diversity is strong local identities, which fuel rebellions against and resistance to hegemons. This factor is most important in preventing or slowing rather than overturning hegemony: the repeated Greek resistance to the expansion of Persia and Rome, for example, foiled the further growth of the first and delayed the rise to hegemony of the other. When combined with others factors, however, such identities may also fuel a pendulum swing toward political diversity: Egypt's and Babylonia's successful revolts against Assyria, to take just one example, came in the wake of Assyria's boondoggling overstretch and the failure of its administrative machinery (especially within Babylonia). India's forest polities, to mention another, repeatedly played a role in hegemonic decline, but again mattered most in hastening imperial rot that had already set in. A final factor, which exists to stabilize some international systems but not others, is an international society built on intersubjectively agreed norms of international behavior. In some cases, such as the systems led by Rome and Qin, the absence of any effective constraints on state behavior is far more important than any rules that might exist. But in others, elaborate systems of international norms do exist, and they seem to play a role in stabilizing their international societies: Kang's picture of early modern East Asia certainly fits this profile, as does the English School (and classical Realist) depiction of the modern European balance of power. Neither hegemony nor balance is the universal historical norm, but either might be normative in a particular international society, and is likely to be more commonly followed in the presence of such normative sanction.

It is important to note that our survey is not comprehensive, and is limited overwhelmingly to political-military sources of international action. Many factors that have been hypothesized as important are discussed little if at all in these pages, and we make no claim regarding their significance or lack thereof. Economic factors, for example, are of obvious importance, but are generally overlooked here. Demographic changes, either from birth and death rates or from immigration, are of unquestioned significance in long-run political changes, but also are outside our purview. Climatic changes, with their enormous implications for both of the above factors, are also sometimes hypothesized to be of great international importance, but are also not discussed here. Technological changes – whether in military, production, or communications technology – are equally important and similarly given little attention here. We make no claim about the relative significance of these; they are all worthy of further examination.

Even with these caveats, however, what we do find is of prime significance. We know now that balance-of-power theory simply does not deserve pride of place in international relations theorizing. Balancing is not the main thing states do. Hegemony, we now know, is a normal condition of the international system, but no more so than diversity or balance. Which direction an international system moves depends simply on the relative strength of forces pushing it in each direction.

Appendix A

The vast majority of the data we present was compiled by David Wilkinson, and so our presentation of it is driven primarily by our assessment of the relevance of that data to our concerns. For the data that we did use, we made only minor adjustments for purposes of consistency and simplicity. First, Wilkinson's data for the East Asian system, unlike all of the others, is coded by quarter-century; we therefore multiplied each quarter by 2.5 to estimate codings by decade. Second, we collapsed Wilkinson's category of 'Tripolarity' into the 'Multipolarity' category, and his 'Empire' category into our 'Hegemony' column, since these distinctions are not critical for our purposes.

Our codings for the classical Mediterranean international system were done as follows. Wilkinson codes the 5th century BCE system as unipolar – led by Persia, but without Persian hegemony over Greece or the central Mediterranean. We judge that this situation continued until the final Macedonian conquest of Greece by Philip II created the Macedonian Empire as a peer rival to Persia, starting after the Battle of Chaeronea (338). Rounding, we identify the decade beginning 340 as a decade of bipolarity. We assign the Macedonian Empire a decade of hegemony – over most of the system, of course, not all of it – corresponding roughly with the decade beginning in 330. The immediate aftermath of Alexander's death created an exceptionally confused and violent situation, but still we judge that the multipolar system of Hellenistic states began soon after Alexander's (starting c. 320 BCE).

Judging the timing of Rome's rise raises additional complex problems. We judge, however, that after the Battle of Magnesia (190 BCE), Rome had decisively defeated all of its peer rivals – Carthage, Macedonia, and the Seleucid Empire – while Ptolemaic Egypt had already fallen to the status of a second-rank power. We therefore date the transformation of the system into a unipolar one led by Rome from 190 BCE. Since Rome's assertion of real sovereignty over most of the rest of the system proceeded in slow stages, it is inherently a matter of judgment at what point the system as a whole can be characterized as hegemonic. However, Ptolemaic Egypt repeatedly intervened in Seleucid politics in the later half of the 2nd century BCE without serious Roman interference, and as late as 87–86 BCE Ptolemy VIII refused aid to the Roman general Lucullus in his campaign against Mithridates of Pontus (see Bevan, 1927), who along with Tigranes of Armenia had emerged as a potential great power. We therefore judge that Rome did not become hegemon over the eastern Mediterranean until Pompey finished off Mithridates and Tigranes and reordered the Levant in the early 60s BCE. We therefore code the transition to Roman hegemony to have occurred early in the decade beginning 70 BCE. We consider Roman hegemony to have lasted until 395 BCE (that is, ending with the decade beginning 390), when with the death of Theodosius the western Roman Empire entered its terminal decline.

To summarize, our classical period codings are as follows.

Decades beginning:

400–350 BCE	Unipolar (Persia 6 – decades)
340 BCE	Bipolar (Macedon-Persia)
330 BCE	Hegemony (Macedon)
320–200 BCE	Multipolar (13 decades)
190–80 BCE	Unipolar (Rome – 12 decades)
70 BCE–380 CE	Hegemony (Rome – 46 decades)

Our codings for the modern system posed fewer problems. Following Hopf (1991), we code the four decades 1520–1559 as bipolar (Charles V's Habsburg Empire vs. the Ottoman Empire). This, plus four decades of the Cold war, yields a total of 8 bipolar decades. The rest of the period is multipolar, except for the unipolar 1990s.

The potentially more controversial questions involve omissions. First, we chose not to use two Wilkinson data sets for periods before 1500 BCE – data sets for Mesopotamia and for Egypt. In the case of the Egyptian data, we judged that since Egypt emerged as a single state so early in the series, the data represents more patterns in *state* unity and decay rather than *international* hegemony and diversity. Including it would have unduly biased the data set toward hegemonic outcomes. The Mesopotamian data unquestionably concerns an international system, but there we simply had doubts about its reliability. The absence of any nonpolar codings, even during periods of major migrations that disrupted the workings of international systems of the time, raises doubts about whether the data may make multipolarity seem unduly common. And the presence of data for the period before Sargon of Akkad in the 26th century BCE raises doubts about the adequacy of the sources. We believe that starting in 1500 BCE, centuries before any of our cases, is going back far enough; and we are much more confident of the quality of the data after that period. These decisions also mean that none of our data sets involve systems comprised exclusively of city-states, which might have different dynamics from systems including territorial states or empires.

Another set of omissions was the medieval period. In the case of medieval Europe, we concluded after some discussion that this period did not represent a state-system at all, so data from the period should not be applied in assessing theories of state-systems. While we recognize that the beginnings of the European system might be pushed back a few centuries (for example, into the period of the Hundred Years' War), none of us claims the expertise necessary to code that period reliably. The same is true for the medieval Middle East: while we believe that this was an interesting and important international system, none of us claims the expertise to code it reliably. For the Mesoamerican and Andean systems of this period, the data do not extend back in time far enough to construct data series of significant length, so these systems were also omitted.

We do not believe that any of these omissions – or even all of them together – significantly biases our analysis. Certainly the omission of Wilkinson's two ancient data sets does not: since the Egyptian data set is overwhelmingly periods of hegemony, while the Mesopotamian system is overwhelmingly periods of multipolarity, adding both would not have significantly changed our conclusions about the relative frequency of balanced and unbalanced systems. The longest relevant historical period still omitted – the medieval Mideast – seems to include significant periods of hegemony or unipolarity (e.g., under the Byzantines, the Arab Caliphates, and the Ottomans) as well as long periods of apparent balance, so again the composite data set does not seem unduly biased by the omission. The other omitted periods represent only a few centuries of time and would not include enough observations to change our data significantly.

Bibliography

Abu-Lughod, Janet L. (1989) *Before European Hegemony: The World System A.D. 1250–1350*. Oxford: Oxford University Press.

Ager, S. (2003) 'An Uneasy Balance: From the Death of Seleukos to the Battle of Raphia', in A. Erskine (ed.) *A Companion to the Hellenistic World*, pp. 35–50. Oxford: Blackwell.

Alfoldi, Andreas (1965) *Early Rome and the Latins*. Ann Arbor: University of Michigan Press.

Ameling, W. (1993) *Karthago: Militar, Staat und Gesellschaft*. Munich: Beck.

Amit, M. (1973) *Great and Small Poleis: A Study in the Relations between the Great Powers and the Small Cities in Ancient Greece*. Brussels: Latomous.

Anderson, Perry (1974) *Passages from Antiquity to Feudalism*. London: New Left Books.

Anderson, Benedict (2002) *The Spectre of Comparisons: Nationalism, Southeast Asia and the World*. London: Verso.

Andreski, Stanislav (1968) *Military Organization and Society*. Berkeley: University of California Press.

Andrewes, A. (1961) 'Thucydides and the Persians', *Historia*, 10: 1–18.

Aron, R. (1973) *Peace and War: A Theory of International Relations*. New York: Doubleday Anchor.

Astin, A.E. (1968) 'Politics and Policies in the Roman Republic', *Inaugural Lecture*, Queen's University, Belfast.

Atwell, William (1982) 'International Bullion Flows and the Chinese Economy circa 1530–1650', *Past and Present*, 95: 68–90.

Austin, M.M. (1986) 'Hellenistic Kings, War, and the Economy', *Classical Quarterly*, 36: 450–66.

Badian, E. (1958a) 'Aetolica', *Latomus*, 17: 197–211.

—— (1958b) *Foreign Clientelae*. Oxford: Oxford University Press.

—— (1993) 'Thucydides and the Outbreak of the Peloponnesian War: A Historian's Brief', in his *From Plataea to Potidaea: Studies in the History and Historiography of the Pentecontaetia*. Baltimore: John Hopkins Press.

Bairoch, Paul (1982) 'International Industrialization Levels from 1750 to 1980', *Journal of European Economic History*, 11(2): 269–334.

Balcer, Jack Martin (1995) *The Persian Conquest of the Greeks 545–450 BC*. Konstanz: Universitatverlag Konstanz.

Barnett, R.D. (1991) 'Urartu', in John Boardman *et al.* (eds) *The Cambridge Ancient History*, 2nd ed., Vol. III, Part 1, *The Prehistory of the Balkans; and the Middle East and the Aegean World, Tenth to Eighth Centuries B.C.* pp. 314–71. Cambridge: Cambridge University Press.

Basham, A.L. (1982) 'Asoka and Buddhism – A Reexamination: Presidential Address Given on the Occasion of the Fourth Conference of the IABS', *Journal of the International Association of Buddhist Studies*, 5(1): 131–43.

Beckwith, C.I. (1992) 'The Impact of the Horse and Silk Trade on the Economies of T'ang China and the Uighur Empire', *Journal of the Economic and Social History of the Orient*, 34: 183–98.

Bennett, Andrew and Alexander George (2005) *Case Studies and Theory Development in the Social Sciences*. Cambridge, Mass.: MIT Press.

Berthold, R.M. (1984) *Rhodes in the Hellenistic Age*. Ithaca: Cornell University Press.

Bevan, E.R. (1902) *The House of Seleucus*. London.

—— (1927) *The House of Ptolemy*. London: Methuen, accessed on-line at http://penelope.uchicago.edu/Thayer/E/Gazetteer/Places/Africa/Egypt/_Texts/BEVHOP/9*.html

Billows, R.A. (1995) *Kings and Colonists: Aspects of Macedonian Imperialism*. Leiden: Brill.

Blumel, W. (2000) 'Ein rhodisches Dekret aus Bargylia', *Epigraphica Anatolica*, 32: 94–6.

Bobbitt, Philip (2002) *The Shield of Achilles: War Peace and the Course of History*. London: Penguin Books.

Boscaro, Adriana (1975) *101 Letters of Hideyoshi*. Tokyo: Sophia University.

Bram, Joseph (1941) *An Analysis of Inca Militarism*. New York NY: J.J. Augustin.

Braund, David (1984) *Rome and the Friendly King: the Character of the Client Kingship*. London: Croom Helm.

Brinkman, J.A. (1984) *Prelude to Empire: Babylonian Society and Politics, 747–626 B.C.* Philadelphia, PA: Occasional Publications of the Babylonian Fund.

—— (1991) 'Babylonia in the Shadow of Assyria', in John Boardman *et al.* (eds) *The Cambridge Ancient History*, 2nd ed., vol. III, Part 2, *The Assyrian and Babylonian Empires and other States of the Near East, from the Eighth to the Sixth Centuries B.C.* Cambridge: Cambridge University Press.

—— (1997) 'Unfolding the Drama of the Assyrian Empire', in *Assyria 1995: Proceedings of the 10th Anniversary Symposium of the Neo-Assyrian Text Corpus Project* (ed. S. Parpola and R.M. Whiting). Helsinki: University of Helsinki.

Briscoe, J. (1973) *A Commentary on Livy, Books XXXI–XXXIII*. Oxford: Oxford University Press.

Brooks, Stephen G. (1999) 'The Globalization of Production and the Changing Benefits of Conquest', *Journal of Conflict Resolution*, 43(4): 646–70.

Bull, Hedley and Adam Watson (1984) *The Expansion of International Society*. Oxford: Oxford University Press.

Bunce, Valerie (1985) 'The Empire Strikes Back: The Evolution of the Eastern Bloc from a Soviet Asset to a Soviet Liability', *International Organization*, 39(1): 1–46.

Burn, A.R. (1962) *Persia and the Greeks*. London: Arnold.

Burns, Thomas S. (2003) *Rome and the Barbarians, 100 B.C.–A.D. 400*. Baltimore: Johns Hopkins University Press.

Bush, George W. (2002) *The National Security Strategy of the United States*. Washington, DC: The White House.

Butterfield, Herbert (1966) 'The Balance of Power', in H. Butterfield and M. Wight, *Diplomatic Investigations: Essays in the Theory of International Politics*. London: Allen and Unwin.

Buttinger, Joseph (1958) *The Smaller Dragon: A Political History of Vietnam*. New York: Praeger.

Buzan Barry (1993) 'From International System to International Society: Structural Realism and Regime Theory Meet the English School', *International Organization*, 47(3): 327–52.

Buzan, Barry and Richard Little (1996) 'Reconceptualizing Anarchy: Structural Realism Meets World History', *European Journal of International Relations*, 2(4): 426–7.

────── (2000) *International Systems in World History: Remaking the Study of International Relations*. Oxford: Oxford University Press.

Buzan, Barry, Charles A. Jones and Richard Little (1993) *The Logic of Anarchy: Neorealism to Structural Realism*. New York: Columbia University Press.

Campbell, B. (2002) 'Power Without Limit: "The Romans Always Win"', in A. Chaniotis and P. Ducrey (eds) *Army and Power in the Ancient World*, pp. 167–80. Stuttgart: Franz Steiner.

Capon, Edmund (1989) *Tang China*. London: Macdonald Orbis.

Carrasco, Pedro (1999) *The Tenochca Empire of Ancient Mexico: the Triple Alliance of Tenochtitlan, Tetzcoco, and Tlapcopan*. Norman, OK: Oklahoma University Press.

Cartledge, Paul (1977) 'Hoplites and Heroes: Sparta's Contribution to the Technique of Ancient War', *Journal of Helleniuc Studies*, 97: 11–27.

Casson, Lionel (1994) *Ships and Seafaring in Ancient Times*. London: British Museum Press.

Cawkwell, G.L. (1997a) *Thucydides And The Peloponnesian War*. London: Routledge.

────── (1997b) 'The Peace Between Athens and Persia', *Phoenix*, 51: 115–30.

Cha, Victor (1998) 'Defining Security in East Asia: History, Hotspots, and Horizon-gazing', in Eunmee Kim (ed.) *The Four Asian Tigers: Economic Development and the Global Political Economy*, pp. 33–60. San Diego: Academic Press.

Chaniotis, Angelos (2005) *Warfare in the Hellenistic World*. Oxford: Blackwell.

Chapman, Graham P. (2000) *The Geopolitics of South Asia: From the Early Empires to India, Pakistan, and Bangladesh*. Aldershot: Ashgate.

Chen, Enlin (1991) *Xianqin junshi zhidu yanjiu (A Study of the Military System in the Pre-Qin Period)*. Changchun: Jilin Wenshi chubanshe.

Christensen, T.J. (1993) 'System Stability and the Security of the Most Vulnerable Significant Actor', in J. Snyder and R. Jervis (eds) *Coping With Complexity in the International System*, pp. 329–56. Boulder, Colo.: Westview Press.

────── (1996) *Useful Adversaries: Grant Strategy, Domestic Mobilization, and Sino-American Conflict*. Princeton: Princeton University Press.

Christiansen, Tomas J. and Jack Snyder (1990) 'Chain Gangs and Passed Bucks: Predicting Alliance Patterns in Multipolarity', *International Organization*, 44(2): 137–68.

Cioffi-Revilla, Claudio (1996) 'Origins and Evolution of War and Politics', *International Studies Quarterly*, 40(1): 1–22.

Cioffi-Revilla, Claudio and Todd Landman (1999) 'Evolution of Maya Politics in the Ancient Mesoamerican System', *International Studies Quarterly*, 43(4): 559–98.

Cipolla, Carlo M. (1965) *Guns, Sails and Empires – Technological Innovation and the Early Phases of European Expansion 1400–1700*. New York: Minerva Press.

Clark, Ian (2005) *Legitimacy in International Society*. Oxford: Oxford University Press.

Clendinnen, Inga (1995 [1991]) *Aztecs: an Interpretation*. Cambridge: Cambridge University Press; Canto.

Coedes, G. (1969) *The Making of Southeast Asia*, trans. H.M. Wright, Berkeley: University of California Press.

Cohen, Edward E. (2000) *The Athenian Nation*. Princeton: Princeton University Press.

Cohen, Raymond and Raymond Westbrook (2000) *Amarna Diplomacy: The Beginnings of International Relations*. Baltimore: Johns Hopkins University Press.

Cole, Steven W. (1996) *Nippur in Late Assyrian Times, 755–612 B.C.* Helskini: The Neo-Assyrian Text Corpus Project.

Collier, George A. (1982) 'In the Shadow of Empire: New Directions in Mesoamerican and Andean Ethnohistory', in George A. Collier, Renato I. Rosaldo, and John D. Wirth (eds) *The Inca and Aztec States, 1400–1800: Anthropology and History*. New York NY: Academic Press.

Conrad, Geoffrey W. and Arthur A. Demarest (1984) *Religion and Empire: the Dynamics of Aztec and Inca Expansionism*. Cambridge: Cambridge University Press.

Cornell, T.J. (1989) 'The Conquest of Italy', in *The Cambridge Ancient History*, Vol. VII Part 2, *The Rise of Rome to 220 B.C.*, 2nd edition, edited by A.E. Astin, F.W. Walbank, M.W. Frederiksen and R.M. Ogilvie. Cambridge, UK: Cambridge University Press.

—— (1991) 'Rome: The History of an Anachronism', in *City-States in Classical Antiquity and Medieval Italy*, edited by A. Molho, K. Raaflaub and J. Emlen. Ann Arbor: University of Michigan Press.

—— (1996) 'Hannibal's Legacy: The Effects of the Hannibalic War in Italy', in T.J. Cornell, B. Rankov and P. Sabin (eds) *The Second Punic War: A Reappraisal*, pp. 97–117. London: Institute of Classical Studies.

Crawford, Michael (1992) *The Roman Republic*, 2nd edition. Cambridge: MA: Harvard University Press.

Creel, Herrlee G. (1970a) *The Origins of Statecraft in China*. Chicago: University of Chicago Press.

—— (1970b) 'The Beginnings of Bureaucracy in China: The Origins of the Hsien', in *What is Taoism? And Other Studies in Chinese Cultural History*. Chicago: Chicago University Press, 121–59.

Cumings, Bruce (1996) 'The Historical Origins of North Korean Foreign Policy', (Paper prepared for the Conference on North Korean Foreign Policy in the Post-Cold War Era).

Curtin, Jeremiah (1972) *The Mongols: A History*. Westport, CT: Greenwood Press.

Cushman, Jennifer W. (1993) *Fields from the Sea: Chinese Junk Trade with Siam during the Late Eighteenth and Early Nineteenth Centuries*. Ithaca, N.Y.: Southeast Asia Program, Cornell University.

D'Altroy, Terence (2002) *The Incas*. Malden MA and Oxford: Blackwell.

Davis, Paul K. (1996) *Encyclopedia of Invasions and Conquests: From Ancient Times to the Present*. Santa Barbara: ABC-CLIO.

de Ste Croix G.E.M. (1972) *The Origins of the Peloponnesian War*. London, Duckworth.

Deininger, Jurgen (1980) Explaining the Change from Republic to Principate in Rome. *Comparative Civilizations Review*, 4: 77–99.

Dehio, Ludwig (1962) *The Precarious Balance*. New York: Vintage.

Delbruck, Hans (1975) *Warfare in Antiquity. Vol. I. History of the Art of War*, translated by Walter J. Renfroe, Jr. Lincoln: University of Nebraska Press.

Deng, Gang (1997) 'The Foreign Staple Trade of China in the Pre-Modern Era', *International History Review*, 19(2): 253–85.

Derow, P.S. (1979) 'Polybius, Rome, and the East', *Journal of Roman Studies*, 69: 1–15.

——— (2003) 'The Arrival of Rome: From the Illyrian Wars to the Fall of Macedon', in A. Erskine (ed.) *A Companion to the Hellenistic World*, pp. 51–70. Oxford: Blackwell.

Deudney, Daniel (2000a) 'Regrounding Realism: Anarchy, Security, and Changing Material Contexts', *Security Studies*, 10(1): 1–42.

——— (2000b) 'Geopolitics as Theory: Historical Security Materialism', *European Journal of International Relations*, 6(1): 77–107.

——— (2007) *Bounding Power: Republican Security Theory from the Polis to the Global Village*. Princeton: Princeton University Press.

Dirks, Nicholas (1989) 'The Original Caste: Power, History, and Hierarchy in South Asia', *Contributions to Indian Sociology*, 23(1): 59–77.

——— (1992) 'Castes of Mind', *Representations*, 37: 56–78.

Doniger, Wendy and Brian K. Smith (trans.) (1991) *The Laws of Manu*. London: Penguin Books.

Dorey, T.A. (1960) 'The Alleged Aetolian Embassy to Rome', *Classical Review*, 10: 9.

Doyle, Michael W. (1986) *Empires*. Ithaca: Cornell University Press.

———. (1997) *Ways of War and Peace*. New York and London: W.W. Norton & Company.

Drekmeier, Charles (1962) *Kingship and Community in Early India*. Stanford: Stanford University Press.

Dreyer, B. (2003) 'Der "Raubvertrag" des Jahres 203/2v Chr.: Das Inschriftenfragment von Bargylia und der Brief von Amyzon', *Epigraphica Anotolica*, 34: 119–38.

Dumont, Louis, Basia M. Gulati (trans.) (1990) *Homo Hierarchicus: The Caste System and Its Implications*. Chicago: University of Chicago Press.

Dupuy, R. Ernest and Trevor N. Dupuy (1993) *The Harper Encyclopedia of Military History: From 3500 BC to the Present*, 4th ed. New York: HarperCollins.

Duyvendak, J.J.L. (trans. with an intro.) (1963 [1928]) *The Book of Lord Shang: A Classic of the Chinese School of Law*. Chicago: The University of Chicago Press.

Eckstein, A.M. (1987) *Senate and General: Individual Decision-Making and Roman Foreign Relations, 264–194 B.C.* Berkeley/Los Angeles: University of California Press.

——— (1999) 'The Pharos Inscription and the Question of Roman Treaties of Alliance Overseas in the Third Century B.C', *Classical Philology*, 94: 395–418.

——— (2002) 'Greek Mediation in the First Macedonian War (209–205 B.C.)', *Historia*, 52: 268–97.

——— (2003) 'Thucydides and the Outbreak of the Peloponnesian War and the Foundations of International Relations Systems Theory', *International History Review*, 25(4): 757–74.

—— (2005) 'The Pact Between the Kings, Polybius 15.20.6, and Polybius' View of the Outbreak of the Second Macedonian War', *Classical Philology*, 100: 228–42.

—— (2006) *Mediterranean Anarchy, Interstate War, and the Rise of Rome*. Berkeley/Los Angeles: University of California Press.

Eddy, Samuel K. (1973) 'The Cold War Between Athens and Persia', *Classical Philology*, 68(4): 241–258.

Elisonas, Jurgis (1988) 'The inseparable trinity: Japan's relations with China and Korea', in John Hall (ed.) *The Cambridge History of Japan: Early Modern Japan*, pp. 235–300. Cambridge: Cambridge University Press.

Ellis, Peter Berresford (1998) *Celt and Roman: The Celts of Italy*. London: Constable.

Elster, Jon (1989) *Nuts and Bolts for the Social Sciences*. New York: Cambridge University Press.

Elton, Hugh (1996) *Frontiers of the Roman Empire*. Bloomington: University of Indiana Press.

Embree, Ainslie T. (1977) 'Frontiers into Boundaries: From the Traditional to the Modern State', in Richard G. Fox (ed.) *Realm and Region in Traditional India*. Durham, N.C.: Duke University Press.

Erdosy, George (1995) 'City States of North India and Pakistan at the Time of the Buddha', in F.R. Allchin (ed.) *The Archaeology of Early Historic South Asia: The Emergence of Cities and States*, pp. 99–122. Cambridge: Cambridge University Press.

Errington, R.M. (1971) 'The Alleged Syro-Macedonian Pact and the Origins of the Second Macedonian War', *Athenaeum*, 49: 336–54.

—— (1972) *The Dawn of Empire: Rome's Rise to World Power*. Ithaca: Cornell University Press.

—— (1986) 'Antiochos III, Zeuxis und Euromos', *Epigraphica Anatolica*, 17: 1–8.

Fairbank, John (ed.) (1968) *The Chinese World Order*. Cambridge, Mass.: Harvard University Press.

Ferrary, J.L. (1988) *Philhellènisme et impérialisme: Aspects idéologiques de la conquête romaine du monde hellénistique*. Rome: MEFR.

Ferrill, Arthur (1986) *The Fall of the Roman Empire: The Military Explanation*. London: Thames and Hudson.

Finley, M.I. (1983) *Politics in the Ancient World*. Cambridge, UK: Cambridge University Press.

Figueira, Thomas J. (1998) *The Power of Money: Coinage and Politics in the Athenian Empire*. Philadelphia: University of Pennsylvania Press.

——. (1991) *Athens and Aigina in the Age of Imperial Colonization*. Baltimore: John Hopkins University Press.

Finkelstein, Israel and Neil Asher Silberman (2001) *The Bible Unearthed: Archaeology's New Vision of Ancient Israel and the Origins of its Sacred Texts*. New York: Simon and Schuster.

Fliess, P.J. (1966) *Thucydides and the Politics of Bipolarity*. Baton Rouge: Louisiana State University Press.

Floris, George A. (1962) 'A Note on Dacoits in India', *Comparative Studies in Society and History*, 4(4): 467–72.

Flower, Michael A. (2000) 'From Simonides to Isocrates: The Fifth Century Origins of Fourth-Century Panhellenism', *Classical Antiquity*, 19(1): 65–101.

Forrest, George (1986) 'Greece: The History of the Archaic Period', in John Boardman, Jasper Griffin and Oswyn Murray (eds) *The Oxford History of the Classical World*. Oxford: Oxford University Press.

Fowler, William R. and John D. Monaghan (1996) 'The Maya', in Barbara A. Tennenbaum (ed.) *Encyclopedia of Latin American History and Culture*. New York: Charles Scribner's Sons.

Frank, Andre Gunder (1998) *ReOrient: Global Economy in the Asian Age*. Berkeley: University of California Press.

Freeman, Edward A. (1893) *History of Federal Government in Greece and Italy*, 2nd edition, edited by J.B. Bury. London: Macmillan.

Friedberg, A.L. (2000) *In the Shadow of the Garrison State: America's Anti-Statism and Its Cold War Grand Strategy*. Princeton: Princeton University Press.

Fussman, Gerard (1988) 'Central and Provincial Administration in Ancient India: The Problem of the Mauryan Empire', *The Indian Historical Review*, 14: 41–72.

Fustel de Coulanges (1864) *The Ancient City: A Study of the Religion, Laws and Institutions of Greece and Rome*. Garden City, NY: Anchor.

Gabba, E. (1994) 'Rome and Italy: The Social War', in *The Cambridge Ancient History. Vol. IX. The Last Age of the Roman Republic, 146–43 B.C.*, edited by J.A. Crook, Andrew Lintott and Elizabeth Rawson. Cambridge, UK: Cambridge University Press.

Gao, Rui (1995) *Zhongguo shanggu junshishi* (*Military History of Ancient China*). Beijing: Junshi kexue chubanshe.

Garlan, Y. (1975) *War in the Ancient World: A Social History*, translated by Janet Lloyd. London: Chatto and Windus.

Gelzer, Matthias (1968) *Caesar: Politician and Statesman*. Oxford: Blackwell.

Georges, Pericles B. (2000) 'Persia Ionia under Darius: The Revolt Reconsiderd', *Historia*, 49(1): 1–39.

Gera, D. (1998) *Judaea and Mediterranean Politics, 219 to 161 B.C.E.* Leiden: Brill.

Ghoshal, U.N. (1959) *A History of Indian Political Ideas: The Ancient Period and the Period of Transition to the Middle Ages*. London: Oxford University Press.

Gibson, Charles (1964) *The Aztecs under Spanish Rule: a history of the Indians of the Valley of Mexico*. Stanford CA: Stanford University Press.

Gilovich, Thomas, Dale W. Griffin and Daniel Kahneman (eds) (2002) *Heuristics and Biases: The Psychology of Intuitive Judgment*. Cambridge: Cambridge University Press.

Gilpin, Robert (1981) *War and Change in World Politics*. Cambridge: Cambridge University Press.

Gilpin, R. (1988) 'Theory of Hegemonic War', *Journal of Interdisciplinary History*, 18: 591–613.

Glaser, Charles L. and Chaim Kaufman (1998) 'What is the Offense-Defense Balance and Can We Measure it?', *International Security*, 22(4): 44–82.

——— (1998/99) 'Correspondence: Taking Offense at Offense-Defense Theory', *International Security*, 23(3): 200–6.

Gold, Ann Grodzins and Bhoju Ram Gojur (2002) *In The Time of Trees and Sorrows*. Durham & London: Duke University Press.

Goldin, Paul R. (2001) 'Han Feizi's Doctrine of Self-Interest', *Asian Philosophy*, 11(3): 151–9.

Goldsworthy, Adrian Keith (1996) *The Roman Army at War, 100BC–AD200*. Oxford: Clarendon.

——— (2000) *The Punic Wars*. London: Cassell.

Goyal, S.R. (2000) *The Kautiliya Arthasastra: Its Author, Date, and Relevance for the Maurya Period*. Jodhpur: Kusumanjali Book World.

Grainger, J.D. (2002) *The Roman War of Antiochos the Great.* Leiden: Brill.

Grayson, A.K. (1991a) 'Assyria: Ashur-Dan II to Ashur-Nirari V (934–745 B.C.)', in John Boardman *et al.* (eds) *The Cambridge Ancient History,* 2nd ed., vol. III, Part 1, *The Prehistory of the Balkans; and the Middle East and the Aegean World, Tenth to Eighth Centuries B.C.,* pp. 238–81. Cambridge: Cambridge University Press.

—— (1991b) 'Assyria: Tiglath-pileser III to Sargon II (744–705 B.C.)', in John Boardman *et al.* (eds) *The Cambridge Ancient History,* 2nd ed., vol. III, Part 2, *The Assyrian and Babylonian Empires and other States of the Near East, from the Eighth to the Sixth Centuries B.C.,* pp. 71–102. Cambridge: Cambridge University Press.

—— (1991c) 'Assyria: Sennacherib and Esarhaddon (704–6690 B.C.)', in John Boardman *et al.* (eds) *The Cambridge Ancient History,* 2nd ed., vol. III, Part 2, *The Assyrian and Babylonian Empires and other States of the Near East, from the Eighth to the Sixth Centuries B.C.,* pp. 103–41. Cambridge: Cambridge University Press.

—— (1996) *Assyrian Rulers of the Early First Millennium BC II (858–745 BC).* Royal Inscriptions of Mesopotamia, Assyrian Periods, Vol. 3 Toronto: University of Toronto Press.

Green, Peter (1996) *The Greco-Persian Wars.* Berkeley: University of California Press.

Griffith, G.T. (1935) 'An Early Motive of Roman Imperialism', *Cambridge Historical Journal,* 5: 1–14.

Gruen, E.S. (1984) *The Hellenistic World and the Coming of Rome.* Berkeley/Los Angeles: University of California Press.

Gruen, Eric S. (1990) The Imperial Policy of Augustus. In *Between Republic and Empire: Interpretations of Augustus and His Principate,* edited by Kurt A. Raaflaub and Mark Toher. Berkeley: University of California.

Guha, Sumit (1996) 'Forest Polities and Agrarian Empires: The Khandesh Bhils, c. 1700–1850', *The Indian Economic and Social History Review,* 33(2): 133–53.

—— (1999) *Environment and Ethnicity in India, 1200–1991.* Cambridge: Cambridge University Press.

Gulick, Edward Vose (1955) *Europe's Classical Balance of Power.* New York: W.W. Norton.

Ha, U-bong (1989) Choson Hugi Silhakja-ui Ilbon gwan yongu *(A Study of Late Choson Silhakja's Views on Japan).* Seoul: Iljisa.

—— (1994) 'Choson jeongi-ui daeil gwangye (Early Choson's Foreign Policy Toward Japan)', in Cho Hang-rae, Ha U-bong, and Son Seung-chol (eds) *Kangjwa hanilgwangye-sa (Lectures on Korea-Japan Relations).* Seoul: Hyonumsa.

Haas, Ernst B. (1953) 'The Balance of Power: Prescription, Concept or Propaganda', *World Politics,* (5)4: 442–77.

Habicht, C. (1997) *Athens from Alexander to Antony.* Cambridge, Mass.: Harvard University Press.

Hall, John (1968) *Japan: From Prehistory to Modern Times.* New York: Delacorte Press.

Halladay, A.J. (1982) 'Hoplites and Heresies', *Journal of Hellenic Studies,* 102: 94–103.

Hamashita, Takeshia (1994) 'The Tribute Trade System and Modern Asia', in A.J.H. Latham and Heita Kawakatsu (eds) *Japanese Industrialization and the Asian Economy*. London: Routledge.

Hamnett, Brian (1999) *A Concise History of Mexico*. Cambridge: Cambridge University Press.

Han, Myung-ki (1999) Imjin Yeoran-gwa Han-jung gwangye (*The Imjin intervention and Sino-Korean relations*). Seoul: Yuksa Bipyoungsa.

Hansen, E.V. (1947) *The Attalids of Pergamum*. Ithaca: Cornell University Press.

Hansen, Morgens Herman (2003) 'Theses about the Greek Polis in the Archaic and Classical Periods: A Report on the Results Obtained by the Copenhagen Polis Centre 1993–2003', *Historia*, 52(3): 257–82.

Hanson, Victor Davis (2002) *Carnage and Culture: Landmark Battles in the Rise of Western Power*. New York: Random House.

Hardiman, David (1994) 'Power in the Forests: The Dangs, 1820–1940', in David Arnold and David Hardiman (eds) *Subaltern Studies VIII: Essays in Honour of Ranajit Guha*, pp. 89–147. Delhi: Oxford University Press.

Harris, Olivia (1995) ' "The Coming of the White People": Reflections on the Mythologisation of History in Latin America', *Bulletin of Latin American Research*, 14(1): 9–24.

Harris, William V. (1979) *War and Imperialism in Republican Rome, 327–70 BC*. Oxford: Oxford University Press.

Hassig, R. (1992) *War and Society in Ancient Mesoamerica*. Berkeley, CA: University of California Press.

——— (1999) 'The Aztec World', in K. Raaflaub and N. Rosenstein (eds) *War and Society in the Ancient and Medieval Worlds*, pp. 361–87. Cambridge, Mass: Harvard University Press.

Heather, P. (2005) *The Fall of the Roman Empire: A New History of Rome and the Barbarians*. New York: Oxford University Press.

Herf, J. (1990) *War by Other Means: West Germany and the Euromissile Crisis*. New York: The Free Press.

Hölbl, G. (2001) *A History of Ptolemaic Egypt*. London: Routledge.

Holleaux, M. (1935) *Rome, la Grece, et les monarchies hellenistiqus aux IIIe. siecle av. J-C. (273–205)*. Paris: Editions E. de Boccard.

Holloway, Steven W. (2002) *Assur is king! Assur is king!: religion in the exercise of power in the Neo-Assyrian Empire*. Leiden and Boston: Brill.

Holsti, K.J. (1991) *Peace and War: Armed Conflicts and International Order*. Cambridge: Cambridge University Press.

Hopkins, Keith (1978) *Conquerors and Slaves: Sociological Studies in Roman History I*. Cambridge: Cambridge University Press.

Hopf, Ted (1991) 'Polarity, the offense-defense balance, and war', *American Political Science Review*, 85(2): 475–93.

Howe, Christopher (1996) *The Origins of Japanese Trade Supremacy: Development and Technology in Asia from 1540 to the Pacific War*. London: Hurts.

Hsu, Cho-yun (1965) *Ancient China in Transition: An Analysis of Social Mobility*. California: Stanford University Press.

——— (1997) 'War and Peace in Ancient China: The History of Chinese Interstate/International Relations', Occasional Paper Number 75, Washington: The Woodrow Wilson Center Asia Program.

Hubert, H. (1987) *The Greatness and Decline of the Celts*, translated by M.R. Dobie. London: Constable.

Hui, Victoria Tin-bor (2004) 'Toward a Dynamic Theory of International Politics: Insights from Comparing the Ancient Chinese and Early Modern European Systems', *International Organization*, 58(1): 175–205.

—— (2005) *War and State Formation in Ancient China and Early Modern Europe*. Cambridge: Cambridge University Press.

Ibn Khaldun (1967) Bedouin Civilization, Savage Nations and Tribes and their Conditions of Life, including Basic Explanatory Statements, in *The Muqaddimah: An Introduction to History*. Princeton: Princeton University Press.

Ikeda, Satoshi (1996) 'The History of the Capitalist World-System vs. the History of East-Southeast Asia', *Review*, 19(1): 49–78.

Inden, Ronald (1990) *Imagining India*. Bloomington and Indianapolis: Indiana University Press.

Ishii, Yoneo (1998) The Junk Trade from Southeast Asia: translations from the Tosen Fusetsu-gaki, 1674–1723. Singapore: Institute of Southeast Asian Studies.

Jackson, Robert H. (1990) *Quasi-states: Sovereignty, international relations, and the third world*. Cambridge: Cambridge University Press.

James, T.G.H. (1991) 'Egypt: the Twenty-fifth and Twenty-sixth Dynasties', in John Boardman *et al.* (eds) *The Cambridge Ancient History*, 2ⁿᵈ ed., vol. III, Part 2, *The Assyrian and Babylonian Empires and other States of the Near East, from the Eighth to the Sixth Centuries B.C.*, pp. 677–750. Cambridge: Cambridge University Press.

Jervis, Robert (1978) 'Cooperation under the Security Dilemma', *World Politics*, 30(2): 167–214.

Johnson, Chalmers (2004) *The Sorrows of Empire: Militarism, Secrecy and the End of the Republic*. New York: Henry Holt.

Johnston, Alastair Iain (1994) *Cultural Realism*. Princeton: Princeton University Press.

Jones, D.M. (1994) 'Balancing and Bandwagoning in Militarized Interstate Disputes', in F.W. Wayman and P.F. Diehl (eds) *Reconstructing Realpolitik*. Ann Arbor: University of Michigan Press.

Kagan, Donald (1969) *The Outbreak of the Peleoponnesian War*. Ithaca, NY: Cornell University Press.

Kahneman, Daniel, Paul Slovic and Amos Tversky (eds) (1982) *Judgment under Uncertainty: Heuristics and Biases*. Cambridge: Cambridge University Press.

Kallet-Marx, R. (1995) *Hegemony to Empire: The Development of the Roman Imperium in the East from 148 to 62 B.C.* Berkeley/Los Angeles: University of California Press.

Kamen, Henry (2002) *Spain's Long Road to Empire: the Making of a World Power, 1492–1763*. London: Allen Lane.

Kang, David C. (2002) *Crony Capitalism: Corruption and Development in South Korea and the Philippines*. Cambridge, MA: Cambridge University Press.

Kang, Etsuko (1997) *Diplomacy and ideology in Japanese-Korean relations: from the fifteenth to the eighteenth century*. New York: St. Martin's Press.

Kangle, R.P. (1965) *The Kautiliya Arthasastra, Part III, A Study*. Delhi: Motilal Banarsidass Publishers.

—— (trans.) (1972) *The Kautiliya Arthasastra, Part II, An English Translation with Critical and Explanatory Notes*, 2nd edn. Delhi: Motilal Banarsidass Publishers.

Kaplan, Morton A. (1957) *System and Process in International Politics*. New York: Wiley.

Kaufman, Stuart J. (1997) 'The Fragmentation and Consolidation of International Systems', *International Organization*, 51(2): 173–208.

Kazui, Tashiro (1982) 'Foreign Relations During the Edo Period: Sakoku Reexamined', *Journal of Japanese Studies*, 8(2): 283–306.

Keay, John (2000) *India: A History*. New York: Atlantic Monthly Press.

Kennedy, Paul (1987) *The Rise and Fall of the Great Powers: Economic Change and Military Conflict from 1500 to 2000*. New York: Random House.

Kim, Key-hiuk (1980) *The Last Phase of the East Asian World Order*. Berkeley: University of California Press.

Kim, Seonmin (2006) 'Ginseng and Border Trespassing between Qing China and Choson Korea', paper presented at the annual meetings of the Association for Asian Studies, San Diego, CA, April 6–9.

Klein, Herbert S. (2003) *A Concise History of Bolivia*. Cambridge: Cambridge University Press.

Klein, Peter (1989) 'The China seas and the World Economy between the Sixteenth and Nineteenth Centuries: the Changing Structures of Trade', in Carl-Ludwig Holtfrerich (ed.) *Interactions in the World Economy: Perspectives from International Economic History*. New York: New York University Press.

Krasner, Stephen (1999) *Sovereignty: Organized Hypocrisy*. Princeton: Princeton University Press.

Kuhrt, Amélie (1995) *The Ancient Near East c. 3000–330 BC*, Vol. II. London: Routledge.

Kulke, Hermann (1997) 'The Early and Imperial Kingdom: A Processural Model of Integrative State Formation in Early Medieval India', in Hermann Kulke (ed.) *The State in India, 1000–1700*, pp. 1–22. Delhi: Oxford University Press.

Kulke, Hermann and Dietmar Rothermund (1998) *A History of India*, 3rd edn. London and New York: Routledge.

Kwanten, Luc (1979) *Imperial Nomads*. Philadelphia: University of Pennsylvania Press.

Labs, Eric J. (1992) 'Do Weak States Bandwagon?', *Securities Studies*, 1(3): 383–416.

—— (1997) 'Beyond Victory: Offensive Realism and the Expansion of War Aims', *Security Studies*, 6(4): 1–49.

Lam, Truong Buu (1968) 'Intervention versus Tribute in Sino-Vietnamese Relations', in John Fairbank (ed.) *The Chinese World Order: traditional China's foreign relations*, pp. 165–79. Cambridge, Mass.: Harvard University Press.

Lancel, Serge (1997) *Carthage: A History*. Oxford: Blackwell.

Larsen, J.A.O. (1967) *Greek Federal States*. Oxford: Oxford University Press.

Lake, David A. (1996) 'Anarchy, Hierarchy, and the Variety of International Relations', *International Organization*, 50(1): 1–33.

Lampela, A. (1998) *Rome and the Ptolemies of Egypt: The Development of their Political Relations, 273–80 B.C.* Helsinki: Finnish Society of Sciences and Letters.

Law, Bimala Churn (1973) *Tribes in Ancient India*, 2nd edn. Poona: Bhandarkar Oriental Series.

Law, Narenda Nath (1920) *Inter-state Relations in Ancient India*. London: Calcutta Oriental Series.

Layne, Christopher (1997) 'From Preponderance to Offshore Balancing: America's Future Grand Strategy', *International Security*, 22(1): 86–124.

—— (2004) 'The War on Terrorism and the Balance of Power', in T.V. Paul, James J. Wirtz and Michel Fortmann (eds) *Balance of Power: Theory and Practice in the 21st Century*. Stanford: Stanford University Press.

—— (2006) *The Peace of Illusions: American Grand Strategy from 1940 to the Present*. Ithaca: Cornell University Press.

Lazenby, J.F. (1998a) *Hannibal's War: A Military History*. Norman: University of Oklahoma Press.

—— (1998b) 'Was Maharbal Right?', in T.J. Cornell, B. Rankov and P. Sabin (eds) *The Second Punic War: A Reappraisal*, pp. 39–48. London: Institute of Classical Studies.

Lebow, R.N. (1991) 'Thucydides, Power Transition Theory, and the Causes of War', in Richard Ned Lebow and Barry S. Strauss (eds) *Hegemonic Rivalry: From Thucydides to the Nuclear Age*. Boulder: Westview.

—— (2000) 'Contingency, Catalysis and International Systems Change', *Political Science Quarterly*, 105: 1–26.

—— (2004) *The Tragic Vision of Politics: Ethics, Interests and Orders*. Cambridge: Cambridge University Press.

Lebow, Richard Ned and Barry S. Strauss (1991) (eds) *Hegemonic Rivalry: From Thucydides to the Nuclear Age*. Boulder: Westview Press.

Ledyard, Gari (1988–89) 'Confucianism and War: the Korean Security Crisis of 1598', *The Journal of Korean Studies*, 6: 81–119.

—— (2006a) posting on the Korea Web, March 22 (Koreanstudies@koreaweb.ws).

—— (2006b) posting to the Korean Web, March 16 (Koreanstudies@koreaweb.ws).

Lee, John (1999) 'Trade and Economy in Preindustrial East Asia, c. 1500–1800: East Asia in the Age of Global Integration', *Journal of Asian Studies*, 58(1): 2–26.

Lee, Ki-baek (1984) *A New History of Korea*, trans. Edward Wagner. Cambridge, Mass.: Harvard University Press.

León-Portilla, Miguel (1984) 'Mesoamerica before 1519', in Leslie Bethel (ed.) *The Cambridge History of Latin America*, Vol. 1. Cambridge: Cambridge University Press.

Lemke, Douglas (2002) *Regions of War and Peace*. Cambridge: Cambridge University Press.

Levy, Jack S. (2001) 'Balances and Balancing: Concepts. Propositions and Research Design', in John A. Vasquez and Colin Elman (eds) *Realism and the Balancing of Power: A New Debate*. Upper Saddle River: Prentice Hall

—— (2003) 'Balances and Balancing: Concepts, Propositions and Research Design', in *Realism and the Balancing of Power: A New Debate*, edited by John A. Vasquez and Colin Elman. Saddle River, N.J.: Prentice-Hall.

—— (2004) 'What do Great Powers Balance Against and When?', in T.V. Paul, J.J. Wirtz and M. Fortmann (eds) *Balance of Power: Theory and Practice in the 21st Century*. Stanford: Stanford University Press.

Levy, Jack S. and William R. Thompson (2003) 'Balancing at Sea: Do States Coalesce around Leading Maritime Powers', Annual Meeting of the American Political Science Association, Phil. Pa 2003.

———— (2005) 'Hegemonic Threats and Great-Power Balancing in Europe, 1495–1999', *Security Studies*, 14(1): 1–31.

Levathes, Louise (1994) *When China Ruled the Seas: The Treasure Fleet of the Dragon Throne, 1405–1433*. Oxford: Oxford University Press.

Lévêque, P. (1968) 'La guerre a l'époque hellénistique', in J.-P. Vernant (ed.) *Problèmes de la guerre en grèce ancienne*, pp. 261–87. Paris.: Hatchet.

Lewis, David M. (1977) *Sparta and Persia*. Lieden: E.J. Brill.

Lewis, Mark E. (1990) *Sanctioned Violence in Early China*. Albany: State University of New York Press.

———— (1999) 'Warring States Political History', in Michael Loewe and Edward L. Shaughnessy (eds) *The Cambridge History of Ancient China: From the Origins of Civilization to 221 B.C.*, pp. 587–650. New York: Cambridge University Press.

Liberman, Peter (1993) 'The Spoils of Conquest', *International Security*, 18(2): 125–53.

———— (1996) *Does Conquest Pay? The Exploitation of Occupied Industrial Societies*. Princeton: Princeton University Press.

Lieber, Keir A. and Gerard Alexander (2005) 'Waiting for Balancing: Why the World is Not Pushing Back', *International Security*, 30(1): 109–39.

Lieberman, Victor (1993) 'Local Integration and Eurasian Analogies: Structuring Southeast Asian History, c. 1350–c. 1830', *Modern Asian Studies*, 27(3): 475–572.

Lin, Jianming (1992) *Qin shi (A History of Qin)*. Taipei: Wunan chubanshe.

Lipinski, Edward (2000) *The Aramaeans: Their Ancient History, Culture, Religion*. Leuven: Peeters Publishers and Department of Oriental Studies.

Lister, Frederick K. (1997) *The Early Security Confederations: From the Ancient Greeks to the United Colonies of New England*, Westport, Conn. and London: Greenwood Press.

Little, Richard (2007) *The Balance of Power in International Relations: Myths, Metaphors, and Models*. Cambridge: Cambridge University Press.

Liverani, Mario (1988) 'The growth of the Assyrian Empire in the Banut/Middle Euphrates Area: A new paradigm', *State Archives of Assyria Bulletin*, 2(2): 81–98.

———— (1992) *Studies on the Annals of Ashurnasirpal II: 2: Topographical Analysis*. Rome: University di Roma.

———— (2001) *International Relations in the Ancient Near East, 1600–1100 BC*. London: Palgrave.

Livy, Titus (1960) *The Early History of Rome*, translated by Aubrey de Selincourt. Harmondsworth: Penguin.

———— (1965) *The War with Hannibal*, translated by Aubrey de Selincourt. Harmondsworth: Penguin.

———— (1976) *Rome and the Mediterranean*, translated by Henry Bettenson. Harmondsworth: Penguin.

———— (1982) *Rome and Italy*, translated by Betty Radice. Harmondsworth: Penguin.

Lockhart, James (1992) *The Nahuas after the Conquest: a Social and Cultural History of the Indians of Central Mexico, Sixteenth through Eighteenth Centuries*. Stanford CA: Stanford University Press.

Lomas, Kathryn (1993) *Rome and the Western Greeks, 350 BC-AD 200: Conquest and Acculturation in Southern Italy*. London: Routledge.

Lupher, D.A. (2003) *Romans in the New World: Classical Models in Sixteenth-Century Spanish America*. Ann Arbor: University of Michigan Press.

Luttwak, Edward N. (1976) *The Grand Strategy of the Roman Empire from the First Century AD to the Third*. Baltimore: Johns Hopkins University Press.

Ma, J. (2000) 'Fighting *Poleis* of the Hellenistic World', in H. van Wees (ed.) *War and Violence in Ancient Greece*, pp. 337–76. London: The Classical Press of Wales.

—— (2000/2002) *Antiochos III and the Cities of Western Asia Minor*. Oxford: Oxford University Press.

Machiavelli, Niccolo (1970 [1531]) *Discourses*, translated by Leslie J. Walker and Brian Richardson. Baltimore: Penguin.

Maddison, Angus (1983) 'A Comparison of the Levels of GDP Per Capita in Developed and Developing Countries, 1700–1980', *Journal of Economic History*, 43(1): 27–42.

Magie, D. (1939) 'The "Agreement" Between Philip V and Antiochus III for the Partition of the Ptolemaic Empire', *Journal of Roman Studies*, 29: 32–44.

Majumdar, R.C., H.C. Raychaudhuri and Kalikinkar Datta (1953) *An Advanced History of India*. London: Macmillan and Co., Limited.

Mandell, S. (1989) 'The Isthmian Declaration and the Early Stages of Roman Imperialism in the Near East', *Classical Bulletin*, 65: 89–94.

Mann, Michael (2003) *Incoherent Empire*. London: Verso.

March, James G. and Johan Olsen (1989) *Rediscovering Institutions: The Organizational Basis of Politics*. New York: Free Press.

Marr, David (1981) 'Sino-Vietnamese Relations', *Australian Journal of Chinese Affairs*, 10(6): 45–64.

Mattingly, Harold B. (1999) Review of Figueira (1998) in *The American Journal of Archaeology*, 103(4): 782–3.

McEwan, Gordon F. (1996) 'The Incas', in Barbara A. Tennenbaum (ed.) *Encyclopedia of Latin American History and Culture*. New York: Charles Scribner's Sons.

McNeill, William H. (1963) *The Rise of the West: A history of the human community*. Chicago: University of Chicago Press.

McShane, R. (1964) *The Foreign Policy of the Attalids of Pergamum*. Champagne-Urbana: University of Illinois Press.

Mearsheimer, John J. (2001) *The Tragedy of Great Power Politics*. New York: W.W. Norton.

Meiggs, Russell (1972) *The Athenian Empire*. Oxford: Clarendon Press.

Menzies, Gavin (2003 [2002]) *1421: the Year China Discovered the World*. London: Bantam Books.

Meritt, B.D. (1936) 'Greek Inscriptions, no. 15: Decree in Honor of Cephisodorus', *Hesperia*, 5: 419–26.

Millar, Fergus (1967) *The Roman Empire and Its Neighbors, 31 BC–AD 337*. Cambridge, MA: Harvard University Press.

—— (1998) *The Crowd in Rome During the Late Republic*. Ann Arbor: University of Michigan Press.

—— (2002) *The Roman Republic in Political Thought*. Hanover: University Press of New England.

Millard, Alan (1994) *The Eponyms of the Assyrian Empire 910–612 BC*. State Archives of Assyria Studies Helsinki: Department of Asian and African Studies, University of Helsinki, Neo-Assyrian Text Corpus Project.

Min, Duck-gi, Son Seung-chol, Ha U-bong, Lee Hun and Chuung Song-il (2000) 'Hanil-gan Pyoryuminae gwanhan yongu (A Study on the Pyoryummin between Korea and Japan)', in Min Duck-gi *et al.* (eds) *Hanilkwangye-ui sahhakheo (Aspects in the history of Korea-Japan relations)*. Seoul: Gukhakjaryowon.

Mitchell T.C. (1991) 'Israel and Judah from the Coming of Assyrian Domination until the Fall of Samaria, and the Struggle for Independence in Judah (c. 750–700 B.C.)', in John Boardman *et al.* (eds) *The Cambridge Ancient History*, 2nd ed., Vol. III, Part 1, *The Prehistory of the Balkans; and the Middle East and the Aegean World, Tenth to Eighth Centuries B.C.*, pp. 322–70. Cambridge: Cambridge University Press.

Modelski, George (1964) 'Kautilya: Foreign Policy and International System in the Ancient Hindu World', *American Political Science Review*, 63(3): 549–60.

Modelski, George and William R. Thompson (1999) 'The Long and the Short of Global Politics in the Twenty-first Century: An Evolutionary Approach', *International Studies Review*, 1(2): 109–40.

Mommsen, T. (1907) *Römische Geschichte I.* 7th ed. Berlin: Weidmann.

—— (1911) *History of Rome. Vol. II*, translated by W.P. Dickson. New York: J.M. Dent and Sons.

Montesquieu (1965 [1734]) *Considerations on the Causes of The Greatness of the Romans and their Decline*. Ithaca: Cornell University Press.

Morgenthau, Hans J. (1978) *Politics Among Nations: The Struggle for Power and Peace*, 5th ed. New York: Alfred A. Knopf.

Mote, Frederick (ed.) (1988) *The Cambridge History of China: Volume 7, The Ming Dynasty, 1368–1644*, Part 1. Cambridge: Cambridge University Press.

Moul, William (2002) 'Power parity, preponderance, and war between great powers, 1816–1989', *Journal of Conflict Resolution*, 46(4): 468–89.

Neuman, Stephanie G. (ed.) (1998) *International Relations Theory and the Third World*. New York: St. Martin's Press.

Nicholson, H.B. (1996) 'The Aztecs', in Barbara A. Tennenbaum (ed.) *Encyclopedia of Latin American History and Culture*. New York NY: Charles Scribner's Sons.

Nicolet, Claude (1980) *The World of the Citizen in Republican Rome*. Berkeley: University of California Press.

North, Douglass C. (1990) *Institutions, Institutional Change, and Economic Performance*. Cambridge: Cambridge University Press.

North, Douglass and Robert P. Thomas (1973) *The Rise of the Western World: A New Economic History*. New York: Cambridge University Press.

Nye, Joseph S. (2003) 'Limits of American Power', *Political Science Quarterly*, 117(4): 545–59.

Oates, David (1968) *Studies in the Ancient History of Northern Iraq*. London: Oxford University Press.

Oates, Joan (1991) 'The Fall of Assyria (635–609 B.C.)', in John Boardman *et al.* (eds) *The Cambridge Ancient History*, 2nd ed., vol. III, Part 2, *The Assyrian and Babylonian Empires and other States of the Near East, from the Eighth to the Sixth Centuries B.C.*, pp. 162–93. Cambridge: Cambridge University Press.

Olivelle, Patrick (trans.) (1999) *Dharmasutras: The Law Codes of Apastamba, Gautama, Baudhayana, and Vasistha*. Oxford: Oxford University Press.

Olson, Jr., Mancur (1965) *The Logic of Collective Action: Public Goods and the Theory of Groups*. Cambridge: Harvard University Press.

Organski, A.F.K. and Jacek Kugler (1980) *The War Ledger*. Chicago: University of Chicago Press.

Osiander, Andreas (1994) *The States System of Europe, 1640–1990: Peacemaking and the Conditions of International Stability*. Oxford: Clarendon Press.

———— (2001) 'Sovereignty, International Relations, and the Westphalian Myth', *International Organization*, 55(2): 251–301.

Ostwald, Martin (1982) *Autonomia, its genesis and early history*. Chico: Ca. Scholars Press.

Pape, Robert A. (2005) 'Soft Balancing against the United States', *International Security*, 30(1): 7–45.

Paley, Samuel M. (1976) *King of the World: Ashur-nasir-pal II of Assyria 883–859 B.C.* New York: The Brooklyn Museum.

Parasher, Aloka (1991) *Mlecchas in Early India: A Study in Attitudes towards Outsiders up to AD 600*. New Delhi: Munshiram Manoharlal Publishers.

Parker, Bradley J. (1997) 'Garrisoning the Empire: Aspects of the Construction and Maintenance of Forts on the Assyrian Frontier', *Iraq*, LIX: 77–87.

Passerini, A. (1931) 'Le relazioni di Roma con l'oriente negli anni 201–200', *Athenaeum*, 9: 260–90.

Pathak, Akhileshwar (2002) *Laws, Strategies, Ideologies: Legislating Forests in Colonial India*. New Delhi: Oxford University Press.

Paul, T.V. (2005) 'Soft Balancing in the Age of U.S. Primacy', *International Security*, 30(1): 46–71.

Perez Collados, José Maria (1998) *Los discursos politicos del México originario*. Universidad Nacional Autónoma de México: México.

Philipson, Coleman (1911) *The International Law and Custom of Ancient Greece and Rome*. London: Macmillan.

Piotrovsky, Boris B. (1969) *The Ancient Civilization of Urartu* (tr. James Hogarth). New York: Cowles.

Pocock, J.G.A. (2003) *Barbarism and Religion. Vol. III. The First Decline and Fall*. Cambridge, UK: Cambridge University Press.

Polybius (1923) *Histories. Vol. III*, translated by W.R. Paton. Cambridge, MA: Harvard University Press.

Pomeroy, Sarah B., *et al.* (1999) *Ancient Greece: A Political, Social and Cultural History*. New York: Oxford University Press.

Porter, Barbara Nevling (1993) *Images, Power, Politics: Figurative Aspects of Esarhaddon's Babylonian Policy*. Philadelphia: American Philosophical Society.

Powell, Robert (1999) *In the Shadow of Power; States and Strategies in International Politics*. Princeton: Princeton University Press.

Powell, Walter W. and Paul J. DiMaggio (1991) *The New Institutionalism in Organizational Analysis*. Chicago: University of Chicago Press.

Quester, George (1977) *Offense and Defense in the International Systems*. New York: John Wiley.

Raaflaub, Kurt A. (1986) 'The Conflict of the Orders in Archaic Rome: A Comprehensive and Comparative Approach', in *Social Struggles in Archaic Rome: New Perspectives on the Conflict of the Orders*, edited by Kurt Raaflaub. Berkeley: University of California Press.

———— (1991) 'City-State, Territory and Empire in Classical Antiquity', in Anthony Molho, Kurt Raaflaub and Julia Emlen *City-States in Classical Antiquity and Medieval Italy*. Stuttgart: Franz Steiner Verlag.

—— (1996) 'Born to be Wolves? Origins of Roman Imperialism', in R.W. Wallace and E.M. Harris (eds) *Transitions to Empire: Essays in Greco-Roman History, 360–146 B.C. in Honor of E. Badian*, pp. 273–314. Norman, Okla.: University of Oklahoma Press.

Raditsa, L. (1972) 'Bella Macedonica', *Aufstieg und Niedergang der römischen Welt* I: 564–89.

Ramaswamy, T.N. (1994) *Essentials of Indian Statecraft: Kautilya's Arthasastra for Contemporary Readers*. New Delhi: Munshiram Manoharlal Publishers.

Rankin, H.D. (1987) *Celts and the Classical World*. London: Croom Helm.

Rawlings, H.R. (1976) 'Antiochus III and Rhodes', *American Journal of Ancient History*, 1: 2–28.

Rawson, E. (1986) 'The Expanson of Rome', in *The Oxford History of the Graeco-Roman World*, pp. 420–35. Oxford: Oxford University Press.

Raychaudhuri, Hemchandra (1997) *Political History of Ancient India*, 8th edn. Oxford: Oxford University Press.

Reid, J.S. (1915) Problems of the Second Punic War: III. Rome and Her Italian Allies. *The Journal of Roman Studies*, 5: 87–124.

Reid, Anthony (1993) *Southeast Asia in the Age of Commerce, 1450–1680, Volume 2: Expansion and Crisis*. New Haven: Yale University Press.

Reus-Smit, Christian (1999) *The Moral Purpose of the State: Culture, Social Identity, and Institutional Rationality in International Relations*. Princeton: Princeton University Press.

Rhodes, P.J. (1985) *The Athenian Empire*. Oxford: Clarendon Press.

Rhys Davids, T.W. (1935) 'The Early History of the Buddhists', in E.J. Rapson (ed.) *The Cambridge History of India, Volume I, Ancient India*, pp. 171–97. Cambridge: Cambridge University Press.

—— (1997; 1902) *Buddhist India*. Delhi: Motilal Banarsidass Publishers.

Robertson, Noel D. (1980) 'The True Nature of the Delian League', *American Journal of Ancient History*, 5: 64–96 and 110–33.

Robinson, Frederick B. (1978) *Adaptation to Colonial Rule by the 'Wild Tribes' of the Bombay Deccan, 1818–1880: From Political Competition to Social Banditry*. Dissertation. University of Minnesota.

Rosecrance, Richard (1986) *The Rise of the Trading State: Commerce and Conquest in the Modern World*. New York: Basic Books.

Rosecrance, Richard and Chih-Cheng Lo (2003) 'Balancing, stability, and war: the mysterious case of the Napoleonic international system', *International Studies Quarterly*, 40(4): 479–500.

Rosen, Stephen Peter (1996) *Societies and Military Power: India and Its Armies*. Ithaca and London: Cornell University Press.

—— (2003) 'Imperial Choices', in A. Bacevich (ed.) *The Imperial Tense: Prospects and Problems of American Empire*, pp. 211–26. Chicago: Ivan R. Dee.

Rosenstein, Nathan (1999) 'Republican Rome', in *War and Society in the Ancient and Medieval Worlds: Asia, the Mediterranean, Europe, and Mesopotamia*, edited by Kurt Raaflaub and Nathan Rosenstein. Cambridge, MA: Harvard University Press.

Rostworowski de Díez Canseco, Maria (1999) *History of the Inca Realm*. Cambridge: Cambridge University Press.

—— (2000) 'The Incas', in Laura Laurenich Minelli (ed.) *The Inca World: the Development of Pre-Columbian Peru, A.D. 1000–1534*. Norman, OK: University of Oklahoma Press.

Roux, Georges (1964) *Ancient Iraq*. London: George Allen and Unwin.
Saggs, H.W.F. (1962) *The Greatness that was Babylon: A Survey of the Ancient Civilization of the Tigris-Euphrates Valley*. New York: Hawthorn Books.
—— (1963) 'Assyrian Warfare in the Sargonid Period', *Iraq*, 25: 145–54.
—— (1984) *The might that was Assyria*. London: Sidgwick & Jackson.
Salmon, E.T. (1967) *Samnium and the Samnites*. Cambridge, UK: Cambridge University Press.
Sanderson, Stephen K. (1995) *Social Transformations: A General Theory of Historical Development*. Oxford: Blackwell.
Sandhu, Gurcharan Singh (2000) *A Military History of Ancient India*. New Delhi: Vision Books.
Sanjun daxue (Armed Forces University) (1976) *Zhongguo lidai zhanzhengshi (History of Wars in China Through Successive Dynasties)*, vols. 1 and 2. Taipei: Liming wenhua chubanshe.
Sartori, Giovanni (1970) 'Concept Misformation in Comparative Politics', *International Political Science Review*, 64(4): 1033–53.
Sawyer, Ralph D. (trans.) (1994) *Sun Tzu: The Art of War*. Boulder: Westview Press.
—— (1998) *The Tao of Spycraft: Intelligence Theory and Practice in Traditional China*. Boulder: Westview Press.
Schmidt, Karl J. (1995) *An Atlas and Survey of South Asian History*. Armonk, N.Y. and London: M.E. Sharpe.
Schmitt, H.H. (1974) 'Polybios und die Gleichgewicht der Mächte', *Entretiens Fondation Hardt*, 20: 67–102.
Schroeder, Paul J. (1994) *The Transformation of European Politics: 1763–1848*. Oxford: Clarendon Press.
Schweller, Randall L. (1994) 'Bandwagoning for Profit: Bringing the Revisionist State Back In', *International Security*, 19(1): 72–107.
—— (1998) *Deadly Imbalances: Tripolarity and Hitler's Strategy of World Conquest*. New York: Columbia University Press.
—— (2006) *Unanswered Threats: Political Constraints on the Balance of Power*. Princeton: Princeton University Press.
Scullard, H.H. (1967) *The Etruscan Cities and Rome*. Ithaca: Cornell University Press.
—— (1989) 'The Carthaginians in Spain', in *The Cambridge Ancient History*. Vol. VIII. *Rome and the Mediterranean to 133 B.C.*, 2nd edition, edited by A.E. Astin, F.W. Walbank, M.W. Frederiksen and R.M. Ogilvie. Cambridge, UK: Cambridge University Press.
Seabury, Paul (ed.) (1965) *Balance of Power*. San Francisco: Chandler Publishing Company.
Sealey, R. (1975) 'The Causes of the Peloponnesian War', *Classical Philology*, 70pp.
Seneviratne, Sudharshan (1981) 'Kalinga and Andhra: The Process of Secondary State Formation in Early India', in Henri J.M. Claessen and Peter Skalnik (eds) *The Study of the State*. The Hague: Mouton Publishers, pp. 54–69.
Shamasastry, R. (trans.) (1961) *Kautilya's Arthasastra*, 7th edn. Mysore: Mysore Printing and Publishing House.
Sharma, J.P. (1968) *Republics in Ancient India, c.1500 B.C.–500 B.C.* Leiden: E.J. Brill.

Sharma, R.S. (1968) *Aspects of Political Ideas and Institutions in Ancient India*, 2nd edn. Delhi: Motilal Banarsidass.

Sherwin-White, A.N. (1939) *The Roman Citizenship*. Oxford: Oxford University Press.

—— (1984) *Roman Foreign Policy in the East, 168 BC to AD 1*. London: Duckworth.

Shively, Donald, *et al*. (1999) *The Cambridge History of Japan: Volume 2, Heian Japan*. Cambridge: Cambridge University Press.

Shoji, Kawazoe (1990) 'Japan and East Asia', in Kozo Yamamura (ed.) *The Cambridge History of Japan, volume 3: Medieval Japan*, pp. 396–446. Cambridge: Cambridge University Press.

Shu, Immanuel (1995) *The Rise of Modern China*. Oxford: Oxford University Press.

Shulman, David (1980) 'On South Asian Bandits and Kings', *Indian Economic and Social History Review*, 17(3): 283–306.

Singh, Sarva Daman (1965) *Ancient Indian Warfare with Special Reference to the Vedic Period*. Leiden: E.J. Brill.

Skaria, Ajay (1999) *Hybrid Histories: Forests, Frontiers, and Wildness in Western India*. Delhi: Oxford University Press.

—— (2003) 'Being *Jangli*: The Politics of Wildness', in P.J. Marshall (ed.) *The Eighteenth Century in India: Evolution or Revolution?* New Delhi: Oxford University Press, pp. 293–318.

Smith, M.E. (2001) 'The Aztec Empire and the Mesoamerican World System', in Susan E. Alcock, Terence N. D'Altroy, Kathleen D. Morrison and Carla M. Sinopoli (eds) *Empires: Comparative Perspectives from Archaeology and History*, pp. 128–54. Cambridge: Cambridge University Press.

Smith, R.E. (1955) *The Failure of the Roman Republic*. Cambridge, UK: Cambridge University Press.

Smits, Gregory (1999) *Visions of Ryukyu: Identity and Ideology in Early-Modern Thought and Politics*. Honolulu, HI: University of Hawaii Press.

Snyder, Jack (1991) *Myths of Empire: Domestic Politics and International Ambition*. Ithaca: Cornell University Press.

Son, Seung-chol (1994) *Choson sidae hanil gwangywe yonku (Korea-Japan relations during the Choson period)*. Seoul: Jisungui Sam.

—— (1999) *Gunsae Choson-ui Hanil gwagye yonku (Korea-Japan relations during the pre-modern Choson era)*. Seoul: Kukhakjaryowon.

Soustelle, Jacques (2002 [1955, 1961]) *Daily Life of the Aztec on the Eve of the Spanish Conquest*. London: Phoenix Press.

Spykman, Nicholas John (1942) *American Strategy in World Politics: The United States and the Balance of Power*. New York: Harcourt, Brace.

Starr, Chester G. (1974) *Political Intelligence in Classical Greece*. Leiden: E.J. Brill.

—— (1986) *Individual and Community: The Rise of the Polis 800–500 BC*. New York: Oxford University Press.

—— (1989) *The Influence of Sea Power on Ancient History*. New York: Oxford University Press.

Stein, Burton (1998) *A History of India*. Oxford: Blackwell.

Sterling, R.W. (1974) *Macropolitics: International Security in a Global Society*. New York.

Strauss, Barry S. (1991) 'Of Balances, Bandwagons, and Ancient Greeks', in Richard Ned Lebow and Barry S. Strauss (eds) *Hegemonic Rivalry: From Thucydides to the Nuclear Age*. Boulder: Westview Press.

—— (1997) 'The Art of Alliance and the Peloponnesian War', in Charles D. Hamilton and Peter Krentz, *Polis and Polemos: Essays on Politics, War and History in Ancient Greece in Honour of Donald Kagan*, pp. 127–46. Claremont: California, Regina Books.

Subrahmanyam, Sanjay (2003) 'Making Sense of India Historiography', *The Indian Economic and Social History Review*, 39(2–3): 121–30.

Sullivan, Vickie B. (1996) *Machiavelli's Three Romes*. DeKalb: Northern Illinois University Press.

Syme, Ronald (1952) *The Roman Revolution*. Oxford: Oxford University Press.

Tadmor, Hayim (1994) *The Inscriptions of Tiglath-pileser III King of Assyria*. Jerusalem: The Israel Academy of Science and Humanities.

Tammen, Ronald L., *et al.* (2000) *Power Transitions: Strategies for the 21st Century*. Chatham, NJ: Chatham House Press.

Taylor, Keith (1976) 'The Rise of Dai viet and the Establishment of Thang-Long', in Kenneth Hall and John K. Whitmore (eds) *Explorations in Early Southeast Asian History: The Origins of Southeast Asian Statecraft*, pp. 149–92. Ann Arbor, MI: University of Michigan Press.

—— (1983) *The Birth of Vietnam*. Berkeley: University of California Press.

Taylor, L.R. (1966) *Roman Voting Assemblies*. Ann Arbor: University of Michigan Press.

Thapar, Romila (1966) *A History of India: Volume One*. London: Penguin Books.

—— (1971) 'The Image of the Barbarian in Early India', *Comparative Studies in Society and History*, 13(4): 409–10.

—— (1981) 'The State as Empire', in Henri J.M. Claessen and Peter Skalnik (eds) *The Study of the State*, pp. 409–26. The Hague: Mouton Publishers.

—— (1997) *Asoka and the Decline of the Mauryas*. Oxford: Oxford University Press.

Thompson, William R. (1992) 'Dehio, Long Cycles, and the Geohistorical Context of Structural Transition', *World Politics*, 45(1).

—— (1996) *Leading Sectors and World Powers: The Coevolution of Global Politics and Economics*. Columbia: University of South Carolina Press.

Thucydides (1951) *The Peloponnesian War*, tr. Crawley. New York: Modern Library.

—— (1972) *History of the Peloponnesian War*, trans. Rex Warner (rev edn). London: Penguin.

Tilly, Charles (1985) 'War Making and State Making as Organized Crime', in Peter B. Evans, Dietrich Rueschemeyer, and Theda Skocpol (eds) *Bringing the State Back In*, pp. 169–91. Cambridge: Cambridge University Press.

Toby, Ronald P. (1991) *State and Diplomacy in Early Modern Japan: Asia in the Development of the Tokugawa Bakufu*. Stanford: Stanford University Press.

Todd, Emmanuel (2002) *After the Empire: the Breakdown of the American Order*. New York: Columbia University Press.

Townsend, Richard F. (2000 [1993]). *The Aztecs*. London: Thames & Hudson.

Unger, Roberto M. (1987) *Plasticity into Power: Comparative-Historical Studies on the Institutional Conditions of Economic and Military Success*. New York: Cambridge University Press.

Van de Ven, Hans J. (1996) 'War and the Making of Modern China', *Modern Asian Studies*, 30(4): 737–56.

Van Evera, Stephen (1998/99) 'Offense, Defense, and the Causes of War', *International Security*, 22(4): 5–43.

——— (1999) *Causes of War: Structures of Power and the Roots of International Conflict* Ithaca. NY: Cornell University Press.

van Leur, J.C. (1955) *Indonesian Trade and Society: Essays in Asian Social and Economic History*. The Hague and Bandung: W. van Hoeve.

van Wees, H. (1992) *Status Warriors: War, Violence and Society in Homer and History*. Amsterdam: H.G. Giebey.

Veyne, P. (1975) 'Y a-t'il eu une imperialisme romaine?' *Melanges d'Ecole Francais de Rome*, 85: 793–855.

Viraphol, Sarasin (1977) *Tribute and Profit: Sino-Siamese Trade 1652–1853*. Cambridge, Mass.: Harvard University Press.

von Fritz, Kurt (1954) *The Theory of the Mixed Constitution in Antiquity*. New York: Columbia University Press.

von Glahn, Richard (1996) 'Myth and Reality of China's Seventeenth Century Monetary Crisis', *Journal of Economic History*, 56(2): 429–54.

Walbank, F.W. (1940) *Philip V of Macedon*. Cambridge: Cambridge University Press.

——— (1954) *A Historical Commentary on Polybius*. Oxford: Oxford University Press.

——— (1967) *A Historical Commentary on Polybius*, II. Oxford: Oxford University Press.

——— (1985) '*Symploke*: Its Role in Polybius' Histories', in *Selected Papers in Greek and Roman History and Historiography*, pp. 313–24. Cambridge: Cambridge University Press.

——— (1993) 'Η ΤΩΝ ΟΛΩΝ ΔΥΝΑΣΤΕΙΑ and the Antigonids', *Archaia Makedonia*. 5: 1721–30. Thessalonica.

——— (2002) 'Polybius and Macedonia', in F.W. Walbank (ed.) *Polybius, Rome, and the Hellenistic World: Essays and Reflections*. Cambridge: Cambridge University Press.

Walker, Richard L. (1953) *The Multi-State System of Ancient China*. Westport: Greenwood Press.

Walshe, Maurice (1995) (trans.) *The Long Discourses of the Buddha, a Translation of the Digha Nikaya*. Boston: Wisdom Publications.

Walt, Stephen M. (1987) *The Origins of Alliances*. Ithaca: Cornell University Press.

——— (2002) 'Beyond Bin Laden', *International Security*, 26(3): 56–78.

Waltz, Kenneth N. (1979) *Theory of International Politics*. Reading, Mass.: Addison-Wesley.

——— 1986) 'Reflections on *Theory of International Politics*: A Response to My Critics', in Robert O. Keohane (ed.) *Neorealism and Its Critics*, pp. 322–45 New York: Columbia University Press.

——— (1993) 'The Emerging Structure of International Politics', *International Security*, 18(2): 44–79.

——— (2000a) 'Globalization and American Power', *The National Interest*, (Spring).

——— (2000b) 'Structural Realism after the Cold War', *International Security*, 25(1): 5–41.

Warder, A.K. (1970) *Indian Buddhism*. Delhi: Motilal Banarsidass.

Wardman, Alan (1982) *Religion and Statecraft among the Romans*. London: Granada.

Warmington, B.H. (1960) *Carthage*. London: Robert Hale.

Warrior, V. (1996) *The Initiation of the Second Macedonian War*. Wiesbaden: Franz Steiner.

Watson, Adam (1984) 'New States in the Americas', in Hedley Bull and Adam Watson (eds) *The Expansion of International Society*. Oxford: Clarendon.

—— (1992) *The Evolution of International Society: A Comparative Historical Analysis*. London and New York: Routledge.

—— (2007) *Hegemony and History*. London: Routledge.

Weir, Fred (2002) 'Chechnya's Warrior Tradition', *Christian Science Monitor*, 26 March.

Wendt, Alexander and Daniel Friedheim (1995) 'Hierarchy under Anarchy: Informal Empire and the East German State', *International Organization*, 49(4): 689–721.

Wendt, Alexander (1999) *Social Theory of International Politics*. Cambridge: Cambridge University Press.

Whittaker, C.R. (1978) 'Carthaginian Imperialism in the Fifth and Fourth Centuries', in *Imperialism in the Ancient World*, edited by P.D.A. Garnsey and C.R. Whittaker. Cambridge, UK: Cambridge University Press.

—— (1994) *Frontiers of the Roman Empire: A Social and Economic Study*. Baltimore: Johns Hopkins University Press.

Wickersham, John (1994) *Hegemony and Greek Historians*. Lanham, Matryland: Rowman and Littlefield.

Wight, Martin (1977) *Systems of States*. Leicester: Leicester University Press.

Wilkinson, David (1999) 'Unipolarity Without Hegemony', *International Studies Review*, 1(1): 141–72.

—— (2002) 'The Polarity Structure of the Central World System/Civilization, 1500–700 B.C.'. Paper presented at the International Studies Association Annual Meeting, March, New Orleans, Louisiana.

—— (2004) 'Analytical and Empirical Issues in the Study of Power-Polarity Configuration Sequences', Presentation to a Conference of a Working Group on Analyzing Complex Macrosystems as Dynamic Networks, Santa Fe Institute, April 28–May 2.

Williams, J.H.C. (2001) *Beyond the Rubicon: Romans and Gauls in Republican Italy*. Oxford: Oxford University Press.

Williams, Stephen (1985) *Diocletian and the Roman Recovery*. New York: Methuen.

Wink, André (1984) 'Sovereignty and Universal Dominion in South Asia', *Indian Economic and Social History Review*, 21(3): 265–92.

Wohlforth, William C. (1999) 'The Stability of a Unipolar World', *International Security*, 24(1): 1–36.

—— (2001) 'The Russian-Soviet Empire: A Test of Neorealism', *Review of International Studies*, 27(5): 213–35.

—— (2002) 'U.S. Strategy in a Unipolar World', in G. John Ikenberry (ed.) *America Unrivaled: The Future of the Balance of Power*, pp. 98–118. Ithaca: Cornell University Press.

―――― (2003) 'Measuring Power – and the Power of Theories', in *Realism and the Balancing of Power: A New Debate*, edited by John A. Vasquez and Colin Elman. Saddle River, NJ: Prentice-Hall.

Woodside, Alexander (1971) *Vietnam and the Chinese Model: A Comparative Study of the Nguyen and Ch'ing Civil Government in the First Half of the Nineteenth Century*. Cambridge, Mass.: Harvard University Press.

Wray, William (n.d.) 'The 17th Century Japanese Diaspora: Questions of Boundary and Policy', ms., University of British Columbia.

Wyatt, David (1984) *Thailand: A Short History*. New Haven, CT: Yale University Press.

Yadin, Yigael (1963) *The Art of Warfare in Biblical Lands in Light of Archeological Study*. New York: McGraw Hill.

Yamamura, Kozo (1990a) 'Introduction', in Kozo Yamamura (ed.) *The Cambridge History of Japan: Volume 3, Medieval Japan*, pp. 1–45. Cambridge: Cambridge University Press.

―――― (1990b) 'The Growth of Commerce in Medieval Japan', in Kozo Yamamura (ed.) *The Cambridge History of Japan, Volume 3: Medieval Japan*, 3rd edition, pp. 344–95. Cambridge: Cambridge University Press.

Yang, Kuan (trans. and ed.) (1977) Li, Yu-ning, *Shang Yang's Reforms and State Control in China*, White Plains: M.E. Sharpe.

―――― (1986) *Zhanguo shi (History of the Warring States)*. Taipei: Gufon chubanshe.

Yang, Lien-sheng (1968) 'Historical notes on the Chinese World Order', in John Fairbank (ed.) *The Chinese World Order: traditional China's foreign relations*, pp. 20–33. Cambridge, Mass.: Harvard University Press.

Yates, Robin D.S. (1987) 'Social Status in the Ch'in: Evidence from the Yun-meng Legal Documents, Part One: Commoners', *Harvard Journal of Asiatic Studies*, 47(1): 197–237.

Zhang, Xiaosheng and Wenyan Liu (1988) *Zhongguo Gudai Zhanzheng Tonglan (An Overview of Wars in Ancient China)*. Beijing: Changzheng chubanshe.

Zimansky, Paul E. (1985) *Ecology and Empire: The Structure of the Urartian State*. Studies in Ancient Oriental Civilization no. 41. Chicago: Oriental Institute of the University of Chicago.

Index